The Biblical Spirit

by the same author
Galatians
John: Gospel of the New Creation
Covenant and Creation
Search for Order
Faith of Israel

by William Dumbrell with editorial support from Russell Bailey
Genesis 1–11
2 Corinthians: A New Covenant Commentary
Revelation: A New Covenant Commentary
Hebrews: A New Covenant Commentary
Romans (second edition): A New Covenant Commentary

William J Dumbrell (Th.D., Harvard University) was for many years Vice-Principal of Moore Theological College, Sydney. At Regent College in Vancouver, he served as Academic Dean and Professor of Biblical Studies. He also lectured at Trinity Theological College in Singapore and various theological colleges in Sydney including Macquarie Christian Studies Institute, Southern Cross College, Emmaus Bible College, Tabor College and Presbyterian Theological Centre.

Russell Bailey (M.C.S., Regent College) is Headmaster of Redeemer Baptist School and an Elder of Redeemer Baptist Church. He was Dr Dumbrell's Teaching Assistant at Regent College, Vancouver.

The Biblical Spirit

by
William J. Dumbrell

with
Russell Bailey

WIPF & STOCK · Eugene, Oregon

Wipf and Stock Publishers
199 W 8th Ave, Suite 3
Eugene, OR 97401

The Biblical Spirit
By Dumbrell, William and Bailey, Russell
Copyright©2016 by Dumbrell, William
ISBN 13: 978-1-5326-4321-7
Publication date 11/14/2017
Previously published by Redeemer Baptist Press, 2016

Preface

Bill Dumbrell has lived with a burden—especially in the senior years of his ministry—to explore and share his understanding of a unitary, Bible-wide theology of the Spirit particularly in regard to the work of regeneration or covenant inclusion. His desire has been for a more balanced emphasis on the person and presence of the Spirit both in academic theology and in pastoral ministry.

To always discover afresh the living, intimate presence of God through the Holy Spirit is as much needed by the Christian today as it was needed by Adam and Eve to become living beings at creation. To live and minister as the body of Jesus Christ in the world, the fullness of the Holy Spirit is as much needed in the body of believers today as was evident in the first century church. Just as the Spirit is the principle of life in creation, likewise, the Spirit recreates new life in the new creation. The Spirit is the powerful presence of God in Israel, imparting wisdom, strengthening leaders and enabling the skill of craftsmen in sanctified service. And the ministries of teaching, administration, healing, pastoral care and good works in the church throughout the ages are also dependent on the sovereign distribution of the gifts of the Spirit.

Any presentation of a theology of the Spirit has the potential to polarise viewpoints. Perhaps some will decide that this text is not lively enough in embracing the various emphases rediscovered in the charismatic contribution to the church in recent decades. Others may view the particular theological contribution of this text as too radical in its challenge to what may be an over-simplified evangelical understanding of the discontinuity between old and new covenants—or between the apostolic age and the present.

It is our hope that many will be encouraged—perhaps even inspired—by the expectation of the present and future powerful activity of the Spirit in transformation towards the image of God in the believer's experience of Jesus' resurrection life.

This text began as a Word file transferred from Bill to me a few years ago, with freedom given to me by Bill to re-express his theology and discuss any differences. Unfortunately, it has not been possible in recent months to discuss the detail of my editing with Bill. Nor has it been possible to work through issues that have arisen where Bill had not included what I considered to be key texts. I have also made some minor modifications, unfortunately without the normal robust consultation, where it seemed that Bill's text may have inadvertently contradicted an obvious interpretation of Scripture. So perhaps if you disagree strongly with a particular point in the text, you can blame me—if you are strongly in agreement, you can thank Bill!

I am sure that Bill would like me to thank the devotion of Norma whose persistence ensured that this text reached publication. In his recent publications, Bill has also thanked the members of Redeemer Baptist Church who have contributed their expertise voluntarily to assist Bill's teaching and publication ministry.

And I would like to thank Bill for spending his life in God's Word. Many of us have benefited in Christ from Bill's obedience to God's call on his life. I pray that this publication will add to that blessing.

Russell Bailey
North Parramatta
April, 2016

Contents

Preface v
Introduction
One Biblical Theology of the Spirit 1
The Biblical Spirit
Old Testament 3
   The Action of the Spirit 5
      The Spirit as the Life Principle 8
      The Spirit's Relationship to God 9
      The Spirit and Divine Rule 9
      The Spirit and Prophetic Inspiration 10
      Wisdom and Spirit 11
   The Spirit in Regeneration 12
   The Spirit in Leadership 17
      Judges to 2 Samuel 17
      The Prophets: Elijah to Isaiah 18
   The Spirit in Isaiah's visions of
   Jerusalem and New Jerusalem 19
      Spirit and New Creation (Isaiah 11) 19
      The Spirit is the Instrument of Renewal (Isaiah 32 & 43) 20
      The Servant of the Lord is Divinely Empowered with the Spirit 20
      Yahweh's Intimate Presence as Spirit (Isaiah 63) 21
   The Spirit and Individuality in the Psalms 23
   The Role of the Spirit in the Future Revival of Israel 25
      National Covenantal Experience (Jeremiah 31:33–34) 26
      The Outpouring of the Spirit and Israel's Future (Joel 2) 34
      God's Indwelling Spirit Vivifies New Covenant Obedience (Ezekiel) 35
   The Fulfilment of Promises of a Spirit-Controlled Future 38

The Biblical Spirit
New Testament 43
   Matthew 44
      The Spirit's role in re-beginning Israel's history (Matthew 1–3) 44
      Jesus' ministry of two baptisms: Spirit and fire 45
      The seal of the Spirit at Jesus baptism (3:13–17) 51
      Jesus is directed by the Spirit into the wilderness (4:1–11) 56
      The Spirit will speak through the disciples (10:17–20) 57
      The Spirit-endowed Servant (12:15–21) 58

  Blasphemy against the Spirit (12:22–32) 58
  In the name of the Father, the Son and the Spirit (28:18–20) 59
Mark 60
  The gift of the Spirit for Jesus' ministry (1:9–13) 60
  Signs of Jesus' Spirit-filled ministry (1:24–3:24) 61
Luke 63
  Filled with or full of the Holy Spirit 63
  The Spirit in the birth narratives of John and Jesus (1:39–2:52) 68
  Zachariah is filled with the Spirit (1:57–80) 68
  The Spirit led Simeon into the Temple (2:21–40) 69
  The Messianic baptism of the Holy Spirit and fire (3:15–22) 71
  The ministry of the Spirit anointed Messiah (4:14–30) 72
  Disciples and the Spirit in the ministry of Jesus (Luke 9–10) 80
  The Father gives the Holy Spirit to all who ask (11:9–13) 81
  Blasphemy against the Holy Spirit (12:8–12) 82
  The judgment message is mediated by the Spirit (12:49–51) 82
  The promised coming of the Spirit (24:49–53) 82
John 84
  Jesus is anointed by and will baptise with the Spirit (1:19–34) 84
  The requirement to be born of the Spirit (3:1–12) 86
  Worship through personal relationship in Spirit and truth (John 4) 94
  The Spirit gives life (6:63) 96
  The Spirit as living water pouring out to heal the world (7:39) 96
  The Father will send the Spirit to the disciples (John 14) 101
  The vine is about the abiding indwelling of the Spirit (15:1–11) 107
  The Spirit enables Jesus' ministry to a hostile world (15:18–16:3) 109
  The coming of the Spirit (16:4–15) 112
  The identification of the Paraclete 115
  The Paraclete and the disciples 116
  The relationship of believers to the Paraclete (14:16–18) 117
  The Paraclete and the world (16:1–16) 118
  Spirit of intercession 119
  Jesus 'gave up the Spirit' (19:30) 121
  Jesus bequeaths the abiding Spirit of prophecy (20:19–23) 121
Acts 131
  The baptism of the Spirit for new covenant witness (Acts 1) 131
  The baptism of the Spirit promoting close family relationship (Acts 2) . . . 137
  Pentecost and the new covenant gift of the Spirit 138
  The Pentecost blessing of Christ's life-giving Spirit 141
  Other tongues commence the Spirit's world harvest (2:5–13) 142

Fulfilment of prophecy concerning the Spirit (2:14–40)............... 143
The significance of Pentecost:
redemptive and sanctifying experience........................... 149
The significance of Pentecost:
reception of the Spirit... 154
The significance of Pentecost:
Christ coming to the church in the Spirit 155
The significance of Pentecost:
union with Christ 156
The significance of Pentecost:
the Spirit of prophecy... 157
All things in common is a result of receiving the Spirit (2:41–47) 158
Peter and John filled with the Spirit before the Sanhedrin (4:5–22) 158
Filled with the Spirit again for prophecy (4:23–31)................... 159
Ananias and Sapphira lie to the Spirit (5:1–11) 159
Israel needs the gifts of repentance and the Spirit (5:17–42) 160
Stephen is a deacon full of the Spirit (Acts 6–7)..................... 160
Missionary expansion empowered by the Spirit (8:1–3)............... 162
The Spirit at work in Christ-like ministry in Samaria (8:4–25) 163
The Spirit directs Philip to the Ethiopian treasurer (8:26–39) 165
Saul is filled with the Spirit for Gentile ministry (9:1–19a) 166
The comfort of the Paraclete multiplying the church (9:31–43) 167
The Spirit directs Peter to table fellowship with Gentiles (10:1–43) 168
The Spirit falls on Gentiles (10:44–48).............................. 169
Peter tells Jerusalem that the Spirit fell on Gentiles (11:1–18).......... 170
The Spirit is central to continuity in salvation history (11:19–30)........ 172
The Spirit sends Barnabas and Saul out on mission (13:1–12).......... 175
The Spirit convinces the Council at Jerusalem (Acts 15) 177
The Spirit directs movement of the mission to Europe (16:6–10)........ 177
Apollos must understand the work of the Spirit (18:24–28)............ 178
Receiving the Spirit is the essence of life in Christ (19:1–7)............ 178
The Spirit appoints elders and directs mission plans (20:13–28)......... 179
The Spirit prepares Paul for future imprisonment (21:10–11).......... 180
The Spirit inspires all Scripture (Acts 28) 180
Romans... 182
Spirit of holiness as the sphere of encountering Jesus (1:1–7) 182
True circumcision is of the heart, by the Spirit (2:25–29)............... 186
The Spirit pours the love of God into our hearts (Romans 5) 186
New life in the Spirit (Romans 8).................................. 187
Flesh verses Spirit in the new covenant (8:1–11) 188
The Spirit as personal 193

    Led by the Spirit as sons indwelt by the Spirit (8:12–17) 195
    We have the eschatological firstfruits of the Spirit (8:23–30) 196
    Resurrection: the goal of the Spirit's activity in the believer 197
    In Christ, by the Spirit (Romans 9–11) 199
    Bearing the imprint of the Spirit of Christ at work (Romans 14–15) 199
1 Corinthians 202
    The Spirit's persuasive power (2:4) 202
    God's wisdom revealed through his Spirit (2:6–16) 203
    The congregation is the temple for God's Spirit (3:1–4) 209
    The Spirit is with the assembled congregation (5:1–13) 211
    The Spirit is the covenant God with us (6:1–11) 212
    Excursus: The Temple as Spirit's Presence 215
    Paul relies on the Spirit in all his communication (7:1–16) 216
    The Spirit enables a true confession about Jesus (12:1–3) 216
    Many gifts expressing unity in the one Spirit (12:4–6) 219
    Different manifestations of one Spirit for all (12:7–11) 220
    Gifts of the Spirit 223
    Baptised by one Spirit into one body of Christ (12:12–31) 226
    Tongues is a gift of the Spirit but is not the priority (14:1–40) 233
    The last Adam—a life-giving Spirit (15:1–58) 234
    The Spirit in the resurrection of Christ and believers 235
    The Spirit in the believers' future resurrection 236
    The Spirit is the efficacious agent for the new resurrection body 237
    The Spirit is the instrumental cause of eternal resurrection 244
    Resurrection change worked on believers by the Spirit 246
    Resurrection of Christ and believers by the Spirit under God 248
    Life in the Spirit even in the dead body of sin 249
2 Corinthians 250
    The Spirit guarantees sonship and integrity (1:22) 250
    God engraves Christ on human hearts by the Spirit (3:1–3) 250
    Covenant without the Spirit must kill (3:4–6) 252
    The glory of Spirit-filled covenant commitment (3:7–11) 257
    Free full covenant fellowship by the Spirit (3:16–17) 261
    New covenant transformation by the Spirit (3:18) 263
    The Spirit reveals divine treasure through clay jars (4:1–18) 265
    Heavenly expectation and guarantee of the Spirit (5:1–5) 265
    New creation—the sovereign activity of the Spirit (5:17) 268
    Ministry credentials formed by the Holy Spirit (6:1–10) 270
    A different gospel confers a different spirit (11:1–33) 271
    The communion of the Spirit (13:14) 272
Galatians 274

We receive the blessing of God—the Spirit—by faith (3:1–14) 274
The Spirit of Jesus in us cries out 'Abba, Father' (4:1–7) 276
The promise to Abraham is the gift of the Spirit (4:21–5:1) 278
The Spirit is the guarantee of our final justification (5:2–6) 279
Freedom in the Spirit is the basis of the moral life (5:16–25). 279
Excursus: The ethics of life in the Spirit under the new covenant 281
The Spirit enables us to fulfil Christ's law of love (6:1–10) 283

Ephesians 284
Blessings are released in us through the Spirit (1:3–14) 284
God grants the Spirit of wisdom and revelation (1:15–23). 287
Common life in Christ through the Spirit (2:1–22). 288
The mystery revealed by the Spirit (3:1–21). 289
The gifts and graces of unity in the Spirit (4:1–16) 290
Communion with the Spirit can be grieved or spoilt (4:30). 291
The fruit of the Spirit is walking in love (5:9,18) 294
Empowered by the Spirit to withstand the devil (6:10–20). 296

Philippians 297
Common fellowship and mutual love in the shared Spirit of Christ. 297

Colossians 299
Love in the Spirit (1:8) 299

1 Thessalonians 301
The powerful presence of the Spirit in ministry (1:5–6) 301
Relationship with God in the Spirit is intimate (4:8). 302
Do not quench the Spirit (5:19–22) 302

2 Thessalonians 304
God chooses, the Lord loves, the Spirit sanctifies (2:13). 304

1 Timothy. 305
Christ's justification (resurrection) in the Spirit (3:16) 305
The Spirit warns about false doctrine (4:1–4). 306

2 Timothy. 308
A Spirit of power and of love and of a sound mind (1:6–7) 308
Excursus: Sanctification occurs by agency of the Spirit. 309
Excursus: Glorification of the believer's body by the Spirit. 309

Titus 311
Christian initiation is one activity of the Spirit (3:5) 311

Hebrews 312
The witness of signs and wonders and gifts of the Spirit (2:4) 312
The Holy Spirit speaks through Scripture (3:7–11) 312
Partaking of the heavenly gift of the Holy Spirit (6:4–6). 312
The Holy Spirit reveals the benefits of the new covenant (9:8). 315

  The Holy Spirit cleanses the conscience (9:14) 316
  The Holy Spirit witnesses the new covenant to us (10:15–18) 317
  To sin wilfully is to insult the Spirit (10:28–29) 318
1 Peter 319
  The Spirit applies the benefits of the gospel of God (1:2–4) 319
  Preaching the gospel requires Spirit empowerment (1:11–12) 320
  The Spirit of glory resting on persecuted believers (4:14) 320
2 Peter 321
  The Spirit inspired men to write infallible Scripture (1:21) 321
1 John 322
  The anointing of the Spirit abides in the believer (2:20–27) 322
  The Spirit communicates the indwelling Christ to us (3:24) 322
  Evidences of the indwelling Spirit of God (4:1–21) 322
  The witness of the Spirit on earth and in heaven (5:6–8) 323
Jude 325
  Those who cause divisions do not have the Spirit (19–20) 325
Revelation 327
  John is in the Spirit and the Spirit is speaking to the churches 327
  The seven Spirits represent the fullness of God at work in the world 328
  The Spirit's message is for overcomers at the Parousia 330
  The Spirit of prophecy (19:10) 331
  The Spirit and bride together pray for the Parousia (22:17) 332

Bibliography 335

Introduction
One Biblical Theology of the Spirit

The Old Testament was the Bible for the writers of the New Testament, hence the writers of the New Testament draw on the Old Testament with regard to the work of the Spirit. The presupposition of this study is that there is one biblical theology of the Holy Spirit which is further personalised in the New Testament and developed in view of the movement, after the cross, from the nation as God's covenant people to the church as God's covenant people. This unitary biblical theology of the Spirit does not prescind development of the doctrine of the Spirit in the New Testament—including new applications of Old Testament pneumatology—but it does prohibit the emergence of doctrines of the Spirit that are different from doctrines already presented in the Old Testament. Biblical doctrines about the Spirit are applied to different communities in each of the Testaments. The Old Testament applies the biblical doctrine of the Spirit to the nation of Israel which was specially chosen by God to fulfil a divine purpose in the world. In this theological application of spiritual principles to a nation, the Spirit is corporate and only marginally personal. The New Testament begins with the gospels still applying the biblical doctrine of the Spirit to the Old Testament entity of the nation of Israel, but application of the biblical doctrine of the Spirit to the individual also begins to emerge. From Acts onwards the individual is still not the prime application, rather, the application is the corporate church(es) as the body of Christ in the world. In both Testaments, the Spirit represents God and Christ in demonstrable action in the world.

The important point is the consistency of the expression of the divine mind—in both Testaments—to the world through persons of the Trinity who are both divine and personal. Scholarship has often been loath to accept this unitary view of a bible-wide doctrine of Trinitarian expression because the second person of the Trinity seems not to appear in the Old Testament and the activity of the Spirit is generally reported in a non-personal way in the Old Testament. Thus some scholars propound a view that the doctrine of the Spirit begins with the outpouring of the personal Spirit, the Spirit of Christ, at Pentecost. This view presupposes a difference in redemption between the two Testaments with the gospel emerging only in the New Testament, that is, this view incorrectly perceives a theological difference between the four gospels (on the one hand) and the Old Testament (on the other). But both Jesus and Paul ministered the gospel on the basis of a fuller understanding of the Old Testament than we possess.

Jesus said to Nicodemus 'unless one is born again (regenerated), he cannot see the kingdom of God' (John 3:3). Jesus clarifies further—when it is clear that Nicodemus does not understand—that genetic heritage is not the basis of covenant inclusion, saying: 'unless one is born of water and the Spirit, he cannot enter the kingdom of God' (John 3:5) and 'that which is born of the flesh is flesh, and that which is born of the Spirit is spirit' (John 3:6). Jesus is telling an Old Testament Jewish teacher that inclusion within the covenant (in the kingdom of God, Old or New covenant) involves the work of the Spirit in regeneration. Nicodemus' reading of the Old Testament has thus far been unenlightened as, even though he is 'the (most prominent?) teacher of Israel' (John 3:10), Nicodemus appears to be unaware that the personal work of the Spirit has always been essential for inclusion within God's covenant.

Like Nicodemus, the modern reader could miss the importance of the personal work of the Spirit in the Old Testament, specifically in regard to the work of regeneration or covenant inclusion. An exploration of covenant inclusion in the Old Testament will therefore involve an exposition of the work of the Spirit in the Old Testament.

The Biblical Spirit
Old Testament

The Action of the Spirit

The words *qadash* (Hebrew, to be set apart or consecrated) and *hagiazein* (Greek, sanctified) convey the idea of separation with undertones of possession. In this regard, sanctification repossesses things that have been put to other uses than God's glory so that they might reflect God's glory. When God is sanctified in his people then his Spirit is poured out on them (Ezekiel 39:27,29). The early divine covenants were sealed to re-create and re-establish the family bond between God and his people so that God's people would express the family likeness. The Sinai Covenant effects the adoption of Israel into God's family (cf. Romans 9:4; Hosea 11:1). This intended relationship is provided by grace. Israel is God's son and is to show forth his praises, that is, to be increasingly the image of God's glory. The promise of the covenant was: I will be your God and you will be my people (Exodus 6:7); or I am your Father and you are my son (Exodus 4:22; Deuteronomy 32:6). The heart of the relationship is: I the Lord (your Father) am holy, therefore you (my children) are to express the family likeness and image, so you are to be holy too (Leviticus 11:44–45; 19:2; 20:7). The motive of the covenant is for God's people to express the divine image. So the glory of the old covenant can be compared with the glory of the new covenant, that is, just as the glory of the old covenant is to live God's word by the Spirit (Isaiah 59:21) so the glory of the new covenant is the work of Christ through the ministry of the Spirit by which God's people express God's glory (2 Corinthians 3:18). This revelation of the glory of God's person and character is the motive for sanctification: we are to be holy and he will make us so (Exodus 31:13; cf. Leviticus 20:8; 21:8). The pattern of holiness arises from imperatives of obedience stemming from indicatives of grace. God has redeemed his people from bondage, so they are to be conformed to his pattern (Exodus 20: 2ff.).

The Hebrew word *ruach* means air in motion, that is, wind or breath but with the sense of a mysterious and powerful effect mediating the presence of Yahweh. In the Old Testament, the Spirit was: the source of divine miraculous power and prophetic inspiration;[1] the conveyor of wisdom and

---

1   Numbers 11:25,26,29; 1 Samuel 10:6,10; 19:20,23; 2 Chronicles 20:14; 24:20; Ezekiel 2:2; 3:12,14,24; 8:3; 11:1,24; 37:1; 43:5; Joel 2:28; Zechariah 4:6.

understanding;[2] the operative presence of God in creation;[3] the imminent presence of the divine in the affairs of men;[4] the breath of life proceeding from God;[5] and associated with God's powerful presence and control.[6] The Spirit is depicted in the Old Testament performing a creative role, conveying divine energy. But the Old Testament does not provide a static identity between Yahweh and his Spirit,[7] rather—in the Old Testament—the Spirit provided the contrast between humanity or flesh (characterised by inertia and lack of power) and deity.[8] The Spirit is God active as he relates to his world creation and his people by the breath (*ruach*) of his mouth. The divine word and the divine breath were not distinguished in their active, efficacious involvement in the creation process.

Thus *ruach* is not only the principle of existence but also, as full vitality, makes the difference between half life (evidenced by hunger, grieving or fainting) and real 'spirited' living. Hill remarks that strong or weak breathing is the clue to understanding the Hebrew sense of *ruach* as full vitality or the lack of it.[9] The Spirit is not power from God but the power of God accomplishing his purposes in his world and through men. 'Spirit of God' thus means God in effective relationship with and in control of creation. The Spirit acting in creation through men is a paradigm for God's continuing supervision of creation. To experience the Spirit of God is to experience God as Spirit and, hence, to experience Yahweh's rule.

The concept of the Spirit maintained the theology of the omnipresence and immanence of God in spite of growing belief in his transcendence because, by the Spirit: God could be everywhere operating for good in the midst of his people; and the Spirit of God is the breath of the Almighty in man such that the vital life essence in man is from the deity (Job 33:4; 34:14;

---

2   Genesis 41:38; Exodus 31:3; Deuteronomy 34:9; Nehemiah 9:20; Daniel 4:9,18; 5:11,14; Zechariah 7:12.

3   Genesis 1:2; Job 26:13.

4   Daniel 4:8; Numbers 27:18; 1 Samuel 16:13; Haggai 2:5.

5   Genesis 6:3; Job 33:14.

6   Judges 6:34; 13:25; 14:6,19; 15:14; Psalm 104:30; 139:7.

7   Fatehi, 2000, 57.

8   The Spirit's creative role is referenced in: Genesis 1:2; Psalms 33:6; 104:30; Job 26:13; 33:4; 34:14. The Spirit's recreative role is referenced in: Psalms 51:12–14; 143:10; Nehemiah 9:20; Isaiah 32:15; 44:3–5; Ezekiel 36:26–27.

9   Fatehi, 2000, 53.

Psalm 33:6). The Spirit is divine—the third person of the Trinity—but this did not refer to God as he was in himself but, rather, God communicating his presence to creation as divine energy (as opposed to divine immateriality). This divine energy of the Spirit of God is demonstrated through Joseph as the source of good government for Egypt (Genesis 41:30–38).[10] The Spirit gave expression to the will of God in creation and redemption, and the Spirit will be the instrument in God's providential will to bring creation to its final perfection.

Consistently throughout the Old Testament, the Spirit is identified as: the power fulfilling the purposes of God in the divine governance of Israel (cf. Isaiah 31:3); the divine power of sustenance and renewal (Isaiah 44:1–5; Ezekiel 37:14); and creating, renewing and guiding human awareness and experience of God with God's blessing (Psalm 51:10). A portion of the Spirit on Moses was transferred to seventy elders who had been chosen to assist in judging the children of Israel (Numbers 11:17,25). Joshua was commissioned by Moses to be his successor because Joshua possessed the Spirit (Numbers 27:18). The Spirit provided inspiration or charismatic power in the Judges period and equipped Israel's kings for leadership including the provision of detailed direction (1 Samuel 10:6,10; 11:6; 16:13–14; 2 Samuel 23:2). The Spirit gave spiritual direction for Israel through the early prophets: protecting Elijah (1 Kings 18:12); rebuking unbelief (1 Kings 22:24–28); as an endowment for fidelity (1 Chronicles 12:18); strengthening trust (2 Chronicles 15:1); and answering prayer (2 Chronicles 20:14; 24:20).

After the exile, experience of the Spirit was more explicitly perceived: actively involved in creation (Job 26:4; Ezekiel 2:2; 3:24; 11:5); as a prophetic gift (Zechariah 4:6; 7:12); to give instruction (Nehemiah 9:20); being provoked (Psalm 106:32–3); and involved in the creation and ongoing maintenance of life (Psalm 104:29–31).

In the Old Testament, reception of the Spirit comes as an outpouring of blessing from on high (Isaiah 32:15; Ezekiel 39:29; Joel 2:28–29). It is not possible to give counsel to the Spirit (Isaiah 40:13) for the Spirit is the divine messenger (Isaiah 48:16) who rests on the Messiah (Isaiah 61:1). Humanity grieves the Spirit (Isaiah 63:10) but, even so, humanity may be transported by the Spirit (Ezekiel 11:1,24; 37:1; 43:5). A new Spirit is God's gift to Israel (Ezekiel 36:26; Joel 2:28–29). In all of these activities within the

---

10   cf. Exodus 35:31; Numbers 27:18; Daniel 4:8.

history of Israel—either national or personal or in creation generally—the Spirit is the communicating presence of Yahweh.

The Spirit as the Life Principle

The Spirit of God is the principle of life (*nesham, nephesh ruach hayyim*) in both human beings and animals. The Anointed of the Lord, under whose shadow Israel lives, is called the 'breath (*ruach*) of our nostrils'—that is, the Spirit is necessary for Israel's existence (Lamentations 4:20). When the *ruach* is withdrawn, death ensues (Psalm 104:29). Yahweh both gives and takes away breath and is the source of life for all creatures.[11] Yahweh is the God of the spirits (or vital breath) of all flesh (Numbers 16:22; 27:16). At death, the *ruach* returns to God (Ecclesiastes 12:7; Psalm 31:5).

The divine word and the divine breath are virtually synonymous (cf. Psalm 33:6). Creation is by the Spirit's life-giving breath. So when the *ruach* which has been given is withdrawn, the vital breath or principle of existence is withdrawn and the result is loss of strength and consciousness (Judges 15:14; Psalms 31:5; 104:29; Ecclesiastes 12:7)—and, ultimately, death. The presence or absence of *ruach*, evidenced as strong or weak breathing, forms either dispirited or spirited living.[12]

Man in the image of God was made a living soul by divine inbreathing (Genesis 1:27; 2:7).[13] The quickening function attributed to the Spirit is the inbreathing of the Spirit so when God sends forth his Spirit (Psalm 104:29-30) the face of the earth is renewed and living creatures are created. The breath of our nostrils (Lamentations 4:20) is appositional to the anointed (Spirit) of the Lord. Thus the Spirit is identified as the breath of life in the creation of man and also the source of life in the regeneration of both man (Ezekiel 37:5) and the cosmos (Psalm 104:30; Isaiah 32:15). The Spirit is the divine power that influences and guides man in living a righteous life and, accordingly, the Spirit brings about moral and religious renewal (in particular, in the messianic age). The Spirit mediates God's presence (cf.

---

11 That is, through the Spirit. Man became a living soul (nesham, Genesis 2:7) through the divine life-giving breath. Hill points out (1967, 214) that the divine breath and the divine word are not really distinguished, that is, both are efficacious entities involved in the creation process.

12 Hill, 1967, 215.

13 Hill (1967, 164) draws attention to God-given nephesh as the seat of all appetites, emotions and passions.

Ezekiel 39:29), indeed, the Spirit is the fullness of the divine being in and with God's people. God himself is present with his people in his Spirit.

The Spirit's Relationship to God

Consistent with Genesis 1:2, the Spirit is the Trinitarian presence of God in the world evidenced in power for action, prophetic utterance, heroic exploits, or righteous living. Actions performed by the Exodus presence cloud are attributed to the Spirit (cf. Haggai 2:5). Throughout the Old Testament, the Spirit is expressed in divine, creative, energising power in the lives of human individuals and communities. But the inner life or personality of Yahweh is never revealed by the Spirit,[14] rather, the Spirit is always an extension of Yahweh's personality (not an explanation of Yahweh's personality). According to Fatehi, *ruach* in the sense of human breath was a relatively late idea in the Old Testament.[15]

Therefore—for these writers of the Old Testament—Spirit of God refers to: God accomplishing his purposes in his world through men (by his Spirit); and God relating effectively with, and within, his creation (by the presence of his Spirit). To experience the Spirit of God is to experience God as Spirit.

The Spirit and Divine Rule

The Spirit is associated in the Old Testament with divine rule through divinely appointed leaders—and God's powerful presence and control. The divine Spirit endowed Israel's kings and is also upon the Servant of the Lord (Isaiah 42:1; 48:16; 61:1; cf. the Messiah, Isaiah 11) with power for surrogate rule. The Spirit also inspired craftsman with special skills or anointed leadership roles. The Spirit is God in action in creation and the source of life in regeneration.[16]

The Spirit is God as he relates to his world and his people, that is, God relating to what is other than himself. But *ruach* never refers to Yahweh as he is in himself (his essence), rather, *ruach* refers to God as he communicates to the world his power, his life, his anger, his will, his very presence. In Isaiah 40:13, *ruach* is the intelligent centre of God's being—the creative

---

14 Westermann cites Psalm 139:7 and Nehemiah 9:30 to support this view.
15 Fatehi, 2000, 54.
16 Fatehi (2000, 22) argues that the description of the resurrected Jesus as a 'life-giving Spirit' refers to Jesus exercising full power and control over the lives of believers.

mind which was active in planning the work of creation (cf. Isaiah 30:1–2). The Spirit is the purposeful power with which God planned and created the world.

In the period of the Judges, the Spirit's work is seen in the intermittent surge of divine power equipping the early judges for heroic actions. Yahweh led his people through judges who were moved by his Spirit, indeed, charismatic leadership preserved Israel during the period of the judges. In Old Testament Israel, the Spirit led through the anointed king thereby enabling God to lead his people as their ultimate king. The Spirit will enable the messianic king to rule over God's people with wisdom, understanding and power (Isaiah 11:2).

The Spirit and Prophetic Inspiration

Yahweh's covenant promise to be with his people is realised through the presence of the Holy Spirit among them, demonstrating his covenant lordship. The voice of the Spirit through prophecy was recognised as the voice of Yahweh himself (Ezekiel 36:23–29): guiding, correcting, teaching and leading. In Psalm 139:7, 'your Spirit' is synonymous with 'your presence'. These writers speak of the Spirit of God accomplishing God's purposes in his world through men. To experience the Spirit is to experience God exercising his lordship over his people. The point of the stories of Moses, Joshua, the early judges, the kings, or the prophets is that the Lord himself was leading his people through his Spirit. Early accounts of Spirit-anointed prophetic ministry emphasised ecstatic experience (cf. Numbers 11:24–30; 1 Samuel 10:10; 2 Chronicles 24:20; cf. Isaiah 48:16; Ezekiel 11:5; Micah 3:8).

Through the presence of the Lord's Spirit, the covenant formula is activated or, indeed, deactivated when they 'grieved' the Spirit by their disobedience (Isaiah 63:10). Yahweh's covenant lordship is realised through the new work of the Spirit (Ezekiel 36:23–29). Hence, 'I am Yahweh' refers to knowing and experiencing Yahweh as the sovereign Lord who communicates his presence by the Spirit. So the Spirit is God conveying to creation gifted capacities and powers beyond normal experience and capacity.[17]

---

17 In prophetic inspiration or prophetic prediction in the history of Israel (Ezekiel 11:24; 36:26; 37:1; 39:29; 43:5; Joel 2:28–29; Zechariah 4:6).

Wisdom and Spirit

Wisdom in Proverbs 1–9 is not merely a literary personification—not a hypostasis—but a personal or quasi-divine entity distinct from God. Wisdom pours out her spirit (cf. Spirit, Proverbs 1:23). Spirit is either the source of the words or the inspirer of the words, or both. 'My Spirit' is the Spirit who imparts wisdom. The Spirit is, therefore, the medium or immediate source of wisdom; that is, transcendent wisdom makes herself available through her Spirit.[18]

Thus the Old Testament activity of the Spirit is both personal and divine in directing the people of God. Only a personal Spirit could engage in high-level rational activity in relationship to other persons.[19] Even so, the partial and sporadic presentation of the Spirit's activity in the Old Testament is prophesied to become full, widespread experience of the Spirit (cf. Ezekiel 36:25–27; Joel 2:28ff.) under the new covenant. The fulfilment of this prophetic expectation will be in the New Testament presentation of God in Christ.

---

18 The Old Testament wisdom literature supports this contention (cf. Fatehi, 2000, 102, n 65).

19 Ferguson, 1996, 16–21.

The Spirit in Regeneration[20]

A theology of the Spirit must relate to the history of redemption from the fall to the new creation since God and Christ (cf. John 1:1–3) express their will for the world through the Spirit. The work of the Spirit in the Old Testament brings into view the history of Israel and her covenants. Covenant theology (established by Genesis 6:18) asserts God's covenant intention in Genesis 2 and follows a connected covenant chain through the Old Testament towards Jesus' new covenant (Luke 22:20).

The divine work of personal restoration into the image of God begins with the fall. Immediately after the fall, the dire needs of the world are revealed (Genesis 4). The second generation of humans become aware that the fruit of toil should evoke spontaneous, sacrificial thanksgiving to God as the provider. The unexplained inauguration of a sacrificial system reveals an instinctive desire to be related to God and to recognise God as the giver of life. Almost immediately after the fall, humanity began to call on the name of Yahweh (Genesis 4:26), that is, to acknowledge the Creator in worship and recognise that he undergirds the basic processes of life and the future. But the human world was also bent on self-destruction (Genesis 6:11f.) so—as man refused to live within the God-given creation order—God chose to make a new beginning through a covenant with Noah (Genesis 6:18) which pointed back to the divine basis for creation (Genesis 1:26–28)[21] along with the expanded terms of the covenant plan for human history (Genesis 2). This original, creation covenant is the basis on which the created world will endure. Successive covenants with Abraham[22] and Israel formalise movement, in the context of redemptive history and under God's control, to the new Eden (Revelation 22:1–5).

The divine covenants of the Bible (including Jesus' new covenant in the upper room) are all unilateral arrangements (like the divine covenant with

---

20 Ferguson (1996, 16–21) states that the Spirit's work was moral, redemptive and ethical.

21 The evidence for the creation character of the covenant recalled in Genesis 6:18 rests on the uniform backward recall associated with the Hiphil of the Hebrew verb used in all its Old Testament references.

22 The covenant with Abram, a Sethite, represents the divine continuation of the covenant with creation (Genesis 6:18) with world blessing in view. The Abram covenant exhibited the beginning of world evangelism, expressing God's intention to bring in a new creation.

creation), without the ratifier's (acceptor's) negotiation.²³ But all the Old Testament covenants depend on the original conception of purpose that is signalled by Genesis 6:18 which recall the Creator's pledge in creation to bring in a perfect world for humanity. This perfect world will be like Eden (Genesis 2), that is, Eden is the model for the future.²⁴ So the covenants take us from Abraham to the new creation and exhibit revelational milestones in the expression of the divine intention. In the purposes of God, Israel is to continue with the Abrahamic commission (cf. Genesis 12:3) to bring in a new world after God's decision to begin again after the flood. But Israel fails in this commission and this failure of Israel reflects the failure of human history to bring in God's totally ordered new creation.

Beginning with Abraham, Scripture plots the intended course of God's intervention by successive covenant indications of divine intentions for national Israel. But, following the covenant with God at the cutting of the new tablets—replacing the broken tablets (Exodus 34:10)—continued defection from God's covenant is to be expected.²⁵ A succession of Old Testament covenants leads to Jesus' commitment to the Divine new covenant (the remedy for world defection, cf. Luke 22:20). This revelation of biblical covenants is the agenda to which, in both Testaments, the Spirit will respond with the breath of spiritual life in regeneration or the absence of spiritual life when the Spirit departs.

The place and purpose of the Sinai covenant as an extension of the Abrahamic covenant²⁶ is important. Biblical covenants are concerned with human expression and development. The Sinai covenant required human response to the Ten Commandments²⁷ with a right response possible upon reception of the individual gift of the Spirit (in both Testaments).²⁸ The Ten

---

23 The covenant with Abram is the only divine covenant in the Old Testament which has two parties, perhaps dur to the important position of that covenant in the framework of eschatology.

24 cf. Dumbrell, 1984 and 2013. Genesis 6:18, referring back to Genesis 2, has the final new creation in mind.

25 The the covenant of Exodus 34:10 placed Israel under severe restrictions for the remainder of her history. That covenant is concluded by the cross of Jesus.

26 Israel is now to carry the intended blessing of the Abraham covenant to the world.

27 The Commandments were a description for Israel of the ideal life, that is, a life produced by divine grace.

28 The Ten Commandments were communicated in the second person singular and, therefore, directed at individual compliance. As time progressed, a remnant came to

Commandments develop the character of human response to the divine covenant in a lifestyle which was the divine intention at creation for humanity.[29] Each of the Ten Commandments is evident in Scripture prior to the Ten being delivered (Exodus 20). The exhibition of the divine intention for humanity through covenant obedience in the Promised Land was to be Israel's mission to the world. But, from the covenant default of the golden calf sin (Exodus 32) onwards, Israel completely failed to express the Commandments. So the work of the Spirit in regeneration needed to be expanded from the required individual response (Exodus 20:1–17) to a grace-filled national Decalogue life.

True identification with the divine covenant required an individual response, through grace, to the covenant rescue from Egypt as a divine act of God (Exodus 20:2). The one, biblical gospel (cf. Mark 1:14–15) is the first commandment to respond to God's action of redemption with singular devotion (Exodus 20:2–3). Hence, obedience to the Commandments as the response to grace was the way of life for Old Testament believers within Israel who accepted the gospel. Hence, national Israel was always divided into believers who were enlivened by the Spirit to act in obedience to the Law and unbelievers who did not have a personal relationship with the God who had rescued Israel.[30]

The Decalogue (ten words) must be interpreted in the light of its prologue—indeed, interpreted in the light of the name of God which gives the understanding of his nature as the I Am in control of past, present and future. The beginning of the relationship between God and humanity is always that he is able to deliver from bondage. The basis and intention of the Decalogue is that God is the God who redeems from any sort of slavery. So the ethic in response to the Decalogue is not grim obedience but, rather, gratitude for the gift of freedom. The Decalogue explains to Israelites individually the dimensions of grace already received and the significance for personal living of the great redemption from slavery. So the Commandments are an invitation to a lifestyle in touch with the God who frees from slavery.

---

be in Israel who were faithful to God in obedience to his commandments.

29 cf. the New Testament indication of the purpose of the Ten Commandments (Romans 1:18–32; 2:12–16), cf. Dumbrell, 2005, 5–6.

30 cf. Romans 9:6; 11:1–6.

The introduction to the Ten Words is a summary of God's grace as it is revealed in the Bible, commencing with the 'I am' divine name (Exodus 3:14) which fosters trust for the future. The Ten Words are not a demand but a set of directions for Eden living in a new Promised Land. So biblical 'law' comes in a framework of grace. If there is no framework of grace from the God whom Israel now knows, then there is no impetus for the new way of life that is being communicated to individual heads of families for the nation. Thus—in the Ten Words and its prologue—gospel precedes 'law', that is, law is a call to a grace-filled life through the Spirit. God saves Israel then provides instructions for a life-style designed to produce maximum blessing (the Sinai covenant). The Decalogue is addressed to those who have just become, by a great redemption, a kingdom of God society. The commandments set forth basic conditions for inclusion in this community of saved Israel.

Law (Torah) interpreted grace. Under the Sinai covenant, law operates by being placed in the individual heart (cf. Deuteronomy 6:6) so that the individual keeps the law in response to grace. But this ideal state relationship with God through law had been fatally impaired by the fall. Consistent with the theology of law operating from within the heart, the predicted national exile for Israel could only be averted by Yahweh circumcising the national heart (Deuteronomy 30:3-6)—that is, when the law is placed in the national heart. But this heart circumcision was never the experience of the nation of Israel in the Old Testament, indeed, after Judah's return from the Babylonian exile the nation re-established pre-exilic practices which had led the nation into exile.

Exodus 25–31 applied and interpreted the covenant, emphasising the priestly character of Israel's kingdom including the essential place of worship of her sovereign Lord. The building of the tabernacle expressed the reality of divine rule and, being portable, it led the movement to the Promised Land. The 'rest' to be enjoyed by Israel in the Promised Land remained elusive throughout the Old Testament but there is a promised fulfilment in an eternal Sabbath rest for the people of God (Hebrews 4:9) as the new Eden experience for the new Israel to come (Revelation 21–22).

Deuteronomy is about the life that is offered to Israel in the Promised Land—an abundant life lacking nothing—provided Israel took the land over and dismissed its inhabitants. Israel was to be Yahweh's world sanctuary re-presenting the ideal of Eden. But entry into the Promised Land was in fact followed by a period of absolute disorder. The writer surveying the period of the judges is appalled by the social and religious disintegration of the period. Even so, Israel was preserved in the period of the judges for a future purpose by the continued intervention of Israel's deity through the Spirit (Judges 3:10; 6:34; 11:29) culminating in the Spirit-led forays of Samson (Judges 13:25; 14:19; 15:14,19). Despite the glaring apostasy of the time, the ideal of Israel (with Yahweh continuing to be their God) was preserved.

The Spirit in Leadership

Judges to 2 Samuel

The Spirit enabled Moses and Joshua to lead (Numbers 11:10–30; 27:16–23; Deuteronomy 34:9) and the Spirit's work is seen in the intermittent surge of divine power which equipped the early judges—and Israel's first king—for their heroic actions (Othniel, Judges 3:10; Gideon, Judges 6:34; Jephthah, Judges 11:29; Samson, Judges 13:25; 14:6,19; 15:14ff; Saul, 1 Samuel 11:6).

The Song of Hannah (1 Samuel 2:1–10) reformulated the ideal of divine leadership for Israel. Prior to Samuel's ministry (1 Samuel 4–6), the focus is the manifestation of the divine power of Yahweh over Israel in crisis. But Israel didn't ever learn from that object lesson. Samuel is then presented as Israel's saviour from both external and internal threats (1 Samuel 7). The transition to kingship occurred by the interposition of the Spirit (1 Samuel 10:6,10; 11:6) but Saul's reign is unsteady (1 Samuel 8–16). Kingship is then engrafted into the Sinai covenant—in which Yahweh covenanted to be the God of the children of Israel (Exodus 20:1)—with Saul (1 Samuel 10:10) and then David (1 Samuel 16:13) authorised through the Spirit to act as Yahweh's representatives. When Saul is dismissed as Yahweh's representative, the Spirit is withdrawn (1 Samuel 16:14).

Control by the Spirit was the ideal of Israelite kingship under covenant, but only Saul and David—of all the kings of national Israel—exhibit election, anointing, Spirit endowment, and prowess. All four of these features of a covenant king is evident in Jesus the Messiah. In the Old Testament, Davidic messiahship describes, eschatologically, the ideal ruler under the Spirit bringing about the desired conditions of the eschaton (the new Israel kingdom of God).

Not only Saul's reign but also David's reign clearly demonstrate that the expectations of the messiah could not be fulfilled by a human. In the case of David—after becoming king over all Israel (2 Samuel 5:1–5)—he makes Jerusalem, the former Jebusite city, his capital. But the development of 2 Samuel shows that David is unable to fulfil the divine requirement of his office as God's covenant king, despite the fact that the succession to messiahship is through David's line (2 Samuel 7).

The promise of a Messiah for Israel from the house of David is not withdrawn, indeed, Davidic kingship continues to be linked to the physical blessings of the Covenant with Creation (Genesis 6:18) even though David's physical line ceased to be kings after Jerusalem fell to the Babylonian king Nebuchadnezzar (circa 587BC). But this expected Messiah through David's line (2 Samuel 23:2ff.) will only be fulfilled by Jesus of Nazareth whose coming and call fully expressed the divine requirements of the office of covenant king.

The Prophets: Elijah to Isaiah

Jerusalem, David's capital, became a world centre (cf. 1 Kings 4:34; 10:24) during the united kingdom. After the kingdom split into Israel and Judah, the northern kingdom narratives feature the prophets Elijah and Elisha (1Kings 17 to 2 Kings 2). Elijah's prophetic triumphs in 1 Kings 18 are followed by a retreat to Sinai (the mountain of God, 1 Kings 19:8; cf. Exodus 3:1; 4:27) in which Elijah is transformed into a Moses-like figure.

1 and 2 Kings survey the Davidic Empire from its rise to its fall while the C8 BC prophets—Amos, Micah and Isaiah—faced with the impending exile of the North and the continuing apostasy of the South, reassess the theological role of Jerusalem as they consider the divine choice of and purpose for Israel. These prophets redefine the roles of Jerusalem and Israel. God's covenant appears to be in jeopardy when David's capital city Jerusalem is physically punished. But the emergent carriers of hope for the future new Jerusalem (Isaiah 65:18) will be a remnant of believers within the faithless Israelite nation.

Amos addressed the question of Jerusalem's religious significance for the whole of Israel and Micah—similar to Isaiah—pronounced judgement on Israel and Judah. Their prophecies about God's redemptive action are directed towards the faithful remnant.

The Spirit in Isaiah's visions of Jerusalem and New Jerusalem

The building of the temple in Jerusalem (Mount Zion) enabled older creation and salvation traditions to be transferred to the temple. Zion is closely connected with Davidic kingship (Psalm 132). From his temple/palace, Yahweh would protect Israel's king—Yahweh's anointed—and Zion will become the world mountain, the world centre where heaven and earth meet. Zion is the place where healing and peace are brought to world society. Zion appears to be inviolable after David's capture of Jerusalem, giving rise to the doctrine of Yahweh's enthronement as the King of Glory in Zion (Psalm 24:7–10).

The role of Jerusalem and her function within God's plan are the themes that bind Isaiah's prophecies together as a theological unity. 2:2–4 foreshadow Zion's elevation in the latter days, with the cherished expectation for Jerusalem as the divine city of God with the temple and the Davidic royal city. In Isaiah, the temple becomes the major symbol carrying Israel's hopes for the future, hence the veneration of Zion as the cosmic mountain of the divine abode.

Spirit and New Creation (Isaiah 11)

The messianic shoot to emerge from the stem of Jesse (11:1–2) will be endowed by the Spirit of the Lord with the Spirit of wisdom and understanding thereby bringing about the divine ideal for the world. This new messianic David will possess the Spirit permanently. The messiah will also possess the Spirit of counsel and might, and the Spirit of knowledge and fear of the Lord. Possessing these gifts of the Spirit, the messianic king will make appropriate judgements and carry them out. The outcome of messianic reign is: righteous judgement for the poor; fair decisions for the meek of the earth (11:4); all creation denuded of wickedness and threats of violence (11:4–9); the earth full of the knowledge of the Lord as the waters cover the sea (11:9); the remnant of Yahweh's people gathered from their dispersion (11:11); and nations of the remnant included in the covenant will flock to the banner of the messianic king in the New Jerusalem and peace will then prevail from New Jerusalem (11:12).

The Spirit is the Instrument of Renewal (Isaiah 32 & 43)

The righteous king will rule in righteousness and justice (32:1-8) but imminent judgement on Jerusalem will precede future hope. An oracle addressed to the complacent women of Israel (11:9) expects doom on the ground, indicating the coming exile. Desolation is to last until there is an eschatological outpouring of the Spirit of God to change the world and people (32:15). Then a truly righteous king will be reigning over Israel (32:1) who will do what all the world's rulers have failed to do (32:2-8). The whole created world will be affected by his righteous reign effected by the pouring out of God's Spirit. Everything is transformed. Justice and righteousness and peace now benefit the land as it is inundated with the outpoured Spirit (32:15-18). All nature is transformed by the Spirit's power and presence.

Against the backdrop of a devastated Israel (32:9-14), God will bring renewal (32:15). The Spirit poured out from on high is the instrument of this renewal as he brings justice and righteousness (32:16) forever (32:17). The effects of this justice and righteousness will be peace, quietness and trust forever (32:17).

The Spirit is to be poured out 'on your descendants' with blessings poured out 'on your offspring' (44:3), with the Spirit presented symbolically as life-giving water that refreshes parched earth (44:1-5). Consequently, the earth is renewed (32:15-18) as the people of God are renewed (44:1-5). Isaiah thus prophesies the reordering of all creation (40-66).

The Servant of the Lord is Divinely Empowered with the Spirit

The heavens exhort Israel to turn from apostasy (40:12-41:29) and then, continuing this exhortation, Yahweh introduces his Servant whom he divinely empowers with the Spirit (42:1) for a mission to bring about world justice (42:4). The Servant will not cease to strive until he has established justice in the earth, manifesting the complete success of Yahweh's supremacy in the processes of history. Yahweh's eschatological divine rule through the Spirit-anointed Servant will operate from the New Jerusalem. The Servant is given as a covenant to the people, an indication that through him God will implement justice in all the earth and pour blessing on future Israel.

The pronounced individuality of the Servant passage (52:13-53:12) indicates that the Servant community, upon whom Israel's hopes reposed, has been reduced to one. The Servant represents faithful Israel when he bears sin for the many (53:12). The consequence of this ministry (Isaiah 54) is a covenant of peace, pointing forward to Zion's unchallengeable supremacy in the imposition of the new covenant and final new order. This new life will flow from new Jerusalem, the new Eden, as waters of life (Isaiah 55). God's promises extend to all who come in obedience to Mount Zion. The suffering and death of Yahweh's Spirit-endowed Servant will achieve: the covenant of peace; the restoration of Zion; the new exodus; and the return of the exiles (Isaiah 53). The Servant will usher in the new era (Isaiah 54), the age of the new creation, with an eternal covenant of peace.

Isaiah 56–66, which is predominantly post-exilic, carries forward the eschatology of hope presented in Isaiah 40–55. Isaiah 61 opens with the commissioning of a Servant-like figure—by Yahweh's Spirit (61:1–3)—who will bring a message of new hope to the poor Jewish community residing in Palestine as they are waiting for the fulfilment of Biblical promises. Directed by the Spirit, the message is that the Servant will bind up the broken-hearted and release the captives. Then the world will pay homage to the bride, Zion; and the world will witness the salvation bestowed on the people of God (61:10–11). Because of what God had done to save Israel, but not for any of Israel's achievements, the nations will come in pilgrimage to serve God. Israel's future is cast in the covenant imagery of marriage (62:4b–5). The divine intention is to fulfil all the promises made to Zion (62:6–9).

Yahweh's Intimate Presence as Spirit (Isaiah 63)

Yahweh's intimate presence as Spirit is not impersonal substance (cf. 32:15).[31] God 'sends' his *ruach* or his angel or his word but God expresses himself by his Spirit. The LXX of 63:9 is rendered by the NRSV 'it was no messenger or angel but his presence that saved them'.[32] The presence of the Lord's Spirit activates the covenant and the rejection of divine communication through the Spirit puts the covenant at risk (63:10).[33]

In the Exodus narrative, the covenant blessing of rest was ascribed to the presence of the Lord's *panim* (face, Exodus 14:19; 33:11,14,20). But in Isaiah 63, the covenant blessing of God's personal presence is ascribed to

---

31 The strong argument against a view of the Spirit as impersonal substance must be mounted from the New Testament, in particular, the Spirit loves (Romans 15:30), can be grieved (Ephesians 4:30), and possesses a will (1 Corintians 12:11). The Old Testament also refers to the Spirit as regenerative (cf. Ezekiel 37:14; Isaiah 44:3a).

32 Fatehi, 2000, 55.

33 Hill, 1967, 228.

the Spirit as an extension of God's own being (63:11–12).[34] Terms such as his glory (cf. 6:3), his breath (30:28), and his Spirit (34:16; 48:16) all refer to Yahweh himself in action. The significance of the Lord's personal leading of Israel in the exodus is repeated in the eschaton according to Isaiah's prophecy: 'thus you led your people to make for yourself a glorious name' (63:14). At times, the Spirit may seem to refer to impersonal substance but the reference is metaphorical of the Spirit being 'sent'. The relational character of the Spirit of God in the Old Testament ensures that the Spirit is never regarded as an entity distinct or separable from Yahweh but, rather, as an extension of Yahweh's personality.[35]

---

[34] cf. 1 Samuel 10:6–7 where the presence of the Spirit is equated with the presence of God.

[35] cf. Fatehi (2000, 53) where the Spirit mediates God's presence.

The Spirit and Individuality in the Psalms

Individuals learn the direction for a way of life required by Biblical covenants through the Spirit. Individual, godly experience in the Old Testament requires the law to be in the heart (cf. Psalm 51). Psalm 51 begins with a comprehensive analysis of sin as rebellion, that is, sin is a breach of the covenant (51:4). David's repentance unfolds when he recognises that his sin has placed him under the judgement of God (51:4) and in danger of being cast out from the presence of God, that is, in danger of being separated from the indwelling presence of the Spirit (51:11).[36] True repentance involves a broken personal spirit (51:17) because self-sufficiency and self-defence have been broken down. The outcome of a broken spirit is God's personal presence in his Spirit. This gift of the Spirit provides inner strength for righteous living. Real repentance brought about by the Spirit is evidenced in a new concern for holiness, that is, a new desire for: heart-reality and a clean life (51:6–7); purity and renewal (51:10); a desire to serve and save others (51:13); and a personal plea to God, 'Take not your Holy Spirit from me' (51:11).

Sinclair Ferguson remarks that David's plea to God—not to take back his Spirit—demonstrates that David is fearful of being removed from the divine office into which the Holy Spirit had installed him as king of Israel (1 Samuel 16:12–13).[37] But David's plea is that God will restore to him the joy of salvation (51:11–12), indeed, what's at stake is more than Samuel's official anointing. Whereas the Old Testament does not state concisely that the gift of the Spirit is directly associated with personal salvation or general covenant connection, even so, David realises that his personal and national gifts cannot continue without the Spirit's ministry in restoration.

In 51:10, the clean heart is dependent on God's movement in a new creation (*bara*, 'I create'). David asks God to 'renew an upright Spirit within me' as David is well aware of the Spirit's personal indwelling and theocratic presence. In the Old Testament, a national change of heart required circumcision of the heart (Jeremiah 4:4; 9:25–26b), that is, a complete life-change in the hearts of individuals (cf. 37:31; 40:8). What follows from the

---

36 David's 'take not thy Holy Spirit from me' (51:11) indicates his understanding not only of how God's grace comes but also how it could be lost.

37 Ferguson, 1996, 24.

law in the heart is the believers' experience of new creation. Indeed, David's future is forgiveness (2 Samuel 12:13).

With the law in the heart, the Psalmist proclaims that 'his steps do not slip'(37:31). The statement that the Lord's law is in David's heart is preceded by his affirmation: 'I delight to do your will, O, my God' (40:8). The Bible—Old and New Testament—wrestles with the tension between the law being in the heart and the obedience that ought to arise therefrom. Old Testament believers exult that the joy of the law is in the heart for they love the law (cf. Psalm 119).[38] So the spiritual possession of the law in the heart was the experience of believing Israelites who knew the Spirit in the Old Testament and received forgiveness of sins, at least in part, through the Old Testament means of sacrificial grace.

All spiritual renewal comes from God through the Spirit. Old Testament experience—such as the (representative) faith of Abraham and the piety of the Psalms—are expressions of New Testament teaching about the Spirit's sovereign work of inner renewal and personal transformation (119:37). The Spirit's inner renewal and personal transformation was not often experienced in Old Testament Israel but there is, nevertheless, continuity in the experience of God's grace through the abiding presence of the Holy Spirit from the Old Testament to the New Testament. The law in the heart is an Old Testament understanding of the outcome of spiritual regeneration (Jeremiah 31:33; cf. Ezekiel 36:26–27). This law in the heart is not just individual because the prophecy says that God will give the nation, collectively, a new heart.

---

38 cf. 119:16,24,47,69b,70b,77b,92a,97,119b,127a,140,163b,167b,174.

The Role of the Spirit in the Future Revival of Israel

How is the law in the heart in the Old Testament, that is, what is the personal role of the Spirit in the Old Testament? Jeremiah 31:33–34 present the new covenant replacement for the Jewish covenants (to be implemented by the death of Jesus). This new covenant will come into operation because of Israel's default with regard to the Sinai and Mosaic covenants. The law (*torah*, Jeremiah 31:33), referring to the Sinai code (the Decalogue), will be in the heart in the new age of the new covenant. Is this interior location of the *torah* in opposition to the external location of the law on two tables of stone in the old age (cf. Exodus 24:12)? Will the interiorised, personalised *torah*—now written on the heart of the individual in the new age—thereby become denationalised? It should be noted that the word 'heart' in the Old Testament refers comprehensively to all inward aspects of personal psychology including, most frequently, thought processes that direct both attitudes and actions. Heart may also refer to moral awareness (conscience) including personal responsibility for decisions and actions.

James Hamilton argues that there is evidence for a distinction between regeneration by the Holy Spirit and indwelling of the Holy Spirit in the Old Testament.[39] But Hamilton overlooks the personalised evidence to which I have referred when he makes the observation that, in the Old Testament, someone who has the Spirit is different from other Old Testament believers. This conclusion is based on the recorded experience of mediators and leaders of the old covenant. These prophets and political leaders were given the Spirit on an individual basis for the national good or for specific national agendas. But I suggest that ordinary Israelites understood that a right response to covenant was always dependant on individual salvation and that, consequently, individual salvation is an experience that is common to both Testaments. Indeed, the Old Testament calls on the individual to ensure that the law is in the heart (cf. Deuteronomy 6:5) but the individual cannot put the law in the heart for only God can lodge the law in the heart.

---

39 Hamilton (2006. 11–121) rightly discerns a distinction between regeneration and indwelling throughout the Bible. Regeneration is God's action in absolute life-change resulting from a recognition that the law is in the heart. Whereas there is not much evidence for this absolute life-change in the Old Testament, it can nevertheless be seen in the personalised literature of the Psalms. Hamilton overlooks the strongly personalised evidence for regeneration in the Psalms.

That there is a special conferral or anointing of the Spirit on Israel's leadership—as distinct from believers in general—is true, for the Spirit is given in peculiar ways for particular purposes (cf. Joshua, Deuteronomy 34:9) or for a special task. But this conferral of the Spirit for the public purpose of Israel as a world witness did not necessarily produce a correlation with personal conduct reflecting law in the heart. Hamilton's review of these cases of particular anointing leaves out the personal literature (cf. the Psalms) representing believer-style experience of regeneration by and indwelling of the Holy Spirit in the Old Testament.

God acted in the Exodus to save the nation of Israel and then called the nation to live according to the externally written covenant, that is, as those who were controlled by the Spirit. But the actual covenant experience of believers was awareness of the indwelling Spirit.[40] Hence there is evidence in the Old Testament for both regeneration (the new life brought about by salvation) and the Spirit's personal indwelling.

National Covenantal Experience (Jeremiah 31:33–34)

Jeremiah's prophecy of the new covenant closes with the conventional Sinai covenant formula, with God saying 'I will be their God, and they shall be my people' (31:33). This well-known formula functions as a conclusion to the revue of the past (old covenant) and a pause to prepare for what is new in 31:34. Accordingly—like the Sinai/Mosaic covenant (31:33) which expected personalised evidence of the Spirit, with individuals required to implement the covenant—God's purpose in the new era is to put his law in the hearts of all the saved so that, like the Old Testament, believers are called to obedience. But externality increasingly characterised Israelite religion as it moved away from original covenant intentions in the Old Testament so 31:33 indicates that God's plan in the new covenant is to return to the original intent of the Sinai covenant. But 31:34 goes beyond the Sinai covenant by indicating the fulfilment, in the new age, of what was always required with regard to personal regeneration and true membership of the Old Testament covenants.[41] The radical newness of the new covenant is what happens beyond 31:33–34.

---

40 We could point to the unity of experience expected from the nation in the torah (Deuteronomy 4–11) contrasted with the reality of personal disobedience, that is, the vast majority of individual Israelites not observing the torah (Deuteronomy 9:6–14).

41 Scott Hafemann (1996, 14–28) agrees with my contention that Jeremiah 31:33 does not contain the newness of the covenant but, rather, expresses what was always

Hamilton argues for regeneration and against indwelling under the old covenant, that is, he agrees that general spiritual change occurs in the Old Testament but refuses to accept that there is any personal indwelling of God's Spirit before Pentecost. So Hamilton appears to be arguing that the Old Testament believer could not personally know that change had occurred as the Spirit could not be personally known. But if the Spirit cannot be known by Old Testament believers then regeneration only provides moral stimulation, that is, regeneration is no more than a new disposition. But there is evidence of personal heart renewal in individual Old Testament believers.

In short, the disassociation of indwelling from regeneration in the Old Testament is not a satisfactory position but it would be equally unsatisfactory to suggest that Pentecost adds nothing to personal experience of the Spirit. Moreover, both regeneration and indwelling represent once and for all change in the life of an individual as evidenced in David who is aware of a new spiritual presence associated with regeneration (Psalm 51:10).

M. M. B. Turner has suggested that, in the new covenant, a true understanding of Jesus' mission from baptism to glorification must come progressively through the Spirit experienced in the Word.[42] In John's gospel, this progressive understanding of indwelling becomes a natural process towards full personal awareness developing within those who have already experienced regeneration. Turner thus understands the command 'to receive the Spirit' (John 20:22) to refer to a climactic event in a progressive process. A profound personal sequence of change and growth is needed to take believers from the Garden (Genesis 2) to the Cross and beyond. The growth of faith and personal experience in the Old Testament reaches its climax in the post-cross full sanctification by the word of truth (cf. John 17:18–19). The disciples at the end of the gospel are now confronted by the risen Lord and commissioned anew in the upper room so they now come into an understanding of Jesus' message at a much deeper level. The cross and the resurrection then provide all that is needed to complete the salvation gift of the Spirit. This view of progressive understanding and climactic reception of the Spirit seems to accord with the inchoate position of the Old Testament.

---

required for true covenant experience in the Old Testament.
42 cf. Turner, 1998, 99.

Partly concurring with Hamilton but more fully with Turner, I believe that the Biblical evidence is that regeneration is a work of the Spirit that brings about an irreversible change (cf. Jesus to Israel, John 10:27-28) which is a complete new beginning. The Old Testament includes some awareness of a personal work of the Spirit, that is, indwelling is attested freely in many Psalms and sometimes in the historical narrative (cf. Hannah's prayer, 1 Samuel 2).

Personalised spiritual witness for personal spiritual indwelling is evident in the Old Testament though not prominent because of the emphasis on adducing reasons for Israel's disastrous failure as a nation, even though much of its leadership had been given the gift of the Spirit. As stated, 31:33 expresses continuity with past experience, that is, in the Old Testament Yahweh both initiated and maintained the covenant and his maintenance of the covenant was not conditional upon Israel's obedience. Rabbinic theology suggested that a person could withdraw from the covenant without cancelling the obligation. Historically, even when faced with national disobedience, God remained faithful to his covenant promises. Israel intentionally rejected God's right to direct the affairs of the nation and this was a rejection of the covenant by Israel so—in order to maintain God's national covenant with Israel—covenant maintenance was finally not contingent upon Israel's obedience but upon God's commitment.

The new covenant, like the old, is God's gift. Furthermore, the new covenant will not be a total change without connection to the past (31:33). But in the new covenant, all true covenant members will receive the fullness of the Spirit so that the consummation of history for the saved in the new creation will be the total infilling of the Spirit with believers totally led by the Spirit.

Wonderful spiritual experience had been possible under the Old Testament covenants and progressively more so for believers identified as 'the remnant' by Isaiah (with a previous brief mention in Amos). After Sinai there were always two Israels: national Israel which had never been a covenant nation since the golden calf episode (Exodus 32); and individual Israelite believers who were open to the work of God through the Spirit, like Hannah (1 Samuel 1-2). The bulk of the nation, including national leaders, remained spiritually unmoved throughout Old Testament history. Indeed, national Israel finally severed any connection with God's covenant when—at the cross, rejecting Jesus—the Israelites proclaimed that they had no king but the Roman Caesar.

Prior to Jeremiah's new covenant prophecy, there was already a remnant of believers with the law in their hearts (cf. 31:33; the law in the heart is not the new element in the new covenant). These believers with the law in their hearts lived in a sinful world and succumbed to sin themselves from time to time. Believers in both Testaments, until the advent of the new creation, are always in need of divine forgiveness which is made available to them through sacrifice.[43] But Jeremiah concludes his prophecy about the new covenant with the words 'their sin I will remember no more' (31:34). Here is a new element in the new age heralded by the return of Christ, that is, the fulfilment of the new covenant effects the final defeat of sin and death so that all believers are relieved from the propensity to sin and instead will only seek to reflect the will of God always.

The demands of the new covenant must be met by the infusion of divine grace. That is, just as there was an explicit law pertaining to the old covenant (Exodus 20:2ff), in the same way there is a connection between covenant and law in Jeremiah's new covenant prophecy. The problem is that historic, national Israel had never kept the law of the covenant. But neither will believers under the new covenant be able to live without sin (1 John 1:8). The law that will be put in the heart (31:33) in the new covenant is the same creational Exodus law which had been required of national Israel and put into individual hearts in the old covenant for personal expression of commitment to Yahweh. But—whether old or new covenant, until the consummation of the new covenant in the return of Christ—all still sin.

The condition for spiritual experience described in 31:33 (namely, the law of the Lord in the heart) is the basis for all spiritual experience in both Testaments. But there is significantly new content in 31:34 where believers are transformed by the Spirit so that they will always express outwardly the interiorised divine will (31:33). 31:34 begins with *we lo ... 'od* (and no longer). *We* (and) indicates an affirmation or continuation of 31:33 but *lo ... 'od* (no longer) presumes the emergence of a new situation—so believers will 'no longer' need the instructional framework of intermediaries like

---

43 There was a sacrificial system given by God in the Old Testament which provided forgiveness for any who confessed their sin. This Old Testament system looked forward to the atonement of the cross, and New Testament forgiveness (1 John 1:8–9) looked back to cover the needs of all who confessed.

priests and prophets, rather, in the new situation all will know God directly and personally. The need for instruction characterised imperfect old covenant relationships (cf. Deuteronomy 6:7; Joshua 1:8; Psalm 1:2). But the tension between the law being in the heart, and the outward response to instruction because the law is in the heart, is a problem which confronts writers of both Old and New Testaments. In the New Testament, believers who walk in the Spirit must also strive against the flesh. But 31:34 goes beyond the Bible's record of personal experience because the limitations of sin have been transcended in the new birth so that believers have now changed, that is, they now have perfected human natures.

The democratisation prophecy of 31:34, whereby all become prophets, is not totally fulfilled in the New Testament era with the outpouring of the gift of the Spirit. The final, important factor which controls the era of the new covenant is contained in the elaboration of 31:34, namely—unlike the era when forgiveness of sins was so necessary and extensive—God will no longer need to act against believers because God will forgive their iniquity and remember their sin no more.

The forgiveness of sins in the Old Testament was obtained through the institutionalised sacrificial system. God forgave on the condition of repentance. But there is no mention of any such precondition in the new age (31:34), rather, it appears that sin has been dealt with once and for all. So in the new age there will be no need for any more action against sin, that is, the Spirit will not need to strive with human flesh (cf. Galatians 5:16–18). In the new age, the fall has no influence because sin is no longer remembered. This is not simply prophetic hyperbole or the psychological attitude of God—forgiving by forgetting sin—in the new age. Rather, in the new age no action needs to be taken against sin because sin is defeated.

The contrast in 31:34 is not between wide divine grace in the new age versus limited divine grace in the old age, rather, the change under the new covenant is so extensive that sin will not occur for God will be universally honoured in human conduct. This is a supposition of unfettered mutual fellowship between God and men, that is, a community in which there is no need for instruction and no breach of fellowship between God and men. The harmony in new creation society prevents the possibility of any tension threatening relationships. In the New Testament, post-cross entry into the new covenant is by regeneration through the Spirit but the post cross era is not a sin-free situation until the end of history. The new covenant, inaugurated by Jesus' death and resurrection, operates in the New Testament as individual regeneration in which believers are being changed by the Lord—who is the Spirit—that is, gradually transformed into the image of God in a work of the Spirit that will be completed when Jesus returns. In the meantime, just as the saints of Israel were gradually transformed by the benefits of the sacrificial system, we are similarly being transformed by the Spirit's application of the benefits of Jesus' sacrificial death to us (2 Corinthians 3:18; cf. 1 John 1:9). But under the fully operative new covenant in the new creation, saved new Israel will have new life in the abiding presence of God. This abiding presence of God in the new creation contrasts with the sporadic, external activity reported of the Spirit in the Old Testament.

Jeffrey J Niehaus refutes the view that the law in the heart indicated regeneration and, hence, was evidence of the Spirit's indwelling in the Old Testament. Niehaus' view—that indwelling was not possible before the Pentecost gift of the Spirit—commands wide support. Niehaus concludes: 'the idea of putting the law on one's heart in the Mosaic covenant is very much a matter of individual application'.[44] But I have argued that God's commitment under the new covenant to put the law in the heart for all believers is an ideal position which had also been the intent of the Sinai covenant, as indicated by God's second person singular address (Exodus 20) with families and individuals in view.[45] I argue that the new covenant should be viewed as a transformation of the Sinai covenant with a different Israel.[46] Niehaus cites Deuteronomy 6:4-6 and 11:18 as indicating that the individual person himself places divine communication (the words of God) in the heart (the *Shema*), that is, there is careful attention to what God has said coupled with the command to bind the words on the hands and the forehead. But the language seems to indicate that the words from God requiring particular care are already known, that is, are already in the heart as they have been placed in the heart by God.

Niehaus turns the demand to heed important revelation (Deuteronomy 6:4-6) into a view that, in the Old Testament, it is the Israelites themselves who put the law in their hearts.[47] Niehaus states that 'the idea that God himself will write the law on our hearts is uniquely applied to the future

---

44 Niehaus, 2007, 267.
45 Dumbrell, 1984, 80.
46 cf. Jeremiah 31:31-34; cf. Dumbrell, 2005, 4-5.
47 Niehaus, 2007, 267-8, n.21.

in the Old Testament'. But the future tense in this promise does not refer to a remote future! Niehaus argues that the only passage which indicates that God will 'write' the law on people's hearts is Jeremiah's new covenant passage (31:33).[48] So, for Niehaus, God writing the law on the heart is the newness of the new covenant following many identified contexts in which Israelites are enjoined to write the law 'on the table of thine heart' (cf. Proverbs 3:3; cf. 7:3). Indeed, in the Old and New Testaments, God often calls on the individual (or the nation comprised of individuals) to internalise the law (to put the law on the heart). This call is often repeated in prophetic preaching, indeed, the Old Testament recognises the stubbornness of the human heart when responding to the divine will.[49] We may 'put' the will of God in our heart but divine placement and divine power is necessary for the effect to be real!

However, there are examples where the obvious conclusion is that God has placed the law in the heart, such as 'I delight to do your will, O my God: your law is within my heart' (Psalm 40:8). The Old Testament Psalmist cites a spiritual change and provides a reason for the change. Niehaus only refers to the second half of Psalm 40:8 but the commitment of the individual to the will of God results from the law being placed by God in the heart.[50] Niehaus only refers to the first half of Psalm 37:31 (which is like Psalm 40:8) in his discussion, again leaving out the result of the placement of the law. Niehaus then asserts that neither Psalm 40:8 nor Psalm 37:31 declares whether God or the psalmist had 'fixed it (that is, God's law) there (in the heart)'.[51] However, both texts infer that delight in doing the law of God results from divine enlightenment!

Niehaus also refers to David's prayer to 'create (*bara*) in me a clean heart, O God' (Psalm 51:10)[52] but, again, he does not refer to the second half of the verse or following verses, namely: 'and renew a steadfast spirit within me' (Psalm 51:10b); 'do not cast me away from your presence (Psalm 51:11a); and 'do not take Your Holy Spirit from me' (Psalm 51:11b). Psalm 51:10 indicates a 'this world' outcome though not an ideal state which, indeed, David never achieved in this life. Niehaus suggests that David's plea

---

48 Niehaus, 2007, 268 (n.32).
49 cf. Deuteronomy 9:5; Jeremiah 17:9.
50 Niehaus, 2007, 267 (n. 21).
51 Niehaus, 2007, 267.
52 Niehaus, 2007, 269.

had nothing to do with spiritual reality but the context suggests that David's appeal for spiritual renewal—which must come from God by indwelling transformation—would then be demonstrated outwardly in his reign. The plea for the Holy Spirit may simply be a plea for the retention of David's kingship however, even so, the Holy Spirit was divinely given and essential for the continuation of David's reign.

Furthermore, Niehaus does not mention Isaiah 51:7, namely: 'Listen to me, you who know righteousness; a people in whose heart is my law'. There is a necessary connection between: righteousness, being right with God, a mark of regeneration in both New and Old Testaments (a state of being that humans cannot possibly achieve); and the law in the heart which is a mark of an indwelt spirit. Both righteousness and the law in the heart are the work of the Holy Spirit. Indeed, the context of Isaiah 51:7 is that God's law proceeds directly from God (Isaiah 51:4), presumably in Israelite witness. Did the individual put God's law in the heart to produce right conduct (according to God) by the strength of will? This is Niehaus' view but the process of continuing sanctification can only be the work of the Spirit. During this process there will be individual surrender to sin from time to time until the Parousia when obedience becomes complete because believers' bodies will then be entirely controlled by the Spirit. Hence the call—included in both Old and New Testaments—for the sinner to seek divine forgiveness within the relevant covenant structure.

Niehaus' examination of the Old Testament evidence is faulty because the one God is God of both Testaments (cf. Romans 3:29–30). Salvation in both Testaments stems from the work of the Spirit creating trust in God's sovereignty which results in regeneration and the will of God placed by the Spirit at the centre of personal being. There are not two ways of salvation in the two Testaments. There is one biblical gospel and one work of the Holy Spirit in regeneration. This is why Jesus expressed amazement that Nicodemus, *the* (pre-eminent) teacher of Israel, did not know (John 3:10) that the requirement for new birth (John 3:5) was already presented in the Old Testament (Ezekiel 36:25–27).

Whereas in Israel human birth conveyed nominal admittance into the national covenant, nevertheless, personal redemption required regeneration by the Holy Spirit.[53] But Niehaus' view of Israel placing the law in its own heart appears to be a works view of salvation. So I believe that the

---

53 cf. Gaffin, 1980, 26.

prophetic new covenant formulas (31:31–34; Ezekiel 36:25–27) state what Israel was always intended to be, that is, a nation of individuals in whose heart the Spirit dwelt communicating delight in the law of the Lord.

Whereas all Israelites were born into the Sinai covenant, true covenant experience required regeneration by the indwelling Spirit. Paul asserts that the mark of a true Jew (not, in the context, a Christian Jew) always was inward (Romans 2:28–29). Paul's understanding of the Old Testament is that true circumcision was always a matter of the heart (Deuteronomy 10:16; Jeremiah 9:25–26), that is, obedience has always been by the Spirit and not by the letter. So believers, under the old covenant, required the law in their hearts (cf. Isaiah 51:7). The unity of the Bible suggests that true (old or new) covenant spiritual experience always required divine spiritual awakening to enable true obedience to the will of God.

The Outpouring of the Spirit and Israel's Future (Joel 2)

Joel prophesied in the context of a national disaster which he saw as the judgement of God. Joel described an invasion of locusts which may have been literal or, alternatively, a metaphorical description of an invading enemy army. There has been a devouring devastation (2:3), frightening appearances and noise (2:4–5), panic in the face of the enemy (2:6), invasion of cities and houses (2:7–9), and an attack that seems to make the ground shiver as the sky turns black (2:10). Behind all of this Joel sees the day of the Lord (1:15) with darkness that symbolises the dread presence of God's wrath (2:10–11). Finally, this army of locusts is none other than the Lord's army under the Lord's command (2:11)[54] and—at the head of the army—the Lord appeals to people to turn to him in repentance (2:12).

Then a massive act of national repentance takes place (2:18–27). First, after the devouring army—the great and terrible judgment of God (2:11)—the nations say of Israel, 'where is their God?' (2:17). But then God takes pity on his people (2:18) so that in the future the world will know of God's amazing forgiveness by the outpouring of the Spirit (2:28–29). This future coming of the Spirit will be marked by universal, cosmic, saving events (2:30–32). 2:28–29 depicts the fulfilment of Numbers 11:29 whereby all the Lord's people become prophets with God's Spirit on them: men and women, young and old, even male and female slaves. There will be no distinctions

---

54 cf. Wright, 2006, 141.

in gender, age or class with regard to who receives the Spirit: all have equal access to this promise.

The cosmic effect of the outpouring of the Spirit is earth-shaking, expressing the ultimate power of God (2:30-31). The climax is salvation for all who call on the name of the Lord (2:32), that is, judgement is followed by deliverance for whoever calls on the Messiah as Lord (2:32). Joel's prophecy did not get a response from national Israel but, on the day of Pentecost after the cross, Joel's prophecy is the reference for bringing into being the new Israel (Acts 2:17-21).

God's Indwelling Spirit Vivifies New Covenant Obedience (Ezekiel)

11:19-20 presents the meaning of spiritual renewal, involving regeneration with inward renewal. God promises to: regather the whole house of Israel; give them the Promised Land; and give them one heart with a new spirit within, resulting in covenant obedience (11:20, cf. 18:31).

36:16ff begins with the factors which led to the operation of the covenant curses and consequent exile for Israel which, as a nation, lost the Promised Land (36:16-20; cf. Deuteronomy 30:1-10). But the curses are followed by redemption as God re-gathers Israel to bring them home (36:24). This depends on the prior infusion of divine grace. The restoration emphasis in 36:21-24 is like Jeremiah in that the restoration and renewal of the covenant are contingent not on performance by Israel but on divine fidelity. Three great issues provide the basis for divine action on Israel's behalf: God's concern that 'his holy name' (36:21, his character displayed) should be honoured by the integrity of divine action in accordance with the Lord's promises to Israel; that there is no ground for national pride in Israel's situation, rather, God's constancy is the basis for divine action (36:22); and that there be an open, divine demonstration to the nations revealing God's purposes for the world so that divine holiness might be vindicated among the nations (36:23). Ezekiel then announces the catalogue of successive acts by which a restoration is to be effected (36:24ff): people and land will again be bound together by an exodus (36:24), then the taint of contaminating influences (as befits the restored sanctuary situation of Israel) is removed by ritual cleansing (36:25). There is both inward change and a formal separation of Israel from her environment. The cleansing sprinkling of the new covenant (36:25) is like the sprinkling at Sinai that brought about the inauguration of Israel's covenant (cf. Exodus 24:6).

Mere separation from the past, however, will not account for the shape of the future. 36:26 reveals the inward transaction by which the new arrangement will be effected. A new heart (new inner disposition) is given to Israel for the new age—the heart of flesh is taken away and a new spirit, namely, God's Spirit (36:27) is put within enabling obedience to the covenant (statutes and ordinances). Whereas this is a promise for the future, it is nevertheless delivered to people who understood the significance of the promise offered. The promised new heart will enable obedience because the indwelling Spirit fulfils all the expectations raised by Old Testament covenants. The nation with a new heart and a new Spirit will be a light to the Gentiles. According to Ezekiel, therefore, obedience to the divine will is the issue with regard to the law. So the law is a matter for the heart in both new and old dispensations and therefore, in Ezekiel, regeneration and indwelling are virtually indistinguishable.

36:25-27 is a little more detailed than Jeremiah 31:31-34 because the renewal (36:26) is effected by the Holy Spirit, resulting in a renewed spirit in man (36:27). In the Old Testament the spirit of a man is the point of divine contact, that is, man viewed as spirit is man from the view of divine possibility—as opposed to man viewed as soul where man is mortal and exposed to disintegration. This corresponds with the Pauline 'spirit' versus 'flesh'. The new age will emphasise the enabling direction of God through the Spirit within the human situation. Ezekiel's prophecy is not about the spiritual reformation of man but, rather, the insertion of the divine nature into man. Ezekiel emphasises inward Spirit renewal for the people of God as a whole thereby effecting the democratisation of leadership in the establishment of a kingdom of priests. This is the restored Israel depicted by Peter in his Pentecost speech (Acts 2). While personal regeneration and the gift of the Spirit was always necessary for covenant identification under the Old Testament covenants, Ezekiel presents a new situation in which Israel is fully transformed as the renewed people of God.

In making God the author of this new obedience, Ezekiel expands and illuminates Jeremiah's description of the new covenant. But the goal is the same: new life in the restored land (cf. 36:35). 36:28-38 virtually describes the consummation of the original divine promise to Israel at Sinai, namely, rest in the Promised Land. The transformation of the people of God by the Spirit proceeds concurrently with—and effects the renewal of—their environment such that the renewal of the creature in Israel progressively brings about the renewal of creation (cf. Romans 8:19).

37:1–14 provides further reflection on the process of renewal. The prophet is taken to 'the valley' (37:1) where judgement on Israel was originally pronounced (3:22) when Ezekiel was commissioned. The nation is now lifeless bones as the result of the prophet's ministry. The prophetic response to the divine question—can life come into these bones in exile? (37:3)—recognises not only the inadequacy of human judgement but also the prophetic recognition of the power of God to begin again. With a clear allusion to Genesis 2:7 in Ezekiel 37:5, the new creation follows in two stages until not only form but also life is given to the national body. The divine explanation of this profound transformation is action taken by 'my', that is, God's Spirit (37:14).

The political significance of this renewal of God's army is the reunion of Judah and Israel (37:15–28), that is, in the new era the entire nation is again in the Promised Land (37:22) under a Davidic prince (37:24). The new circumstance is an everlasting covenant of peace with Israel (37:26) that fulfils the covenant with creation (Genesis 6:18). The Abrahamic or creation promises of being blessed and multiplied (37:26) are re-invoked and the sanctuary, Edenic character of the divine presence dwelling with Israel follows (37:27). The result of Israel's election is witness to the world (37:28).

Yahweh, the God of the spirits (vital breath) of all flesh (Numbers 16:22; 27:16), effects Israel's restoration (39:29) and—at death—*ruach* returns to him (Ecclesiastes 12:7; Psalm 31:5). The Spirit of God is not only purposeful divine power (Genesis 1:2) but also (at the same time) the creating and vivifying *ruach* (breath, like wind) of God (cf. 'by the word of the Lord the heavens were made and all their host by the breath [*ruach*] of his mouth', Psalm 33:6).[55] The divine word and the divine breath are not really distinguishable for they are active, efficacious entities involved in the creation process.

---

55 Cole, 2007, 214.

The Fulfilment of Promises of a Spirit-Controlled Future

The eschatological function of the Spirit is to extend God's works in the soteriological sphere. Through prophetic signs, the Spirit: heralds the near approach of the future world (cf. Joel 3:1ff); equips the Messiah as a permanent possession (cf. Isaiah 11:2; 28:6; 42:1; 61:1); and appears as the source of the future new Israel in ethic-religious renewal (Isaiah 32:15-17; 44:3; 59:21; Ezekiel 36:27; 37:14; 39:29). It is Jehovah who sends the Spirit to introduce and continue the eschatological state. In the Old Testament, the word Spirit is the comprehensive form for the transcendental or supernatural reality projecting himself into human experience. The Spirit is sovereign over the individual—blowing 'where it listeth' like the wind—a concrete force coming from above to direct believers towards a higher world (like Jeremiah who sits alone because of Jehovah's hand, Jeremiah 15:17). The promise of a Spirit-controlled future for Israel is realised by the gift of the Spirit of Christ to the restored Israel at Pentecost.

The activity of the Spirit in the Old Testament is both divine and personal for only a personal Spirit could engage in a high-level rational/spiritual activity in relationship to other persons so as to direct the people of God as God intends. The activity of the Spirit in leadership in the Old Testament was sporadic, theocratic, selective and (to some degree) external. But various Psalms (cf. Isaiah 51:7) demonstrate both individual regeneration (righteousness, that is, right standing before God) and the law indwelling the heart. Much personalised evidence makes it difficult to separate regeneration and indwelling in the Old Testament.

The early divine covenants were sealed to re-create and re-establish the family bond between God and his people so that the people would express the family likeness. The Sinai Covenant adopts Israel into God's own family (cf. Romans 9:4; Hosea 11:1) by grace. Israel was God's son and is to show forth his praises, bearing increasing family resemblance as the image of God's glory. The promise of the covenant was 'I will be your God and you will be my people' or 'I am your Father and you are my son'. The heart of the covenant is 'I the Lord (your Father) am holy; therefore you (my children) are to express the family likeness and image so you are to be holy, too' (Leviticus 11:44-45; 19:2; 20:7). The old covenant glory is surpassed by the new covenant transformation of the heart which is the work of Christ and subsequent ministry of the Spirit (2 Corinthians 3:18). God's revealed person and character provide the motive for sanctification. We are to be holy for God makes us holy (Exodus 31:13 cf. Leviticus 20:8; 21:8), that is, holiness arises from imperatives of obedience stemming from indicatives of grace. God has redeemed his people from bondage so that they can be conformed to his pattern (Exodus 20:1-2).

Moses desired to see a fuller coming of the Spirit affecting the whole people of God (Numbers 11:29) but the fulfilment of that promise awaited the demise of Israelite nationalism. In the new covenant the Spirit will be poured out in a universal, personal manner upon a non-national Israel (Joel 2:28ff; Ezekiel 36:24-32).

The story of the Spirit is incomplete but implicit in the Old Testament. The Spirit possesses the divine attributes and bears the divine nature. Believers await the central promise of the new covenant (cf. Ezekiel 36:27; cf. Joel 2:28) in the great future of the Day of the Spirit. The Messiah would come, filled with the Spirit (Isaiah 11:1f; 42:1ff; 61:1ff). Luke's gospel chronicles this fulfilment (Luke 1:1): John the Baptist was filled with the Spirit from birth, restoring prophecy to Israel (Luke 1:15); the overshadowing of Mary by the Spirit was the beginning of the new creation (Luke 1:35); Elizabeth and Zechariah are filled with the Spirit (Luke 1:41,67); and Simeon, in whose life the Holy Spirit was already present, understood the inner significance of the coming of the Messiah. Salvation had dawned with the Christ-child. The promised Messiah had come, the one on whom the Spirit would rest (Isaiah 11:2)—in the coming of Jesus, the day of the Spirit had fully dawned. The new covenant brings the full day of the Spirit into human experience.

The New Testament (new covenant) revelation requires a Christian reading of the Old Testament. The Old Testament recognised that a profound inner transformation was necessary to obey God, indeed, John Goldingay asserts that Romans 4 and Hebrews 11 point to an equivalence between Old and New Testament believers.[56] Jesus also points to this equivalence in John 3. Graham Cole agrees that Old Testament believers were regenerated and indwelt by the Spirit, the experience being described as 'circumcision of the heart'.[57] I have argued that faith in the divine basis of salvation was the same for Old and New Testament believers. Graham Cole suggests that Old

---

56   Goldingay, 1996, 14-28.
57   Cole, 2007, 143.

Testament believers lived between promise and fulfilment (Isaiah 11; 32; 42; 44; Ezekiel 36-37; 39; Joel 2)—but this is also true of New Testament believers awaiting the consummation of the kingdom in the return of Christ.

Old Testament language of 'circumcised hearts' replacing 'hearts of stone' moves in the same conceptual field as New Testament language of regeneration and new birth.[58] It is clear from Pentecost, however, that further gifts have been bestowed on God's people in this changed national situation. The Spirit moved Old Testament Israelite believers but the New Testament development is worldwide commitment by the people of God to the promise of the new covenant.

Spiritual union with Christ is the new covenant blessing that could not be enjoyed until Christ's death. Old Testament believers were regenerated, justified and sanctified on the basis of Christ's future work but their mode of covenant fellowship was provisional as it lacked the permanence of union with the glorified Christ. Becoming God's sons through the Spirit of adoption comes with the new covenant. Old Testament personal experience of God—such as the (representative) faith of Abraham, and the piety and prayers of the Psalms—are expressions of the Spirit's sovereign work of inner renewal and personal transformation (as detailed in the New Testament). The experience of covenant believers in Old Testament Israel was personal experience of God mediated by the Spirit and this model for Old Testament piety was continuous with the piety mediated by the Spirit in the New Testament.[59] Indeed, New Testament believers were not capable of more sublime praise or deeper devotion or greater fervency of prayer than, for instance, the Psalms of David which was used as a resource in old covenant Israel for sharing personal conviction and experience of God.

Whereas covenant membership was assumed in Old Testament Israel from birth, the delight in the law of God—that is, the vivification of formal covenant membership—occurred when, by the Spirit through regeneration, Old Testament believers had the law written on the heart such that obedience to the covenant resulted (cf. John 3:3). The difference between membership of the Sinai covenant and membership of the new covenant is the loss of national Israel's election by their rejection of Jesus (John 19:15). Thenceforward membership of the new covenant is no longer associated with birth but comes only by regeneration by Spirit baptism. Moreover, in

---

58 Cole, 2007, 145.

59 Gaffin, 1979, 37ff.

the new covenant the Spirit is poured out on all flesh (Acts 2:17). Regeneration by the Spirit through the word brings humanity from the fall into the kingdom of God.

In the New Testament, by resurrection, Christ became the life-giving Spirit so that the Spirit is now vitally present among the people of God. The universal Spirit in the New Testament community is now poured out on Israel and the nations (Jews and Gentiles) so the blessing of Abraham has now come on all flesh (Galatians 3:14). The Spirit was taken away from national Israel and—in an unprecedented worldwide function of the Spirit—given to a nation producing the fruits of the Spirit (Matthew 21:43). Christ is the life-giving Spirit at Pentecost and this Spirit is fundamental in world mission. The Spirit in the Old Testament had worked within Israel to provide a people for God's name in addition to being the agent of God in the preservation of the created order. In the New Testament also, the Spirit actions the divine purposes relayed through the covenant with creation (Genesis 6:18) to its fruition in the new creation.

The Biblical Spirit
New Testament

Matthew

The Spirit's role in re-beginning Israel's history (Matthew 1–3)

1:18 includes a word that could be either *genesis* (genealogy) or *gennesis* (birth), depending on which source document is relied on. If *genesis* (now the genealogy of Jesus Christ, cf. 1:1) is read for 1:18–25, then Matthew's emphasis is that the conception of Jesus begins a fourth period of Israelite history (cf. 1:17) or a re-beginning of Israel's history. This fourth period is initiated by God through the activity of the Holy Spirit in the virgin conception of Jesus in Mary's womb (1:18). There is no historical conclusion to this re-beginning of Israel's history in which Jesus will achieve the call and purpose of Israel as Jesus is both Son of David and Son of Abraham (1:1), that is, Jesus will fulfil the covenant promises connected with both David and Abraham.

Approximately thirty years after the birth of Jesus, John the Baptist (the Baptist) is at the Jordan River calling for Israel to turn from its disobedient past and place her faith in God's future revealed in Jesus. The Baptist's prophetic purpose was to reconstitute all Israel under covenant renewal like Elijah's ministry as the prophet of the covenant. The Baptist was prophetically invoking Israel—like Elijah had done centuries before—to stop hesitating between two opinions and to get back to the God of the covenant (cf. 1 Kings 18:21).

It appears that the Baptist was baptising on the Transjordan side of the Jordan (John 3:26), that is, he was inviting Israel to re-enter the Promised Land by crossing the Jordan again. But, this time, Israel was to cross as the people of God now fitted for re-entry by repentance. The Baptist depicts Israel as a sinful nation, like Gentiles, requiring the same cleansing as the proselyte who comes to join the people of God. So the universal pollution of all who are outside a covenant of grace is also Israel's position for the Israelites had broken the covenant and now have a universal need to repent.

The Baptist only baptised with water—which was a sign of spiritual inauguration—but the mightier one who came after the Baptist (Jesus) would baptise them with Spirit and with fire (3:11). The Baptist's message was not only judgment, for his baptism also indicated repentance and therefore raised the possibility of forgiveness (3:6,8; Mark 1:4). The judgement of the coming one (Jesus), by the work of the same Spirit, would bring either affirmation (reception into the people of God) or rejection (dismissal from the people of God). The Baptist saw his baptism as a promise of forgiveness and salvation to the penitent, and probably thought of the coming baptism as similar fulfilment of the promise of forgiveness and salvation.

The Baptist probably coined the double function metaphor of the coming one's baptism, that is, not of water but of both Spirit and fire. The function of baptising with the Spirit occurs in all four gospels (3:11; Mark 1:8; Luke 3:16; John 1:33). Whereas the absence of fire from Mark and John is in accord with the absence of reference to judgment in the Baptist tradition in these two evangelists, the threefold repetition of 'fire' in 3:10–12 associates judgement with Spirit baptism. Mark's omission of any reference to 'fire' in the baptism administered by Jesus may indicate a connection with the Pentecost tradition of Spirit baptism only (not Spirit and fire baptism).

Jesus' ministry of two baptisms: Spirit and fire

To 'baptise in the Spirit and fire' signified the fearful effects of God's wrath on Israel's sin and presumption. This baptism would be purgative: purifying those who repented and consuming those who did not. Thus Jesus' ministry of two baptisms would include both judgment and mercy for national Israel. But Pentecost would be a baptism by Spirit—not of fire symbolising judgment and purification in Jewish thought[60]—on believers, that is, on remnant Israel. In the Old Testament, Spirit (*ruach*) could denote either judgment or blessing (cf. Isaiah 4:4; Jeremiah 4:11f; 1QSb 5:24ff). *Ruach* is also used with the apocalyptic metaphor of the river of judgment (cf. Isaiah 30:27f). Just as the Baptist practiced baptism in the river Jordan as a way of symbolising end time tribulation so also the metaphor of Jesus' baptism in Spirit and fire also depicts the tribulation.

The Baptist's reference to baptism of Spirit and fire may not refer to Pentecost (Acts 2) since the Baptist was addressing a representative group of national Israel about the continuance of their national role. But Pentecost refers to the emergence of the new Christian Israel with the Spirit coming upon believers only. Jesus' reminder about the character of the disciples' ministry after his ascension points to a promise yet to be fulfilled (Acts 1:5), anticipating the Pentecost experience but without reference to the 'fire' associated with the baptism and gift of the Spirit. The tongues of fire that descended in the upper room (Acts 2) were visible signs of theophany, not fulfilment of earlier expectation.

---

60 cf. Numbers 31:23; Isaiah 66:15ff; Amos 7:4; Malachi 3:2f; 4:1.

According to the Baptist's prophecy, the baptism of Jesus would betoken God's powerful intervention in the history of Israel through Jesus' ministry concluded by the cross. Jesus' message would divide and, finally, end the nation. Having regard to the national covenant with Israel, 'spirit and fire' may have referred to the cleansing and purification that could remove national Israel's dross by bringing its disobedience to judgement in a significant event in Jesus' ministry. Jesus referred to his approaching death as a baptism (cf. Mark 10:38; Luke 12:50). Baptism is the word used to refer to Jesus' experience of suffering in a particular event associated with a cup of wrath that has to be drunk (Mark 10:38-39). Jesus unites fire with a judgement experience in Luke's gospel: 'I came to cast fire upon the earth and would that it were already kindled; I have a baptism to be baptised with and how I am constrained until it is completed' (Luke 12:49-50). In the Garden of Gethsemane, Jesus will find that baptism repugnant but he will accept God's will.

The fire that Jesus longs to cast on the earth seems to refer to the coming judgment of the cross—which national Israel could not avert—mediated by the Spirit, separating the righteous from the wicked, causing strife and division (cf. Luke 3:16 where fire, Spirit and baptism are linked). Jesus' own fiery baptism (Luke 12:50) by which he was constrained was the cross which would fan the flames of division within Israel into a conflagration. Israel and all humanity would have to undergo such a baptism themselves by being brought before the cross (cf. John 12:31-32). Jesus did not come to bring peace; indeed, the cross would bring division, not unity, even within families. The decision for humanity in regard to the cross would bring either divine acceptance or divine rejection.

Jesus died as Israel's Messiah, that is, as representative Israel. Jesus' baptism of the Spirit and fire—his cross—would be representative. The cross would cleanse Israel: bringing her before God's judgement bar (cf. John 12:32); potentially separating her from her past; and inviting her to enter a new future. This baptism of Spirit and fire brings Israel and the entire world before the judgement bar of the cross, thereby separate 'wheat and chaff' not merely within Israel but also within humanity at large. Historically, Jesus' baptism would terminate national Israel's connection with covenant and produce a believing Israel upon whom the Spirit rests with all of God's promises benefiting them within a new covenant.[61]

Jesus accepted the Baptist's expectation with regard to his ministry, indeed, Jesus endorsed the Baptist's program of restoration by accepting John's baptism thereby identifying with the new Israel community. But Jesus offers an inward, spiritual renewal—the water baptism commanded by Jesus is the beginning of the process of making disciples. The Baptist's baptism was provisional, demanding repentance with 'a view to the remission of sins'. The Baptist's baptismal candidates confessed their sins (3:6) but Matthew doesn't mention forgiveness because, for the nation, forgiveness would be associated with Jesus' forthcoming baptism of the Spirit and fire. Response to the message of the cross would effect the restoration of Israel. The Baptist made no appeal to sacrificial ritual in the Jordan baptisms, rather, covenant renewal for the people of God depended on repentance.

The purgative judgment that the Baptist predicted must first be experienced by Jesus. From the beginning of his ministry, Jesus was aware of the cross where he would drink the cup of God's wrath and suffering (cf. Mark 2:20; Psalm 75:8; Isaiah 51:17–23; Jeremiah 25:15–28). Jesus looked on his imminent death as: God's judgment; the suffering which the saints of the Most High must suffer before their exaltation as regents in God's kingdom (Daniel 7:17–27); and the vicarious suffering necessary before Jesus' vindication by God (Isaiah 53:1–12). This view of Jesus' death was espoused by Jesus himself (cf. Mark 8:31; 9:31; 10:33f,45).

Jesus would suffer the divine judgment himself. So Jesus was not so much the baptiser in Spirit and fire but the one who would be baptised in Spirit and fire thereby enduring the birth pangs of the new age. The hope was that the new age might be brought in fully and that others might either be spared the messianic tribulation or at least be enabled to pass through the river of fiery *ruach*. So Jesus' reinterpretation of the metaphor 'baptised in Spirit and fire' both retains its initiatory significance as the means of bringing in the new age and intensifies its note of judgment and suffering.

Jesus described to his disciples the impending crisis that will end his ministry along with the ongoing judgement resulting from his ministry (Luke 12:49–53). Jesus submitted himself in death to the ordeal of the cross

---

61 Mark 9:49–50 records a saying of Jesus ('Everyone will be salted with fire. Salt is good; but if salt has lost its saltiness, how can you season it?') which indicated that Jesus looked for this fiery purification which would involve everyone.

through which the Spirit would bring him to resurrection (Hebrews 9:14; Romans 1:14). The fire that Jesus longs to cast on earth refers to the judging message of the cross, mediated by the Spirit, which separates the righteous from the wicked and causes strife and division among men.

The Baptist was expecting a divided response to his prophetic invitation from Israel since he spoke of the impending judgement between wheat and chaff (3:12). This divided response would mean rejection of the nation as only a renewed and purified Israel could confidently meet Yahweh the Judge. Paradoxically, Jesus—their potential Saviour whom they rejected—will be Israel's eschatological judge. The Baptist was calling for a reconstituted Israel but he realised the limitations of his baptism which was merely preliminary for the nation. The Baptist's baptism did not only aim at the moral transformation of the individual, although that notion was included, rather his baptismal call had been to all Israel corporately for the reviving of her vocation by restoration of her covenant life.

Beyond the interminable divisions which mark human history there will be final peace for a transformed world (Revelation 21:1ff). Israel and the world must realise the bankrupt condition that will bring them before the divine court. Israel must repent of covenant waywardness—their refusal to be the Israel that God required—and seek reconciliation before the judgement.[62]

Unlike Pentecost which was for the reconstituted believing Israel, the Baptist's message at the Jordan was for Israel as a whole.[63] Jesus spoke of the distance between himself and the Baptist in answer to John's question: 'Are you the Coming One or should we look for another?' (11:3,5; Luke 7: 19,22). The distinctive difference between the message and ministry of the Baptist and Jesus, according to Jesus, is realised eschatology or fulfilment. The Holy Spirit effected Jesus' ministry by the presence and power of God working through him in Israel (Mark 3:29-30) but the response of the Scribes was to interpret the gracious acts of God through Jesus as the work of the prince of evil. Jesus said that the effect of his ministry would be salvation through judgment for those who repent—that is, the grain is gathered into the barn after winnowing—but for those who remained impenitent there would only be judgment, that is, burning in unquenchable fire. So 'baptise in the Spirit and fire' signifies the fearful effects of God's wrath on

---

62 cf. Caird, 1963, 169.

63 cf. Yates, 1960, 58-60.

Israel's sin and presumption: purgative, purifying those who repented, destructive, and consuming those who do not repent.

The Baptist coined the phrase baptism in the Spirit which is included in all four gospels and therefore of considerable importance (3:11; Mark 1:8; Luke 3:16; John 1:33). The phrase referred to judgment (emphasised by the three-fold repetition of fire in 3:10–12). Paradoxically, spirit baptism must also have referred to mercy because the Baptist's message was not solely judgment. Thus the Coming One would gather wheat into the granary as well as burn chaff (3:12; Luke 3:17). Moreover, those whom the Baptist had baptised would also be baptised by the coming One (Mark 1:8). Insofar as John saw his own baptism bearing a promise of forgiveness and salvation to the penitent, the coming baptism was the fulfilment of that promise.

The Baptist tradition 'baptise in Spirit and fire' cannot be taken to mean 'baptise in water (and) in Spirit and fire' because Spirit and fire are elements into which men would be plunged—a river of (apocalyptic) *ruach* and fire. In the Baptist tradition, 'baptise in Spirit and fire' is set in explicit antithesis to John's baptism in water which was a warning and preparation for a much more terrible baptism: an immersion in the fiery breath of God.

The absence of judgment from Jesus' ministry puzzled the Baptist, that is, Jesus was far from the figure of wrath and fire that John anticipated. Proclaiming the kingdom was one thing but what about the Baptist's prophetic conviction that the Coming One would baptise in Spirit and fire? When John indirectly asked Jesus the question 'Are you the Coming One or should we look for another?' (11:3; Luke 7:19), Jesus proclaimed that the shift in the ages (the Baptist had preached that this shift was near at hand) had already taken place. James Dunn notes that Jesus' answer reflects three Isaiah passages which contain both promise of blessing and threat of judgment (Isaiah 35:3–5; 29:18–20; 61:1–2).[64] But Jesus alludes only to the promise of blessing for it is the note of blessing that characterises his ministry. The day of God's judgment is not yet—the year of the Lord's favour is now (Luke 4:18–19).

When Jesus said 'Everyone will be salted with fire' (Mark 9:49), he indicates that he was looking for fiery purification to confront Israel and the world. Jesus also said (Luke 12:49–50):

---

64 Dunn, 1998, 104.

> *I came to cast fire upon the earth and would that it were already kindled. I have a baptism to be baptised with and how I am constrained until it is completed.*

This indicates that Jesus himself will be engulfed in the fiery purification (cf. Mark 10:38).

This Lucan context combining fire and baptism provides the clearest confirmation that the Baptist's prediction about Jesus with regard to judgment and suffering was accepted by Jesus. Jesus depicts himself as the eschatological dispenser of fire (Luke 12:49) as the Baptist had predicted but, furthermore, Jesus is the one who must himself endure the eschatological baptism (Luke 12:50). Jesus longs for the baptism of fire—which he came to administer—to be kindled (accomplished) on himself by his sacrifice of himself which would be the purgation that the human world merited. From that sacrifice would flow the Pentecost gift of the Spirit. Jesus' death would thereby address all human history. Jesus recognised from his water baptism that his would be a baptism of the Spirit and fire, that the purgative judgment which John the Baptist predicted must first be experienced by himself (cf. Mark 2:20; Psalm 75:8; Isaiah 51:17–23; Jeremiah 25:15–28).

Jesus looked on his imminent death as covenantally necessary, accepting John's prediction for his ministry and seeing that he himself would be the instrument of the messianic woes whereby the kingdom would fully come to birth. Jesus saw himself not as the agent who would bring about the end time tribulation on others but rather as the one who would suffer the divine judgment himself. Jesus was not so much the baptiser in Spirit and fire but the one who would himself be baptised in Spirit and fire. Jesus would himself alone endure the birth pangs of the new age in the hope that others might either be spared the messianic tribulation or enabled to pass through the river of fiery *ruach* themselves (cf. Hebrews 2:5–10). Jesus' reinterpretation of the metaphor 'baptised in Spirit and fire' retains its initiatory significance as the means of bringing in the new age—and intensifies its note of judgment and suffering—but also transforms the metaphor from a description of what the coming one would do to an expression of what Jesus' death meant for Jesus himself.

The post-cross baptism of the Spirit inaugurates the believer into the life of union with Christ, which is marked outwardly by water baptism.[65] Re-

---

[65] The Spirit is the inner instructor of the believer: giving and creating faith; making each a child of God; leading them into close communion with God; and filtering their

pentance, the forgiveness of sins and the gift of the Spirit are correlative aspects of the one reality of entrance into Christ and thus into the fellowship of the Father, the Son and the Holy Spirit (28:19; Acts 2:38). Water baptism—a continuing feature in the early church—was carefully distinguished from Spirit baptism. Baptism and the Lord's Supper function as signs in the communication of the gospel so that, in and through these signs, the Christ of the new covenant is to be made known through the Spirit.

The seal of the Spirit at Jesus baptism (3:13–17)

Jesus submitted to John's baptism as a model of the covenant obedience to which the Baptist had called all Israel. Jesus' baptism also indicated his acceptance of his divinely commissioned role to be numbered with the transgressors (Isaiah 53:11–12) by his willingness to undergo a baptism by Spirit and fire. The Baptist's ministry of baptism was the historical context in which the Messiah would be unveiled (John 1:31). Jesus viewed the cross as the fulfilment of his baptism.

Jesus' water baptism was a sign pointing to the cross as fulfilment. As confirmation of this sign—at his water baptism—Jesus received a seal of the Spirit upon the outcome of his ministry (3:16). The Spirit came to equip Jesus to bring what was signified to full realisation in his prophesied baptism on the cross where Jesus would forge a new covenant in his blood. At the heart of this new covenant was the gift of the Spirit (Ezekiel 36:26–27). Jesus' baptism looked towards the purification of Israel and was marked by heaven's confirmation of his role as God's son, that is, as Israel's Messiah (3:17). Jesus' death on the cross would give complete expression to the demands of God on Israel, atoning for Israel and the world but requiring submission from the world to the verdict of the cross on the world. Cleansing and purification would come by accepting this judgement of the cross on the world; or personal, final judgement would come by rejection of the judgement of the cross. For national Israel, acceptance or rejection of the judgement of the cross would mean either continuance or final dismissal as the people of God. Jesus would give complete expression to the existing covenant relationship in the baptism of the cross (3:15). Israel's Messiah, Jesus, took on himself Israel's covenantal need. As representative Israel, Jesus was acting for Israel.

---

prayers. For the believer, possession of the Spirit and sonship go together.

The two events depicted as baptism or analogous to baptism in the New Testament had water ordeals attached to them through which the elect of God passed to deliverance while others fell under a curse, namely: Noah and his family (1 Peter 3:18–22); and Moses and the Israelites (1 Corinthians 10:2). Jesus' prophesied baptism on the cross also bore the character of a water-ordeal (cf. Psalm 69, a messianic psalm which Jesus applied to his sacrifice).[66] On the cross, the great ordeal symbolised by his baptism takes place in reality—he experienced sorrow and desolation, which almost killed him (Mark 14:33–34). The symbolism of Jesus' circumcision (Luke 2:21) and baptism coalesced in the reality of the cross (cf. Colossians 2:11–15). As the divine Servant, Jesus is cut off from the land of the living' (Isaiah 53:8) and oppressed (Isaiah 53:7–8) as the 'iniquity of us all' is placed on his shoulders (Isaiah 53:5–6,8,10).

By this means, forgiveness and salvation are brought to all through Jesus' baptism in the Spirit. Christ underwent the covenant curse so that the blessing given to Abraham might be fulfilled in the gift of the Spirit to those who believed (Galatians 3:13–14). New covenant baptism is into the name of Jesus, that is, new covenant baptism seals and signifies the substance of the faith union with Christ which unites us to him. By faith, the sealing of the Spirit draws our eyes to the inner meaning of the baptism of Jesus on the cross for us. The word of the Spirit, by faith, makes the connection between the sign and the reality of Jesus' baptism on the cross for us (cf. Romans 6). All who are baptised into Christ Jesus are baptised into his death, buried with Jesus, and raised into newness of life in Jesus' resurrection power (Romans 6:4). This baptism referred to by Paul in Romans 6 is both water and Spirit baptism since baptism apart from faith generated by the Spirit cannot carry significance.

Water baptism is often viewed as the response to conversion and testimony to faith in Christ, but this is not the complete New Testament perspective for it minimises the illuminating ministry of the Spirit. Baptism is not just about the individual's own faith commitment, rather, the baptism of the Spirit is submission to the work of the cross with the significance of Jesus' death sealed with Christ's gift. In baptism, the Spirit bears witness to Christ. Paul warns the Corinthians that they must not leave the Lord's Supper unchanged for they eat and drink judgement (1 Corinthians 11:27–30),

---

66 cf. Psalm 69:9 (John 2:17; Romans 15:3); Psalm 69:4 (John 15:25); Psalm 69:25 (Acts 1:20–25); Psalm 69:22–23 (Romans 11:9–10).

that is, by unbelief they transgress against the Spirit. The efficacy of baptism and of the Lord's Supper is in the ministry of the Spirit just as the efficacy of reading and hearing of the Scriptures is the ministry of the Spirit.

Jesus' baptism must be deemed the second most important element in the gospels as this was Jesus' acceptance of Israel's need and his identification with Israel as representative Israel acting for Israel (3:15). Jesus submitted to the Baptist for the sake of all righteousness, completing for Israel the requirements of John's baptism. However, the 'all' of all righteousness is arresting, signifying Jesus' comprehensive, willing acceptance of representative Israel's role as he is commissioned at his baptism. Jesus will fulfil all the elements of the divine plan to enable Israel's ministry to the world for the salvation of the people of God. This commitment of Jesus to ministry and its endorsement by the divine voice will lead to the cross, the way chosen by God as the means to reconcile the world. The resurrection will then implement the inauguration of the new creation to be taken to the world by Pentecost Israel.

Jesus' death on the cross would give complete expression to the demands of God on Israel—atoning for Israel and the world but requiring submission from the world to the verdict of the cross on the world. For the world, submission would mean in prospect and through history the completion of the Eden intention: a new world, a new creation. In the baptism of the cross, Jesus would give complete expression to the existing covenant relationship thereby fulfilling all righteousness (3:15) with regard to the divine intention registered initially by the covenant with creation (Genesis 6:18). Israel's Messiah, in the person of Jesus, accepted Israel's need as his own and—as representative Israel—Jesus acted for Israel to complete national Israel's obligation as the world's representative.

To bring all righteousness (3:15) to complete expression may bring in what God has decreed by creation as right for the world, that is, the final process leading to the fulfilment of the covenant with creation in the new creation. Christ's acceptance of baptism by Spirit and fire for the world, in the divine mind, always required the cross even before the foundation of the world (Revelation 13:8, cf. 17:8). In the progress of revelation, Israel was chosen as world evangelist and Jesus would fulfil this undertaking of God to Abraham (Genesis 12:1–3) and to the world (Genesis 6:18). Thus Jesus would complete the righteous plan of God for Israel and for the world. Jesus submits to covenant judgement for Israel and accepts the cross thereby bringing about total fulfilment of the creation covenant and personal forgiveness for those who understand and accept the message of the cross. The baptism of the cross would bring in the new covenant representing promise and fulfilment of the divine intention for the totality of creation at the end of history in the Garden of God (cf. Genesis 2).

Jesus' baptism for the nation and the world again placed before Israel the possibility, with Jordan forded, of re-entry in covenant into the Promised Land to be the people who would attract the world to its God. Christ's baptism by John for the sake of all righteousness (3:15) has in view the total aims of Jesus' ministry, that is, Christ was willing to undergo the death that Israel had submissively pledged at Sinai (Exodus 24:8–11). Thus Jesus undertook his baptism in Spirit and fire for the world.

The voice from heaven identified Jesus as servant-king (3:17; cf. Psalm 2:7, king; and Isaiah 42:1, servant). Christ submits to the divine will leading to his crucifixion which will highly exalt him and bring about his kingship over the universe (Romans 1:4). This will complete the righteous plan of God for Israel and the world, that is, God's righteousness is in acting through Jesus in complete fidelity to his promised intentions for Israel and—through Israel, that is, through Christ as representative Israel—for the world.

The apocalyptic imagery of the heavens opening (3:16) indicates an entirely fresh initiative from God. In the baptism of Jesus, the kingdom of God had broken into the world from heaven (the transcendently inaccessible spiritual side of the created world). The Spirit of God—said to be silent since the close of the Old Testament prophetic age—came down visibly (3:16; Luke 3:22; John 1:32) as the agent of the divine revelatory intention for Jesus. Through this 'eternal Spirit' (Hebrews 9:14) Jesus offers himself 'without blemish to God'.

The heavenly affirmation of the baptism authorised Jesus for office and commissioned him for ministry (cf. Acts 10:38) as representative Israel. Jesus was commissioned for messianic ministry at his baptism but was full of the Spirit from his conception. The visionary descent of the Spirit as a dove may be an oblique reference to Genesis 8:9–12, in which the end of the flood was an indication of the dawning of a new day of revelation heralding God's peace for all humankind.[67]

---

67 The Spirit of God descending as a dove may be a reference to the beginning of the world in Genesis 1:2 or the new beginning for the world in Genesis 8:19–21. Strack

Jesus' baptism fulfils all righteousness by meeting all the conditions of the Old Testament covenants and opening the way to the new covenant age. The voice from heaven rent the heavens and the descent of the Spirit meant new revelation (cf. Isaiah 64:1). The heavenly voice said 'This is my son the beloved; with whom I am well pleased'. This reference to Psalm 2:7 bestows on God's chosen Israelite king the role of Messiah, the coming victor over the nations, the universal ruler, God's adopted son. 'With whom I am well pleased' is a reference to Isaiah 42:1 where the divine servant was both prophetic and royal, endowed with God's Spirit but also the eschatological Son. The Spirit of God descending was Jesus' anointing as Messiah and his authorisation for ministry so that he would exercise his role of Servant Messiah by the Spirit. Jesus' Servant Messiah ministry achieved the purposes of Israel's election, vindicating the new Israel within history by Jesus' death and exaltation. God implemented his eternal plan through Jesus as Israel.[68] From this point on the Spirit would be with him as the power by which, as Son of Man, Jesus would exercise his defined role.

The good pleasure of God—his delight in his creation with his life-giving conviction that 'it was very good' (Genesis 1:31)—is reborn in the baptismal waters to issue into the ministry of Jesus to Israel. From the baptism, in the person of Jesus, the power of God goes out to confront the world and 'do battle against the forces of negation that crush the hopes of humanity'.[69] Jesus would achieve universal kingship (Psalm 2) through suffering (Isaiah 42), the heavenly communication foreshadowing the ministry of Jesus. After the Servant's ministry, the world will turn in universal submission (Isaiah 2:1-4) to Israel's Torah emanating from Jerusalem, from Israel's king. Jesus rises from the baptismal waters to bring in the new age commissioned by God through the Spirit as the divine Son of God and Messiah. Jesus will complete his messianic ministry by dying and then he will be highly exalted (cf. Luke 24:26). Jesus' kingship of the universe will come but first he must die as the Suffering Servant. The Day of Pentecost equipped believers with power to proclaim that Jesus is the Christ of God, to the ends of the earth.

---

    und Billerbeck (1922, 123-125) present evidence for the dove being a rabbinic image for Israel—and Jesus was the total replacement for Israel.

68 Marcus, 1992, 73.

69 Marcus, 1992, 75.

John's call to Israel was to national repentance—not just the regular turning away from a specific sin act but a definitive repentance by which Israel's Sinai mandate as world evangelist could be renewed. Jesus' baptism identifies with Israel and provides for the fulfilment of her mission. The opening of the heavens denotes a public theophany and a ministry for which the Spirit will provide strength, a messianic kingship achieved through suffering obedience. The commissioning at the baptism is then followed by spiritual preparation for the ministry to follow (4:1–11) as Satan offered the kingdom without the cross at the temptation (4:8–9; cf. Peter is in league with the devil when, at Caesarea Philippi, he posits a cross without suffering, 16:23).

So the Baptist's prophecy was fulfilled at Calvary, not Pentecost, for at Pentecost the Holy Spirit came on believing Jews only. Again, the wrath to come in the Baptist's proclamation is not part of the Pentecost narrative. Pentecost reconstructed Israel for her Abrahamic ministry of blessing the world. The Baptist's message at the Jordan was an ultimatum for Israel as a nation. In Jesus' unique ministry, the Holy Spirit was the presence and power of God in Israel (Mark 3:29ff) for those who would hear. But the Scribes were interpreting the gracious acts of God through Jesus as the work of the prince of evil.

Jesus is directed by the Spirit into the wilderness (4:1-11)

Matthew 4 advances the typology of Jesus as representative Israel. Jesus was full of the Spirit (cf. Luke 1). The Spirit not only equipped Jesus but also directed his ministry. The Spirit drove (4:1; cf. Mark 1:12) Jesus into the wilderness where God had put Israel to the test after the crossing of the Red Sea. This time, in the crucial battle with evil, Jesus as representative Israel would succeed where Old Testament Israel had failed. This earthly success of Jesus over Satan will climax in casting out the prince of this world (John 12:31). The resilience of Satan suggests that these sorts of temptations were presented to Jesus throughout his ministry.

The narrative attests the reality of evil as a personal power, a perversion of goodness. The temptations challenged: the nature of Jesus' call to messiahship; Jesus' obedience as God's Son; Jesus' total dependence on God and trust in his presence; and Jesus' acceptance of God's sovereignty. Jesus' victory over Satan confirmed his divine sonship and his servant vocation before Jesus began his ministry. This victory anticipated the final victory of the cross over evil. The wilderness, the temple and the mountain—the three venues of the temptations—were places associated with eschatological expectations. The temptations (cf. Deuteronomy 6-8) were Satan's appeals for Jesus to freely use his power to conform his messianic ministry to popular expectations, but Jesus was the Son of God and God had given him the Spirit without measure (John 3:34). Filled with the Spirit, Jesus acknowledged the authority of Scripture but then replied from a common human standpoint (cf. man shall not live by bread alone, 4:4). The temptations were about what it meant for Jesus to be the Son of God (if thou be the Son of God, 4:3,6). In the wilderness, Jesus recalled the covenant promises that Israel had forgotten in her sojourn through the wilderness. The ministering angels at the conclusion of this round of temptations hinted at Jesus' final lordship over all creation. Jesus' victory over Satan's temptations confirmed his status both as Son and as Israel. The temptations in the wilderness were the beginning of a battle with Satan that would be ongoing throughout Jesus' ministry.

The first temptation reminds Israel of God's ability to feed them. No contrast is made between natural food and spiritual food. Jesus rejected recourse to messianic power but, instead, put himself in the position of hungry Israelites. God had directed hungry Israel to trust God as the one who is able to sustain life beyond a protracted fast (Deuteronomy 8:3). What is required is faith in God's word in the face of starvation. The second temptation—to leap from the pinnacle of the temple—was meant to force God to intervene for Jesus rather than trust God's providential care. The third temptation was an appeal to sin openly—unlike the first two more subtle temptations—requiring an act of Satan worship in contesting the key issue of who should be God (God or Satan). But God had absolutely prohibited sin. The fullness of the Spirit guided Jesus' human nature which was capable of sinning.[70]

The Spirit will speak through the disciples (10:17-20)

In controversy with adversaries—when arrested—Jesus' disciples are not to worry for they will be given words to say because the Spirit, as a witness of the Father, will speak through them.

---

70 For this paragraph, see Vos, 1948, 365.

The Spirit-endowed Servant (12:15–21)

The character of the Spirit endowed Servant (12:15–21; cf. Isaiah 42:1–4) provided a rationale for Jesus' compassionate action on the Sabbath and for withdrawal from controversy with the Pharisees (12:15). Jesus expressed his implementation of the ministry of the Servant as non-violent intervention to bring justice, that is, rectifying a system that needed reversal.[71]

12:18–21 provide a summary of the nature of Jesus' ministry, indicating quiet acceptance of the rejected in Israel and the extension of the gospel to the Gentiles (anticipating what will occur after Pentecost). This exhibition of the Servant's mercy in humility and lowliness was real leadership as opposed to the religious domination of the Pharisees. Like the Servant whose ministry Jesus now acted out, Jesus' ministry would end in his death for Israel. The end of the quote from Isaiah's prophecy (12:18–21; cf. Isaiah 42:1–4) was ominous for Israel with regard to judgement followed by hope for the Gentiles. Like the faithful Servant of Israel, Jesus' fidelity to his baptismal appointment of kingship through suffering could potentially achieve for Israel and the world a reversal of the course of history and—finally—the eternal heavenly celebration of the Sabbath (cf. Hebrews 4:9). But Israel would not hear the Servant Jesus.

Blasphemy against the Spirit (12:22–32)

The Pharisees ascribed Jesus' Spirit-driven works—that bound Satan, the 'strong man' (cf. 12:29)—to Beelzebub (12:24), prince of the demons. So Jesus warns that the Pharisees were blaspheming the Holy Spirit (12:31–32). Jesus' Spirit-led activities announced that the Kingdom was at hand, that is, Jesus' actions were expressing the Jewish apocalyptic hope of deliverance from evil.[72] To speak against the Son of Man (Jesus' self-designated title) was not as blasphemous because Jesus' opponents thought that 'Son of Man' was merely a term of self-reference.

Jesus pointed out how illogical the Pharisees' criticism was, for it would mean that Satan was divided against himself. Jesus' ministry reflected his character just as the words of the Pharisees, the real blasphemers, reflected their character (12:33–35). The Day of Judgement would declare the Pharisees' blasphemy for their words had been 'careless' (12:36–37), reflecting their inward condition. The activity of the Spirit in Jesus pointed to the fact

---

71 Beaton, 2002, 160.
72 France, 1985, 209.

that the kingdom has come in Jesus, underscoring the severity of their sin of blasphemy. Graham Cole observes that blasphemy against the Spirit is not a temporary episode but, rather, is persistent impenitent unbelief—and the Pharisees in the gospels were continually guilty of this sin.[73] Jesus responded to the associated request by the scribes and Pharisees for signs by explaining that he needs no greater sign from heaven than his own message (12:39-45) for, through Jesus' Spirit empowered ministry, the eschatological rule of God would be realised (12:28; Luke 11:20). In performing miracles by the Spirit of God (12:18), Jesus was the promised harbinger of the Spirit.

In the name of the Father, the Son and the Spirit (28:18-20)

The Trinitarian formula in the command to go into all the world is often considered to be a later liturgical addition. But the reference could be dominical since both John and Luke associate the Spirit with the resurrection thereby linking the three persons of the Godhead. The baptism that Jesus had already embraced for his community is the point of new covenant entry. Jesus' baptism is into the (singular, 28:19) name (of the Father and of the Son and of the Holy Spirit), indicating the oneness of the Godhead to whom believers now owe full allegiance. The participles 'baptising' and 'teaching' are instrumental participles, indicating the manner of making disciples.

The threefold commission to go into the entire world: revokes the limitations of Jesus' historical mission to Israel only (10:5-6); makes baptism the public institutional sign of new covenant ties, replacing Jewish circumcision; and teaches believers to pledge obedience to the 'law of Christ' (28:20; cf. Galatians 6:2), no longer requiring converts to pledge obedience to the Mosaic Torah. Jesus thus legislates for a clear break with national Israel.[74] Jesus promises to be with the disciples until the end of the world, assuring them of continuing relationship through his risen function as the life-giving Spirit.

---

73 Cole, 2007, 177.
74 Meier, 1991, 213. The risen and historical Jesus—an acknowledged member of the Godhead—is presented as the founder of the church.

Mark

1:1 tells the whole story about who Jesus is, indeed, 1:1–3 is the key to Mark's gospel. Mark's 'beginning of the gospel' (1:1) is followed immediately by Old Testament expectations (1:2–3; cf. Malachi 3:1; Isaiah 40:3) which have in view the ministries of Jesus and John the Baptist, whose baptismal work begins the gospel.

The gift of the Spirit for Jesus' ministry (1:9–13)

Mark's interest in the baptism of Jesus is centred on coming up from the waters (1:10a; cf. Isaiah 63:12, in the context of the opening of the heavens in 1:10b). Isaiah 64:1 foreshadowed the onset of a new age with new revelation by a new activity of God through the Spirit (cf. Isaiah 63:14). Isaiah's prophecy (cf. Isaiah 63:7–64:12) recalls Yahweh's exodus intervention and there is a plea for Yahweh to intervene again in response to the penitence of a rebellious people (cf. Isaiah 64:6–12).

Isaiah recalled Israel's first exodus experience, being guided by the Holy Spirit (Isaiah 63:7–14), as part of a wider lament (Isaiah 63:7–64:12) pleading Israel's present position. Isaiah asks for the rending of the heavens (64:1–5a) and new revelation of the divine presence to rescue Israel from apostate leaders and temple functionaries. The advent of this new revelation of the Holy Spirit within Israel suggests a new, divine, second exodus movement towards a new Promised Land. This movement was happening in the plains of Moab beyond the Jordan as John recalled Israel to what she should be. The new age prophesied by Isaiah 64 begins with the death of Jesus when the rending of the veil of the temple (15:38) ends the age of Old Testament Israel. The same verb, *schizo*, is employed both at Jesus' baptism (1:10)—of the rending of the heavens to bring in the age of the new covenant—and at the rending of the veil of the temple (15:38). The world will now behold the glory of God through a new Israel.

The gift of the Spirit to Jesus at his baptism (1:10) was to commission (cf. anoint, Acts 10:38) and empower Jesus for ministry. The descent of the Spirit as a dove symbolised Jesus' identification with Israel. Jesus experienced the descent of the Spirit and the voice from heaven personally, convincing him of the purpose of his ministry and conferring power for his ministry. Jesus would prevail in conflict with the enemies of the people of God and—by his death—Jesus would bring into being a resurrected Israel (cf. Ezekiel 37:1–14), the true Israel, the one people of God (Ezekiel 37:15–28).

The voice of God identified Jesus as Messiah (1:11; cf. Psalm 2:7; Isaiah 42:1). Psalm 2 reflects on the eschatological victory of the Davidic Messiah who sets up his reign from Jerusalem over the defeated rebellious nations. Isaiah 42:1 refers to the ministry of the Servant of God whose victory over the world comes by complete surrender to the divine will and death (Isaiah 53). Jesus' baptism is placed immediately before the temptations, suggesting that the opposition that the Messiah will overcome is demonic. Only divine empowerment on one 'born from above' (cf. Psalm 2:7)—who has more than human stature—could overcome demonic opposition. Mark's gospel states that Jesus is not merely Son of God as a royal figure but also the Son of God as a divine figure, identified with God and yet distinct from him. Son of God and kingship are closely related in Psalm 2. Jesus is Son and Servant. By his death, Jesus makes the divine will accessible and able to be performed by all in a total new covenant inclusion.

Jesus, as Israel's representative—illuminated and led by the Spirit—ushered in the new covenant age and triumphs over demonic hatred (cf. Psalm 2). Defeat of demonic opposition is a theme throughout Jesus' ministry (cf. 1:24). Jesus achieves this victory by total dependence on the word of God as the Servant of God (Isaiah 53). The typology of Jesus' forty days in the wilderness (1:12ff.) corresponds to Israel's forty years in the same wilderness (Deuteronomy 8:2-4) before entry into the Promised Land. Jesus' forty days in the wilderness proved his trustworthiness as Son of God because he had authority over Satan in the power of the Spirit in the wilderness and in later exorcisms. Indeed, Jesus introduces a new era in which the definitive action of God will attest his total world control through the ministry of Jesus (1:15). The wild beasts accompanying Jesus in the wilderness (1:13) do not suggest a reversal of the results of the fall, rather, wild beasts coupled with demons in the wilderness (cf. Isaiah 34:14) emphasise the menacing character of the environment.

Signs of Jesus' Spirit-filled ministry (1:24-3:24)

The healings and exorcisms in Mark (1:24-28,40-43; 3:1-5; 3:10-11,23-24; 5:1-20; 7:24-30; 9:14-29) reveal the presence of the Spirit in the context of continuing cosmic engagement between Satan—under whom all demonic forces were united (3:23,26; cf. 1:13; 5:2,12)—and Jesus filled with the Holy Spirit (1:10,12). The demon identified Jesus as the 'Holy One of God' (1:24), that is, the bearer of the Holy Spirit. The contrast between the combatants was clear, as was the authority exercised by Jesus over Satan's world. By prophetic exception—for the Kingdom of God, demonstrated by the present activity of the Spirit of God with authority over demonic spirits, should come first to remnant Jewish believers (7:27)—a young Greek (gentile) daughter is released from demonic oppression (7:25–26,29–30).

Just as Jesus had exercised authority over evil spirits, so he sent the twelve apostles out to minister with his power over demonic spirits (6:7) and the result of their ministry was that many demons were exorcised and many sick people were healed (6:13). But there was a boy with a mute spirit that the disciples could not heal (9:18) and when they asked Jesus why he was not healed—like the rest—Jesus indicated that the Spirit's power over evil would not always be instantaneous, indeed, sometimes it would be necessary to engage in the time-consuming spiritual disciplines of prayer and fasting before there would be a kingdom of God outcome over evil. Perhaps a process involving time and effort in exercising authority over evil is sometimes necessary now (in this age, before the return of Christ) because of the faithlessness of the present generation before the sons of God are revealed at the return of Christ (when all will be fully led by the Spirit).

Luke

Luke provides key information on the Spirit with regard to the significance of the incarnation and early life of Jesus. With the annunciations of two births, the new age is shown to be beginning in Israel after a long and dispiriting post-exilic history.[75] The annunciation of John the Baptist (1:5-25) corresponds to the annunciation of Jesus (1:26-38).

The narrative about John's birth begins in Jerusalem with a country priest, Zachariah, at home with his wife Elizabeth and then—having regard to Old Testament expectation (cf. Malachi 3:1)—Zechariah is in the temple. Zechariah and Elizabeth were numbered among the many faithful in Israel (1:6; 2:25,37); their conduct demonstrated that they were right with God. Zachariah came to Jerusalem for temple duty to officiate at the burning of incense within the sanctuary, a once-in-a-lifetime privilege for priests. The annunciation by the angel Gabriel to Zachariah about John was a typical Old Testament annunciation to a pious childless couple (cf. 1 Samuel 1-3).[76] Zachariah's wife's barrenness presaged this wondrous birth as the dawn of a new day in Israel for the Holy Spirit would fill this child, John, from his mother's womb (1:15) so that John would be empowered by the Holy Spirit for his divine commission to announce the beginning of the new exodus redemption. The Baptist would be great in the sight of the Lord and, like Elijah (Luke 1:16), he would call many in Israel back to the covenant.

Filled with or full of the Holy Spirit[77]

'Full of the Spirit' in Luke-Acts is a metaphorical expression describing a life that is progressively Spirit filled. 'Full' draws attention to a rich intensity in the quality of a person, defining a noun in the genitive (that is, the person possesses this being or characteristic).[78] Stephen was described as a man full of grace and power (Acts 6:8), that is, Stephen was characterised by these rich qualities in the sight of his fellow men. Both the Baptist and Jesus are described as being full of the Holy Spirit (1:15; 4:1), that is, the power

---

75 Significant events in the infancy narratives raise expectancy in Israel. The birth of Jesus is the unrecognized climax of Israel's call because her Messiah has come to fulfil God's covenants (Creation, Abraham, Sinai, David and the Jeremianic).

76 Litwak, 2005, 74-5.

77 cf. Turner, 1981, 45-63.

78 cf. Tabitha is 'full of good works' (Acts 9:36), that is, Tabitha is marked by good works or crammed full of good works which so abounded that they kept on being produced.

and presence of God's Spirit is clearly manifest in both of their ministries. Being 'filled' with the Spirit, it was evident that the Baptist and Jesus had received spiritual power for their immediate tasks.

The child to be born to Elizabeth would be filled (*pimplemi*) with the Holy Spirit before his birth. Luke is the only New Testament writer to use *pimplemi* (fill) with respect to persons (1:15, the Baptist; 1:41, Elizabeth; 1:67, Zechariah; Acts 2:4, 4:8, 4:31, 9:17 and 13:9, the Holy Spirit; cf. *pleroo*, Acts 13:52). *Pimplemi* (fill) denotes the immediate inspiration and charismatic character of a speech event, not the inception of an enduring endowment.[79]

Judaism stopped short of a hypostasis for the Spirit but still used personal language of him. The clearest presentation of the Holy Spirit as a personal being is in John 14–16 where the Spirit is parallel to Jesus, mediating the Father and Son to the disciples as Jesus had. Jesus was the mediator of the Father and he revealed himself. The Spirit is the mediator of Jesus and he reveals Christ and the Father (not himself). To receive the promised Spirit is to prophesy (Acts 2; Joel 2), that is, to receive the Spirit is to experience some specific activity of God's Spirit. Throughout Acts, receiving the Spirit designated experience of the Spirit in the character promised by Joel. Hence, Pentecost is programmatic of the new age.

When Jesus received the promised Spirit at his ascension, Jesus received the authority and power to administer the gift promised in Joel's prophecy. The Spirit of God given by Jesus reveals God's word and will, and the Spirit of Jesus gives his wisdom (cf. Acts 6:10; Luke 12:12; 21:15). In Acts, to receive the Spirit usually means receiving the Spirit of Prophecy (that is, divine communication designating a precise set of circumstances and time). Jesus received the Spirit at the Jordan at his baptism (3:22) and this reception of the Spirit was affirmed at his ascension (Acts 2:33). The disciples then received the Spirit at Pentecost (Acts 2:3–4) and, perhaps, before Pentecost (9:1; 11:13; John 6:63; 14:17; 20:22). So the Spirit arising from

---

[79] Acts 4:8 (Peter) and Acts 13:9 (Paul) refer to speeches—no more, no less. Acts 4:31 says that they were all filled with the Holy Spirit which provided fresh impulse to begin preaching again with boldness. Acts 2:4 refers to the immediate inspiration of the tongues (glossolalia) miracle, and Peter's speech. Luke uses the aorist phrase to designate short outbursts or intense flashes of Holy Spirit. Acts 9:17 sums up the whole of Paul's life as a constative aorist, that is, a life-long endowment of the Holy Spirit or the whole of Paul's life is an intense flash of Holy Spirit. The disciples who are filled with the Spirit at Acts 2:4 need to be filled again at 4:8,31.

the Incarnation begins a new work in relationship with persons, with each reception fundamentally different.

National repentance was to precede the coming of Yahweh to his people—which is the purpose of the Baptist coming in the spirit and power of Elijah (1:17; cf. Malachi 4:6), that is, as a prophetic preacher (the Baptist is not identified as Elijah). This coming of the Baptist was good news (1:19, the first use of *euaggelizo* in Luke). Until John was born, Zachariah was dumb because of his scepticism (1:19-63) and was unable to pronounce the priestly blessing at the end of his duty. The fulfilment of Gabriel's proclamation occurs with Elizabeth's conception (1:24-25).

The second annunciation (1:26-38)—devoted to the divine character of Jesus' conception—takes the same form as the first annunciation. Gabriel appeared to Mary, like Zachariah, again somewhat like an Old Testament visitation (cf. Judges 13:3-7; Isaiah 7:14). Mary was not greeted in her own right but in terms of what God had done (1:28). Mary states her inability to understand but does not question what God will do (1:29). This parallel annunciation conveyed continuity between Jesus and the Baptist in salvation history but also establishes Jesus' superiority (1:17,32-33).

God will send a saviour to Israel who has a filial relationship with God—a descendant of David who will reign eternally over Israel (1:32-33). These elements fitted Jewish eschatological expectations of the promise of a Messiah. 1:32-33 explain why his name was to be Jesus (1:31, Yahweh saves). As Son of the Most High, Jesus will fulfil the promises of 2 Samuel 7:12-14 by reigning forever. By the ascension, we know that this reign over Israel will extend without end to the whole universe.

Mary appears to be ignorant of 'this' (1:34) heavenly initiative. Her question assumes that the birth is virginal—that is, the birth will occur before a marriage union—the question is about 'how', not 'whether'. The answer is that in this new creative act by the Holy Spirit (1:35), the power of God will be demonstrated. The conception of Jesus marks the conception of the renewal of Israel and the onset of the new creation. The Spirit has been poured out on Israel from on high (cf. Isaiah 32:15) to effect the messianic reign in righteousness. The Spirit will 'overshadow' (*episkiazo*, 1:35) Mary: like the overshadowing cloud symbolising God's presence in the exodus; like the overshadowing activity of the Spirit as the 'mid-wife' of creation (Genesis 1:2). Sinclair Ferguson points out that *episkiazo* is used to translate the Hebrew word *shakan* in the Septuagint (cf. Exodus 40:35 and

29 LXX; Psalm 91:4 and LXX 90:4).[80] *Episkiazo* is used for the glory-cloud of the divine presence during Israel's exodus, that is, the superintending divine power (Psalm 91:4).

The Holy Spirit (Isaiah 63:10-11) led Israel through the wilderness as a pillar of cloud and fire (Exodus 13:21). And the cloud of the glory of the Spirit reappeared in the cloud representing the presence of the glory of God at the tabernacle (Exodus 40:34-38) and in the temple (Isaiah 6:1-4). The cloud of the glory of God is known as the *shekinah*.[81] 'Until the power (Spirit) comes upon you from on high' (24:49) is a further overshadowing, referring to Israel's renewal with the Spirit-conception of Jesus and his birth that represents the first stirrings of the new creation.[82] In a dramatic vision, Ezekiel witnesses the *shekinah* glory of God departing from the temple (Ezekiel 10:1-22) permanently until it returns to the new temple (Ezekiel 43:1-50). The time for returning to the new temple at the birth of the new creation has now come (cf. John 2:18-22). The *shekinah* cloud was absent during the building of the second temple yet the Lord promised that his glory would be seen there (Haggai 2:7-9) and that he would suddenly return to the temple (Malachi 3:1-5). Jesus is that promised glory because the Spirit's glory overshadowed him from the beginning.

The child Jesus would be holy (1:35): an expression of God's essence and distinctiveness as the Son of God. The language consistency between the Holy Spirit overshadowing creation (*sakak*, Genesis 1:2) and the Holy Spirit overshadowing Mary (1:35) at Jesus' conception points to the dramatic inauguration in Jesus of the new creation. Jesus became great because of his divine conception. In his earthly life, Jesus was the descendant of David and therefore the heir to the promises of the Jewish Scriptures including the heir to David's throne over Israel. Even though there was no guiding precedent, Mary nevertheless accepted Gabriel's claim that God's power would achieve all that he had said about the birth of Jesus (1:38, cf. 1 Samuel 1:18).

Luke's use of *episkiazo* (overshadow, 1:35) in the annunciation to Mary echoes both creation and the Exodus. Ferguson proposes that the work of the Spirit in incarnation should be interpreted in a two-fold light.[83] First, the work of the Spirit in incarnation is a divine work of new creation, *de novo*

---

80 Ferguson, 1996, 38.
81 Ferguson, 1996, 40-43.
82 cf. Hawthorne, 1991, 66-67.
83 Ferguson, 1996, 39-40.

but not *ex nihilo*. The Spirit is working on existing material (the humanity of Mary) to produce the last Adam and thereby restore true order (just as the Spirit had brought order and fullness into formlessness and emptiness at the original creation). Second, the work of the Spirit is the beginning of a new work of redemption (the new exodus). The Spirit hovered over the Son of God throughout his temptations and for the whole of his life and ministry (4:1,18). The care of God for his son whom he called out of Egypt (Deuteronomy 8:1ff; Ezekiel 16:1ff; Hosea 11:1) continues in God's care for the incarnate Son (cf. Matthew 2:15), even in his embryonic state in Mary. Jesus' assumption of our weak humanity was also hidden from view and comprehension by the overshadowing of the Spirit.

Ferguson notes that the action of the Holy Spirit to bring Jesus into being without conception (John 1:13) points to a sovereign newness in the work that God is accomplishing.[84] By divine work, the personal divine Logos assumed human nature in the likeness of sinful man (Romans 8:3; cf. Jesus says 'I am from above', John 8:23), but without sinning. Jesus' freedom from guilt and Adam's curse makes his virgin birth essential to our salvation.

The Father sent the Son and the Holy Spirit conceived the Son, therefore, all three members of the Trinity were engaged in the work of redemption by external acts of deity. Jesus' early growth (2:52) draws from Isaiah 11:1–3a. Jesus also fulfilled Isaiah 50:4–5a, indeed, God had said through the prophet Isaiah 'I will put my Spirit on him' (Isaiah 42:1). Luke portrays daily, constant communion with God—that is, Jesus' intimacy with God (cf. 2:49, Jesus said in the temple, 'I must be about my Father's business'). 2:27 narrates the fulfilment of Isaiah 11:2, with the Spirit of the Lord resting on Jesus—the Spirit of wisdom and understanding, counsel and power, knowledge and the fear of the Lord—so that Jesus delighted in the fear of the Lord. Jesus' knowledge of God by the Spirit lent newness, authority, and a sense of reality to his teaching (2:52). Recounting his baptism, Luke portrays Jesus as an anointed priest (the beginning of Jesus' ministry occurred at the age of thirty, 3:23). In his water baptism, Jesus consecrated himself by prayer to his coming death. Jesus was committed to submit to his cross baptism, thereby enabling believers' baptism with the Holy Spirit (3:22; 4:1).

---

84 Ferguson, 1996, 40–43.

The Spirit in the birth narratives of John and Jesus (1:39-2:52)

During Mary's visit to Elizabeth (1:39-41), Elizabeth's loud cry—an indication that Elizabeth was filled with the Holy Spirit (1:41-42a)—declared Mary's blessed status (1:42-45), Mary's special call, and the special call of her son-to-be. Elizabeth's declaration linked Mary with God's plan. The unborn John is also Spirit-filled (1:15) and he moved in the womb to bless Mary (1:41). The phrase 'filled (*pimplemi*) with the Holy Spirit' (1:41) draws attention to the great importance of the occasion.

The Baptist was filled with the Spirit from before birth for prophetic ministry (1:15 and 1:17, the spirit and power of Elijah). However, the Spirit to come on Jesus is the great power of God implementing a new beginning for humanity and their world (cf. 1:35 with Genesis 1:2). The Baptist is to be great 'in the sight of the Lord' (1:15) but Jesus is to be Lord (1:43). The Spirit produces the life of the unique child Jesus so that Gabriel calls him the Son of the Most High (1:32); Elizabeth, inspired by the Spirit (1:41), hails Mary's unborn son as her Lord. Mary is blessed not only because of what will be her special relationship to Jesus (1:43) but also because she believed—with complete commitment—the amazing revelation to her (1:45).

In response to Elizabeth, Mary's praise of God is directed to all generations (1:46-55) because this will be the measure of the ministry of her son, indeed, the blessing of the future to come through this child (1:50-55) is dissociated from any history or expectations for national Israel. With the successive and remote future in mind, the birth of Jesus will be a gift to the whole world throughout history (1:55). The theme of Mary's song concerns the changes in worldly structure and expectations to be brought about by Jesus' birth.

Zachariah is filled with the Spirit (1:57-80)

The account of the birth and early life of the Baptist (1:57-80) corresponds closely to the narrative of Jesus' birth and early life (2:1-52). Zachariah, filled with the Holy Spirit (1:67), prophesied at the birth of John. The narrative comment 'he shall be called' (1:60, RSV)—ascribed to Elizabeth and later attested by Zachariah (1:63)—indicates that the divine hand is in the birth and naming of John, shaping the future course of his ministry. John's name defied family convention yet, obviously, the divine hand is seen in Zachariah's release from dumbness which aroused awe in the whole region (1:65).

The 'song of Zachariah' (1:68-79) celebrates the fulfilment of Gabriel's promise to the Baptist's parents and then elaborates on the significance of the two births: John and Jesus. The song is the answer to the general question 'What then will this child become?' (1:66), a question that arose from the extraordinary events—with Zachariah able to speak again—at John's circumcision. The hymn weaves together quotations and echoes from Law, Prophets, and Psalms in a convergence of scriptural eschatology.

The Spirit led Simeon into the Temple (2:21-40)

Mary dedicated her child to God in a way which was contrary to normal custom (1:22-24, the narrative at this point appears to be a conflation of the rites of purification and presentation of first-born). The presentation of Jesus to God in the temple was exceptional because there was no mention of the required redemption payment for a firstborn son (cf. Exodus 13:2). Jesus' circumcision, which would have taken place at this time (2:21-22), represented his formal entry into the covenant. At this time the Spirit led Simeon into the sanctuary enabling Simeon to recognise the child as the promised Messiah and to provide for him the revelation of Simeon's blessing (2:29-32,34-35).

The canticle and prophecy of Simeon is the theological climax of the infancy narratives. In the Spirit, in the temple (1:27-28, Simeon held the Lord's Christ—for whom he had been waiting for a long time. Simeon may now conclude his ministry after he has proclaimed Jesus' birth as heralding salvation from God prepared for the world through Israel (cf. Isaiah 40:1; 49:6; 61:2). Simeon anticipates the Gentiles coming into the covenant. He had received revelation and guidance by the Holy Spirit and his Spirit-filled prophecy not only acknowledges Jesus but also establishes for the ministry of Jesus a pattern of acceptance and rejection.

The 'consolation of Israel' (2:25)—perhaps hope of the restoration of Israel—came from God in the person of Jesus who is the glory of Israel. Because of Jesus' birth, Israel will reflect as God's people the character and intention of God for the world (2:31). The elective Greek term *laos* (people, 2:31) is used predominantly of Israel in the Old Testament but the interesting use of the plural foreshadows the blessing of covenant inclusion for the Gentiles (or, perhaps, for both Israel and the Gentiles). The Lord's salvation conveys a light for the nations through Israel's witness, that is, through the new revelation of Jesus who is the glory for Israel. A new awareness of God's presence accorded with the fulfilment of expectations generated by previous general revelation and, in particular, the fulfilment of Israel's vocation (2:32; cf. Isaiah 49:6). Salvation is light for the Gentiles and the Gentiles are both witnesses (2:31) and sharers (2:32) in this light. There is divine blessing and glory for Israel in this new revelation for the Gentiles (2:32). The coming of the Messiah to Israel fulfilled God's promise to Abraham which was blessing for all the families of the earth (Genesis 12:3).

Following the blessing, Simeon's prophetic warning (2:34b-35) portended major division among the Jews. 2:29-32 described the positive significance of Jesus and 2:32 prophesied the salvation to come as a result of Jesus' birth but the prophecy to Mary in 2:34 qualifies the encouraging expectation. Not all Israel will accept the salvation offered in the coming of Jesus. The resultant division would not be accidental but, rather, part of God's plan. There would be no middle ground, indeed, the unbelieving part of historic Israel would fall away. Jesus would be a 'sign that will be opposed' (2:34). Within Israel, a believing people of God would arise in continuity with Old Testament believers as a sign of the continuation through Israel of God's plan. National Israel would reject the message of God's salvation through Jesus but a new believing community would accept it. The nation will be humbled in falling from covenant but Christian Israel will rise in new faith. These two Israels will exist side by side as opposed groupings for the remainder of history. Simeon's projection of conflict is a notable feature of the infancy narratives and of the gospel as a whole.

2:35a is parenthetical in that it is only for Mary. The sword—the divine judgement upon Israel—means that the pain of Jesus' rejection and crucifixion would pierce her heart. Simeon's song is a fitting capstone to the infancy narratives. God had made manifest his plan of salvation for Israel and the world. God's plan would not fail but would result in the revelation of the true glory of Israel in the divine servant bringing light to the world in the face of opposition. This plan of God was prepared for Israel throughout her history and would be declared 'in the presence of all peoples' (2:31). The Song of Simeon recognised that Jesus himself was the answer to all expressed hope for salvation for Israel and all the world (cf. Isaiah 42:6; 49:6). Salvation is in the renewal of Israel so that she may be a light to the nations.

After Simeon blessed the amazed parents and disclosed to Mary the division in Israel from her child's future—a future that would bring deep disturbance to Mary—the party returned to Nazareth (2:39) and the narrative refers to the growth and increasing wisdom and favour of the child, Jesus (2:40).

The narrative enclosed by the attestation of Jesus' wisdom (2:40,52) presents a representative account of Jesus' silent years. The twelve year-old Jesus—at an age when a Jewish boy was being prepared to enter the religious community—showed extraordinary discernment in his discussion with the leaders in the temple (2:41–51), which attested his wisdom. Jesus is conscious of being the messianic Son of God and, as such, he was the wise interpreter of Scripture. The narrative assumes his real humanity. The discussion in the temple was about his Father's affairs, perhaps foreshadowing the later episode of Jesus' teaching in the temple (20:1–21:38). Joseph and Mary did not comprehend (2:50), however as they returned to Nazareth they were no doubt more aware of Jesus' distinctiveness and wondered about his future. Jesus' silent years of growth and development is described in terms like those used of the young Samuel (2:52; 1 Samuel 2:26). Sinclair Ferguson suggests that the account of Jesus' childhood points to Jesus being the fulfilment of expectation that the Spirit of the Lord (of knowledge and the fear of the Lord) rests on Jesus as the Messiah (Isaiah 11:2)[85] through the work of the Spirit.

The Messianic baptism of the Holy Spirit and fire (3:15–22)

The Baptist deflects the question about whether he was the Messiah (3:15) by pointing to the significance of the messianic baptism to come. The Messianic baptism of the Holy Spirit and fire will bring the confrontation of eschatological judgment for all, resulting in either salvation or destruction (3:17). From Pentecost onwards, the believer's salvation would come by identification with the cross by which Jesus would absorb the wrath of God directed against a sinful human race.[86]

Luke's baptismal context shows that this was not the first descent of the Spirit on Jesus (1:32,35; cf. 2:41–45) but Jesus' Jordan experience of the Spirit marks him out as the inaugurator of salvation for Israel (cf. 4:16–30). Luke associated the gift of the Spirit and the eschaton with Jesus' birth. By the descent of the Holy Spirit and the divine word at baptism, Jesus now exercised the role of Messianic son/servant (cf. Psalm 2:7; Isaiah 42:1ff). Jesus

---

85 Ferguson, 1996, 44.
86 cf. Gaffin, 1979, 15–16.

inaugurated the new period of salvation for the transformed Israel with the ultimate goal of new creation (cf. 22:20).

The descent of the Holy Spirit in the form of a dove at Jesus' baptism was not only the essential item for messianic ministry but also the authorisation for messianic kingship. The voice from heaven at Jesus' baptism attests that Jesus is not only a kingly Messiah (Psalm 2:7) with authority to rule the nations but also that his office will be achieved through suffering (Isaiah 42:1). The coming of the Holy Spirit on the Messiah is an indication that his office is not hereditary, rather, the Spirit equips Jesus for ministry and the Messiah will share the Spirit with the people of God.

Jesus' baptism is followed by a genealogy tracing Jesus' lineage back to Adam. This genealogical preface extending to the first man indicates the cosmic nature of the wilderness conflict (cf. 4:1–4) and gave to Jesus 'impregnable assurance of his own identity and ministry as Son of God and the inauguration of his suffering Servant-Messiah's commission of empowerment for ministry under the divine Spirit'.[87]

Jesus' identification as a human is clarified in the genealogy (3:23–37). Jesus' link with Adam (3:37) gives the clue to the meaning of Son of God in the genealogy (3:38) as both Adam and Jesus share the common title 'son of God'. Both Adam and Jesus begin their lives as Son of God but Adam contributed disobedience and death. The Son of God theme—evident in the baptism—is continued in the genealogy after the baptism. Jesus, like Adam, is created in righteousness and is head of God's creation and (as Son) the divine representative. With Jesus' coming, one age ends and another begins. Jesus is not only linked with Adam but also linked with all men as the new beginning, as the second Adam (1 Corinthians 15:47).

The ministry of the Spirit anointed Messiah (4:14–30)

The return of Jesus to Galilee is marked by his spreading fame and universal acceptance. This activity of the Spirit (4:1,14) is linked to Jesus' commission at baptism and his victory over Satan in the temptation. This commission and victory are interpreted by what follows in the synagogue (4:16–30). The anointing of the Spirit is for messianic office and the Spirit of Prophecy is the medium of revelation, combining the ideal royal and prophetic figure (Isaiah 42:1–4; 61:1–3). Jesus' fully empowered ministry

---

87 Jesus' endowment for ministry is now complete (Fergusion, 1996, 46).

is not merely a preaching ministry for Jesus will release mankind from the power of evil and restore blessings in the messianic age.

Some incorrectly suppose that when Satan 'departed from him until an opportune time' (4:13), the ministry of Christ was free of temptation up to the passion (which contains the next direct reference to Jesus' trials, 22:28). But the implication of 22:28 is that temptations had been ministry-long, that is, the wilderness battle continued. Indeed, the Greek perfect tense (have continued, 22:28) suggests that the whole of Jesus' earthly ministry was under temptation.

Returning to Nazareth, Jesus is in the synagogue on the Sabbath day as was his custom and the Spirit of God is evidently on him, fulfilling Isaiah's prophecy (Isaiah 42:1). The whole synagogue concentrates on his words. Luke radically expands Mark's Nazareth episode (Mark 6:1-6) and locates it to control the presentation of Jesus' ministry to Israel. Luke altered Mark's chronology to place this pericope in the Nazareth synagogue at the outset of Jesus' ministry including major theological themes of Luke-Acts, namely: the work of the Spirit, the universality of the gospel, the grace of God, and the rejection of Jesus.

4:1,14 mention the activity of the Spirit at the baptism and temptation. The Nazareth synagogue reading also references the Spirit's messianic activity, highlighting the significance throughout his ministry of being anointed by the Spirit. This prelude of Spirit activity was necessary prior to the messianic application of Isaiah 61 to Jesus (4:18-19).[88] Jesus announces himself as the anointed—that is, commissioned by God—Servant figure of Isaiah 61 who will lead Israel into the new age of universal reconciliation (Isaiah 61:5,11). Luke frames the incident in reports about the growing reputation of Jesus (4:14,37) with interest centred on the identity of Jesus.

Jesus attends the synagogue (4:16-21) according to his regular custom as a pious Jew. After the Torah was read, Jesus stood up to read from the prophet Isaiah (61:1-2a, omitting 61:1d 'to heal the broken hearted' and inserting the line 'to set the captives at liberty' from Isaiah 58:6d). Jesus has been uniquely anointed with the Spirit to proclaim and to heal (4:18). The first half of the Nazareth episode reaches a climax when Jesus sat down and said that the prophecy was fulfilled 'today', thereby claiming God's anointing and identifying himself as the predicted Isaiah 61 figure who would

---

88 Brawley, 1987, 7.

inaugurate eschatological fulfilment by preaching good news to the poor. The message says that Jesus is the solution to Israel's predicament.

Jesus' public ministry to Israel began by offering release and freedom under the reign of God with the inauguration of the messianic age. Jesus indicates that he is the expected deliverer, the Messiah, the one who will liberate Israel. He then announces the character of his ministry to Israel, namely, Jesus will: preach good tidings to the poor, proclaim release to the captives, give sight to the blind, and set the oppressed free. These aims are generalised by 'proclaiming the acceptable year of the Lord' (4:19).

At this beginning of his ministry in Nazareth, Jesus challenged the assumption that the Jews had a relationship of privilege with God (4:24–27) thereby offending all in the synagogue. There is a dramatic shift when the townspeople become sceptical as they reflect on the humble origins of Jesus (4:22) but scepticism turns to rage when Jesus announced that the blessing of God is extended to outsiders. Jesus will, indeed, share a common fate with the prophets (4:24–28).

Jesus chose the portion of Scripture from Isaiah with deliberation. In its context, Isaiah 61:1–2 is eschatological and similar in tone to the Servant songs. Indeed, as the Isaianic Servant will perform the tasks of the one who is anointed by the Spirit so Jesus is empowered by the Spirit to carry out royal and prophetic tasks (Isaiah 61:1; cf. 42:1). In the time of Yahweh's favour: comfort will be provided for the oppressed and the afflicted (Isaiah 49:13; 61:1–3); there will be rebuilding and restoration of the land (Isaiah 61:4; 49:8); and there is a response of joy and praise (Isaiah 49:13; cf. 61:3; 62:10). The Aramaic Targum identifies Isaiah 61:1 with the prophet himself but the text then seems to eliminate messianic overtones.[89]

Jesus read Isaiah as a personal statement of his vocation, emphasising two words—'me' and 'release' (Isaiah 61:1)—referring to his person releasing captives like the exodus, that is, his vocation is the restoration of Israel. Jesus asserted that God had sent him as the medium of revelation to exercise the prophetic function of declaring the mind of God by preaching good news to effect liberation from Satanic oppression for those who are poor, captive, blind or broken. Only the Messiah as the one who is uniquely anointed (3:22), utterly filled (4:1), and entirely directed (4:1) by the Holy Spirit has the equipment to fulfil this ministry of liberation.

---

89 Strauss, 1995, 233.

For Jesus, at the beginning of his ministry as reported in Luke (cf. Matthew 5:3–6), the poor are Israel in need of salvation. Jesus identifies himself as the figure in Isaiah 61:1–2 who not only announces the arrival of God's eschatological salvation but also brings it about. What he proclaims in Isaiah 61 is performative, that is, the one who proclaims the prophecy has authority to effect it (cf. Isaiah 58:6). As a world figure, the chief task of the Servant was to bring justice/judgement (Isaiah 42:1,3,4) that was calculated to change the course of Israel's history, in particular, to restore Israel to her Promised Land. Isaiah 61, together with the Servant passages, suggests a function of messianic judgement normally associated with regal or governmental power—the king, priest, or judge. Quoting Isaiah 61 at 4:18–19a defines with precision the significance attached to Jesus' anointing by the Spirit, namely: the primary result of Jesus' unique anointing was preaching the good news and this was the pre-eminent aspect of his mission; and the Spirit-inspired ministry of Jesus would effect salvation for Israel as he uttered words that liberated with power.

Jesus' message of relief from the burdens of life and oppression was at the very heart of his gospel. 4:16–30 and Acts 10:34–38 have similar sequences because Luke understood that the healing of the oppressed was the result of Jesus' conflict with—and victory over—demonic forces that had held the people in captivity. Placing the Nazareth sermon between two encounters with Satan (4:1–13; 31–37) reinforces the important gospel motif of conflict with and victory over Satan. Luke presents the Servant who will both deliver Jacob-Israel from its blindness and deafness and execute Yahweh's purpose for the nations.

The omission of 'to bind up the broken hearted' (Isaiah 61:1d) in Luke's quote (4:18–19)—and replacing that line with 'proclaim the release of the captives' (Isaiah 58:6c)—placed stress on the good news of release. God grants freedom to the prisoners! The exorcism following the proclamation of his ministry (4:31–37) demonstrates that Jesus' ministry is about release from spiritual bondage.[90] This preaching of the good news of 'release' is highlighted by the context of Luke 4 which continues to refer to Jesus' messianic ministry of healing and exorcisms. Jesus ceased reading beyond *dekton* (acceptable, Isaiah 61:2a) perhaps because the remainder of Isaiah

---

90 cf. 6:18; 7:21; 8:2,29; 9:39,42; 13:11.

61 is Zion centred and his Nazareth charge will move in a different direction,[91] namely, personal spiritual commitment to the covenant.

When he rolled up the scroll (4:20) and ascribed its message to himself, he was also referring to the anointing of the Spirit (that is, his baptism) and the conquest of temptation. Since there is little reference to the Spirit in Luke's gospel after this point (10:21; 11:13; 12:10,12), the heavy emphasis on the Spirit at the beginning of the gospel is significant in the Luke-Acts presentation emphasising that Luke understood 'anointed' in messianic terms. In Jesus' 'today', Luke translated the 'nearness of the kingdom' (Mark 1:15) with regard to fulfilment of Scripture (cf. 4:21). The audience reaction that followed was dramatic.

Through Jesus' carefully selected reading from Isaiah, he proclaimed himself by the Spirit as the anointed Servant Messiah who brings liberty to oppressed Israel! Immediately after the message of release (4:18), Jesus pointed to the type of release he had in mind (cf. 10:18). 4:43 identifies the activity of setting at liberty with preaching the good news of the kingdom, so the 'release' refers to his messianic ministry as well as to his healing and exorcisms. And this Servant messenger will deliver Israel from captivity to its disobedience and national humiliation if Israel will listen to him.

As the Servant, Jesus will lead Israel in the new exodus, for the fourth servant song (Isaiah 52:13–53:12) immediately follows the summons to the new exodus (Isaiah 52:11–12).[92] By ending his reading with the phrase 'the year of the Lord's favour' (4:19; cf. Isaiah 61:2a)—which was not the conclusion of the original sentence in Isaiah—Jesus emphasised his role as eschatological fulfiller. Jesus' commentary, 'Today this scripture has been fulfilled in your hearing' (4:21) would have been taken by his audience to mean that the eschatological jubilee year had arrived (Isaiah 61; cf. Leviticus 25). 4:18d, 'to set free the oppressed', would also have heightened Jubilee expectations. The Qumran group also understood Isaiah 61:1–2 as a proclamation of the advent of the kingdom of God in terms of the final jubilee (11Q Melchizedek), in particular, Melchizedek would appear in the 10th jubilee year to proclaim liberty to the captives (cf. Isaiah 52:7).[93] The Qumran fragment represents Melchizedek as the supra-mundane Messiah

---

91 cf. Scheffler, 1993, 4.
92 Strauss, 1995, 286–7.
93 Turner, 1981, 19.

carrying out the will of God for salvation and judgement, and bringing the times of the Gentiles to an end.

Jesus employed the Isaiah passage in the context of an established eschatological Jubilee understanding and Jesus' message resonates with the Jubilee theme of restoration but this connection must not be overemphasised for there is no other allusion to Jubilee in Jesus' ministry. When the monarchy was in place, it was the king's responsibility to announce the Jubilee/Sabbath year release (cf. Jeremiah 34:8-22). However, contrary to what Israel would have expected in a Jubilee year, the disciples will leave all and receive nothing back.[94] Moreover, 4:16-30 draws the messianic portrait of the advent of the kingdom—the gift of the last days—as the universal outpouring of the Spirit on Israel (not a Jubilee).[95] Jesus had received power to promulgate messianic forgiveness and the Spirit would be the gift of life for those in the kingdom in the new age. The Jubilee element simply emphasises the freedom for Israel which will follow Israel's acceptance of Jesus as Messiah. More than that, Jesus' ministry, death, and resurrection will lead to an eternal Jubilee.

The townspeople who thought they knew Jesus' personal background reacted to his reading and interpretation of fulfilment with amazement 'at the gracious words that came from his mouth' (4:22). But is this evaluation positive or negative? *Marturein* (witness) and *thaumazein* (be amazed) point to a positive reaction. However, if the response was positive it is difficult to explain how the innocuous expression of amazement—'is not this Joseph's son?' (4:22)—could provoke Jesus' strong response (doubtless you will say, 4:23). Most scholars take 4:22 positively and suggest that the hint of a Gentile mission that followed (4:23-27) turned the exclusivist crowd against Jesus.

Joachim Jeremias contended that the audience was offended because Jesus stopped short in the reading and did not condemn the Gentiles by adding the announcement of God's vengeance in Isaiah 61:2.[96] However, that suggestion not only violates the context—which is entirely positive, focussing on Israel's restoration—but, in addition, Jesus' response (4:23-24) supplies the reason for the hostility after the relatively favourable reaction of 4:22. Jesus knew that his home town would not accept (*dektos*, 4:24; cf.

---

94 Seccombe, 1982, 54-56
95 Joel 2:28-32; Isaiah 32:15; 44:3-5; Ezekiel 18:31; 36:25-27; 37:14; 39:29.
96 Jeremias, 1958, 44-45.

Acts 10:35) a prophet from among themselves, that is, they would reject his Isaianic servant claims. *Patris* (homeland, 4:24) most naturally refers to Nazareth but may refer to the nation in the context of 4:24–27. Jesus' reference to Elijah highlights the widow of Zarephath (1 Kings 17:8–24), that is, the blessing of God had gone beyond the border of Israel because the prophet was unacceptable at home, in Israel. Likewise, Israel risked losing the blessings that God wished to send. To show that Elijah and Elisha were not acceptable in their *patris*, Jesus contrasted: Elijah's gentile widow with many widows in Israel who were not similarly blessed (4:25); and Elisha's healing for gentile Naaman (2 Kings 5) with many lepers who were not healed in Israel (4:27). By rejecting Jesus, Nazareth became a symbol of Israel's rejection of its prophets.

The undertones for a later Gentile mission are evident in 4:23–27 but they are not pronounced for the stress at this stage is on the good news to Israel's poor. Jesus, like the prophets, proclaimed the acceptable year of the Lord but the people rejected him for he was not acceptable to them. But God's will to save was wider than the reference to the prophet's homeland. Jesus' examples of Elijah and Elisha show that God's will from the beginning was to show mercy to the Gentiles. Moreover, the examples of the two northern prophets (Elijah and Elisha) indicate that Jesus is working with the concept of a united people of God and that Jesus will not exclude the old northern kingdom from ministry. But this prophetic word—together with Jesus' lowly origins and familiarity—were unacceptable to Israel. The rejection of his townsfolk demonstrated his messianic and servant identity and this pattern of initial acceptance followed by national rejection is then prominent in Luke/Acts.

In this context, 4:18–21 probably means that the Spirit-anointed Isaianic prophet inaugurates the expected new exodus, beginning the work of Israel's freedom and movement to the Promised Land. God is now powerfully present in his Spirit-anointed Servant. He will free his people from their wretched estate of slave-poverty, captive-exile, blindness and oppression— and he will shepherd them to Zion's restoration. But the Servant can only act where his message is acceptable (4:24) for it involves willing participation. When the insiders (Israelites) reject him, they will see blessing on outsiders (4:25–27). Jesus' ministry of proclamation was for Israel's salvation to make her a light to the Gentiles (2:25–38). But the Nazareth manifesto also: exhibited Jesus' universal program; anticipated his provocative and startling message; and foreshadowed, by his townspeople's attempt to kill him (4:29), Israel's final rejection of Jesus.

The setting in Luke is both royal messianic and prophetic. The first person language of Isaiah 61:1 is—according to the Targum and other rabbinic literature—reminiscent of a prophetic call as is the charismatic power in proclamation and miracle working. 4:22b-30 also describes Jesus' rejection as a prophet (cf. the proverb, 4:24). Whereas Jesus' rejection by his townspeople and Israel is similar to the rejection of the Old Testament prophets, Jesus' claims were far greater than their claims. Jesus resumed his itinerant ministry (4:31-32) by preaching with authority (which excited amazement) and healing all who were under the power of the devil (4:33-37). Nothing was outside his dominion as he performed wonders by the energy of the Holy Spirit (cf. Matthew 12:28).

The identification of Jesus as a prophet in Luke's writings[97] is supported by Jesus' statements about the suffering of prophets (4:24; 11:47-52; 13:33-34; cf. Acts 7:52). Others refer to Jesus as a great prophet (7:16; 24:19).[98] Jesus is, indeed, much more than an ordinary prophet. The Baptist is described by Jesus as more than a prophet (7:26), fulfilling the role of the eschatological Elijah (1:17; 7:27).

The messiah is endowed with the Spirit (Isaiah 11:2; 42:1; 61:1), anointed (1 Samuel 16:13; 2 Samuel 23:1-2; Psalm 2:2), and chosen by God (Isaiah 42:1; 61:1)—so the Spirit was active in Jesus' proclamation. The Messiah is to: establish justice (Isaiah 9:6; 11:3-5) and righteousness (Isaiah 9:7; 11:4-5); bring comfort and gladness to the poor and oppressed (Isaiah 9:2-7); and be a light to the nations (Isaiah 9:2-7; cf. 11:10) dispelling darkness by freeing the prisoners and releasing the oppressed (cf. Isaiah 58:6). A new exodus of Yahweh's people (Isaiah 11:11-16) will mark his reign. Turner suggests that the Spirit was shared as a power in the ministry of the disciples and the mission of the seventy (cf. 10:21).[99] Where people

---

97 7:16; 13:33-34; 24:19; Acts 3:22-23; 7:37.

98 The hailing of Jesus as the great prophet (7:16) seems to identify him with the expected messianic prophet of Deuteronomy 18:15 (cf. Luke 7:18-28). The silence of Israel's prophecy had been broken dramatically. The Rabbinic belief that the Holy Spirit had been withdrawn from Israel with the demise of Old Testament prophecy is, therefore, invalid. Jesus was not merely a prophet but a prophet like Moses (cf. 3:22) to begin in Israel—like Moses (Acts 3:22ff.; 7:37; cf. Luke 7:24-35; 24:19)—a new covenant era for the people of God (22:20).

99 Turner, 1998, 33-35.

press into the kingdom, this is the effect of the Spirit. Just as the Holy Spirit formerly confronted Israel through the prophets (Isaiah 63:10-13 cf. Acts 7:51) so now they experience the Spirit in Jesus' proclamation and acts of great power.

There is little evidence that the equivalence Servant = Messiah was commonly held in post-exilic Judaism. The Targum identifies the Servant with the Messiah (Isaiah 42:1; 43:10; 52:13; 53:10) but then transfers the suffering either to the Jewish nation (Isaiah 52:14; 53:3,4,8,10), the temple (Isaiah 53:5), the Gentiles (Isaiah 53:3,7,8), or the wicked generally (Isaiah 53:9).[100] Jesus drew together the Servant of Isaiah 40-55 and the prophet herald of Isaiah 61 into a Spirit anointed, Spirit filled, Spirit directed messianic person. Luke announced Jesus as the Davidic messiah in the birth narratives and identified Jesus with Isaiah's redemption vocabulary (light, comfort, son of David; 1:79; 2:25,30,32,38). Jesus is portrayed by Luke as Isaiah's messianic Servant saviour and prophet-herald: Jesus is the one who comes in the name of the Lord (19:38; Psalm 118:26); and Jesus confirms that he is the coming Davidic king by pointing to the signs of eschatological fulfilment (7:18-23; cf. Isaiah 61:1-2; 35:5-7).

Disciples and the Spirit in the ministry of Jesus (Luke 9-10)

The Spirit was active in Jesus' proclamation (cf. 'the words that I speak to you are Spirit and life', John 6:63b). God's people see Jesus teaching with authority and power (4:36), indeed, Jesus was seen as powerful in word by all the people (24:19). Acts 1:2 speaks of Jesus instructing his followers through the Holy Spirit. The Spirit is active in Jesus' words—not merely passing on revealed words but also revealing Himself as the Messianic Son of God through the powerful work of the Spirit. The disciples did not receive the Spirit during Jesus' ministry in the same manner as they did at Pentecost but they came under the influence of Jesus' powerful spiritual presence and this moulded their lives. Disciples on mission received power to heal (9:1). The account of sending the 70 on mission (10:1-12) is like the Old Testament account of sharing the Spirit with Moses (Numbers 11:16-30) in that their authority was received by Spirit as an extension from Jesus (cf. Acts 10:38), that is, the disciples were in some kind of Spirit fellowship with Jesus.

---

100 cf. Strauss, 1995, 244.

The Father gives the Holy Spirit to all who ask (11:9-13)

Jesus' parable emphatically denies that the Father would give evil gifts (11:9-13; cf. the combination of serpent and scorpion as symbolic of demonic powers, 10:19). The 'finger of God' (11:20) represents the Spirit as the power on Jesus to liberate the afflicted. No son who asks the Father for a gift will receive demonic power! Accordingly, Jesus had not been given Beelzebul's power (11:19-20)! The Spirit emerges in Acts as the key to the Father's promise 'which you heard from me '(Acts 1:5 = Luke 24:49), with the fulfilment of the entire promised salvation in view.

Salvation in Luke is the inbreaking of the kingdom of God, that is: God's self-revealing, reconciling and redeeming presence—in strength—bringing to fulfilment the liberating, radical, cleansing transformation of Israel in accordance with Isaianic hopes for Israel's new Exodus. The kingdom commences with an assurance of God's forgiveness but this is only the beginning of his inbreaking reign.

Just as the Father had given the Spirit to Jesus in his baptism, so Jesus promises: if you then, who are evil, know how to give good gifts to your children, how much more will the heavenly Father give the Holy Spirit to those who ask him (11:13). This promise is reiterated just prior to Pentecost (Acts 1:5; cf. Luke 24:49). The generality of this promise unfolds at Pentecost in a new Israel. New gifts enable all who belong in the new covenant to be prophets who apply the will of God through the Spirit towards the new creation (cf. 22:20; Acts 1:3-8).

The disciples can figure out that Jesus is the anointed Messiah because the 'finger of God' (11:20)—that is, the power of the Spirit (cf. Matthew 12:28 where Spirit of God = finger of God; the hand of the Lord was anthropomorphic for the Spirit)—is casting out demons (11:20). The Baptist looked for a sign in God's impending judgement and therefore doubted Jesus' ministry (7:22). But Jesus referred the Baptist's disciples to evidence that his Nazareth announcement is being implemented (4:18-19) and this probably assuaged the Baptist's doubts. Indeed, Jesus thought of himself as a prophet within the prophetic tradition of proclaiming God's intention for the new Israel in the new era. Jesus' reference to the finger of God portrays the might of the Spirit applying the power of God in the age of the new creation which will be ushered in by the resurrection of Jesus.

Blasphemy against the Holy Spirit (12:8-12)

The disciples will suffer at the hands of Jewish leaders who are condemned by Jesus for their hypocrisy. The disciples are to confess Jesus as the Son of Man before human courts and—following their confession—Jesus confesses the disciples before the angels of God in the supreme heavenly court. To deny Jesus as the earthly Son of Man (representative man) is able to be forgiven, at present (cf. Peter after his denials) but to blaspheme against the Holy Spirit—to impute God's operation in Israel through Jesus to sources other than God—is unforgivable. The disciples' witness before human agencies will be prompted by the gift of the Holy Spirit (12:11-12).

The judgment message is mediated by the Spirit (12:49-51)

The Baptist prophesied that Jesus would baptise with the Holy Spirit and with fire. So when Jesus speaks of his own baptism (12:49-51)—having already spoken to Israel about his approaching death as a baptism (cf. 12:50; Mark 10:38)—the suffering of his death (I have a baptism to be baptised with and how I am constrained until it is completed) is associated with a cup of wrath which has to be drunk. The parallelism in 12:49-50 unites fire with judgement which Jesus will ultimately find repugnant but, nevertheless, will also accept.[101] The already kindled fire that Jesus longs to cast on the earth refers to the judgment message of the cross which national Israel could not avert. The judgment message was mediated by the Spirit and separated the righteous from the wicked, resulting in strife and division (cf. 3:16 in which fire, Spirit and baptism are linked). Jesus' fiery baptism (12:50) is the cross and the cross fans the flames of division within Israel into a conflagration. All humanity has to undergo such a baptism, that is, all are brought before the reality of the cross during their life on earth (cf. John 12:31-32). Jesus did not come to bring peace, indeed, the cross would bring division (even within families). Acceptance or rejection of the cross is the divine opportunity for all humanity.

The promised coming of the Spirit (24:49-53)

The Spirit as the Promise from the Father (24:29; cf. 11:13) proceeds through Christ, indeed, Jesus has become Lord of the Spirit. In Acts, the Spirit is the empowering presence of Father and Son in, with, among and to the disciples in the world. The impact of the gift of the Spirit to the disciples

---

101 There is a parallel to 12:49 in The Gospel of Thomas 10.

will be the ongoing work of the anointed Messiah in the world through his disciples.

The conclusion of Luke's gospel states the effect of Jesus' ministry and death on the Messianic community. Richard Gaffin suggests that the disciples' presence in the temple after their return from Bethany—coupled with Jesus' final blessing—signifies evocative public praise for their newly understood significance of Jesus' death and resurrection.[102] Inflamed by new heart-warming, mind opening experience (24:32,45), the disciples perceive the true significance of Christ's death and resurrection. The content of their praise was the gospel. In the temple, the disciples worshipped publicly and openly continually. Luke reports transforming experiences before Pentecost to indicate that it was not Pentecost but—rather—the ministry of Jesus which transformed the disciples.

---

102 Gaffin, 1979, 27–28.

John

Jesus is anointed by and will baptise with the Spirit (1:19-34)

The Prologue to John's gospel (1:1-18) is joined closely by *kai* (and, 1:19) to the survey of the Baptist's ministry (1:19-34) including the Baptist's testimony to Jesus over two days. Two units in loose parallelism (1:19-23 and 1:24-28) comprise day one. The first parallel unit (1:19-23)—the Baptist's testimony before the Jerusalem advocates (cf. 1:6-8)—has a legal style for his witness is under cross-examination. If the Baptist's witness is to reveal God's coming emissary to Israel then his baptism meets the purpose of the gospel, that is, reconstituting Israel under messianic leadership (20:31). The Baptist begins by rejecting the title 'Christ' when questioned by the Jerusalem delegation (1:19-20), thereby denying that he is the Messiah associated with the end-time spiritual renewal by national cleansing (Ezekiel 36:25-27; cf. 37:25-28). The Baptist's emphatic denial is testimony to Jesus, that is: another is the Messiah; another is the end-time prophet; and the Baptist is not Elijah (1:21).

The focus of investigation by religious leaders (including some Pharisees) in the second parallel unit (1:24-28) is: why is John baptising if he is not an accepted, expected eschatological figure? John replies that his baptism was only preliminary, that is, he was only a voice announcing the new exodus end of the present exile to a generation still in the wilderness (1:23; cf. Isaiah 40:3). The Baptist was subordinate to the one to come (1:26-28; cf. 1:15) who will be permanently anointed by the Spirit (1:32) and will in turn baptise with the Holy Spirit (1:33).

By his location in the wilderness and the appropriation of Isaiah 40:3 to himself, the Baptist claims to be an eschatological forerunner for the coming of God himself. The Baptist's function was to call the nation to return from spiritual exile through covenant repentance. Water baptism—usually self-administered by non-Jewish proselytes—indicated the parlous condition of all Israel, that is, they were outside of the covenant because of their disobedience. The Baptist says that he baptises with water (1:26-27), indicating that his mode of baptism is different from the mode used by the coming greater one (1:27,30). John's baptism is, therefore, provisional; the real baptism for Israel is the baptism of the Holy Spirit still to come (1:33). The one standing among them whom they do not know but must come to know is Jesus and Jesus must be known if Israel is to survive as a nation. The descent of the Spirit on Jesus (1:32) is a reference to the unreported baptism of Jesus and confirmation of his Messiahship.[103] The typology of John baptising beyond the eastern side of the Jordan (1:28) references Israel's needs to re-cross the Jordan as a cleansed people to re-occupy the Promised Land.

Two confessions of the Baptist on day two (1:29–34) offset his negations on day one (1:21), namely: Jesus is the Lamb of God (1:29); and Jesus was pre-existent (1:30). Jesus came to the Baptist as the Lamb of God with no need of confession—the vicarious sin-bearer—introducing an important connection between the Passover and the gospel.[104] The connection between Passover and gospel will associate the ministry of Jesus and the cross with the new exodus liberation. Jesus, the ideal Passover victim, resolves and fulfils all Jewish expectations contained in the festival of Passover by assuming upon himself the sin of Israel. As with the Passover sacrifice, Jesus commences a new exodus deliverance and redemption which leads to the Promised Land.[105] The removal of the world's sin by the servant of God (Isaiah 53:6–7) further interprets 'Lamb of God' because the servant of God (Jesus) is the ultimate Passover for Israel, that is, Jesus takes away not only the sin of Israel but also the sin of the world.[106] Since Israel was representative of her world, Christ's death as representative Israel will satisfy the world's need.

The Baptist's call through baptism for repentance finds its reference point on the next day when he recognizes Jesus as Israel's Servant Messiah (1:29). The Baptist had been sent to baptise (1:31)—to prepare for the coming of the Messiah—with a clue from God for recognising the Messiah during his baptism (1:33). Before the descent of the Spirit on Jesus, the Baptist did not know that the Coming One was his cousin. The Baptist's statement 'he who has now taken rank before me' (1:30) attests to his later statement 'he must increase, but I must decrease' (3:30) which, in turn, leads to an assertion of the pre-existence of Jesus (3:31–32). The Baptist had come baptising in order to manifest the Messiah—whose identity was not known to John prior to Jesus' baptism—to Israel (1:31), that is, to pave the way for the reconstitution of Israel under messianic leadership.

---

103 Hill, 1967, 286–7.
104 cf. 1:29–34; 2:23–25; 6:4–14; 11:55–12:8; 13:1–17:26; 19:13–42.
105 Porter, 1994, 406.
106 Hamid-Khani, 2000, 310.

The Baptist saw (Greek perfect tense)—in accordance with his prophecy—the Spirit descend on Jesus (1:32) which awakened him to the awareness that Jesus is not only the Messiah upon whom the Spirit rests permanently (a messianic expectation, 1:32)[107] but also that Jesus is the bearer of the Spirit.[108] The outworking is that Jesus will also give the Spirit (20:22).

All four gospels report the Spirit descending as a 'dove' on Jesus at his baptism. If the dove—as in rabbinic thought—was a figure for Israel, then the descent of the dove marks Jesus out as Israel's hope (1:32). Jesus will accomplish his ministry through the Spirit's gifts and Jesus will baptise with the Spirit (1:33). There is no mention of 'fire' in John's gospel but Jesus' baptism of the Spirit is featured at the beginning of all four gospels (1:33; Matthew 3:11f; Mark 1:8f; Luke 3:15-18), indeed, Jesus' suffering and atoning death is Jesus' baptism of the Spirit to purge and cleanse from all sin. This baptism comes on all humanity through time by reaction to the cross, which is the judgement bar for all and particularly for Israel (12:32; cf. 3:5). The Baptist knew that Jesus is the Messiah through revelation (1:32-33). The Greek perfect tenses (1:34) indicate that, because of this descent of the Spirit on Jesus, the Baptist continues to bear witness to Jesus' messiahship. The textual alternative 'elect one' (instead of the messianic 'Son', 1:34) may be preferable on the grounds of age and diversity. 'Elect one' points to the Isaianic servant (Isaiah 42:1-4), the one on whom Israel's hopes rested and on whom God had placed his Spirit (Isaiah 42:1). Taken as a whole, John's gospel bears out identification with Isaiah 53. Relativising his water baptism, John states that the baptism of the Spirit identifies the believer with the death of Christ.[109]

The requirement to be born of the Spirit (3:1-12)

John 3 is the first important dialogue in John's gospel. Three exchanges in the dialogue between Jesus and Nicodemus include a question or statement from Nicodemus (3:2,4,9) followed by a response from Jesus (3:3,5-8,10-21).[110] Nicodemus comes as one of a group (cf. 'we', 3:2, representing Pharisaic Judaism) who were not in Jesus' circle but, nevertheless, were

---

107 Isaiah 11:2; 61:1-3.

108 1:33; 3:34b; 20:22; cf. Isaiah 11:2.

109 See my remarks on Matthew 3:11 on the nature and purpose of Spirit baptism and its indispensability for Christian identity.

110 cf. Neyrey, 1981, 115-127.

stirred by Jesus' miracles (there were many unreported 'signs', cf. 20:30). Nicodemus is a Pharisee and a member of the Sanhedrin, that is, he is a member of a group implacably opposed to Jesus. So Nicodemus comes from Jesus' enemies on behalf of institutional Israel (cf. plural 'you', 3:7), at night, as representative of those who lived in darkness and fail to see the significance of the light. Towards the end of the gospel, John still identifies Nicodemus as the one who had come to Jesus by night (19:39) perhaps suggesting that Nicodemus was not yet a believer. Nicodemus' confident Christology (3:2) is not wrong but it is inadequate because he is confined by his own categories. The remainder of John 3 elucidates in what sense and with what result Jesus has come 'from God', that is, the Christology of 3:2 is progressively clarified by Jesus' reply.

Jesus attacks Nicodemus' knowledge of the new covenant as inadequate because it does not come from 'above' (3:3) by revelation—that is, from heaven—as is contemporaneously happening in the person of Jesus for Israel. Human reasoning is totally inadequate for a new creation beginning into new covenant relationship (3:1-4). Jesus' use of *anothen* (being born above or again, 3:3) could refer to rebirth either in another place or at a new time or, alternatively, could be deliberately ambiguous since both senses are relevant. Eternal life locates the believer in God's kingdom which is another place in the unending presence of God. And eternal life begins at a point in time after physical birth, after the Holy Spirit's challenge to human decision effecting a new beginning.[111] But how does one see that the kingdom of God has now come and is visible in the person of Jesus?

Nicodemus' lame question (3:4) reveals his inability to understand, to 'know', because he is from 'below'. Jesus' heavenly rebirth from above replaces physical birth and privilege in national Israel, but this language of 'new birth' is unheralded and requires elaboration. Nicodemus understands *anothen* to mean 'again' in the physical sense—he needs to understand *anothen* as also from 'above'! Jesus follows with the need to be born by water and the Spirit to be able to enter (see, experience) the kingdom (3:5), which is a further attack on Nicodemus' 'we know' (3:2) because they cannot 'know' unless they are born again from above.

'Born of water and Spirit' (3:5) is an outward process with inward results. The two Greek nouns governed by one preposition indicate a unitary process with two steps. While 'water' elsewhere in John's gospel can symbolise

---

111 O'Day, 1995, 549.

the Spirit (7:39) which Jesus will pour out on believers (3:5), in this context of an extended reference to the Baptist and his baptism (3:22-24) 'water' is an allusion to what John's necessary but insufficient baptism had required of Israel. Beyond his baptism by water, John had pointed to the need for spiritual regeneration for Israel—that is, an eschatological cleansing. To be born of water *kai* (and, 3:5) Spirit points to both cleansing and inner transformation. Indeed, to be effective, the Baptist's baptism 'for' or with a view to repentance must also lead to inner transformation.

Since Jesus' call for baptism by 'water and Spirit' with the demand for 'new birth' is addressed to Nicodemus as Israel's representative (cf. the plural 'you', 3:11), Jesus is drawing attention to the requirement for change if Israel is to enter into the new covenant. No less than national cleansing is required to produce new creation renewal of Israel (water and Spirit, Ezekiel 36:25-7; cf. Jeremiah's new covenant, Jeremiah 31:31-34).

James Hamilton and others read 'spirit' (as opposed to Spirit, 3:5-8), suggesting that the single governing preposition points to a composite reality. But Hamilton's conclusion is not necessary.[112] Nicodemus ought to have known that the demand for radical national change (3:10) is not only outward sprinkling with clean water but also inward national transformation (Ezekiel 36:25-27; cf. the baptism of John the Baptist). Jesus is speaking to a representative from Israel's leadership, saying that Israel's response to his ministry must be inward national transformation. Nicodemus should have known this—indeed, Israel's leadership should have provided the impetus for national repentance towards re-establishment of the covenant because,

---

112 John 3 is a program placed before the nation where the Holy Spirit is the divine instrumentality operating beyond human cleansing (3:5; cf. Matthew 3:11; Luke 3:16). I have argued on the basis of Luke 12:49-51 and Mark 10:38 that the Baptist's reference to Jesus' baptism is, in fact, his death on the cross. The baptism referred to in John 3 is water baptism looking forward (with a view to, eis, 3:5) repentance. The Baptist's water baptism was preliminary, that is, a covenant call to the nation to heed the ministry of the one who came after him. So Hamilton's view of a composite baptism in 3:5 is wrong both in regard to John's gospel and the Synoptic gospels. The absence of an article before Spirit does not bear syntactical weight for definite support of one composite reality. Further, Hamilton's preference for 'spirit' presumes individualism whereas Jesus constantly referred to the nation (as did the Baptist in the Synoptic parallels). The absence of a co-ordinating definite article between the nouns points, rather, to a unitary process with two separate steps.

presently, the reality for Israel is covenant exclusion because of national disobedience (cf. John 10).[113]

So to be born again by water and Spirit (3:5)[114] is what God requires from Israel as a whole—addressed to Israel through Nicodemus, the representative Pharisee (cf. the plural second person pronouns; 3:3,7,11). The Baptist had said to the Jews, in effect: you are not yet the true people of God, indeed, only those who respond to the call with true repentance will be God's people nominated as the remnant by Old Testament prophets. And Old Testament prophets persistently attacked Israel's reliance on the written covenant and temple cult. Now, because of Israel's lack of repentance, judgment was about to come on Israel (and the world) collectively.[115] Individuals must respond but the intention was the eschatological renewal of Israel, involving (Ezekiel 36:25-27; Jeremiah 31:31-34): the cleansing of the nation; a new national heart; the gift of God's Spirit; and the resultant obedience of the nation. The new spirit (the gift of the Spirit) is how Jeremiah's new covenant will operate in Israel in the last days. Birth through the water of baptism looked forward to a coming one on whom the Spirit rested, who would baptise with the Spirit (3:33).

Ezekiel 36:16-37:14 begins by reviewing the factors that led to the loss of the land, making it clear that the promised restoration would come through God's intention to vindicate his holy name by bringing about his declared purposes through Israel. A new exodus return to the Promised Land (Ezekiel 36:28) would occur as a result of this renewal, with people and land brought together in this great restoration. God would give Israel—sprinkled with clean water (Ezekiel 36:25)—a new corporate heart and a new Spirit for national transformation and obedience which will restore Israel's covenant relationship through spiritual circumcision of the heart (cf. Deuteronomy 10:16; 30:6). The Sinai covenant formula in Ezekiel 36:28 (cf. Exodus 19:5-6) is used to show that complete transformation is required for Israel to be the people of God, that is, to fulfil her commission of being God's instrument in world redemption. Israel failed to submit to Jesus' ministry, that is, they would not undergo the national new birth required for

---

113 John the Baptist's call beyond the Jordan to Israel to be baptised likens the nation of Israel to Gentiles who are outside Israel's covenant.

114 John distinguishes between regeneration and the faith which results from it (1:12-13; 1 John 5:1).

115 Meyer, 1979, 117.

the later outpouring of the Spirit on the new Israel at Pentecost. The Pentecost outpouring of the Spirit: effected personal transformation as required of the new people of God; and then directed their ministry. Bennema also sees Ezekiel 36 and the implementation of a new covenant governing John 3.[116] The initial water and then Spirit baptism expresses the prior necessity for Israel to enter the kingdom under the new covenant and then God's outpouring is the precursor to Israel's full possession of kingdom blessings through the Spirit (Isaiah 44:1–5).

Thus Ezekiel 36 adds further dimensions to the new covenant program sketched at Jeremiah 31:31–34, making the new covenant a further expression of the Sinai/Mosaic covenant formula: 'You shall be my people and I will be your God' (Ezekiel 36:28).[117] Continuities with Sinai include occupancy of land and obedience expressed through Torah (Ezekiel 36:24, land; 36:27, Torah). By this renewal, the Promised Land will become like the garden in Eden (Ezekiel 36:35) and Israel will exercise Adam's world role in this new Eden. Accordingly, in Ezekiel's survey of the full course of redemption, all Israel becomes kings and priests (cf. Revelation 1:6; 5:10; 20:4–6).

Jesus foreshadowed in the upper room the conclusion of a new covenant by his death (Luke 22:20). But how will baptism by the Spirit—which is integral to new covenant inclusion—occur for Israel as a whole (cf. 1:33)? The Synoptic gospels affirm that Jesus' cross is his metaphorical fiery Spirit baptism effecting judgement on the world, Jesus' cross also effects either Israel's cleansing (and restoration) or rejection once the nation looks, as they must, on Jesus who had been pierced by them (Zechariah 12:10). The constraint on Jesus' ministry is that he must first undergo this world judgement (baptism) himself (Mark 10:38; Luke 12:50).[118]

The new covenant language of Ezekiel 36 goes further than Jeremiah 31 in identifying the Spirit in the process of renewal. Jesus' association of the new covenant with his death—together with Ezekiel's connection between new covenant and Spirit—points to the cross as the means whereby the Spirit will effect inner cleansing. At the cross there is either cleansing through judgement, or judgement. In John, Jesus brings the new community into covenant by the Spirit (as heralds of the new covenant) on the

---

116 Bennema, 2002, 170–173.

117 cf. Jesus' anticipated introduction of the New Covenant at Luke 22:20.

118 Cf. Caird, 1963, 167.

resurrection evening in the upper room. Jesus submitted to John's baptism (cf. 1:32) as representative Israel to effect Israel's ministry to the wider world, that is, Jesus' cross becomes Israel's (and the world's) baptism in the Spirit to cleanse or to sear and reject. Thus, the requirement for a new birth for Israel refers to Ezekiel's prophecy about how the new covenant is to come to Israel.

Ezekiel 37:1–14 looks at the program of restoration from another viewpoint: the results of Ezekiel's prophetic ministry of proclaiming judgement against Israel. The valley (Ezekiel 37:1), Ezekiel's call (Ezekiel 3:22), is full of the remains of Israel which consists of dry bones only. The nation has been 'slain' by the prophetic word. Then the divine power creates a national resurrection, a new birth where God breathes his Spirit into the slain bodies (Ezekiel 37:9,14; cf. Genesis 2:7) as he had done into Adam. Israel and Adam are linked because the restoration of Israel (cf. Ezekiel 36) requires a national resurrection from the death of exile (cf. Genesis 3:24; Isaiah 53), that is, a spiritual rebirth for the nation. This resurrection of Israel required by Jesus in 3:5 will also be made possible by Jesus (as Israel) in his death and resurrection.

The results of this rebirth of the nation by the Spirit are seen in Ezekiel 37:15–28 (cf. Jeremiah 31:31,33), namely, Israel becomes a united people of God with the two former warring factions—Israel and Judah—coming together in a national fusion in the Promised Land under Davidic kingship. God concludes an everlasting covenant of peace (cf. Isaiah 54:10) leading to the new creation with new Israel (Ezekiel 37:26) under Davidic messianic leadership (Ezekiel 37:24). This re-invokes the Abrahamic promises of multiplying and blessing them in the land (Ezekiel 37:26). The promise of the tabernacle of God in their midst effects the blessing of the new covenant by God's eternal presence (Ezekiel 37:27). Thus, in Ezekiel 37 penitent Israel is the reconstituted Adam put back once into an Eden locale (cf. Ezekiel 36:35). The true Israel, including believers of both Testaments, will be beneficiaries of these promises at the final transformation when the New Jerusalem is a new Eden (Revelation 22:1–5). True Israel, gathered together through the Spirit, emerges at Pentecost under messianic leadership directed eschatologically towards the transformed universe of the new creation (Romans 8:18–30).

Therefore, John's report on this significant encounter between Jesus and Pharisaism (John 3) relies on a clear understanding of new covenant prophetic typology originating in the Old Testament. Ezekiel's emphasis is individually corporate, like John 3. If the nation of Israel is to survive, individual Israelites must be reborn into a relationship with God but this individual requirement is not the emphasis in John 3. The reality is that not all in Israel will be members of the new Israel (cf. 3:13–18; Romans 9:6), that is, a new community will arise within Israel from the ministry of Jesus to fulfil Ezekiel 34–37.

Yet the demand of 3:5 is a human impossibility because like begets like (3:6). Israel's new birth cannot happen from within Israel but must (*dei*, a divine imperative, 3:7) come from above, by spiritual impetus. Rebirth is not an option for Israel if she is to survive as a people chosen for a mission. Moreover, the plural 'you' (3:7) indicates that—while this demand primarily addresses Israel and her leadership corporately—response is required from individual Israelites. Accordingly, Jesus chides Nicodemus because the demand to be born again should not be a surprise (3:10).

Jesus parallels by example the mysterious and indiscernible nature of spiritual rebirth (3:8). *Pneuma* is ambiguous, meaning either 'wind' or 'spirit'. Like the uncontrollable wind, the course of the Spirit is indiscernible and inexplicable to humans. The origins of this new life cannot be understood from below, rather—like wind—understanding comes by experience (3:8). The whence and whither of this birth from above is correlated with the whence and whither of the origin and destination of the Son of Man, indeed, questions about origins and destination of the Son of Man become the key questions of public ministry.

If the teacher of Israel and the Israel he represents are to enter the kingdom of God (3:5) as Ezekiel prescribed for revived Israel, then Spirit transformation must be experienced individually but reflected nationally (in corporate structure); hence the required individual, outward cleansing with water (cf. Ezekiel 36:25) and inward transformation by the Spirit. Jesus said to Israel through Nicodemus that Israel must submit to John's baptism for spiritual cleansing, thereby establishing the connection between repentance and the reconstitution of Israel. Jesus is the only one who was pre-eminently born by the Spirit from above as representative Israel and Jesus is the only one who makes reconstitution of new Israel possible through his baptism by the Spirit at the cross. In the ministry of Jesus, the restoration of Israel—to which the prophets looked forward—had begun!

Nicodemus' second question (how can these things be, 3:9) further betrays his ignorance for Jesus had answered this question at 3:8. Like the wind, Spirit is felt but the mysteries of its source and destination are hidden. If Nicodemus cannot feel the force of Jesus' analogy, he is flesh from below[119]—indeed, Nicodemus' lack of comprehension (3:9) draws a rebuke from Jesus' (3:10). Nicodemus, 'the' (that is, pre-eminent) teacher of Israel should know how this Old Testament necessity for a spiritual rebirth happens.

The dialogue between Jesus and Nicodemus becomes a monologue by Jesus at 3:11. Jesus communicates unique knowledge, moving from Jesus' testimony to Israel's Scripture to Jesus himself as the descended Son of Man. The switch to the plural first person personal pronoun (we know, 3:11) balances Nicodemus' 'we know' (3:2), turning Nicodemus' opening confident assertion back on him. Jesus—the supreme teacher—then utters authoritative communication between heaven and earth, that is, he reveals heavenly things (3:12) which humankind requires. Israel's pre-eminent teacher had not understood 'earthly things' from what has already been revealed in the Old Testament, indeed, he had found this challenge bewildering (3:12) because it is impossible to decipher an earthly understanding of divine truth. But 3:12-18 provides Jesus' revelation that the man from heaven has come down to be lifted up (3:14) as the complete revelation of God's love for the sinful world. Indeed, Jesus' ministry will climax in being 'lifting up'. The personal significance of the love of God for all is to be revealed for all by the illumination of the Spirit (cf. 6:63).[120]

An astonishingly incomprehensible advance of further truth is now revealed concerning the mission of the Son of Man. Only baptism by water and the Spirit can bring understanding of this new revelation. According to Jesus, God has given the Spirit without measure (6:34). Jesus' ministry provides all that is required to bring in the new creation because Jesus is the recipient of the complete gift of the Spirit, so new life in saving revelation full of grace and truth comes through Jesus—transcending Moses and the prophets. Turner makes the point that, while previous revelation through the prophets was fragmentary, the immeasurable gift of the Spirit to Jesus not only refers to the reception of the Spirit but also to the Spirit's

---

119 Flesh is not the source of sin but, rather, the source of human weakness (cf. Romans 5:18).

120 cf. Turner, 1998, 69.

impartation of the perfection of revelation whereby he utters the words of God.[121] John 3 concludes with faith in Jesus leading to eternal life and unbelief resulting in exclusion from life (that is, the permanent abiding wrath of God; 4:36).

Worship through personal relationship in Spirit and truth (John 4)

John 4 develops the emphasis (cf. John 3) on the new covenant enabling resolution of past national differences (Ezekiel 37:15-23; cf. Acts 8:14-17). As representative Israel, Jesus must undergo and complete new Israel's unity by his death and resurrection. The action of the Spirit in rebirth results in a new Israel acting in unity through the corporate gift of the Spirit.[122] The cross and inbreathing of the Spirit (20:22) bring into being the restored, new Israel. Thus all Israel's hopes are embodied in Jesus.

The theme of Jesus' superiority to a Samaritan holy site dominates John 4. For Jesus, the true holy site is the Spirit within (4:21-24). In the encounter between Jesus and the Samaritan woman, she raises the critical religious issue in dispute between Jews and Samaritans, namely: where is the right place of worship in Palestine (4:20)? The woman raises the question because she now understands that Jesus is an inspired person, a prophet (4:19).

According to Samaritan tradition, Abraham had been prepared to sacrifice Isaac on Mt Gerizim. Samaritans believed that, during the Mosaic period, the Shekinah dwelt with unseen angels over Mt Gerizim. Through Moses, the Lord required a single site—that is, one altar (Deuteronomy 12)—but the location of this one altar was not named. However, immediately preceding this requirement for one altar at one location, Mt Gerizim was named as the place of blessing for Israel (Deuteronomy 11:26-32) as opposed to the curse associated with Mt Ebal. The Samaritans believed that the authority of the fathers condoning worship on Mt Gerizim trumped other Jewish views about Jerusalem as the place where worship was to be offered.

Jesus appealed to the woman to understand that the changed covenant environment meant that the issue she raised was now merely a side issue (4:21) for the time is coming when God will be worshipped as Father and he will accept all true worship, irrespective of ethnic traditions. Jesus tells

---

121 Turner, 1998, 59.

122 Living water, a feature of John 4, is descriptive of life mediated by the Spirit (cf. Carson, 1991, 219).

the woman that Samaritan worship is limited by their inadequate knowledge of God,[123] that the Jerusalem temple is the proper historical place for worship, and that salvation is from (points to in terms of both origin and departure) the Jews (4:22). The contemporary reader knows that the restoration of Israel will include the old North (cf. Acts 8:14–17) but begins in the south, that is, in Jerusalem.

Significantly—speaking in the area where Abraham offered the first sacrifice in the Promised Land (Mt Gerizim)—Jesus transposed the question of worship to a question of eschatology. Jerusalem and Gerizim both become irrelevant, instead, the attitude towards God is what is important. A critical time ('the hour comes and now is', 4:23) has now arrived. The later hour of Jesus' death will bring in worship in Spirit and truth, but such worship is possible now (contemporaneous with the conversation between the Samaritan woman and Jesus) by faith in the person of Jesus. True worshippers, then and now, worship in Spirit responding to the person of Jesus. True worshippers seek truth in conformity to the revealed knowledge of God conveyed and applied by the Spirit, not by human adjudication (4:24).

'God is Spirit' (4:24) is not a metaphysical statement—a definition of being—but describes how God, invisible and unknowable, relates to humans in creative life-giving power through Jesus' word illuminated by the Holy Spirit. A personal relationship with God through the receipt of the Spirit as 'living water' replaces worship based on a place. Jesus, the truth of God revealed, is the new eschatological point of worship; Jesus is the new temple (2:21). The erection of the new temple will indicate, as the building of the Jerusalem temple had done for the Sinai Covenant (1 Kings 8), that God's new covenant promises have come to fruition in new worship. Personal revelation is reflected in worship animated through the Spirit and reflecting the character of God as Spirit.

This new worship renders the institutionalism of temple and sacrifice invalid and unnecessary. The erection of the glory-filled new temple—that is, Jesus' death and resurrection (2:19–21; cf. Exodus 40:34; 1 Kings 8:11)—will mean that God's presence is permanently with believers and hence no other temple is necessary. Revelation in Christ continues and fulfils God's revelation to the Jews (cf. 5:39–40, 45–47). The Old Testament era of sacred mountain and sacred temple is ending. Among the new community of believers, holiness will no longer be tied to sacred times and places. Both

---

[123] The Samaritan Bible contained only the first five books of the Old Testament.

Samaritan and Jewish claims to holy places must now be given up. Indeed, Jesus' reply to the Samaritan woman is announcing the radical end of the Old Testament era for Jesus is greater than Jacob. Jacob was the father of Israel and patriarch of Israel's covenant, but Israel's covenant is now to be superseded by greater revelation.

The Spirit gives life (6:63)

In the controversy engendered by Jesus feeding the five thousand (6:1-14), and the question of the disciples' reservation about him (6:60-64), Jesus claimed that he is the life-giving bread (6:32-40) and his blood is the true drink (6:55). Jesus' teaching and sacrifice (6:62) is from the Spirit and therefore quickens life and transformation when received (6:63). The material did not give life to the material in creation, indeed, inbreathing the Spirit of God enabled man to become a living being.[124] Flesh comes to life by God's Spirit. Likewise, new covenant new creation relies on the Spirit of God to impart life. In the new covenant (as in the old covenant) the material world—including the flesh of man—is not truly alive apart from Spirit inspiration and, hence, the pervasive and continuing presence of the Holy Spirit.

Many disciples turned away when Jesus said that he was the life-giving bread and his blood was the true drink. Confronted with the true source of their life, people would rather not attribute the life in their flesh to the Son through the Spirit of God. It is less confronting to believe that we give life to ourselves by partaking of the elements including air, food and drink. But we cannot create the elements we need for survival and, regardless, merely imbibing these elements cannot impart life in all its fullness. To be an alive human being, we need the indwelling breath of God. Thus when Jesus asks the apostles whether they will continue in ministry with him, Peter replies as the spokesman: 'To whom can we go? You have the words of eternal life' (6:68).

The Spirit as living water pouring out to heal the world (7:39)

On the last and great day of the Feast of Tabernacles, Jesus issued an invitation to come to him and drink from him rivers of living water. Living water in the Old Testament is a metaphor of the creation of life—and in

---

124 Genesis 2:7; cf. 7:22; Job 32:8; 33:4

Judaism living water is a symbol of the Holy Spirit.[125] This flow of living waters from Jesus is the fulfilment in Jesus of the smitten rock (Exodus 17:6) from which living waters flowed.[126] The Messiah became the thirsty one (19:28) so that he could give his thirst-quenching Spirit to those who thirst (19:30). The blood and water that flowed from his side (19:34) correspondingly relate to his sacrifice for sin and the water of new life in the Spirit flowing to believers.[127] The sacrifice for sin and the water of new life in the Spirit is to come (7:39) from the death of Jesus so the Spirit has not yet been given at the time of this Feast of Tabernacles since Jesus was not yet glorified. Jesus' glorification will come. Pentecost brings into being a new Israel with new spiritual leadership and regenerate membership bearing the hallmarks of having received the Spirit. It was not possible to receive this measure of the Spirit until Jesus is glorified and gives the Spirit by his death. This new covenant blessing of the Spirit comes at Pentecost.

During the Feast of Tabernacles, Jesus offered national Israel a new future (7:37–39). Water pouring ceremonies were conducted during the Feast of the Tabernacles, that is—on each of the first seven days of the eight-day festival, at the altar of holocausts in front of the temple[128]—a priest with a golden pitcher poured water drawn from the spring of Gihon. On the last day of the Feast of Tabernacles, in the temple precinct, Jesus speaks. This last (eighth) day is the day of solemn assembly (Numbers 29:35) when no water was poured.[129] Jesus offers to pour into Israel the spiritual water of life on this eighth day when no water was poured. Jesus' teaching alludes to Jewish eighth day expectations for a day of great rejoicing in Israel's future. For the Jews, the day on which God graciously bestowed the season's first rains foreshadows and anticipates God's promise to pour out the spiritual rains of the Messianic age.[130]

If the phrase 'and let the one who believes in me' is taken as the conclusion of 7:37—as opposed to the opening of 7:38—Jesus will be the New

---

125 Hill, 1967, 291.
126 It is debated whether 6:37–38 refers to water flowing from Jesus or from the believer.
127 Ferguson, 1996, 67.
128 Resseguie, 2001, n. 84.
129 Carson, 1991, 321.
130 Grigsby, 1986, 101–8.

Temple source of living water (cf. Ezekiel 47).[131] Jesus then becomes the referent of 'his' in 6:38. This construction harmonises with the general theology of the gospel and with the Old Testament. But even if the text predicates the believer as the immediate source of living waters, Christ remains the ultimate source.

Jesus' invitation (7:37) identifies himself as the answer to the nation's prayers, recalling the invitation of Yahweh in the work of the Servant (Isaiah 55:1-3). In Isaiah, Yahweh's offer to eat and drink in response to coming to the 'waters' refers to imbibing his word and teaching as the sources of life. Elsewhere, God is described as a fountain of living water (Jeremiah 2:13) and the fountain of life (Psalm 36:9).[132] Finally, the New Jerusalem—the divine residence—becomes the source of this living water.[133] The view that Jesus is speaking of himself in 7:37-39 is, therefore, supported in the Old Testament.

At the Feast of Tabernacles, worshipping Jews chanted messianic expectations (Isaiah 12:3) designating God as the source of Israel's salvation. God is represented as the source of living water at Isaiah 12:3, based on the exodus miracle of water struck from the rock on which God stood (Exodus 17:6).[134] Living water flows as eschatological blessing for Israel (cf. Numbers 20:7-11; Isaiah 43:20-21). Jesus was speaking to Jews who were engrossed by the water ceremony symbolism and longing for eschatological waters—envisioned by Isaiah, Ezekiel, Joel and Zechariah—to trickle from the rock underneath the new temple until they gathered strength as rivers of living water reviving the land (cf. Ezekiel 47:1-12). Jesus cries out that these eschatological torrents of living water will flow from him (the new temple, the pierced rock, 7:37; cf. 4:14; 6:35) bringing healing to the world. This indeed happens when Jesus pours out the Spirit at Pentecost.

There is no exact Old Testament parallel to 7:38b, rather, Jesus is referring to the general tenor of several Old Testament passages—an allusion to an Old Testament pattern in which God himself is the eschatological source of the living water. Beyond the Old Testament contexts, Christ confronts

---

131 Grigsby, 1986, 101.

132 Revelation 21:6 and 22:17 reflect the theme of God as the source of living water (cf. Psalms 42:2-3; 78:16; 105:41; Isaiah 12:3; 43:18-21; 48:21; 55:1; Jeremiah 2:13; Joel 3:18; Zechariah 13:1.

133 Isaiah 55:1-2; Ezekiel 47:1-12; Zechariah 14:8 (read at Tabernacles).

134 Forestell, 1974, 29.

contemporary Jews with his claim to provide the spiritual water of life thereby returning the people of God to the expected paradise recreation of the world. This water to flow from Jesus, as prophesied in Ezekiel 47:1-12, flows from the east door of the temple to fertilise arid areas of the Promised Land until it becomes the new covenant 'Garden of Eden' (Ezekiel 36:35).

Ezekiel anticipated the reconstitution of Israel and Israel's worship on God's holy soil (Ezekiel 20:40; 37:24-28). The climax of the Sinai and Exodus events was the erection of the tabernacle on the mountain of revelation following the blueprint provided from heaven (Exodus 25:9) after the re-making of the covenant (Exodus 34). The re-building of the temple (Ezekiel 40-48) follows the removal of all opposition to the kingdom of God and the introduction of the end-time rule under a new covenant (Ezekiel 36:25-27).

Ezekiel's new temple theology is not a blueprint for post-exilic restoration, rather, if Israel is to have a future then Yahweh will do a new thing for Israel with himself at the centre. He alone will become responsible for the future of the people of God—he alone will build the new temple. This new temple will not merely be God with his people but a statement in the world signifying God's reign over the new universe. The immaculate symmetry of the new temple, the absence of any political tensions in the holy city, and the centrality of worship in the new age reflect the exalted doctrine of the holy presence of God in Ezekiel. So never ending blessings flow from the new temple as the product of perfect divine rule and the holy city becomes the world centre (indeed, the navel of the universe) as Yahweh demonstrates to his people his ultimate control over history. Revelation 22:1 picks up on this theme and connects the source of the river of life with the throne of God and the Lamb as 'edenisation' of the world occurs with the onset of the kingdom of God. The rivers of living water (Ezekiel 47:1-12) are the Spirit that Jesus will give proceeding from him as the new temple. These waters will transform not only a Promised Land but also, indeed, the whole world.

Jesus may also have inferred association with Zechariah 14 because, for the Jews, Zechariah promised judgement on oppressor nations (Zechariah 14:1-7, 12-19) when the Lord is king over the whole earth (Zechariah 14:9). Yahweh will then raise up Jerusalem (Zechariah 14:10), make her secure forever (Zechariah 14:11), and collect the wealth of the nations for her (Zechariah 14:14). This New Jerusalem will be the final centre of worship for all the nations, indeed, the nations will come to Jerusalem to celebrate the Feast of Tabernacles (Zechariah 14:16-21).

Zechariah 14 also fits Jesus' understanding that God would establish his kingdom over the nations through Jesus. In Zechariah, Jerusalem is a cup that makes the nations reel (Zechariah 12:2) and a flaming torch which ignites the nations for judgement (Zechariah 12:1-9). At this time of salvation, the Spirit of grace and supplication is poured out on the house of David (Zechariah 12:10). So the inhabitants of Jerusalem will look 'on me'—the one they had pierced—and they 'would mourn for him, as one mourns for an only child, and weep bitterly over him, as one weeps over a firstborn' (Zechariah 12:10). Thus the water pouring ceremonies need to be understood in the light of the blessings to flow from Jesus, for Jesus is the fountain that 'shall be opened, for the house of David and the inhabitants of Jerusalem, to cleanse them from sin and impurity' (Zechariah 13:1; cf. John 19:34). For believers, Jesus is 'a spring of water gushing up to eternal life' (4:14).

The fulfilment of Jesus' claim will arise from his glorification at his death and will involve the intimate new gift of the Spirit. The Jews—confident in the gracious disposition of their God—were waiting for the joyous advent of the season's first rains that would end the physical drought and herald, spiritually, the age of Messianic prosperity with symbolically full wells of salvation. Jesus cries out that he will graciously provide 'rain' which will bring life in the Spirit to all who drink. This drink will spring from his sacrifice of himself.

This overflowing spring/river of living waters is the presence of the Holy Spirit in the life of each person believing in Jesus (7:39; cf. Jesus' comment to the Samaritan woman, 4:21-24). He who comes to drink by faith from Jesus will himself become an intermediate source through whom the living waters—God's Son—will flow. Jesus promises rivers of life-giving water flowing from him to those who hear his word, fulfilling the promises of blessings flowing from the end-time temple (Ezekiel 47:1-12). Jesus is the new temple of glory, the visible reality of God's presence, and the answer to all the expectations in the Feast of Tabernacles. Jesus replaces institutions, localities, festivals and national expectations. As the living new temple, Jesus—on the Day of Pentecost (Acts 2)—will pour out rivers of living water on believers who become the renewed Israel. And Jesus continues to pour out rivers of living water through believers to the world. So John points to the abundant gift of the Spirit to come after Jesus' departure.

The Father will send the Spirit to the disciples (John 14)

The whole tenor of the upper room discourses is that, with the departure of Jesus, the disciples could be in a new relationship 'in Christ' (cf. 14:23). The relationship is to be established between the Father and the disciples (14:1-3) following the necessary death of Jesus. Whereas Jesus does not provide a time for the establishment of this relationship, his remarks about preparing a dwelling for the disciples to receive them probably don't refer to the Parousia since that would be too allusive (that thought is absent elsewhere either in John's gospel or Jewish messianic expectations). Rather, Jesus seems to be referring to his spiritual cleansing and incorporation of the disciples after his resurrection, presupposing the coming of the Spirit at Pentecost.

John 14 discusses issues raised in 14:1-3. 'Let not your hearts be troubled' (14:1a,27d) frames the chapter, forming the general connection between 14:1-3 and 14:27d-31. The disciples are to trust Jesus for the Father's house—with its many possibilities for 'dwelling'—is the goal of Jesus' journey. 'House' can mean 'household' or 'family' (cf. 4:53; 8:35), but house is more likely in this context.

Jesus had earlier used the phrase 'my Father's house' (14:2; cf. 2:16) to speak of the Jerusalem temple, a familiar Old Testament use; but Jesus is probably referring to the heavenly temple in 14:2. In the first half of the gospel, John establishes Jesus as the new temple to be tabernacling temporarily with his people during an earthly ministry. But by his death and resurrection, Jesus is to be the new temple—the permanent sovereign presence of God ruling over his people. In the second half of John's gospel, Jesus lays the foundation for the positive application of the new temple metaphor to believers in the post-cross situation.

There can be no place without preparation. Jesus will prepare a place by making it ready or putting it in order so that the Father's house will be accessible. His Father's house will be accessible by Jesus' death and resurrection whereby Jesus will become the new temple. The Jewish nation will 'destroy this temple' (Jesus' body, 2:19) but the cross and resurrection are necessary precursors for the spiritual experience of Pentecost in prospect for the disciples. Jesus had already indicated that the Spirit—the new inward connection with Jesus as the new temple—could not yet be given until Jesus was glorified on the cross (7:39). But the promise is that the Spirit would be given not only to contemporary disciples but to all believers (14:12; cf. 1:35-51).

But the disciples are not able to make the journey before Jesus prepares the house. Jesus will return to take the disciples with him to his Father's house, but this will only be possible when Jesus has traversed the necessary journey of being lifted up in the cross and resurrection. So the disciples are taught about the heavenly temple in which they will 'abide' (14:2) and are encouraged to see themselves as places in which God himself will dwell by his Spirit (14:17,20,23). The disciples are currently separated from this heavenly temple but may look forward to dwelling in the new temple—in the risen Jesus—which will level out the distance between heaven and earth.[135] The disciples may look forward to their future dwelling with God but now, Jesus says, they may know an interim period of God's dwelling with them through the Holy Spirit. Disciples can know what it means to be a temple themselves, that is, God makes his dwelling in them through the Spirit so that they could be temples exercising their ministry of witnessing to the immanent sovereignty of God.

The goal of Jesus' journey is to effect the disciples' union with him in the Father's house, that is, to take them into fellowship with himself. They are already in fellowship with Jesus physically but the passage contemplates a new spiritual union that is not possible until Jesus departs. The Father's house, this spiritual residence in God and Jesus, is ready now! Jesus promises that—after his journey of preparation—the disciples will become a family in the Father's house, reunited by a deep spiritual bond of being in Jesus himself and in the Father (14:2-3). Jesus is going to prepare a spiritual abode for the disciples within his own person. Jesus' talk about his journey not only forewarns the disciples of the coming reality of the cross but also provides confidence for them beyond the resurrection with regard to their standing in the risen Christ.

The resolution of the question about 'the way' to the Father's house (14:4-6) is even more important in this passage than 'truth' and 'life' as truth and life are not discussed further. Throughout John's gospel, truth—that is, final revelation—leads to eternal life, thereby providing the way.[136]

---

135 Forestell, 1974, 29.

136 Carson, 1991, 491.

Truth provides an understanding of the way, making clear which path leads to life. Once the way is known and followed, arrival at the goal is certain. Jesus is the revelation (truth) leading to the divine life because he is, by his death, completing the way to the Father. Jesus is the goal of the way, replacing previous ways to life in Old Testament law and wisdom. Jesus left himself as revelation, that is, Jesus provides knowledge of the way. So understanding of the truth is given through the Spirit and this understanding of truth consists of knowing the risen Jesus, indeed, the Holy Spirit communicates the presence of the risen Jesus (14:26). Knowledge of the truth reflected in transformed spiritual life will be evidence that the disciples are 'in the way'. In John 14 the 'way' is not an independent way, rather, 'the way' is the post-cross reception of the Spirit that will be Jesus in them.

Jesus repeatedly stressed that access to the Father must come through Jesus. The goal is acceptance into the Father's presence through Jesus as the way. The Father and the Son will be present and active in providing the way for the believer through the Spirit. John's gospel has already disclosed that knowledge of God proceeds only from the Son (1:18) but Jesus' replies to the disciples' questions in John 14 reveal how they may know that they are in the way and how they can remain in the way.

Jesus' assertion that 'to know him is to know the Father' is Jesus' total ministry—the direction of all Jesus' works including his words—from the Father (14:10-11). Jesus' words and works illustrate God's indwelling for Jesus' works were God's works for Jesus never spoke by appeal to his own authority. Only here in John's gospel do we read that the mutual indwelling of Jesus and the Father is such that the Father's works done through Jesus display the Father's power and character. The disciples have heard Jesus' words and seen Jesus' works so now they may believe Jesus' mutual union with the Father.

Jesus calls for a personal commitment from the disciples (*ho pisteuon eis eme*, he who believes on me; 14:12, cf. 14:10-11). If the disciples believe in Jesus then they will extend the ministry of Jesus (14:12) because Jesus is going to the Father—that is, Jesus' going to the Father will provide the power for greater works to come. These greater works continue Jesus' work in the disciples as Jesus' representatives in the world (cf. 17:20; 20:29). The disciples' spiritual discernment of the significance of the cross, resurrection and ascension come not only from having heard directly from Jesus about the kingdom of God for forty post-resurrection days (Acts 1:3) but also from receiving the Spirit at Pentecost for ministry. Jesus' works in the disciples will produce a great number of converts in the world by the power of the Spirit of Christ testifying to Jesus. Jesus is no longer present with them physically but his absence from the disciples produces the gift of the Spirit (cf. 7:39) and, by the Spirit, greater works evidence a clear presence of Jesus refracted post-cross into the world via the disciples.

Jesus indicates that the disciples will continue to remain in the way and produce 'greater works' because his departure will provide more access to Jesus (14:15-17). Their continuing love for Christ expresses the will of God and brings the Comforter who is not a substitute for Jesus but, rather, Jesus himself in them. Love involves a commitment to Christ and willingness to do Christ's will through seeking the welfare of others (14:15). God's love is other regarding, not self-regarding, so loving God means loving neighbours. True love for Jesus will be accompanied by obedience, that is, doing the will of God which always includes obeying the new commandment to love (13:34).

Jesus thus commissions his disciples to carry on his work on earth under the genre of a prophetic commission. This overwhelming task demands the heavenly support provided by Jesus' eschatological gift to the disciples, that is, the promised Holy Spirit. Jesus' upper room teaching (John 14–17) explains how the Spirit will be the disciples' sponsor in the work of prophetic proclamation, indeed, prophetic proclamation is the climactic purpose of the ministry of the Holy Spirit in John's gospel. By the ministry of the Holy Spirit, the disciples are divine messengers and spokespersons: glorifying God; teaching; and interpreting events. The disciples' witness predicts the future but is rejected in the present. Furthermore, the Holy Spirit's permanent presence within the Christian community is the fulfilment of the hope that all the Lord's people would be prophets (Numbers 11:29). Jesus' abiding message to the disciples was that the long-awaited presence of the prophetic Spirit would equip them with heavenly power to proclaim, as prophets, the good news about their Saviour Christ Jesus.

The giving of the Spirit is conditional upon Jesus going to the Father but when the Spirit is given, Jesus comes himself (14:18). The promises in 14:19-24 about Jesus coming to the disciples refer to the coming of the Spirit of Christ—not to the brief post-resurrection appearances or to the second coming—as there is absolute congruence between the work of the Spirit and the work of Christ. Christ has lived on earth but now the Spirit is the source of eschatological life, indeed, Jesus continues to live and is at work in the church by his Spirit. Coming in exaltation to the church in the power of the Spirit is Christ's crowning achievement.

Without the coming of the Spirit, Jesus' work would have been unfinished for Christ is always present with the disciples by and in the Spirit (14:20). The Paraclete has come in response to Jesus' prayer to the Father to enable Jesus to be always resident with his disciples (14:16). The Holy Spirit, as the gift of the Father, strengthens and supports the disciples by personally strengthening their inner awareness of Jesus being with them. Both the Father and the Son are present and active within and among believers in the Spirit.

The Holy Spirit is 'another Paraclete' (14:16), the first Paraclete being Jesus himself. Therefore, the Holy Spirit continues the work of Jesus through the apostles not as a substitute for the incarnate, risen Jesus but as the risen Jesus himself in them. Through the Spirit, the disciples are in Jesus and thus in the way. The Spirit, who is continually with them, produces the love and obedience upon which the disciples' ministry depends. And the Spirit will be with them forever. So the presence of the Spirit—who is the risen Jesus—accounts for the love and related obedience that keep the disciples in the way. Some argue that a dichotomy exists between regeneration (14:15) and indwelling divine presence (14:16) but there is no dichotomy, indeed, 14:17 looks forward to both regeneration and indwelling presence in the work of the Spirit at Pentecost. The Paraclete is the Spirit whose function is to give new life in regeneration. The Paraclete is the life of Christ in the Christian through the Spirit. The identification of the Paraclete with the Spirit indicates that there is a further expectation of indwelling experience, even more than the disciples already have, expanding their capacity for inner direction.

The Father sends the Paraclete as 'another' (*allos*, of the same sort, 14:16) comforter who comes in Christ's name (14:26), indeed, Christ sends him (15:26). The Paraclete, the indwelling Spirit, keeps the disciples in the way by conveying truth inwardly (14:17)—that is, the Spirit applies the revelation of Jesus within as continuing evidence of the spiritual presence of the physically absent Jesus. The Spirit is a distinct person (14:17) who is Jesus' relational and parallel divine presence, intimating the Trinity. The world has rejected and cannot know Christ but as the believer abides in Christ the Spirit can be known (cf. 15:4). Relationship with the Spirit depends on commitment to Jesus. Hence the world, having no relationship with the Father, can have no dealings with the Spirit. For the disciples, the coming of the Spirit enables personal relationship with Jesus and the Father (14:18-20). The Spirit does not perform his own ministry but, rather, continues the ministry of Jesus through the disciples. The departure of Jesus does not leave the disciples orphaned, rather, the Spirit brings understanding. Jesus' death will soon mean that the world will no longer see him (14:19) but the disciples will see Jesus at post-resurrection appearances or through the possession of the Spirit who reveals the risen Christ after Pentecost.

By the gift of the Spirit, the disciples experience the great change of new life in Christ enabling them to 'see' him. 14:20 includes the eschatologically significant resurrection day (that day), supposing the gift of the Spirit in them (Acts 2; cf. John 7:39). John provides a full disclosure of the 'way' involving mutual indwelling of Jesus with the disciples, indeed, incorporating the disciples into the mutual indwelling of Jesus with the Father. This mutual indwelling is permanent. The home which has been prepared and is now made known to the disciples is the heavenly home found contemporaneously in the inner being or spirit of the believer. This new notion of indwelling goes beyond the indwelling evident in the Old Testament.

Assurance of Jesus' continued indwelling is conditional on keeping Jesus' words and—since Jesus' words are also the Father's words—Jesus' words will draw the love of the Father to the disciples. As the Father and Son come to live in the disciples (14:23), the indwelling Spirit will direct the disciples to the truth (16:23). The Father and Son jointly give the Spirit (14:26; 15:26; 16:7), requiring obedience to which they will be disposed because of the continued presence of the Spirit. 14:24 presents the converse of 14:23 with regard to loving Jesus, for where there is no love for Jesus there can be no believing obedience. General moral obedience cannot profit a person if there is no love in relationship with Jesus. Love in relationship with Jesus comes through believing his word, his present discourse, his total revelation. Since Jesus' word is the Father's word, if there is no obedience based on love for Jesus then there is no relationship with the Father. So exclusive access to the Father is through Jesus.

The Old Testament view that the Spirit is merely a mode of Yahweh's presence is upset by the notion that the Paraclete is a parallel figure to Jesus in sustaining the relationship of the disciples with the Father and the Son.

John viewed the Spirit as a divine person who relates to the Father and the exalted Son like Jesus related to the Father in his ministry.

The vine is about the abiding indwelling of the Spirit (15:1-11)

The imagery of the vine (John 15) builds on Jesus' discussion about relationship with him through the Paraclete after his departure (John 14). The vine image offers a detailed and intimate picture of ongoing, sustained relationship with Jesus analogous to Paul's 'Body of Christ' (1 Corinthians 12:27). The theme changes from the coming of 'another Comforter' (14:16)—that is, the post-cross reception of the Spirit—to abiding, permanent relationship to be established with Jesus by the coming of the Spirit. The vine is thus an image of new covenant indwelling, with *meno* (dwell permanently, used more than forty times in John including 15:4,7,9) mostly carrying the theological concept of abiding. The vine imagery thus depicts the indwelling of the Spirit (cf. 14:16, 26).

The relationship of the disciples to national Israel will change with the cross. National Israel as the vine is a strong covenant image in the Old Testament[137] but national Israel had not borne fruit (cf. Ezekiel 17:6-10). Now Jesus is the true vine, a new covenant image, and branches attached to him through the Spirit will bear fruit. Jesus is the true vine—unlike the Old Testament vine Israel—that is, Jesus is the true Israel and Yahweh will take care of his true vine/vineyard (Isaiah 27:2-6; cf. Isaiah 5:1-7). Under Yahweh's care, attached to him, the true Israel will be a fruitful vineyard.

As branches of the vine, the disciples relate to Jesus personally and, through the Spirit, draw their new life from him. So their ethnic relationship with national Israel will have no bearing on their spiritual future. They (cf. in me, 15:2)—unlike national Israel who, as the Old Testament vine, failed to bear fruit—are fruit-bearing branches formed by present attachment to the vine, and by that attachment they have become members of the true Israel. If a branch is not drawing upon the life of the vine then that branch is dead wood and the vinedresser will cut it out (15:2). If the branch is bearing fruit, the vinedresser will cut off whatever hinders optimum flow of life from the vine thereby enabling optimum fruit bearing. In claiming to be the true vine, Jesus is claiming to be the true Israel and claiming that his flock (cf. John 10) will be the continuation of the charter to Israel and the rejection of sinful national Israel. Those who would be part of this new

---

137 cf. Psalm 80:8,14,15; Isaiah 5:1-7; Jeremiah 2:21.

people (new Israel) must be branches drawing on the life of the true vine, that is, continually sanctified through the operation of the Spirit of Christ.

By his death, Jesus becomes the source of eternal life for all for he has life in himself and apart from him there is no life. Jesus' death unites all believing Israel to him as the true Israel. The continuation of the disciples' relationship with Jesus is taken up in terms of their sanctification through the presence of the Spirit (15:2). If the branch located 'in me' (in Jesus, 15:2), is no longer receiving life from the vine (from Jesus) then the vinedresser will remove it. The disciples' life is to grow out from Jesus (*en emoi*, in me; in Jesus, 15:4), enabled to bear fruit because they are already clean by their relationship with the vine. Abiding in Jesus, they reflect Jesus' teaching and his active creative word which called them into the new relationship with Jesus. Bearing fruit—an Old Testament metaphor for doing good works as proof of repentance or reformation (cf. Isaiah 3:10)—now refers to all that will be produced in the branch through connection with Jesus. By direct attachment to the source of life (the vine), since they are continually receiving his life, the disciples will reflect Jesus' character for they must build their life on his word. The roots of this word must go down deep within them to determine their connection to the vine, for disciples cannot claim self-sufficiency. And they will continue this deep relationship with Jesus by obedience (15:10). Their fruit bearing (15:4), the total product of their relationship with Jesus, will provide the evidence of their connection with Jesus (cf. Isaiah 5:1-7). Their loving conduct shows the appropriation of Jesus' life and bears witness as outreach, drawing others to become branches united in Christ.

The present tenses in 15:5 speak of an organic connection with the risen Jesus. Remaining in him will mean continued infusion of new life into a new nature (cf. John 3) by the Spirit (cf. 7:39). So the vine and branches are a compelling illustration of the reality of life in Christ because infusion is not merely continued connection but continued growth and fruitfulness. Apart from connection with Jesus, fruit bearing cannot occur. The results of not abiding, like pruning (15:2), are disastrous. The definite past tense 'cast out' (15:6) indicates the certainty and finality of divine judgement on unbelievers as they will have been cut off from the source of life (cf. Ezekiel 15:1-8 where the failure of the vine to bear fruit meant that the wood was burnt in fire). The vine itself will not be destroyed, that is, a true Israel will continue even though disaster will come to the nation. The warning that unproductive branches will be lopped off and burnt is directed, primarily, to contemporary Jews but there is also secondary application to the future. Without fruitfulness, there is wrath to come.

Jesus will give decisive answers to the disciples' prayers (15:7) arising out of their union with him. These answers are the fruit of the disciples' union with the vine. The test of abiding in Jesus is a life controlled by Jesus' teaching. The task and index of discipleship is fruit bearing by infusion of divine life emanating in witness in mission. This witness and mission continue the work of Jesus thereby glorifying the Father (15:8) because the Son reflects the Father's glory. Fruit bearing, reflecting the character and work of Jesus, identifies Jesus' disciples (cf. Matthew 7:21; Galatians 5:22). From the perspective of Jesus' departure, Jesus' love for the disciples is shown by his continuing indwelling relationship through the Spirit—just as the Father's love for Jesus was his indwelling (abiding) in Jesus.

This relationship of indwelling love is not automatic, rather, the relationship comes into being once a commitment which governs the believer's future has been made (*meinate*, aorist, 15:9). The call to obedience (15:10) stems from the example of the relationship between Jesus and the Father. For the disciples, maintaining a relationship of indwelling love with Jesus will mean obedience because obedience is the product of love reciprocating into further love producing more obedience. Love is not merely an attitude but must show itself in action. This union of love maintained by obedience is the secret of inner, continuing joy (15:11). This joy is not a human emotion but, rather, a divine gift. Jesus' joy is based on what is ahead (cf. Hebrews 12:2). The disciples are now called to share the joy that Jesus will have beyond enduring the cross. Jesus is rejoicing in prospect—they will rejoice in consequence.

The Spirit enables Jesus' ministry to a hostile world (15:18 –16:3)

The disciples operate in the context of world hatred, indeed, the world's hatred of the disciples is not a passing phenomenon. The world rejects Jesus because Jesus reveals their sin—they disobey Jesus as God's Son and agent (14:22). Jesus' presence in the world makes the world culpable because they refused to recognise Jesus' demonstration of the authority of the Creator of the world, God's world, and Israel's Redeemer. There is no excuse for Israel since they had received a full revelation of the Father in Jesus. There is no way forward for Israel other than to turn to Jesus. But both the world and Judaism refuse to have Jesus reign over them (cf. Luke 19:14).

National Israel's institutionalism, Torah and temple are now of no avail since the coming of Jesus has confronted the nation with a decision to either join with Jesus in a new covenant or cease to be the people of God. Incredibly, Israel kills the one sent from God to be their Messiah—as foretold by Scripture! The world's baseless hatred of Jesus was a hatred of the Father, the product of human foolishness.

Jesus argues that his ministry will continue after his departure, for the Paraclete—personalised by the Greek word *ekeinos* (that one, he, 15:26)— will come, sent by the exalted Jesus but emanating from the Father (the Paraclete is the Holy Spirit or Spirit of truth, 15:26).[138] The significance of the Spirit's coming is announced in programmatic terms (15:26-27) with legal language. The Spirit of truth (16:13) will guide them into all truth after Jesus' resurrection. The Spirit will not speak on his own authority but will glorify Christ by taking what is Christ's and declaring it. The Spirit's coming depends on the completion of Jesus' work and his departure from the earth (16:7). And the function of the Spirit is to guide, to speak, to announce and to teach; to be Jesus in them, communicating only what he has heard, reinforcing Jesus' revelation by reminding them of what Jesus said and did (cf. 'all truth', 16:13), being with them in continuing ministry. The Spirit is not adding to Jesus' revelation, that is, there is no independent content from the Spirit nor is there any defence of the disciples by the Spirit. Peace (16:33) is the effect of an indwelling power bequeathed to the disciples by Jesus, equivalent to the Old Testament *shalom*. Hence, peace is the total blessing of the new covenant (cf. Ezekiel 37:26).

A masculine form is used of the Spirit (*ekeinos*, 14:26; 15:26; 16:8, 13- 14) but the masculine personal reference may simply be derived from the masculine *Parakletos*. There are, however, many other New Testament references to the Spirit as personal.[139] 15:26 is clearly Trinitarian, that is, Jesus will send (future, with Pentecost in view) the Spirit proceeding from the

---

138 Some manuscripts read only 'Spirit'. Either way, the Spirit was to be all that Jesus was to them—that is, the truth (1:14,17).

139 Cole, 2007, 66-72. Paul presents the deity of the Spirit in Romans (8:14,16,18- 25,26-27; cf. the mind of the Spirit 8:27) in terms of his regenerating and indwelling sanctifying presence. The Spirit searches the depths of God (1 Corinthians 2:10) and he alone knows the thoughts of God (1 Corinthians 2:11). Cole points out that only God can know God (cf. Philippians 3:3).The Spirit apportions, as he wills, the

Father. This reference to the procession of the Spirit from the Father—without mentioning (in this reference) procession from 'the Son'—becomes a divisive point in Christology between Eastern and Western Christianity (though a textual variant, favoured by the West, added 'and the Son'). But 15:26 is not about mutual relationships within the Trinity, rather, the verse references the Spirit coming from God in apostolic mission revealing Christ. The Spirit's (cf. *ekeinos*, masculine, that one) purpose in coming is to bear witness to Christ, made clear by the concluding phrase 'he will testify of me' (16:26).

The ministry of Jesus had provoked opposition and, likewise, the disciples' witness to Jesus through the Spirit will continue to provoke opposition. Hence the coming of the Spirit has forensic overtones for the Spirit will enable Jesus' ministry of witness to a hostile world to continue to proceed through the disciples as they are in full possession of the substance of Jesus' total ministry (15:26-27). The witness of the disciples' community to Jesus will be a sign of the presence of the Paraclete.

The Paraclete will declare to the world the truth of the mission of Christ. This will be an entirely offensive operation, taking the battle to the world, putting the world on trial (cf. 16:8-13). The testimony of the disciples to the truth will be instrumental as eyewitnesses since they had been with Jesus 'from the beginning' (16:27). Jesus had provided them with a pattern and content which the Spirit would reinforce.

The Paraclete sections in John always bring the disciples' ministry into contact with an antagonistic world, not only continuing the gospel notion of the world on trial but also providing information on the purpose and function of the Paraclete. There will be persecution (16:1-3). Jesus has spoken to warn them about the perils of their future ministry so that they don't fall away. But the disciples all fall away (cf. 20:19)! The disciples will be persecuted by their compatriot Jews as an exercise in 'divine worship' (cf. *latreia* at Romans 9:4, Hebrews 9:1,6). Sadly, their compatriots will engage in persecution with sincere motives—because of basic ignorance of Father and Son—because the world and the Jews are challenged by Jesus' witness.

---

gifts of God. The Spirit is also presented in Trinitarian statements (Matthew 28:19; 2 Corinthians 13:14).

The coming of the Spirit (16:4–15)

Beyond the cross and their restitution, the disciples own hour (*hora*, 16:4)—like Jesus' hour—will come. The world will then have its way with the disciples, persecuting them like Jesus with similar consequences. But beyond death, like Jesus, there will be a triumphant outcome. 'These things' are the sombre facts of persecution after Jesus' departure. The disciples must now understand the shape of the future beyond the cross for the persecutors' 'hour' will come with its supposed victory; but that temporary victory is followed by judgement. So the remembrance of Jesus' prediction during persecution will strengthen the disciples. 'These things' must, therefore, be said before Jesus is gone.

The disciples are too self-absorbed in sorrow (15:6) to press for more detail (cf. 13:36; 14:5) about the important question of Jesus' destination (16:5). The antidote to their sorrow will be the coming of the Paraclete. Jesus makes it clear that his departure is vital ('I tell you the truth', 16:7) for their future ministry since the Paraclete, who will come when Jesus departs, is to represent and mediate through the disciples the person and work of the crucified and risen Jesus. When the Spirit comes, he will continue Jesus' 'trial of the world' through the witness of the disciples (16:8). After the death of Jesus, the Spirit will bring the trial to resolution and secure a conviction involving the history of the Jewish people on the score of sin, righteousness and judgement. The three terms *hamartia*, *dikaiosune* and *krisis* (16:8) appear without the article so they must be interpreted qualitatively. The Paraclete will convict consciences by providing the grounds on which the Judge will pronounce a verdict (*elegcho* means to bring to light, expose or convict; 16:8) on the world—that is, a verdict not only on Judaism but also on the human world as a whole through apostolic witness. *Parakletos* and *elegcho* are forensic terms indicating that the setting is a judicial process before the tribunal of God. The divine verdict will be the post-cross exaltation of Jesus (Philippians 2:9–11).

Apostolic preaching will deliver the divine charges. The Paraclete convicts the world through the mission of the disciples, laying the basis for the guilty verdict at the divine assize on the ground of sin. The world's sin is unbelief that the resurrection is the outcome of Jesus' death. Israel's sin is that it had killed the Son of God, its Messiah, as an insurrectionary!

The Spirit also acts as prosecutor, putting the world on trial for its sin (16:8–11). The Spirit battles to help the world to see its folly in its opposition to God and Christ, for the chief sin that the world is guilty of is unbelief in Jesus' person and ministry. The Spirit will convict the world on the score of righteousness, exposing Judaism's final apostasy in their rejection of Jesus. The covenantal rights of the case—the question of who is in the right, that is, the position of righteousness—will lie with Jesus whom God vindicates by resurrection (cf. 'because I go to my Father', 16:10). Condemnation awaits the human world because Jesus' resurrection has decided in Jesus' favour the lawsuit that Jesus had brought against the world. Finally, the Prince of the World is cast out by the victory of Jesus over death and this will prove that the world is guilty and, indeed, divinely judged (16:11). Satan's defeat at the cross will release the world and Judaism from any necessary subjection to Satan (12:31). The cross is the judgement bar that summonses before it all mankind (12:32).

The verdict of the trial will be that Christ is in the right so Jesus will be exalted—going to the Father (16:10) in triumphant, final ascent. Only the absolutely holy could do what Jesus had done. But now the Spirit operates through Christian proclamation to impact hearers with the power, person, work and teaching of Jesus. The activity of the Spirit of Christ through the disciples in the world to generations will bring in the Garden of God (Genesis 2:8-9) as a reality in the new Eden (Revelation 22:1-5).

Jesus sensed in the upper room that the disciples were not ready to hear all that he wanted to reveal to them (16:12-13). Misunderstandings and misgivings filled the disciples' minds (14:5,8) but the unique relationship between Father, Son and Spirit would guarantee that the apostles and early Christians would understand Jesus' full revelation. After Pentecost, the Spirit will guide the disciples ('you', 16:13-15) into all truth, thereby bringing them further in 'the way' to keep them in Jesus himself and bring them new revelation in continuity with and as a fuller understanding of Jesus' gospel revelation. The Spirit will speak only what he hears (16:13; cf. 14:26). The reference to 'when he has come' (16:13) points not only to Pentecost but also to future application of the total significance of the Christ event by the Spirit leading to apostolic exposition—originating from the Spirit—resulting in the production of the New Testament Canon. The upper room discourse points to this final deposit of New Testament revelation, that is, John is not referring to the task of the early church generally but specifically to the task of those who had been with Jesus from the beginning. Subsequent generations will benefit from re-inspiration of Jesus' inspired teaching and understanding provided by the eye witnesses (2 Timothy 3: 16).

The 'things to come' (16:13) through the Holy Spirit will include an understanding of Jesus' death leading to the new creation (1:1–5). The disciples did not regard Jesus' death as a defeat but, rather, as that which was necessary to complete Jesus' work.[140] The work of the Spirit in showing things to come also points to the announcement of the eschatology of the new order. The Spirit will 're-announce' (*anaggello*, 16:13), that is, confirm what has already been said about the final eschatological event with regard to the unveiling of sin, righteousness and judgement. The Spirit will also announce what is to come, that is, the Spirit will give them spiritual understanding about glorification and the period beyond Pentecost. But the Spirit is the Father's agent so he will not present himself, rather, he will speak 'what he hears' as he draws his authority from the Father in Trinitarian relationship like Jesus.

The Spirit glorifies Christ by communicating what he received from Jesus (cf. *ek tou emou*, 16:14). So the Spirit will lead the disciples to understand the upper room address, to manifest Christ by the application of prior revelation thereby magnifying Christ's work. So the Spirit will not deliver a new word, rather, he will deliver words already given but now filled with divine power. The coming of the Paraclete registers the coming of Jesus. Now Jesus has perfectly reflected the Father's will so the Father will take the truth revealed in Jesus' work and words and show it to the disciples through the Spirit thereby guaranteeing the continuance of Jesus' mission.

Jesus tells the disciples that in the new post-resurrection era there will be no need—in the light of their reception of the Holy Spirit—to raise the questions that they have been asking (16:23).[141] They will have direct access to the Father on the basis of their new relationship with Jesus and they will receive what they ask of the Father in Jesus' name (16:23b). The ongoing role of the Spirit is to communicate the ongoing presence of the Father and Son. To date the disciples had asked nothing of the Father in Jesus' name but when Jesus leaves the world they may then ask the Father directly. And there is fullness of joy in this new direct relationship with the Father (16:24). The new direction in prayer after the resurrection in the new era addresses the Father in the name of the exalted Son, Jesus.

---

140 O'Day, 1995, 772.

141 Barrett, 1978, 494 (on *erotao*, question). cf. 13:24,37; 14:8,22; 16:17–18

The identification of the Paraclete

The Paraclete is the Holy Spirit, a parallel figure to Jesus in the triune God (14:26; cf. 15:26; 16:8-11; 16:13). It is difficult to suggest a precise translation for Paraclete—but counsellor, advocate and helper all contribute to an understanding of Paraclete. So it is better to leave Paraclete untranslated and, instead, recognise the function of the Paraclete with regard to apostolic ministry after the resurrection.

There are four occurrences of *parakletos* (14:16,26; 15:26; 16:7) in conjunction with four occurrences of *pneuma* (Spirit, 14:17; 14:26; 15:26; 16:13) in the New Testament. The only other occurrence of *parakletos* in the New Testament is 1 John 2:1. The *parakletos* comes to someone's aid or defence. Sinclair Ferguson sees the *parakletos* as one who testifies to Christ, with the forensic connotation of the Spirit in the disciples as advocate witness against the world (16:8-11). Ferguson indicates that in contemporary trials the advocate could vindicate the defendant by telling the truth about him—the advocate's relationship with the accused enabled him to speak with authority—in a lawsuit. Having been with Jesus since the beginning of his ministry (and by birth, Matthew 1:20), the Holy Spirit had been the constant intimate companion (eye-witness) of Jesus.[142] But the Paraclete will be 'another Paraclete' (14:16) because the first Paraclete was Jesus, so the Holy Spirit continues the work of Jesus.

Raymond Brown notes that virtually everything that has been said about the Paraclete has been said elsewhere in the gospel about Jesus,[143] namely: Jesus is the Truth and the Paraclete is the Spirit of Truth; Jesus is the Holy One of God and the Spirit is the Holy Spirit; Jesus is the Teacher and so is the Paraclete; Jesus bears witness and the Paraclete is a witness; the world does not recognise Jesus and neither does the world recognise the Paraclete; and Jesus goes to prepare a dwelling place for the disciples (14:2) but the Paraclete comes from the Father to prepare a dwelling-place (*mone*, 14:23) for the disciples with the Father and the Son. As Paraclete (1 John 2:1), Christ makes a home for his people in the presence of the Father; as Paraclete, the Spirit makes a home for the Father and the Son in the believer who becomes individually and ecclesiastically 'a dwelling in which God lives by his Spirit' (Ephesians 2:22). The Spirit is the divine home-maker

---

142 Ferguson, 1996, 36-37.
143 Brown, 1971, 1140.

unrecognised by the world (14:17b). And the Spirit effects new life, growth, nourishment and change.

References to the Paraclete build accumulatively in terms of the Paraclete's task and the disciple's relationship to the Father and Jesus in their post-cross ministry (14:15–15:17). The world is profoundly hostile towards the Paraclete (16:8–11). The first reference says that the Paraclete comes from Jesus (14:16). The second reference says that the Paraclete is the Spirit of truth (15:26), just as Jesus' ministry is characterised as the truth (14:6) and hence as the way to new life. So the Spirit dependent upon Jesus will communicate truth. The Spirit gives faith, animating the disciples' dependence on Jesus. The Paraclete has a didactic function, coming from the Father in Jesus' name—that is, to bear Jesus' name, all that Jesus was—and thus the Spirit comes as a replacement for Jesus (14:26). John viewed the Spirit as a divine figure who relates to the Father just as the exalted Son related in his ministry to the Father.

The Spirit has no program of his own, rather, he functions to glorify Christ and teaches the disciples by reminding them (the explicative *kai*, and, 14:26) about Christ's revelation. The disciples understand Jesus when the indwelling Spirit interprets the revelation that Jesus had already given. The third Paraclete text (15:18–16:3) deals with the persecution of the disciples by the world because the witness of the Paraclete in the disciples is directed against the world (15:26).

The Paraclete and the disciples

Jesus sends the Spirit after asking the Father (14:16,26), and the Father sends the Spirit with the Son as mediator. There is a double sending of the Spirit in the economic Trinity. Nicea (AD 325) and Constantinople (AD 381) affirmed procession of the Spirit from the Father only but the Western church later added 'from the Father and the Son' (the Filioque clause). The Filioque clause had not been agreed on by an ecumenical council but the Western Church understood it as scriptural, particularly after the split between East and West in 1054. The biblical, Western view understands the Spirit to be eternally breathed from the Father through the eternally begotten Son; indeed, John makes reference to both the Father and the Son sending the Spirit. Without the Filioque Clause, we know of the Father's economic and ontological relationship to the Son and Spirit, but we know only of an economic relationship between the Son and the Spirit.

Throughout the New Testament, the economic (functional) relationship within the Trinity illumines the ontological (personhood) relationship. The Spirit proceeds on his mission from both Father and Son, so he proceeds personally within the Godhead (that is, ontologically) from both Father and Son.[144] The gospel states that: the Father sends the Paraclete in Jesus' name (14:26); Jesus sends the Spirit from the Father (15:26); and Jesus sends the Spirit (16:7). There is complete unity between the Father and Son in the coming of the Spirit.

The relationship of believers to the Paraclete (14:16–18)

The Paraclete is to be with and in the disciples (14:17) as the personal presence of Jesus while Jesus is with the Father. When the Spirit comes he illumines the disciples, teaching them inwardly the nature of their relationship to Christ and Christ's relationship to the Father (14:20). In view of this continuity, the Paraclete will come as Jesus had come into the world (5:43; 16:28; 18:37), that is, from the Father. Indeed, the Father gives the Paraclete at Jesus' request as the Father had given the Son (3:16) and the Father sends the Paraclete as the Father sent the Son (3:17). The Paraclete is sent in Jesus' name (14:26) so the Paraclete's relation to Jesus is like Jesus' relation to the Father.

The disciples have the privilege of knowing and recognising the Paraclete just as it had been a special privilege for them to know and recognise Jesus. The Paraclete is to be with them and remain with them and, therefore, Jesus will remain with them and be in them (14:20,23; 15:4,5; 17:23,26). The Paraclete declares to the disciples the things to come, such as the truth about Jesus as the Messiah (4:25–26). The Paraclete glorifies Jesus just as Jesus glorifies the Father. The world cannot accept the Paraclete just as the world could not accept Jesus (5:43; 12:48). Since the Paraclete can only come when Jesus goes, the Paraclete is the presence of Jesus when Jesus is absent—indeed, the first passage containing Jesus' promise of the Paraclete (14:16–17) is followed by Jesus saying 'I am coming back to you'.

So when the Spirit comes, the disciples will understand Jesus' saying 'I am in my Father and you are in me and I am in you' (14:20) and they will also understand the mutual indwelling of one another by the persons of the Trinity being expressed in mutual harmony and love. The Spirit effects the realisation that the Son dwells face to face with, in the bosom of, the Father

---

144 cf. Cole, 2007, 29, 76–78, 199–202.

(1:1,18). In this way, the Spirit displays the glory of the Son. The Spirit also teaches the disciples that they are in Christ and that Christ dwells in them. Indeed, the disciples will not lose Christ by his going—rather, they will gain more in their existential union with Christ. Accordingly, union with Christ is a central theme of the rest of the New Testament.

The Paraclete is not Jesus, nor is he an intercessor, nor is he in heaven. The disciples will recognise the Spirit (14:17) for he will: be within the disciples; remain with them; teach them everything (14:26); guide them as the Spirit of Jesus (cf. Romans 8:9); take what belongs to Jesus to declare it to them (16:14); glorify Jesus by bearing witness on Jesus' behalf (16:14); and remind the disciples of all that Jesus told them (14:26). The Spirit attests Scripture but brings no positive revelation of his own. The Spirit's work is Christocentric, that is, he will not attest any departure from Jesus' existing revelation. The world cannot accept the Spirit (14:17) for it neither knows nor recognises him, indeed, the Spirit bears witness to Jesus against the background of the world's hatred demonstrated in the persecution of the disciples.

The Paraclete and the world (16:1-16)

With the fourth mention of the Paraclete (16:7), the Paraclete theme reaches its climax (16:8-11). John 16 begins with the prospect of world hostility against Jesus' representatives (16:1-4). D. E. Holwerda recognised that 16:8-11 provides the key to the post-cross role of the Paraclete,[145] namely, to put the world on trial through the ministry of the disciples as Jesus had done in his public ministry to Israel. The natural meaning of *elegchein* (convict, 16:8) is to convict by testifying successfully against. The Spirit will take what belongs to Jesus to declare it to the disciples and glorify Jesus (16:14) by revealing Jesus in a hostile world which neither knows nor recognises the Spirit (14:17). The peace which is to come from this gift of the Spirit is not a peace that the world can give (14:26,27). In the context of the hostile and difficult world, the Paraclete will bear witness on Jesus' behalf. The disciples, too, must bear witness (15:26-27).

When Jesus commissioned his disciples to continue his work on earth—the genre is a prophetic commission—he was looking forward both to the

---

145 Turner (1977, 231-42) agrees with Holwerda that the term parakletos is essentially forensic. The Spirit mediates the presence of the Father, prosecuting Jesus' case through apostles and disciples post-cross against the *kosmos*.

resurrection and to Pentecost. The teaching ministry of the Spirit to the disciples effects recall of Jesus' ministry (14:26; 16:13). The disciples feared that Jesus' departure would mean that they would know less of Christ and that their intimacy with Christ would end. But Jesus taught them that through the Spirit they would know Jesus better, and understand more about Jesus and their relationship with him.

The overwhelming task in the disciples' prophetic commission will require heavenly support and sponsorship, provided by Jesus in his eschatological gift of the promised Holy Spirit. Jesus' upper room teaching explains exactly how the Spirit will be their sponsor in the work of prophetic proclamation. This is the climactic purpose of the ministry of the Holy Spirit in John's gospel. The Holy Spirit functions as: a divine messenger and spokesperson, one who glorifies Jesus, a teacher, an interpreter of events, a witness who predicts the future, and one whose message the world rejects. Furthermore, the Holy Spirit's permanent presence within the Christian community is the fulfilment of the hope that all of the Lord's people would be prophets (Numbers 11:29). Jesus' message to the disciples was that the Spirit would equip them from above. This long-awaited abiding presence of the prophetic Spirit will enable the disciples to proclaim as prophets the good news of their Saviour. Jesus thus prepares the disciples for his departure and their future post-cross ministry under the influence of the Spirit-Paraclete (16:12–31).

Spirit of intercession

The Paraclete is also the Spirit of Intercession. Prayer expresses worship, adoration and personal need. No one can call Jesus 'Lord' or God 'Father' except by the Spirit (1 Corinthians 12:3; Galatians 4:6). Like Jesus, in the Spirit, the disciples will be able to rejoice in the works of God (Luke 10:21). Praying in the Spirit is prayer that conforms to the will and purpose of the Spirit. Prayer also expresses weakness and need as we recognise our powerlessness. We make requests to God because we cannot meet them ourselves. Paul recognises his profound weaknesses (2 Corinthians 12). When the believer is subject to weaknesses that make coherent petition impossible, prayer becomes but a groan (Romans 8:26). But this groan is an indication of the presence and ministry of the Spirit! This is probably not referring to speaking in tongues or ecstatic utterance in the congregation, rather, the groan is the complete frustration and weakness of the believer—too weak to be coherent but the Spirit intercedes! The communion of the Spirit points to blessings which provide grace for all in need. In the believers' weaknesses, God reveals his power through the Spirit (2 Corinthians 12:9 cf. 1 Corinthians 1:25b,27b). So the Spirit is another Paraclete like Christ.

Some of the functions of the Holy Spirit are not those of the Paraclete, so the Paraclete is definitively the post-resurrection gift of the Holy Spirit. The Father gives the Paraclete at Jesus' request to those who ask him (Luke 11:13), indeed, God has poured out the Spirit through Jesus Christ (Titus 3:6). Some of the functions of the Holy Spirit such as regeneration and forgiveness of sins are not assigned to the Paraclete. So John's distinctive title for the Holy Spirit—Paraclete—indicates a specialised focus of the work of the Holy Spirit (cf. the noun *paraklesis* used to describe the ministry of the Spirit in Acts 9:31).

But the world will not believe, even with the Paraclete at the disciples' side (14:17). It is not the function of the Paraclete to defend the apostles in the world, rather, through the disciples the Paraclete will bear witness to Jesus (15:26) as in a courtroom. The world's hatred of Jesus—personalised in the gospel by the Jews' hatred of Jesus—will continue to be expressed through persecution of the disciples. At the disciples' trial, the Spirit will give them courage to bear testimony, that is, the Spirit is not a spokesman for the disciples but a spokesman through them.[146] Accordingly, the phrase *te paraklesei tou hagiou pneumatos* (the comfort of the Holy Spirit, Acts 9:31) is used for growth resulting from Christian ministry.

The Paraclete is a Christocentric, conserving, preserving force in revelation who takes what is the Son's and declares it to the apostles in accordance with Jesus' saying: 'All that the Father has is mine; therefore I said that he will take what is mine and declare it to you'. Perfect cooperation between God, Christ and Spirit will guarantee that the apostles and early Christians receive revelation from God through Christ and the Holy Spirit—they will not miss out by Jesus' going, rather, they will receive much by Jesus' glorification.

The forensic role of the Paraclete on behalf of the disciples ensures that they are not left as orphans. The Paraclete strengthens the disciples' witness in the world, that is, the Spirit acts through the disciples as the chief witness after the death of Jesus in the continued cosmic trial. Jesus' departure will be to the disciples' advantage for the Paraclete will convict the world

---

146 Brown, 1966, 117.

of sin, righteousness and imminent judgment and thus bring assurance to the disciples that their Lord has won the decisive victory over sin, the flesh and the devil.

Jesus 'gave up the Spirit' (19:30)

Concluding the horrific ordeal of the cross, Jesus' last words from the cross were 'It is finished'. He then 'gave up the Spirit'. Normally this is taken to be the onset of death as Jesus surrenders the vital power of existence. Some, however, perceive that Jesus is bequeathing the Holy Spirit in this moment of glorification in death.[147]

Jesus bequeaths the abiding Spirit of prophecy (20:19-23)

The commissioning narrative of the wounded, risen Jesus in the upper room on the first evening of the resurrection (20:19-23) deserves special attention. The form is reminiscent of Old Testament prophetic commissioning narratives, with: introduction (20:19); confrontation by the deity (20:19-20); reaction of fear or unworthiness (20:19-20a); and the act of commissioning with divine reassurance by the gift of the Spirit (20:21-23). Individual expression of inability is the only missing prophetic-call item, though the context provides this. The commission is not confined to the apostles. The Christian community—given the power to bind and loose—will continue Jesus' judgment. The enormous consequences of Christian witness are spelt out. The context of prophetic commission and the tandem relationship between Jesus and the Paraclete emphasise the continuity of function, mediating to believers the ministry of the risen Jesus from heaven through the Spirit. For Jesus is the prophet par excellence who provides the model for the prophetic spirit.

The figure of Moses may also lie behind John's description of Jesus' bequeathing his Spirit to his disciples. In the Moses narrative, the Lord bestowed on the seventy elders the Spirit of prophecy that was on Moses (Numbers 11:24f). In addition, at the end of his farewell discourse, Moses' handed on some of his authority to his successor Joshua who was full of the Spirit (Deuteronomy 34:9; cf. Numbers 27:18-23). But throughout John's

---

[147] Hill (1967, 286) suggests that the gift of the Spirit became possible at this moment of Jesus' glorification. Cole (2007,166) takes his lead from Hebrews 9:14 (how much more will the blood of Christ, who through the eternal Spirit offered himself without blemish to God, purify our conscience from dead works to serve the living God?) to rightly conclude that the cross was a Trinitarian event.

gospel there is a contrast between Moses and Jesus: Jesus is the fulfilment of Torah because he has seen the Father and explains him (1:17-18); and manna was given through Moses but Jesus is the true manna from heaven (6:32-35). So Jesus supersedes Moses. Terms such as light, life, bread and water—previously applied to the Torah—are now applied to Jesus. In accordance with this contrast between Jesus and Moses, Jesus does not impart the temporary Spirit of prophecy that Moses had bequeathed, rather, Jesus bequeaths the permanent abiding Spirit to enable God's people to prophetically proclaim the good news of the new age. So the bequeathing of the Spirit (20:22) gives finality to the promise of 7:37-39.

The repetition of the peace greeting (20:19,21) underscores the importance of the commissioning. The resurrected Jesus comes as the life-giving Spirit and breathes on his disciples (20:21-23) as God had breathed life into Adam (Genesis 2:7) thereby indicating the onset of the new creation. Jesus is equipping his disciples for ministry with his own indwelling Spirit so that they may be an extension of himself, ministering forgiveness of sins within the promises of the new covenant. Jesus' offer of salvation to the world through his representatives is open-ended until the end of history when history will give way to the endless reign of the Kingdom of God.

Two Greek verbs—*apostello* and *pempo* (both meaning send, 20:21)—convey Jesus' commission to the disciples. Some suggest that there is a difference in emphasis between the two verbs, with *apostello* conveying function and *pempo* conveying relationship, but the frequency with which John uses these two relatively synonymous verbs makes the distinction unlikely. The force of the perfect tense of *apostello* (*apestalken*, as the Father has sent me, 20:21) should not be missed. Jesus has now completed his personal mission but he will continue it through the mission of the disciples. The Greek perfect tense indicates that Jesus is still the sent one who is continuing his mission through the present tense sending (*pempo*) of the disciples into a hostile world, as his agents, in the same way that the Father had sent him. This sending involves, like Jesus, knowledge of the Father and participation in the life of the Father. The disciples are to be one in nature with the Father, bound by the same Spirit as the sender, to do the will of the Father. The disciples are to be dependent upon and reflect Jesus' teaching.

Jesus breathed on his disciples (20:22), as God had breathed on Adam (Genesis 2:7), for new creation thereby equipping them for a ministry of forgiveness and judgment—like Jesus' ministry—with his own Spirit. The new covenant offer in the coming of the Spirit was the indwelling of Jesus. Jesus' infusing them with the Holy Spirit is not the baptism of the Spirit referred to by John the Baptist (1:33) since the gift in 20:22-23 is for the pronouncement of forgiveness of sins. Neither is this infusion the gift referred to at 7:39 since Jesus has not yet been fully glorified at the ascension. Many suggest that the infusion (20:20-22) is an anticipation of Pentecost but the Greek aorist imperative 'receive the Holy Spirit' rules out any notion of later fulfilment or delivery of a promise. The disciples receive the gift in John 20 without being bidden to wait for it in Jerusalem. Indeed, there is little correspondence in 20:19-23 to the promise concerning the coming of the Paraclete, which is a promise referring to Pentecost. When he is glorified, the evangelist reveals, Jesus will give the Spirit (7:39); but 'glorify' requires 'lifting up' in death, resurrection and exaltation. John 21 witnesses to Jesus' further appearances after the resurrection but the coming of the Paraclete is dependent on Jesus' going so the Paraclete obviously has not yet come.

Jesus' commission in 20:21-23 is not specifically an apostolic commission because all in the upper room receive it. The New Testament gives authority to bind and loose to the believing community as a whole (20:23; cf. Matthew 18:18). The exercise of the authority to forgive or withhold forgiveness by the believing community perpetuates the judgement for which Jesus came into the world. The gift of forgiveness (20:23) is the consequence of a witness to Christ. The delegated authority to forgive depends on (by the Greek perfect tenses) prior heavenly forgiveness (cf. Matthew 16:18-19) so Jesus did not transfer to the disciples the power to forgive, rather, they pronounce that divine forgiveness had been given or withheld. This commissioning by Jesus is not 'ordination' since there is no office involved.

B. F. Westcott spoke of 20:22 as the paschal gift of new life to the community by regeneration which was necessary before Pentecost.[148] But the evidence of the gospel presumes the disciples' regeneration prior to the passion (cf. 13:10).

With regard to the infusion of the Holy Spirit, Ezekiel 37:9 (LXX) uses the same combination of words (*pneuma*, spirit; and *emphusao*, breathe in) used by Jesus (20:22). In Ezekiel, the inbreathing effects new life in Israel after the word of judgement pronounced by the prophet on Israel by which Israel lay dead in exile. The prophet Ezekiel is taken to the valley where he had received his commission (cf. Ezekiel 3:22) to see the effects of the

---

148 Westcott, 1908, 351.

prophetic word of judgement. He watches as the Spirit breathes into lifeless Israel, who then rise as a mighty army (Ezekiel 37:9-10; cf. *emphusao* in Genesis 2:7 LXX where the breathing of God's Spirit into man at creation brings initial life to humankind). So the infusion of the Spirit at Ezekiel 37:9 was the means whereby Israel, as a new creation, was resurrected for ministry with the aim of including the world in its covenant relationship (cf. Exodus 19:5-6). 20:22 reports the culmination of the ministry of Jesus, bringing into being the assertion of 1:12, that—with the nation rejecting their covenant king (19:15)—beginning life is being breathed into the core of the New Israel, the children of God.

The new covenant language of Ezekiel 36-37 goes further than Jeremiah 31:31-34 in the clear association of Spirit in the process of renewal. Jesus' association of the new covenant with his death—together with Ezekiel's yoking of new covenant with Spirit—points to the cross on which Jesus undergoes the fire of judgement as the means whereby the Spirit will effect cleansing through judgement or by judgement. The occasion in John's gospel when Jesus brings the new community into covenant standing by the Spirit as heralds of the new covenant is this resurrection evening in the upper room. Jesus was baptised as representative Israel in John's baptism (cf. 1:32). Through Jesus the burden of sin is paid and there is the climactic revelation of God's loving desire to reconcile the world unto himself. The magnitude of reconciliation by the cross brings into being the new Israel through the Spirit. The debt had been paid and God's willingness to pardon has been revealed.

Jesus' public ministry (John 2-12) ended in the rejection of Israel. The quote from Isaiah 53:1 at John 12:38 referred to unbelief and the following quote from Isaiah 6:9-10 at John 12:40 referred to the reason for the unbelief, namely, the nation of Israel disbelieved the ministry of Jesus (cf. Isaiah 6:1-13) because of the projected rejection of the nation and the creation of remnant Israel as the true prophetic continuity. Pentecost would begin a prophetic mission for this community but, before Pentecost, the impress of the new creation (cf. 1:1-3) that characterised the incarnation is seen in this climactic action of Jesus breathing his Spirit on them in the upper room. Thus Jesus brings into being, in fulfilment of Ezekiel 37:1-14, the true Israel which results from his ministry (cf. 1:12). The mission of true Israel is to announce the great reconciliation of the world which has occurred at the cross with the removal of divine wrath and the potential for all to be included in the new covenant. The cross and resurrection had also opened the way for a new age to bring into being the final new world. Jesus has called into being an alternative Israel as a new creation, a result that John's gospel had always envisaged (cf. 1:12–13). John does not record any immediate change in the disciples following this upper room commission, indeed, they revert to their old way of life (21:3). Nothing will happen in their ministry until they are empowered for ministry (Acts 2) but the potential is clear.

Thomas, absent on the first Sunday resurrection evening (20:24), demanded physical proof that the others had in fact seen Jesus on the second Sunday. On that second Sunday evening Jesus appeared and offered evidence to Thomas who responded to Jesus—not to God, as per the Greek dative pronoun *autoi*, 20:28—with the gospel's climactic Christological confession: 'my Lord and my God'. This represents a complete confession of the covenant name Yahweh, both Lord (cf. LXX) and Elohim (the general name in the Old Testament for God as Creator). Jesus accepts Thomas' worship (cf. 21:29a) proclaiming a beatitude on those who will believe without seeing, those for whom the apostolic testimony is sufficient. By faith and through the Spirit of Christ in them, later believers will have the same immediacy of the divine presence as those disciples who saw Jesus face to face in the upper room but this sense of immediate presence is not a needed prerequisite for faith. The differentiating fact for the disciples is not seeing Jesus but believing his word. And the promise is that when Jesus left the world his presence in believers continues.

20:22 is the last mention of *pneuma* in John and the relationship to Genesis 2:7—linking the creation of humanity to the new creation—is important. The mediation of the Spirit through the resurrected Jesus is the summarising and crowning entry of John's gospel particularly in view of the ministry of the Spirit presaged in John 14–16. The greater works foreshadowed by Jesus for the disciples will be enabled through this infusion of the Spirit. The gift of the Spirit binds the sending of the disciples to the resurrected one. No longer will their relationship to Jesus be by seeing but, rather, the activity of the Spirit will determine their relationship.

Nevertheless, 20:19–23 is not the fulfilment of the promise of the Paraclete to be given by the glorified Jesus since the ascension had not yet taken place. Some suppose that the ascension had taken place between the meeting with Mary Magdalene (20:17ff) and the appearance of Jesus in the evening to the disciples (20:19ff) for it is not otherwise clear why Jesus gives to Mary Magdalene the commission to report to the disciples his imminent ascension. Among the foreshadowed indications of the victorious completion of Jesus' ministry were joy and peace (14:27; 16:22,33) which are evident in the upper room after Jesus is recognised. So, according to this supposition, Jesus gives the disciples the Spirit in this upper room account after his glorification (cf. 7:39). Is not the sequence of Paraclete reception thereby completed?

But John's gospel does not view the crucifixion, resurrection and ascension as discrete events in the career of Jesus. All these final events are included in the notion of his return to the Father. Furthermore, between 20:17 and 20:19 there is no alteration in the condition of Jesus so it seems that Jesus had not yet ascended. Why did Jesus command Mary not to keep clinging to him (20:17) if the ascension is not about to occur? What is the relationship between 'cling' and 'I have not yet ascended'? Was it that there was more pressing business for Mary than this temporary reverence? Do the words to Mary emphasise that this is not yet Jesus' permanent mode of presence with the disciples who must await the Paraclete? Jesus is certainly not depreciating the touch as if the earthly were something inferior. Is it now not possible for Mary and others to relate to him in the same old way? Is she offering to him the reverence which is only due to him after the Ascension? Or is the simple answer that there is no need to cling to Jesus because he is still here?

Others suggest that Thomas' confession (20:28) proves that Jesus was already the glorified and thus ascended Lord since the confession forms an inclusion with the beginning of the gospel (1:1) and is the high Christological point of the gospel. However, it is much more theologically compelling if Jesus is recognised as God before the ascension than after. And Jesus' later meeting with Thomas seems to be the usual sort of earthly meeting where disciples could hear and see Jesus. The second upper room evening meeting does not close an epoch for the time of not seeing Jesus has not yet come—so it seems that Jesus has not yet ascended. And the fact that the Spirit is called the Holy Spirit at 20:22 does not mean that Jesus has already ascended since Holy Spirit also occurs at 14:26.

In John's gifting narrative the Holy Spirit is breathed into the disciples but the presence of Jesus is only temporary (the Paraclete abides with them forever, cf. 14:16), that is, Jesus will withdraw himself from the disciples again so their peace and joy in the upper room are at best provisional (14:26-27; 15:11). There is yet to be a real absence of Jesus, a lacuna that the Spirit (Paraclete) would fulfil. Furthermore, the functions of the Paraclete are also different from—more personal than—this infusing for the ministry of forgiveness of sins, indeed, the Paraclete's only connection with sin (16:8ff) uses *hamartia* (sin) which John normally uses to refer to hostile unbelief. So there is very little to connect the upper room gift of the Spirit (20:20-22) with the promise of the Paraclete as the conditions for the gift of the Paraclete have not been fulfilled (14:26,16; 16:7,13). Moreover, the Paraclete's ministry is absent from 20:20 to the end of the gospel. Thomas does not believe the witness of the disciples (cf. 16:8-15), indeed, it is a resurrection appearance that convinces him. John 21 includes further resurrection appearances and each appearance of Jesus delays the coming of the Paraclete. John does not record the coming of the Paraclete.

Did the command to receive the Spirit (20:22) refer to the future gift of the Paraclete? This attempt to harmonise Luke and John was condemned in AD 381 by the council of Constantinople. D. A. Carson is the most recent, plausible advocate of this view.[149] Carson suggests that: the verb *enephusen* (20:22) means, simply, Jesus expired a deep breath (rather than Jesus insufflated them); the command to receive the Spirit does not mean immediate reception, like other imperatives used by Jesus which cannot be fully undertaken at the instance of the command; and the commissioning of the disciples is like Luke 24:36-49 in which the context is a future gift of the Spirit.[150] But John does not indicate that Jesus' expiration refers only to future experience.

Four different approaches agree that the Spirit is given in some different way at 20:22 than at Pentecost.[151] First, Calvin opted for 20:22 referring to 'an earnest of Pentecost' in which the Spirit was given to the apostles in such a way that they were only sprinkled with His grace and not saturated with full power. But this view circumscribes the difficulty. Hoskyns correctly perceived that the infusing with the Spirit was about inauguration,

---

149 Carson, 1991, 649-56. However, Carson's view is not acceptable since *enephusen*, a rare verb, had not lost its prepositional function (cf. Genesis 2:7; Nahum 2:2; Ezekiel 22:20; 37:9; Wisdom 15:11).
150 But see Turner (1977, 29) with regard to *ekpnein* (expire) which would have been sufficient if John just wanted to say that Jesus emitted a deep breath.
151 cf. Turner, 1977, 32-4.

not empowering for mission. Secondly, John Chrysostom opted for a gift of apostolic power to forgive sins but the context does not confine the gift of the Spirit to the apostles (cf. 17:18–21), rather, this gift is for all Christians. Likewise, there is no evidence that forgiveness is a right limited to the apostles, rather, the task of judgment is assigned to the whole community. The command to forgive or to retain sins continues the judgment ministry of Jesus and presupposes the consequences of Christian witness. Thirdly, Westcott opted for the communication of a new life that is essential for Pentecost. Fourthly, others opt for regeneration of the Spirit in the upper room—which must precede Spirit baptism—with *enephusen* evoking Genesis 2:7, for Jesus breathed the breathe of life into creation (and into the disciples). Forestell suggests further that 20:22 is neither a Johannine Pentecost nor the fulfilment of the promise of the Paraclete, on the contrary, 20:21–23 portray both giving life to believers and forming Christian community as a fulfilment of gospel expectations.[152]

Porsch and Schnackenburg correctly observe that the closing scenes of the gospel indicate that the Paraclete is not yet active. 20:22 thus presents the gift that will become the Paraclete after the resurrection appearances,[153] but Turner points out that it is not clear how the Spirit will become the Paraclete when he does not yet act as the Paraclete. But they have received the Spirit so some activity of the Spirit has already commenced.

Turner suggests that 20:22 cannot refer to the gift of the Paraclete as gifting the Paraclete depends on Jesus going away to the Father (16:7). Turner's view is sound because: the Paraclete was to be for the disciples the replacement for Jesus himself; the Paraclete would be sent after Jesus' glorification which had not yet occurred; and Jesus had promised that he would see them again after he went away (14:23). Others point out the comparison of the Paraclete's ministry of directing the disciples with Old Testament prophetic ministry.[154] Pentecost and Acts 2 inaugurate this prophetic ministry of the new Israel congregation. Indeed, it is beyond the chronological horizons of the gospel (Acts 2) that the disciples receive the Spirit as the Paraclete. Turner suggests that John depicts the new birth of the disciples as a process reaching its climax after the resurrection (20:22 being climactic).

---

152 Forestell, 1974.
153 cf. Turner, 1998, 100.
154 Isaacs, 1983, 391–407.

In this view, the words receive the Spirit would be interpretative of the disciples' commission of John 17 such that 20:22 fulfils 17:19.

But Turner's view is too personalised in the corporate context of John's gospel. *Emphusao* is *hapax* in the New Testament (20:22) so key Old Testament contexts (Genesis 2:7; Ezekiel 37:9) are necessary to understand John's carefully selected use of this verb. In Ezekiel 37 a new Israel arises from the debacle of the old as a result of the judgment of God upon the nation within history. Likewise, Ezekiel 37:9 depends on the context of Genesis 2:7 in which God infuses Adam with life to bring about the new creation.

The infusion of the Holy Spirit at 20:22 is the location in the fourth gospel where the new creation that has been in prospect since 1:1 (cf. 1:12; 20:31) has occurred. The gift of the Spirit in 20:22 brings into being the new Israel (cf. Ezekiel 37) which is equipped with further authority and power in Acts 1-2 (following the inauguration of the new covenant). This belief structure is created by the Spirit; indeed, Turner correctly notes that 'for John, a true understanding of Jesus' mission from baptism to glorification is only available through the Spirit experienced in the word; this alone is the source of life'.[155] For John, new birth means incorporation into a new community brought into being by the ministry, death and resurrection of Jesus the Messiah of Israel—for salvation is of the Jews. The reception of the Paraclete by the new prophetic group in Acts 2, in fulfilment of the promise for empowerment, will continue Israel's ministry of witness. This ministry of witness is the purpose for which the group in John 20 was called into being. This new Israel is the community established by the forgiveness of sins through the gift of the prophetic Spirit. The restoration of Israel occurs on the Day of Pentecost when the Gentiles are also incorporated, fulfilling in the new covenant the purpose of the Old Testament covenants. The Day of Pentecost is also the commencement of the ministry of the Paraclete by whose influence the Apostles begin to convict the world of sin, righteousness and judgement to come.

A consistent doctrine of the Holy Spirit emerges from John's gospel, with Spirit and the construction of Israel intertwined (cf. John 1-12). The gift of the Paraclete foreshadowed in the upper room provides for the witness of the newly constituted community (cf. 20:22) to the world at large. The Paraclete is the source of teaching enabling worship in Spirit and truth—an advocate who provides the way to the Father through the Son. So in Acts

---

155 Turner, 1977, 40.

2 the prophetic Spirit comes to the new Israel, now fully reinstituted by the full complement of twelve apostles. Eschatological Israel assembled at Pentecost, through the prophetic Spirit (Paraclete), announces that God had made this same Jesus whom the world crucified both Lord and Christ.

Acts

The baptism of the Spirit for new covenant witness (Acts 1)

The dedication in 1:1-2 summarises the first Lukan volume and links the two volumes by the activity of the Holy Spirit. The mention of the Holy Spirit also provides an introduction to what will happen in the second volume. In accordance with the close connection between Spirit and kingdom in the Bible, the Holy Spirit is involved both at the beginning (1:2) and the end (28:25) 'through the Scriptures'. The mention of the Holy Spirit is coupled with the departure of Jesus (1:2), indicating the manner of continuing communication to take place between the risen Jesus and the chosen apostles who form—as Jesus' legatees and earthly successors—the nucleus of the restored, new covenant Israel. The apostles carry Jesus' message, leading to progressive empowering for mission in the developing church. The close link in the mission of Jesus with his disciples throughout Acts is the Spirit, indeed, the Acts of the Apostles continues Jesus' ministry through the Spirit.

1:3-8 is an important summary. The disciples' prior reception of the Spirit for ministry through Jesus (John 20:19-23) means that they are further empowered to preach the kingdom after Pentecost. The risen Jesus' commission is to direct the gift of the Spirit promised by Joel to the work of new Israel in implementing the new covenant (cf. Luke 22:20).

The departure from the gospel begins at 1:4-5. Jesus is eating with the disciples (sharing salt, *sunalizomenos*, 1:4) when he reminds them that they heard about the Father's promise of the Spirit from Jesus. This promise could refer back to Luke 24:49—but 1:4 and Luke 24:49 may be variant reports of the same event. Early in his ministry, Jesus had told the disciples: 'if you then who are evil, know how to give good gifts to your children, how much more will the heavenly Father give the Holy Spirit to those who ask him' (Luke 11:13). This promise about the gift of the Holy Spirit comes after the prayer Jesus taught them which enabled the disciples to address God as Father (Luke 11:2-4). There are frequent, post Luke 11:13 references to the Spirit as God's gift (2:38; 8:20; 10:45; 11:17 cf. 5:32). Prior to the cross, Jesus had declared the Father's readiness to give the Spirit to the disciples (Luke 11:13). After the resurrection, Jesus indicates that the coming of this gift of the Spirit for the disciples is imminent (1:4-5).

The disciples were to wait in Jerusalem—the city where Jesus died—for the Father's promise, God's Spirit, to be conveyed through Jesus (1:4–5 cf.2:33). Christianity needed to originate in Jerusalem to be the authentic new covenant Israel.[156] Salvation was always about Zion's (Jerusalem's) restoration. Beginning in Jerusalem, the good news would then be taken to the nations (1:8).

The structure of the sentence in 1:4–5 permits the view that they had heard about the promise of the Spirit from Jesus. This was the Father's promise and had in view the promised salvation for which the Spirit emerges as the key in Acts. However, 1:4 broadly paraphrases what John the Baptist said (Luke 3:16) but without the Baptist's reference to 'fire'. It is generally assumed that the fire had been absorbed by the cross, however, the tongues of fire (2:1–4) argue against this view. But the Baptist's parallel metaphor is of unquenchable fire for failure to receive Jesus (Matthew 3:12; Luke 3:17). Jesus refers to what he had been promised (1:5) which may refer to Luke 24:49, however, if Luke 24:49 is a variant of 1:5 then 1:5 may refer to Luke 11:13 or 12:12 which are worded in such a way as to encourage the reader to see them fulfilled in Acts 2.

Prior to Acts, for the upper room community who had accepted Jesus as Messiah: Jesus had drunk the cup of God's wrath; the messianic woes had been endured; and the new covenant had come into effect. Their entry into the new covenant age—and the entry of those who accept their message—is without the fiery refining which Jesus had experienced himself for the world. The fire, which Jesus by his death had cast on all unrepentant humanity (Luke 12:49), begins its confrontational progress in the Acts of the Apostles.

Baptism by water (1:5; 11:16) is a metaphor for something else, a rite which looks for further fulfilment, namely: further outpouring or filling of the Spirit, an experience aptly described—in language drawn from the rite of water baptism—as baptised by the Spirit. This baptism by the Spirit was initiatory for it enabled the disciples to participate in the new age. Later baptism in the Spirit (cf. Cornelius and his group, 10:44–48) provided

---

156 By its rejection of Jesus (John 19:15), the Old Testament entity of Israel as a covenant nation ceased to exist. Jesus' death introduced the new covenant (Luke 22:20) with a Christian Israel whose profile is being put together in Acts and the remainder of the New Testament. While national Israel continues to be addressed in Acts—offering membership of the new covenant—the New Testament identifies Christians as the new Israel.

forgiveness, salvation and membership in the new community conferred by the new covenant promise of Pentecost. Presumably, baptism by fire is still to be experienced by those who refuse the forgiveness available throughout history by the personal acceptance of the significance of Jesus' crucifixion. So the baptism of the Spirit at 1:5 without fire appears to refer to the upper room believers who are already cleansed by the messianic forgiveness of the cross. 2:3-4 (cf. Luke 12:50) records a further experience of the Holy Spirit at Pentecost for the disciples beyond that referred to in Luke 3:16, John 20:22 or John 13:10. The experience at 2:4 confirms their baptism in the Spirit and forgiveness by personal identification with the work of the cross, a further gift empowering them for ministry.

The disciples ask Jesus (1:6), 'Lord is this the time when you will restore the kingdom to Israel?'. This question comes between verses dealing with the gift of the Holy Spirit, so the gift in Jesus' mind is the gift of the Spirit that will initiate restoration and times of world witness for new Israel. Did the disciples mean the restoration of Israel as the people of God with the gift of the Holy Spirit (2:1-4) shedding messianic blessing on the Christian group? It is highly unlikely that, after forty days with Jesus on the subject of the kingdom, the disciples would ask a nationalistic question. When told that this further reception of the Holy Spirit was coming, the disciples may have thought—naturally and logically—about what else should come with these last days, since the prophetic role of the initial upper room group was about to commence. However, when the disciples ask whether Jesus will restore the kingdom to Israel, Jesus did not give a direct answer.

But Jesus' reply (1:7-8) to the disciples' leading question (1:6) offers new content to be developed in Acts. The apostles are to remain in Jerusalem until they receive power. Jesus' followers may have supposed that the messianic reign over Israel and then the world was about to begin, and they were right, but the 'how' needs to be understood. Jesus rebukes the disciples' interest in times and seasons and directs their attention to their responsibilities for the mission that will soon begin. This mission will inaugurate the coming of the kingdom in human experience and thus bring into being the new Israel. Jesus had previously corrected a supposition that God's reign would appear immediately upon his arrival in Jerusalem (Luke 19:11ff.)—his resurrection had revived these premature hopes.

Jesus' reply (1:7) is non-committal. He corrects the disciples' desire to know the times and seasons but he does not give an answer to their question because they are not to know the details, rather, they are to engage in the ministry of witness to the widening world (1:8). The kingdom in all its fullness will not come immediately but their part in its restoration commences now with mission. Like Old Testament Israel (Isaiah 43:10), the new community was to bear witness to the divine intention. The suggestion that the Spirit is the substitute in Acts for the imminent expectation of the Parousia cannot be correct for Jesus' word about the coming of the Spirit prompts the disciples' question about the restoration of the kingdom of Israel (1:6). If the supposition in the disciples question is national restoration for Israel in her own land (cf. Jeremiah 16:15; 24:6; 50:19, where the LXX uses the cognate verb *apokathistemi*)—if there were lingering nationalistic ideas—then, presumably, Jesus' response (1:8) would have corrected their supposition.

Jesus' answer (1:7-8) does not imply that Israel is beyond restoration but, rather, that the timing of that restoration and the form of Israel after the restoration is in the hands of God and the Messiah (cf. 3:19-21). The restoration of Israel is not the disciples' problem. With the imminent coming of the promised Spirit, questions about the completion of God's purpose through the reign of Jesus naturally arise. However, this promise of the Holy Spirit was for the new Israel to be restored now—and the rest of Acts traces the process.

Jesus rejects the supposition that the kingdom will come immediately but he does not deny the disciples' concern about the restoration of Israel's witness. Peter, instructed by Jesus and inspired by the Spirit, speaks to the people of Jerusalem about times of restoration involving all that God spoke through the prophets (3:20-21)—including the eschatological sending of Messiah Jesus from heaven. The close connection between 1:6 and 3:19-21 is indicated by common references to times and seasons and the use of the unusual root *apokathistano*, with Acts 3 making fulfilment (for Israel) dependent on national repentance. Acts will deal with Israel's intransigence but her failure to repent will not mean the absolute rejection of 'Israel' by the end of Acts. Luke/Acts underscores a restored non-national Israel as the continuing carrier of the promises of God. 1:6-8 cannot be a narrow nationalistic question because Israel had already relinquished the national covenant (John 19:15).

Jesus spoke to apostles (1:8; cf. 1:2) who were already empowered by the Spirit as the new people of God—comprising both Jews and Gentiles—to bear witness initially to national Israel in the area defined by Jesus. Luke uses *martus* (witness) in Acts only of those who saw the risen Lord (1:21ff; 10:36-39). The *martus* is not to know all the details, rather, together they will function as witness to the widening world (1:8), an obligation devolved on Israel under the Sinai Covenant. The Spirit will empower the *martus* community for witness. Israel's witness role (Isaiah 43:10,12) is now, since Pentecost, the new covenant (new Israel's) community's world role. The Spirit of Jesus in mission will work by witness to the divinely revealed word.

David Pao points to the eschatological projection (Isaiah 2:2-4) which mandates that the 'word of the Lord will go forth' from Jerusalem.[157] Pao traces this development through Acts from Jerusalem to the nations (cf. 6:7; 12:24; 19:20), with growth occurring in each case in the community of believers and then further implementation of the new community's task to spread missionary witness. Such implementation is dependent on the coming of the Holy Spirit. Pao notes that this gift of the Spirit will create a situation where Israel's desolation will continue until 'a Spirit from on high comes upon us' (cf. Isaiah 32:15). The coming of the Pentecost Spirit signifies the beginning of the restoration of new Israel at the beginning of the new age, and also the apostles' commission for ministry. Turner makes the same comment on Isaiah 32:15, associating the witness theme of 1:8 with Isaiah 43:10-12; 49:6.[158] But Pao's suggestion that Pentecost fulfils John's prophecy of a baptism in Spirit and fire—with fire signifying the coming of the Spirit on the apostles as power for Israel's cleansing and restoration—is, as previously noted, doubtful.

Jesus' words are a command to move progressively into the world, and the Acts of the Apostles bears witness to the beginning of this movement but not to its fulfilment as Luke only deals with the spread of the gospel as far as the imperial centre in Rome. 13:47 defines Israel's mission in terms of Isaiah 49:6 so the phrase 'to the ends of the earth' means ministry to the Gentiles—and, hence, to the widening world. This answers the 'how' of restoration of non-national new Israel (cf. 2:39). The apostles' ministry is to the world at large in fulfilment of the covenant with Abraham, indeed, Jesus calls on the disciples to fulfil the eschatological witness mandate delivered to Old Testament Israel. The mission must begin in Jerusalem and move out from Jerusalem (1:8) for the new and decisive event of salvation

---

157 Pao, 2000, 92.
158 Turner, 1998, 50.

took place in Jerusalem. But the apostolic witness is not about the place of national Israel in God's purposes, rather, restored new Israel's witness is to the word of God creating new life in its journey from Jerusalem to the ends of the earth.

It is odd that Luke never uses the missionary commission (1:8) to impel the apostles to go to the Gentiles. Indeed, Paul uses the missionary commission of Old Testament Israel (13:47) to justify his work. The prior reference to the Gentile mission (Luke 24:47) left no room for doubt about Jesus' intention in Acts 1. The tension about Peter's reluctance to go to the Gentiles (1:8; 10:1-48) is the historical tension between what ought to happen and what actually happened. The Gentile mission passes for extraordinary among the Jews, which is indicative of the factuality of the Acts account since the Spirit must bring the apostles to think about Gentile mission even after Pentecost! The mission does not automatically unfold.

By the guidance of God (10:9-16)—and with the outpouring of the gift of the Spirit and the enterprise of others (8:5-8; 11:19-21; 15:12-21)—mission will mean that restored Israel does go out. This outgoing missionary activity of new Israel is a departure from the centripetal program of Old Testament, national Israel signifying the end of national Israel as the geographical centre for divine revelation. After the formal end of the nation in AD 70 there will be no geographical Promised Land into which converts may come! As far as participation in the mission was concerned, apart from Peter, the twelve were non-participants and even reluctant to get involved. They lead and guide the Jerusalem community but are not active in missionary enterprise even in Judea. The twelve remain in Jerusalem even when the church is scattered by persecution. In short, mission was not an organisational response by the early church community to the supposed delay of the Parousia, on the contrary, the direct involvement of the Spirit of Jesus is necessary for the community of the restored new Israel to engage in covenant witness (cf. Acts 10).

Movement out from Jerusalem (1:8) indicates that the age of Old Testament nationalism—when Israel was to witness to the world by being a kingdom of God people within a Promised Land—had been terminated by Israel's rejection of Jesus (John 19:15). During his ministry, Jesus constantly threatened the end of national Israel as the covenant community because of Israel's continuing disobedience. Paul wrote that the gift of God's call to Israel was 'without recall' (Romans 11:29) but God's gift of election for Israel was never to be for absolute privilege, rather, national Israel was called for witness to the world.[159] The call to witness was without recall! National Israel had consistently rejected this commission but the restored Christian Israel of Acts will now fulfil the commission by worldwide mission.

God's rejection of the Jewish nation, not the people, will be evident from the destruction of the Jerusalem Temple predicted by Jesus (cf. Mark 13). But whereas salvation will come to individual Israelites (cf. Romans 10:9–13), nevertheless, salvation will not come to the nation as a whole.[160] The disciples take over the vocation of the Isaianic servant to: bear witness (cf. Isaiah 49:6) to the ends of the earth (cf. Luke 24:47; cf. 2:32; Acts 13:47; where 'ends of the earth' = Gentiles); raise up Jacob; and restore the remnant of Israel. The disciples will not know the times or the seasons but they will receive power to mission, that is, the Spirit will act in the disciples as the power of Israel's cleansing and restoration. So Jesus' words in 1:8 renew both the vocation of Israel to be a light to lighten the Gentiles and her prophetic calling to the world. According to Jesus, the restoration of Israel occurs through the Spirit. The Holy Spirit inspired the Scripture (1:16; cf. 4:25; 28:25) so the prophetic Spirit is the authority with regard to the divine will and purpose expressed in Scripture. Acts 1 closes with the election of Matthias to complete the apostolic circle of the new Israel. The choice is by God with no mention of the Spirit. But the implicit claim for the church to be the new Israel has been made and will be developed through Pentecost.

The baptism of the Spirit promoting close family relationship (Acts 2)

The events of Pentecost show the significance of the Spirit as the Spirit of prophecy empowering the new Israel community for witness. Pentecost reflects the ongoing availability of redemption as a result of the cross through Jesus' life-giving Spirit. The apostles receive power to preach the presence of the Kingdom of God, that is, to continue the ministry of Jesus. The addressees of 1:4–5,8 are supplied with the power of the Spirit (2:4) necessary for their anticipated ministry (cf. John 20:22–23). The coming of the Spirit results in powerful preaching and conversion of large numbers.

---

159 cf. Exodus 19:5–6; Dumbrell, 2002, 37–38; 2005, 110–117.

160 On the long-term future of the nation, see Dumbrell (2005, 97–119). On the place of the Jewish covenant and the Mosaic Law in the post-cross period, see Dumbrell 2005, 26–27; 32–34; 75–77.

But the Spirit is more than a necessary means to fulfil a task, rather, the Spirit enables the experience of God as Father so the presence of the Spirit promotes a close family relationship among the new Israel with God. The Spirit conveys the blessings of salvation (2:38-40).

Jesus highlighted the importance of Pentecost (1:8) for the promise of baptism in the Holy Spirit—to be given at Pentecost—leads to proclamation of new life in the risen Jesus. Jesus' promise is a Spirit baptism (1:5) but there is no mention of fire (cf. Luke 3:16) because Pentecost is not a baptism of the Spirit and fire for the assembled disciples, rather, new believers are baptised. Indeed, Spirit baptism is applicable to all people from Pentecost forward who recognise that, at the cross: Jesus bore all of their sin; forgiveness can be found; and the result is a new way of life. However, rejection of the cross raises the prospect of a baptism by fire and the human experience of the finality of divine rejection.

Pentecost and the new covenant gift of the Spirit

Pentecost was the day that Moses received the law on Mt Sinai and gave the law as God's gift to Israel. In Old Testament Israel, the feast of Pentecost celebrated covenant renewal. In Acts 2, Pentecost marks the transition from the old to the new covenant. Suddenly, on the day of Pentecost, a mysterious sound like a strong wind accompanied by tongues of fire introduced the day—like the Sinai revelation where the Lord descended in fire with thunder and lightning (Exodus 19:16,18). Both Sinai and Pentecost are covenant introductions, indeed, the Moses/Sinai parallels make Pentecost (2:3) the affirmation of the new covenant.

Wind could symbolise the breath of resurrection life and fire could symbolise eschatological judgment, or they could simply indicate divine presence. The wind and fire theophany affirms the existence of the new covenant. The coming of the Spirit empowers the community ('all' 120, 2:1; cf. 1:15) for its ministry in this new beginning of salvation history. I. H. Marshall has pointed out that the number 120 (1:15) was the minimum number of men required to establish a community with its own council—so the early Christians could be considered a new community.[161]

The wind and fire theophany is not regeneration 'baptism of the Spirit'. Baptism of the Spirit is confrontation with the cross in the light of the resurrection and exaltation effecting either cleansing or rejection. The new

---

161 Marshall, 1977, 351.

Israel had been gathered to the cross (John 12:32) and had already received new life for ministry (John 20:21-23).[162] The allusions to Moses/Sinai in Acts 2 suggest that the gift of the Spirit was of foundational importance for prophetic ministry in the life of new Israel. At Pentecost—though it is perhaps too simplistic to view it this way—the emphasis changes from law to Spirit in the church, that is, the Spirit is the new covenant guide replacing Jewish law. However, whereas the Spirit offered at Pentecost is the same Spirit as in the Old Testament (God's gift of salvation required the same work of the Spirit in both Testaments with the same recognition of God as Lord and King), the constituency receiving the gift of the Spirit and the purpose of the gift are both more extensive in the new covenant. The gift of the Spirit is now specifically individual and worldwide.

After Pentecost, the mission of the church is a movement of the Spirit. In Acts, not only are there five separate accounts of a bestowal of the Spirit (2:1-12; 4:28-31; 8:15; 10:44; 19:6) but the Spirit also intervenes at every critical stage of the mission (8:29,39; 10:19; 11:12; 13:2,4; 16:6,7; 19:2; 20:23). Luke reports that the gift of the Holy Spirit (1:4) initiates and gives shape to mission at Pentecost providing the expected restoration of Israel to her prophetic vocation (Isaiah 42:6; 49:6).

The language of the Spirit's coming at Pentecost ('from heaven', 'rush of a violent wind', 'tongues as of fire', 2:2-3) emphasises that the coming was a divine act—like circumstances surrounding the granting of the Sinai Covenant—for wind and fire evidenced divine appearances (theophanies) from Sinai onwards. In fulfilment of 1:5, the previously regenerate disciples (cf. John 13:10) in the upper room were not only regenerate by the Spirit but were also all filled with the Spirit and then commissioned and gifted for their ministry.[163] Indeed, the gathered Galileans (2:7) began to speak in other tongues (cf. 2:8)!

Pentecost publicly marks the transition from the old covenant—to which the 120 previously belonged (John 20:19-23)—to the new covenant, that is, Pentecost marks the threshold of the last days and the commencement of the new day of salvation. The future eschatological life now invades the present evil age in a proleptic manner, that is, the end of the ages has dawned on

---

162 cf. Dumbrell, 2006, 183-186.
163 Luke's use of *pleroo* (filled, Luke 1:15; Acts 2:4; 4:8,31; 9:17; 13:9) indicates a more permanent endowment than *pimplemi* which indicates a filling for a special occasion (cf. Turner, 1981, 54).

those who have the Spirit and are in Christ (1 Corinthians 10:11). The gift of the Spirit is: the central element of the new covenant promise (Ezekiel 36:27); the essence of the promise given to Abraham (Galatians 3:14); and the promise to Christ, at his baptism, that his ministry would implement the divine plan for the new creation (Matthew 3:13ff; Isaiah 52:15; 53:12). The fulfilment of the 'great commission' (Matthew 28:19-20) begins to take place at Pentecost through the Spirit. The resurrected Jesus now becomes the life-giving Spirit (cf. 1 Corinthians 15:45) and Abraham's seed in all the nations of the earth will now be blessed (Genesis 12:3; Galatians 3:13-14).

Sinclair Ferguson suggests that Pentecost reverses Babel,[164] that is, the preceding scattering of the nations (Genesis 10-11) becomes the community of reconciled humanity in the new people of God who are one community of Jews and Gentiles. But Pentecost is not a reversal of Babel because it does not finally remedy the confusion of tongues, rather, it projects that occurrence in the final new creation reality. With the Pentecost outpouring of the Holy Spirit, the last days have commenced and eschatological reversal of the effects of sin begin to appear in the one reconciled people of Jews and Gentiles—possessing one Lord, one faith, and one Spirit baptism (Ephesians 4:5)—now united by the Spirit and preaching reconciliation. So the hearing of foreign tongues is a sign of God's promised judgement (Deuteronomy 28:49; Jeremiah 5:15), an indication that the kingdom is being taken from national Israel and given to a people who will produce the fruit of the kingdom (Matthew 21:43). National Israel now begins to experience a partial hardening until the fullness of the Gentiles is brought in.[165] At Sinai, Moses descended with the law. But as Christ ascended from the cross, the Spirit of Christ descended to write the law in the hearts of new believers.

Peter's preaching indicates that Joel's prophecy about the distribution of the Spirit had been fulfilled (cf. 2:17), that is, the longed-for Day of the Lord had arrived and the power of the age to come has been released. The Spirit had been poured out without geographical and ethnic limitation—the boundaries of the exclusive Mosaic covenant is now obsolete. All of the Lord's people now possessed the knowledge formerly only possessed

---

164 Ferguson, 1996, 45-63. The new covenant promises now begin to be fulfilled (Romans 8:3-4; 2 Corinthians 3:7-11).

165 cf. Davis, 1952, 228-231. Before the cross, the future was still open for Israel but not after since this partial hardening will not later be removed (Romans 2:5, cf. Dumbrell, 2005,111), that is, final judgement follows this hardening.

by prophets, as desired by Moses (Numbers 11:29). 'Prophecy' becomes a metonymy for sharing the Spirit. Jeremias suggests that contemporary Judaism understood that those who possessed the Spirit were prophets.[166] So on this Pentecost Feast of the firstfruits, the firstfruits of the new people signal the end of one law and the arrival of a new mode of relating that would produce the gift of the Ten Words as fruit in the life of new Israel.

Pentecost is the once and for all re-establishment of the basis for Abrahamic universal spiritual outreach. From Pentecost on, the Spirit is present and active in the covenant community, and the Spirit is the means of the establishment of the world church as the new covenant people of God. Because of the Spirit given at Pentecost, the new covenant people of God is the body of Christ—a dwelling place of God in the Spirit (Ephesians 2:22), the temple of God in which the Spirit of God dwells (1 Corinthians 3:16). The Pentecost language miracle indicated the world domain of the gospel. This beginning of world mission, and the place of the apostles as coordinators, was integral and not repeatable. Pentecost supplied gospel content and direction but left the continuing presentation of the gospel open to adaption.

The Pentecost blessing of Christ's life-giving Spirit

The outpouring of the Spirit was the essence of the fulfilment of the old covenant (2:39; Galatians 3:14; Ephesians 1:13) and thereby would bring into being the operation of the new covenant. At the Jordan, Jesus was given the Spirit for his messianic task so that he could give the promised gift of the Father to the church. Pentecost is Christ's personal coming as the life-giving Spirit in his exalted resurrection life. There is a coalescence and congruence between Jesus and the Spirit so that the work of the Spirit is not an addendum to the work of Christ but a continuing presentation of Christ. The Spirit's coming shows that Christ is the source of eschatological life now, through the Spirit, living in the church (cf. Matthew 28:20) as the life-giving Spirit active in the new covenant community. Acts is not a random sampling of Christian piety and practice, rather, Luke points to the establishment of the new covenant church of Jews and Gentiles through the apostles and those with them. They implement Jesus' program (1:8) when the Holy Spirit comes at Pentecost, indeed, 1:8 supplies the initial impetus for the foundational spread of the gospel and its continued progress. Acts 8, 10, 11 and 19 take place not as extensions of Pentecost but as a result of

---

166 Jeremias, 1971, 78.

what took place at Pentecost and none of these post-Pentecost events emphasise individual believers.

The gift of the Spirit is the exalted Christ himself—as the head of the new creation—equipping the church for his ministry as the last Adam, resulting from the operation of the new covenant. The Spirit is always related to the body of Christ, that is, the church is the place where the Spirit is present in his diverse working. The Spirit is not the creator of the body of Christ, rather, the Spirit is the gift granted to all believers as a result of being in the body (1 Corinthians 12:13). To belong to Christ is to have the Spirit (Romans 8:9) and to be joined to the Lord is to have one Spirit with him (1 Corinthians 6:17).

Other tongues commence the Spirit's world harvest (2:5-13)

The audience at Pentecost are Jews (cf. 2:5,14,22). The first occurrence of the gift of the Spirit to Gentiles is 10:44. The first aim of the gospel is to address the message to Israel—that is, representatively, all the house of Israel is to hear this message of renewal and eschatological blessing. The promised Holy Spirit, given to restore Israel, initiates the action of Acts by invoking at Pentecost the mission that continues through the rest of the book. At the Spirit's arrival at Pentecost there is an outburst of speech that communicates with Jews from every nation under heaven in their native languages. This is a communication miracle. Pentecost was a festival celebrating the fulfilment of the wheat harvest and, accordingly, restored Israel by the gift of the Spirit looked to a ministry of bringing in a worldwide harvest of Christian believers.

The world will be affected by the Pentecost event since Jews 'from every nation under heaven' (2:5) were represented. What has happened to Israel is a paradigm for the world in accordance with the prophecy that the Spirit is to descend in these last days on 'all flesh' (2:17). Pentecost sets the character of the new age by prescribing the way that God will meet his new people. So further 'mini-Pentecosts' occur at crucial points of missionary expansion (cf. 8:14-17; 10:44-47; 11:15-17). The Jerusalem council notes this connection (15:7-9) and the Spirit is again strikingly active at Ephesus (19:1-7) where he incorporates a John the Baptist group into the faith.

Through the Spirit, Jesus directs the work of the church. The Spirit is not merely a personal gift to believers, rather, the Spirit is the link on earth between Jesus and the disciples to convey the message (cf. 2:5-21) of the mighty works of power that are now happening through the gift of Jesus. Up to Christ's resurrection, the Spirit was the Spirit of God. But—post-resurrection—Christ majorly became the Spirit, that is, the Spirit is the means through whom Jesus continues his messianic forgiveness. This paradoxical force of the presence of God in history at Pentecost leads to mocking, amazement and perplexity in the crowd of onlookers.

Pentecost is the miracle that brings about a repentant, re-established Israel added to the Old Testament nucleus of already existing believers. There can be no witness to the ends of the earth until God's claim on the whole house of Israel is reasserted. 'All' in 2:1 is the group of disciples mentioned at 1:15, that is, the representative true Israel who all receive the Holy Spirit at Pentecost for ministry (2:1-4). This provides the answer to the question 'what does this mean' (2:12-13). The emerging, energised early church is end-time Israel. Peter speaks on behalf of the twelve and the larger gathering who were the first to receive the Spirit. His audience is Israel (2:14,22,36) but they now need to minister in Israel's new covenant role. The interpretation of the outpouring event (2:17-21) as the fulfilment of Joel 2:28-32 is provided by Peter. The associated gift of prophecy (2:18) is intended for the desperate situation of the nation.

Fulfilment of prophecy concerning the Spirit (2:14-40)

The behaviour of the disciples calls for explanation (2:12-13). The crowd was divided between wonder, excitement and mocking when Peter began to speak. First, in inverse order, Peter responds to the crowd's mocking (2:15). Then, referring to the manifestations of the Spirit as the fulfilment of Joel's prophecy (2:16-21), Peter relates the whole episode to the recent events of the death and resurrection of Jesus (2:22-36). The climactic announcement of Peter's exegesis of Scripture reveals the crucial importance of Pentecost to all the house of Israel (2:36), that is, to the audience of Jews from every nation under heaven (2:5) including Israel's Diaspora. The formal speech opens (2:14) and closes (2:36) with Peter's outreach to all Israel, with the follow through dialogue (2:37-40) representing an integral result for Jerusalem and Judea from Peter's speech.

2:14 includes all those dwelling in Jerusalem, that is, Jews from every nation under heaven dwelling in Jerusalem (2:5). The concluding 'let the entire house of Israel know with certainty' (2:36) rephrases the opening 'all who dwell in Jerusalem, let this be known to you' (2:14). Peter's speech thus shows a concern for all Jews to hear the gospel to bring about the restoration of Israel as a united people under its Messiah, committed as a chosen people for witness to Christ.

These Jews from every nation under heaven are amazed when they hear about the mighty acts of God spoken by Galileans in their many languages. The long list of peoples and lands underlines the diversity of the Pentecost audience, representing a broad sampling of people from the four corners of the then known world. This global emphasis includes representatives from Mesopotamia, Arabia, Asia, Europe and Africa gathered in Jerusalem. The restoration of Israel began with the appointment of Matthias (1:26) and now involves the spiritual return of the diaspora Jews from the four corners of the earth (cf. Isaiah 11:11).

The diverse, worldwide, Jewish audience verifies both the language miracle and the global scope of the mission. These devout Jews on pilgrimage in Jerusalem had raised the question, 'Whatever could this mean?' (2:12). Peter's response—which is as inspired as the language miracle (2:5-13)—points to their promised Messiah. The global Jewish audience are representatives of their homelands so this new covenant mission has power to cross ethnic and religious frontiers. These Jewish hearers were no doubt acquainted with the recent Passover crucifixion of a supposed messianic pretender, indeed, they are included in Peter's accusation (2:23,36) since Jesus' death is attributed to those living at that time in Jerusalem (both Jews and Gentiles).

Peter addresses the question of the fulfilment of scripture (2:16-21; cf. Joel 2:28-32), showing the significance of the events for his globally diverse Jewish audience. The Pentecost gift has fulfilled a prophecy of the coming of the Spirit on all Israel as a covenant blessing associated with the arrival of the Day of the Lord,[167] bringing judgement on the nations and vindication to Israel. God declared 'I will pour out my Spirit' (2:17; Joel 2:28), that is, the personal presence of the transcendent God. In the new covenant community, Spirit is no longer restricted to Israel but now includes Israel and the nations as the Spirit is poured out on all flesh. Indeed, the Spirit had been taken from the old Israel and given to new Israel (a nation producing fruits, Matthew 21:43). The unprecedented worldwide ministry of Christ

---

167 The Spirit confers—to the new covenant community—the eschatological gift of prophecy, that is, the gift of communicating the new covenant. The generality of the gift is indicated by gender, age and social strata (slaves) inclusions (2:18).

is enabled by the life giving Spirit—the third person of the Trinity—establishing the eschatological lordship of Christ over all creation such that the blessing of Abraham has now come through the Spirit to the Gentiles (Galatians 3:14).

Jesus' programmatic speech at Nazareth (Luke 4:16–27) introduced and anticipated the character of his ministry, interpreting the coming of the Spirit on Jesus in terms of messianic activity in Israel. Peter's reference to the coming of the Spirit at Pentecost sets the tone for missionary activity in Acts. Peter's 'in the last days' (2:17) reinterprets Joel's 'then afterward' (Joel 2:28), indicating that Peter perceived the eschatological outpouring of the Spirit to be ushering in the 'last days' in accordance with post-resurrection teaching on the kingdom of God received from Jesus. Both speaking in other tongues and Peter's speech are included at Pentecost as prophetic speech inspired by the outpouring of God's Spirit. Indeed, Peter adds 'and they shall prophesy' (2:18) to Joel's prophecy, indicating new covenant prophetic proclamation—of God's revelation in Christ to all—by all in the Christian community including Gentiles. So Spirit in the new covenant community is no longer restricted to Israel but includes all flesh, that is, Israel and the nations.

The eschatological gift of the Spirit is: the equipment of the church for ministry beyond conversion; the climactic event that the prophetic figure of Moses had wished for all Israel (Numbers 11:29); and the sign to gauge the appearance of the last days (2:17). The charter of Israel anticipated in Joel 2:28–32 is to be an eschatological, prophetic, witnessing community. Judaism knew of a messianic figure who would receive revelation and wisdom through the Spirit, and would be empowered by the Spirit. But Peter's speech tells of something entirely unparalleled with his Christological interpretive comment at the end of the Joel citation that 'all who call upon the name of the Lord shall be saved' (2:21).

Peter speaks of a Messiah who directs the activity of the Spirit in such a way that he can be described as giving the Spirit and the author of specific charismata among the people of God. Peter says that Jesus had 'poured out this that you both see and hear' (2:33; cf. 2:1–4). In the Old Testament, God endows the activity of specific men with his *ruach* (Spirit) thereby making them his instruments to reveal his will and empowering them for specific tasks. In the same way, Jesus is revealing and empowering in the lives of his disciples. Just as the Spirit mediated God's activity and presence among his people in the Old Testament, in the same way the Spirit is now the sign of Jesus' presence and activity in the new covenant community (2:33). And this gift of the Spirit is directly connected with the death of Christ.

This divine Christology speaks of Jesus directing God's Spirit, which is tantamount to calling Jesus God. Jesus' functions are so aligned with Yahweh that both Jesus and Yahweh pour out the Spirit (2:17,33)—hence, Jesus is the Lord referred to in the Joel citation (Joel 2:28–32) upon whom the Jews (and all others) must now call to be saved.[168] Only a minority from national Israel, either living in Palestine or scattered abroad, will respond to Peter's call.

The repeat manifestations of the Spirit in Acts—and the witnessing that these manifestations occasion—express the eschatological character of the church. Jesus had received the gift of the Spirit and now has lordship over that gift, that is, Jesus now gives the Spirit to the church. The phrase to 'receive the Spirit' denotes the beginning of a new function of the Spirit in and through believers, beyond the gift of personal conversion which was already an activity of the Spirit in the Old Testament.

The Spirit of prophecy promised through Joel has now become the Spirit of Jesus (5:9). The basic gift of the Spirit is regeneration and witness however, in addition, the Spirit now distributes individual and varied charisma (cf. 2:33) thereby directing the church's mission to outsiders and giving charismatic wisdom and revelation where needed for the defence and propagation of the gospel. The Spirit is the link between Jesus in heaven and his disciples on earth, that is, the Paraclete promised in John's gospel. Thus—through the Spirit—Jesus directs and empowers the church's edification and mission to outsiders, and continues to announce his ministry of messianic release. The Spirit is the very life of the church! At Pentecost, the outpouring of the Spirit has come on Jews only but Gentiles are already also in view to receive this gift (1:8; 2:39).

The second major section in the text cited from Joel (Acts 2:19–20) points to the appearance of wonders and signs prior to the coming of the glorious Day of the Lord. Peter adds the word 'signs' to Joel's prophecy (2:19; cf. Joel 2:30), formulating the 'wonders and signs' terminology as a response to faith. Peter employs a common LXX phrase, 'signs and wonders', used to describe the effect of the word of God in the exodus. The phrase then becomes commonplace in Acts to refer to the miracles that

---

168 Turner, 1982, 180-181.

attend the apostles' presence and preaching. *Terata* (wonders) never occurs in the New Testament without *semeia* (signs)—usually as 'signs and wonders', but the word order in Peter's Pentecost speech is 'wonders and signs'. Peter's wonders and signs may refer to: eschatological portents of the day (cf. 'wonders in the heavens above', 2:19); the gifts of the Holy Spirit (cf. 2:4); apostolic signs and wonders recorded later in Acts; or, most likely, the ministry of Jesus (cf. 'wonders and signs' referring to Jesus' life attested by miracles, 2:22). Wonders and signs in Jesus' ministry include: the cosmic disturbances associated with the death of Christ, that is, wonders in the heavens above; or the spectacular miracles (signs) during Jesus' earthly ministry. 'Blood, smoke and fire' (2:19) could also be an apocalyptic phrase referring to the ministry of Jesus as the breaking in of the age to come. Alternatively, the specific referent in Peter's phrase 'wonders and signs' may be intentionally vague to include some or all of the abovementioned possibilities. Indeed, 2:19–21 may refer to the Pentecost effect of bringing into being the new, witnessing Israel alluded to in 2:17–18.

Joel 2:28–32 is programmatic of restored Israel's ministry to Israel—and beyond—on display in the Acts of the Apostles. Ministry occurs as God is pleased to pour out his Spirit with accompanying signs and wonders, enabling his new sons and daughters to prophesy. The analogy with the exodus portents is that the people of God are on the move with a new covenant to direct their future into a New Canaan where new Israel may claim the blessing of 'rest' in God's presence. New Israel will become new people at the commencement of the new creation brought into being by the death-resurrection-ascension of Jesus.

Salvation in Christ sums up this great development in eschatological reality for the new community. In the light of catastrophic portents heralding the historical intervention of Yahweh (2:19–20), Peter concludes the Joel citation with salvation being received by all who call on the name of Jesus (2:21). The divine Christology in Peter's speech declares that salvation will come to everyone who has faith in who Jesus really is. The crowd would immediately think of 'Lord' (2:21) as Yahweh but Peter's use of 'Lord' refers to the elevation of Jesus who is now Lord. Indeed, 2:22 begins a compact, carefully constructed argument leading to the Christological affirmation: 'God has made him both Lord and Messiah, this Jesus whom you crucified' (2:36). The summary of the life, death, resurrection and exaltation of Jesus

(2:22–36) is followed by the hearers' response (2:37) and Peter's call to repentance (2:38–40).

Peter not only proclaims Jesus' authority but also reveals the intolerable situation of the audience who share responsibility for the crucifixion. The audience rapport expands from men (2:22) to brothers (2:29) to the whole house of Israel (2:36). Peter's speech includes a summary of Jesus' life, Jesus' death at the hands of men acting outside of the law (*anomos*, 2:23), Jesus' resurrection (2:24,32), and Jesus' climactic exaltation (2:36). Peter's speech is not only proclamation but also supporting explanation. The significance of the Pentecost event witnessed by the whole house of Israel is not only evidence of Jesus' resurrection but also that the exalted Jesus has poured out the Father's promised gift of the Holy Spirit (2:33). The effect on the disciples witnessed by the crowd—and the miracle of hearing in their own languages—was evidence of a mighty divine intervention.

God had loosed the bonds of death (2:24) in Jesus' resurrection. Peter bases his explanation for Jesus' resurrection (2:25–31) on two important messianic Psalms (16 and 132). Promises to David concerning the eschatological Son of David (2:25–28; cf. Psalm 16:8–11) predict that raising the Messiah from the dead (Psalm 16:10–11) would fulfil the divine oath (Psalm 132:11) that one of David's descendants would sit on his throne forever (2:30; cf. 2 Samuel 7:13). David, indeed, had died and been buried (2:29)—but he had spoken prophetically of the resurrection of the Messiah (2:31–32; cf. Psalm 16:8–11).

Peter moves from Jesus' resurrection to Jesus' exaltation (2:33). Jesus, having received the gift of the Spirit, had initiated the gift of prophetic preaching of the advent of the kingdom to the new Israel and directs the work of the church in preaching messianic forgiveness.

The allusion to Psalm 68 in 2:33 (receiving gifts) adds force to the argument (cf. *oun*, therefore, 2:33) that the risen Jesus must be the eschatological son of David (2:25–31) of whom David spoke in Psalm 16:8–11. Gifts are given to the Messiah (2:33; Psalm 68:18) consequent upon his resurrection and his necessary exaltation. The Targum's paraphrase 'you have ascended to heaven' (Psalm 68:18) refers to Moses the prophet, with the elaboration 'you have taken captivity captive and you have learned the words of the Torah and you have given gifts to men' (cf. Ephesians 4:8–10). But, in context, Psalm 68:18 refers to the victorious ascent of Yahweh to the heavenly Zion to receive the tribute of the vanquished. Furthermore,

Acts 2 interprets Psalm 68:18 as referring to the ascent of Jesus to heaven to receive gifts that he has now given to humankind. God had raised Jesus and Jesus had ascended on high to the right hand of God (2:33)—but David did not ascend on high (2:34).

The significance of Pentecost: redemptive and sanctifying experience

The 'promised Holy Spirit' received by Jesus is the gift promised by Joel which fulfils Moses' wistful desire: 'Would that all the Lord's people were prophets and that the Lord would put his Spirit on them' (Numbers 11:29). In the future, according to Joel, the Spirit of prophecy—which is divine revelation to witness to Jesus, or communicating God's word directly to man, or wisdom, or a revelatory dream or vision—would not be confined to the prophets and leaders of Israel. The gift of the prophetic Spirit could be given to all. Pentecost fulfils this hope and Peter underscores the universality of the promise available to all flesh (2:38). The promise of the gift of the Spirit brings remission of sins and the power to transform and redirect lives.

The concept that Jesus being exalted on high has received the gift of the Spirit (2:33) is metaphorical but there is also a real referent. The phrase 'receive the Spirit' denotes the beginning of some new nexus of functions or activities of the Spirit in a man's life. 2:33 refers to the new activities described by Joel (Acts 2:17–21). Jesus has now received Joel's promise in the sense that he has the power to administer the operation of the Spirit as the Spirit of prophecy. Jesus is now Lord over this gift of the Spirit to be given to the church now that he is exalted to the right hand of God. Having received from the Father the promised Holy Spirit, Jesus then poured this gift out to the church resulting in spiritual gifting. Jesus must have received the gift of the Spirit from the Father who is the Lord of the Spirit. So the Spirit of God has now also become the Spirit of Jesus (16:7) and Jesus—indicating divine Christology—is now able to distribute individual charismata of the Holy Spirit. Thus, through the Spirit, Jesus: directs and empowers the church's mission (2:4,33; 4:8,31; 8:29; 11:12; 13:2,4,9; 16:6ff); gives charismatic wisdom and revelation for the propagation or defence of the gospel (6:3,5,10); and directs, sanctifies and builds up the church (5:1–11; 9:10ff,31; 11:28; 13:52; 15:28).

The crowd had witnessed the pouring out of the Spirit foreshadowed by Joel, and Israel should understand this Pentecost gift of the Spirit as part of the fulfilment and renewal of Israel's covenant. The one whom David addresses as 'my Lord' (2:34; cf. Psalm 110:1) is none other than the exalted Jesus who has now been given dominion over his enemies (2:35) including the last enemy, death. Therefore, Jesus is the redeemer upon whom people must call for salvation. David had unknowingly foretold Jesus' resurrection (Psalm 110:1) and, indeed, Jesus' resurrection established his identity as the Davidic messiah—David's eschatological heir—who is now Lord.

In the Old Testament, God's Spirit referenced the personal presence of the transcendent God. So the Pentecost audience must have been astounded when Peter declared that Jesus received and poured out the Spirit (2:33), that is, the Spirit now proceeds from Christ as from the Father. But only God can act through his Spirit, exercising lordship over and through the Spirit. So if Jesus is now presiding over and directing God's self-revealing vitality then in some sense Jesus has become Lord of the Spirit (cf. Luke 24:49). Thus Spirit in Acts is the self-manifesting and empowering presence of both the Father and the Son. Hence, Christologically, Jesus is one with the Lord God of Joel 2:28-32. So Jesus, at one with the Father, sends the Spirit (2:17; 5:31-2; 11:15-17) just as Jesus said he would (cf. John 14:16-17). The Spirit of God, now the Spirit of Jesus, is the executive power of Jesus' presence as the Messiah. Jesus Christ, at one with the Father in this gifting, has now poured out the Spirit from the throne of God and henceforward—through believers—the Spirit is the means of Jesus' promised continued presence and activity (John 14:28).

Jerusalem residents and rulers were blind to God's purpose and acted to get rid of Jesus. Whereas they were responsible for their actions, nevertheless, their act contributed to God's purpose of enthroning Jesus as Messiah (2:36). 'Therefore' (2:36) indicates that Peter is drawing Christological conclusions from the preceding statements of Jesus' resurrection and heavenly session as messianic king. Enthroned as Lord and Messiah, Jesus will fulfil all the promises made to Israel. God has granted the newly enthroned ruler universal power to rule and judge (Psalm 110:2,6). All the house of Israel should recognise the ascension paradox that the crucified Jesus is now Lord (2:34; cf. Psalm 110:1) and Christ, that is, God and Messiah. Lord, the Greek Old Testament terminology for Yahweh, is now applied to Jesus (2:36). Through the restored Israel, Christ Jesus the Lord will offer salvation to the world (cf. 2:38). The ascension conclusively underscores the deity of

Jesus; the ascension is the fact which supports Peter's theological, Christological conclusions.

Following the Pentecost speech with its disclosure about Jesus (2:36), the crowd who had sought explanation for the Pentecost event 'were cut to the heart' (2:37)—that is, the Jerusalem Jews were moved to repentance because the enthroned Messiah is now pouring out benefits to the Messiah's people (2:37–39). Peter's call to repentance indicates that this offer of release from sins (2:38) and new life with the gift of the Spirit is still available for Israel as a whole in new covenant but especially for Jerusalem, and then the world beyond Israel.

The link between the Spirit and water baptism (2:38) is purposive (with a view to), not causal (because of the forgiveness of sins). The people should repent and accept baptism with a view to receiving the promise of Spirit baptism which identifies believers with the work of the cross. It is the work of the cross that brings about the forgiveness of sins. Peter's offer 'in the name of Jesus' (2:38) appeals to the royal power and authority of the Jewish Messiah and water baptism declares commitment in the name of Jesus leading to further identification with Jesus' death and exaltation. The baptism of the Spirit and forgiveness of sins occurs in regeneration (Luke 12:50; Mark 10:38; John 3). Water baptism is always 'with a view to' the reception of Spirit baptism which may accompany water baptism. Spirit baptism requires the penetration of the work of the cross in the believer's life.

Jesus has now poured out the Spirit on all his followers for ministry. Previously, the Spirit had rested on Jesus during his earthly ministry but not on his followers but God now saves Jews and Gentiles through Jesus' promised messianic reign. If the Jewish nation rejects this promise of the reign of Jesus then the pathos is that the promise which had belonged especially to Israel will be lost by Israel. Accordingly, as Israel continued to reject Jesus' reign, Pentecost also laid the foundation for apostolic ministry to the Gentiles.

Peter concluded his speech by recalling the Abrahamic covenant (2:38–39). 'For the promise is for *you*' (2:39) lifts the pronoun into the emphatic position, balancing the previously emphatic pronoun 'whom *you* crucified' (2:36). The promise of the gift of the Spirit is offered universally (2:39) through time (to your children) and space (in other places) but is first offered to Israel (for you and your children). But reconstituted missionary Israel will be a light to lighten the Gentiles and therefore the contours of the promise extend beyond national Israel to 'all who are far away'—that is, the promise extends to the Gentiles (cf. Ephesians 2:17), to 'all whom the Lord our God will call' (2:39). Peter calls on Israel to come out of the perverted and crooked generation, that is, out from bankrupt national Israel (2:40). These converted Jews provide the nucleus of the new theocratic Christian community.

Remission of sins (justification) is the gift of the Spirit (2:38; 1 Corinthians 12:13), that is, new life through repentance and faith is the gift of the Spirit. In Acts 1-13, the giving of the Spirit to the church is part of the once and for all accomplishment of redemption (*historia salutis*, 2:38) and the gift of the Spirit to believers is part of the ongoing individual application of redemption (*ordo salutis*). Pentecost integrates the church into the once and for all work of Christ, that is, the gift of the Spirit is integrated in the experience of all united to Christ. So the Spirit is the power given to all believers to redirect and transform all Christian experience.

But Pentecost is only a partial realisation of Joel's words for the divine promise says, 'I will pour out my Spirit upon all flesh'. Joel refers only to Israel but the promise in Acts 2 is universal (cf. 'and all flesh will see the salvation of God', Luke 2:31-32; 3:6). The gift was intended for much more than a relatively small group at Pentecost. Subsequent narratives in Acts provide an emphasis on the fuller realisation of this promise, for the response of new groups to the word of God brings similar outpourings of the Spirit because the promise is that all who call out to Jesus will be saved. However there is a distinct Jewish reluctance to move beyond Jerusalem and Judea until Acts 10.

The end of the ages has dawned on those who have the Spirit—who are in Christ—for the gift of the Spirit is the central element in the new covenant promise (Ezekiel 36:27). Sinclair Ferguson defines the Spirit's task as the restoration of divine glory in the world, that is, restoring glory in a creation in which all has fallen short of God's glory.[169] In Christ, the radiance of God's glory is to be restored (2 Corinthians 3:18).

The upper room believers gathered at Pentecost had believed in the earthly Jesus and then in the exalted Jesus. Henceforward from Pentecost, new believers would believe in both the earthly and the exalted Jesus at once. The universal gift is the Holy Spirit. So to believe at Caesarea (Acts 10) involves entering into the same blessing as the crowd received at

---

169 Ferguson, 1996, 91.

Pentecost. Certain manifestations of tongues and prophecy (10:46; 19:6; cf. 8:17) were not evidences of a second distinctly existential experience but, rather, were signs of a redemptive-historical breakthrough in the new covenant era reaching a further significant staging post in the advance of 1:8. Acts 19 (Ephesus) identifies a transition from the world of the old covenant and John's baptism to the world of the new covenant and Spirit baptism. Pentecost as a point in redemptive history is not repeatable, rather, the New Testament points to faith reached by believers because of the outpouring at Pentecost. Because of the outpouring on Jews at Pentecost, Gentiles at Caesarea receive the same gift.

The coming of the Spirit was the evidence of the enthronement of Christ just as the resurrection had been evidence of the efficacy of the atonement. Paul indicates that all believers are baptised with the Spirit and drink the water of the Spirit (1 Corinthians 12:13).

At Pentecost, the Spirit comes as the Spirit of the exalted Christ. And the experience in every baptism of the Spirit (1:5; 2:17–18,33; 10:45; 11:16)—and in each gifting of the Spirit (2:38; 11:17)—is of the exalted Christ. Peter draws the analogy between Pentecost and Cornelius (cf. 11:15–17) because the coming of the Spirit to the Cornelius household marks the breakthrough of the gospel to the Gentile world, as confirmed by the Jerusalem church (cf. 11:18). Peter identifies the experience at Caesarea with the upper room group at Pentecost (2:4; 11:15; cf. John 19:22–23). There seems to be a distinct second stage experience in the case of the Samaritans and Ephesians (8:12,15–17; 19:1–7). Pentecost was an entire Christ-event encompassing Jesus' death, resurrection and ascension. Indeed, Acts records Jesus' actions as the exalted Lord extending the Pentecost blessing but many suggest that Acts does not propose a two-stage Christian experience—like the apostles'—as normative for future Christians. Indeed, Pentecost cannot be repeated for Pentecost was a redemptive gift primarily directed to the restored Israel (2:1–4). Even so, the visible coming of the life-giving Spirit is evidence of the enthronement of Christ just as the resurrection is evidence of the efficacy of the atonement. Therefore, while the historical features of Pentecost are not repeatable, the redemptive and sanctifying experiences of Pentecost are repeatable. Now in Christ the radiance of God's glory is restored in the believer through the Spirit received by faith (2 Corinthians 3:18).

The significance of Pentecost: reception of the Spirit

Pentecost, as the once and for all establishment of redemption in Christ, signifies the onset of the new covenant as suggested by the analogies between Sinai and Pentecost (cf. 2:1–2). Thus Pentecost signifies redemption accomplished, so the assembled believers—previously regenerate through the Spirit during the ministry of Jesus—now become new covenant members and are gifted with the prophetic Spirit. At Pentecost, the exalted Christ comes in his exalted life as the life-giving Spirit presenting his resurrection life. Like Cornelius, from Pentecost on Jews and Gentiles who believe through the Spirit will also receive with regeneration ministry gifts that Christ conferred through the Spirit at Pentecost. Ministry will occur on the basis of divine intervention through the death of Jesus bringing in a new covenant age. Luke documents how the Pentecost revelation reaches the ends of the earth.

The question of the 'content' of the reception of the Spirit at Pentecost for believers is a contested one. For some, Jesus was the only person who possessed the Spirit before Pentecost—and that by virtue of his baptism in the Jordan. Indeed, Jesus was the only person who possessed the Spirit for ministry prior to Pentecost apart from occasions on which the disciples successfully conducted some ministry which relied on contact with Jesus conveying gifts. But prior to Pentecost the disciples were regenerate: their names are written in heaven (Luke 10:20–22); they are fully cleansed (John 13:10); they share Christ's glory (John 17:22–23); and they are now able to receive further gifts of the Spirit (John 14–16).

The Pentecostal audience is comprised of two groups: the upper room believers (1:15); and the wider audience that Peter addresses (2:37–39). The upper room believers are previously regenerated but at Pentecost are further gifted for ministry and received into the new Israel formed at Pentecost. The second group of Peter's audience who responded seem to be like Cornelius, that is, individually regenerated and gifted for ministry by the Spirit at their conversion into the new Israel (cf. 10:47). But this view is not generally accepted, rather, personal spiritual transformation is generally perceived to be a new movement in the New Testament which is not present in the Old Testament.

On and from Pentecost, new believers have the law written on their hearts by the Spirit (Jeremiah 31:34) and receive gifts for ministry. But until the return of Jesus, believers are not free from sin—rather, believers within new Israel are forgiven because of the continuing benefits of the cross (1 John 1:9, 2:2). The transformation will be complete at the return of Christ when all believers will be sinless like Jesus.

The significance of Pentecost: Christ coming to the church in the Spirit

The major differences between the Old and New Testaments (commencing at Pentecost) are: the Spirit is now the universal Spirit; the new covenant is no longer restricted to Israel but includes the nations; the Spirit is now poured out on all flesh (2:17); the blessing of Abraham has come to the Gentiles (Galatians 3:14); the Spirit of the kingdom has been taken away from Israel and given to new Israel who produce the fruits of God's kingdom (Matthew 21:43); and the Spirit of Pentecost is the Spirit of mission. But both testaments are united in the belief in the coming of the kingdom of God, that is, the eschatological lordship of Christ over all creation.

Pentecost was part of the once and for all accomplishment of redemption so baptism with the Spirit at Pentecost is a unique event of epochal significance in the history of redemption. At Pentecost, the church was established as the new covenant people when Christ came personally to the Church in the form of a life-giving Spirit.[170] Further, the coming of the Spirit will emphasise the absolute congruence of the work of the Spirit and the work of Christ as totally interrelated. Christ is now the source of eschatological life, living and working in the church in the Spirit. Christ's coming in exaltation to the church in the power of the Spirit is the crowning achievement of his work.

Pentecost means nothing less than the establishment of the church as the new covenant people of God and the body of Christ. The body of Christ is the dwelling place of God in the Spirit (Ephesians 2:22), that is, the temple of God in which the Spirit of God dwells (1 Corinthians 3:16). All who are incorporated into that Spirit-baptised body share in the gift of the Spirit (1 Corinthians 12:13; Roman 8:9-10). The notion of union with Christ is fundamental for understanding the Spirit's ministry in redemption.

---

170 Gaffin (1979, 19-20) suggests that the nexus between Christ and the Spirit was so complete that the two became equated—made one in the giving of life to the Church as the visible first fruits of Christ's resurrection. The Spirit poured out on the church at Pentecost is the resurrection life of the exalted Christ.

Regeneration is a present reality but the believer awaits its consummation. Justification is an already accomplished and perfect reality as a new status—freed by divine pronouncement from the wrath to come—but this status must be maintained by demonstration of the fruit of the Spirit. Sanctification continues the work of the Spirit and involves a radical break with the dominion of Satan (1 Corinthians 6:11; Romans 6:1–14), developing progressively to final perfection at the return of Christ (cf. 1 Thessalonians 5:23). Glorification has already begun at regeneration and continues through the indwelling Spirit of grace and glory (1 Peter 4:13), reaching its fullness at the return of Christ when believers are fully transformed into the image of Christ. Adoption as sons awaits final acceptance, to be conferred with the redemption of our bodies (Romans 8:23; cf. 1 Corinthians 15:51–53). At the final judgement, justified believers who have longed for his appearing (2 Timothy 4:8) will receive from the righteous judge (the Lord) the crown of righteousness which is full transformation in a body entirely controlled by the Spirit.

The significance of Pentecost: union with Christ

Union with Christ is the great privilege of the believer from Pentecost onwards. Union with Christ is Christ's incarnation in the believer's flesh, that is, we remain in Christ's resurrected life so that he might provide the salvation needed and bring us to full humanness in him. Our union with Christ means that, by heavenly transformation, we will in the future share his perfect heavenly humanness and now our personal condition is progressively changed by the Spirit's work of sanctification towards the full image of Christ (cf. Philippians 3:21). Our true and final life is hidden with Christ in God (Colossians 3:3). Full humanness, heavenly transformation and progressive sanctification are possible only through the indwelling of the Christ by the Spirit by faith. This does not compromise the grace of God in salvation since it is because of God that we are in Christ Jesus (1 Corinthians 1:30) and are being sanctified in that union by the Spirit. Believers were chosen in Christ before the creation of the world so that, blessed in covenant union with him, they might live for the praise of his glory (Ephesians 1:3–4,11–12). And God's choice of us is related to his pre-creation choice of Christ as the God-human mediator.

This union with Christ by the indwelling Spirit is a central theme in Paul's gospel. Christ died for (*huper*) us (Romans 5:6,8). 'With Christ' carries the idea of participation: in his crucifixion (cf. Galatians 2:20); in his burial (Romans 6:4); and in his life (Romans 6:8). Union with Christ is a summary of what it means to be a Christian which is counter parallel to being 'in Adam' as a sinful human being. Adam's sin devolved on humanity by being born in his likeness and 'according to his image' (Genesis 5:3), determining our existence through sin leading to death. Like Adam, we are able to refuse God's will and follow our own choices leading to death but righteousness in Christ through the Spirit will lead to life and complete union with Christ in God at Jesus' return.

The significance of Pentecost: the Spirit of prophecy

The notion of the Spirit as the Spirit of prophecy—divine illumination in wisdom and knowledge directing the lives of God's servants in many and different ways—is prominent for Luke-Acts. This notion was typically Christian but not Jewish.

The Spirit is the power behind apostolic witness to Jesus (cf. 1:8; Luke 24:49). But the empowering of authoritative preaching is not a single activity of the Spirit, rather, authoritative preaching is the effect of different activities of the Spirit. Accordingly, the Spirit may grant to the speaker direct revelation to inform the content of the preaching such as Peter's vision at Joppa informing his preaching in Cornelius' household (Acts 10, the only such occurrence in Acts). Or the Spirit may give to the speaker charismatic wisdom such as Stephen—fulfilling Jesus' prophecy (Luke 21:5)—where the wisdom is not new revelatory content but enhanced insight about the relationship between Israel's history, the Christ event and the hearer's response to Christ combined with the ability to speak clearly and provocatively (6:3,5,10). The influx of the Spirit gave to Stephen charismatic assurance and boldness to speak. This boldness is also evident in Peter's short address before the Jewish rulers (4:8-12), indeed, the reaction of the rulers focused on Peter's boldness which is a referent to the charisma he received. Prophecy, whether oral or written in a letter, was a regular feature of New Testament Christianity (Ephesians 4:11–16). In the Old Testament, prophecy was restricted to a few; but in the New Testament, prophecy is the

Spirit communicating to all believers as they all now share the Spirit of the knowledge of Christ in God.

Pentecost delimits those who now belong to the true Israel. Their faith by the Spirit is in the divinely powered earthly ministry of Jesus or in his message and presence communicated by the disciples who are filled with the Spirit after Pentecost. Thus Jesus continues to direct the life of the Church through the Spirit.

All things in common is a result of receiving the Spirit (2:41-47)

The gift of the Spirit creates awe (2:43) and leads to the ministry of proclamation of the word as the whole church is filled with the Holy Spirit (4:29-31). The Jerusalem community of restored Israel is formed through the apostles' Spirit-empowered ministry of words, wonders and signs (2:43). The result of receiving the Spirit is a community life of unity and sharing, with all things held in common (2:40-47). The Greek imperfect tense verbs denote the continuing nature of fellowship in the restored Israel and what such fellowship would produce: devoted to the teaching of the apostles; helping those in need out of the common pool of resources; and sharing common meals in their homes. This demonstrated *koinonia* (partnership, 2:42) in a concrete example of unity.

Peter and John filled with the Spirit before the Sanhedrin (4:5-22)

The apostles are questioned regarding the authority enabling the healing miracle for the lame man: 'by what power' and, the equivalent question, 'by what name' (4:7). Peter's defence is given under empowerment with boldness from the Holy Spirit (4:8-12). The Sanhedrin could not deny the miracle, the more so since the man who had been healed was present (4:9,14). So, instead, the question was the source of the authority for the healing. Peter forthrightly named the authority as the power—that is, the name (4:10)—of the risen Jesus Messiah who had been crucified by order of this same council at Caiaphas' expedient suggestion (John 11:50), but also subsequently raised to life by God. So Jesus was rejected by the builders, Israel's leaders (4:11; Psalm 118:22)—originally in the Psalm the builders rejecting the cornerstone were the heathen—but Israel's messianic king Jesus (the stone of the Psalm) has nevertheless become the stone holding together the new temple building (Mark 14:58-61). Peter's reference to the rejected stone—recalling Jesus' earlier temple address for much the same audience (Luke 20:9-18)—indicated the pitch of Peter's boldness. Indeed,

Peter concludes that salvation is available only in this rejected but resurrected Jesus; that is, Jesus is the only one who can deliver from the final judgement (4:12).

The new Spirit-inspired boldness of the apostles' Christian witness—and the quality of their defence without the benefit of rabbinic training (4:13)—impressed the Sanhedrin and they could not discredit the miracle. So they ordered the apostles to stop preaching (4:15-22) because they realised that the only way to stop the spread of this new movement was to contain the word of witness in Jesus' name (4:17). Peter and John vehemently refused because they owed obedience to a much higher authority (4:19-20). Peter and John are then threatened and then released by the Sanhedrin.

Filled with the Spirit again for prophecy (4:23-31)

When Peter and John returned to the congregation of believers, the whole church prayed together echoing the language of the Old Testament (cf. Isaiah 37:16-20). Unity in the Spirit and assurance that God was at work in their midst characterised the early Christian community. Their prayer shows that the power of God has moved from the temple to the gathered Christian group which is now the true house of prayer, indeed, the Christian group prays to the one who is the new temple. Their prayer is for boldness in the context of persecution—not for deliverance from persecution (4:29)—in order that they may continue ministry through the power of Jesus (4:30). The presence of the Holy Spirit among them, being individually renewed as they are filled with the Spirit again for ministry, answers their prayer as they continue to speak God's word with boldness (4:31).

Ananias and Sapphira lie to the Spirit (5:1-11)

The 'but' with which this narrative begins causes us to pause and reflect. The Ananias and Sapphira story—upon which great issues in the early church turned—is in contrast to Barnabas' generosity (4:36-37) and is a heinous breach of early Christian fellowship (cf. 4:32-35). The apostles were not profiting from their spiritual elevation but now the first storm of human rage from outside the Church (Acts 4) is complemented by corruption within the church. Ananias professed to make a very significant donation from property sold but only contributed part of the sale price. Peter tells Ananias that he had lied to the Holy Spirit (5:3), that is, he had lied to God (5:4). The church had been so guided by the Spirit that failure to obey church rules was a sin against the Holy Spirit and thus against God!

The unusual word 'kept back' (5:2) refers to the Old Testament story of Achan (Joshua 7)—both Achan and Ananias similarly deceitfully hold back resources which had been dedicated to God. Lack of total commitment has serious consequences. Peter's prophetic, Spirit-inspired insight recognised that the deception had been levelled not merely against church agreement but also against the Spirit's guiding presence so God's judgement falls on both the husband and his complicit wife. As a result, a godly awe descended on the assembly (*ekklesia*, 5:11) and corruption is checked. *Ekklesia* is used in the LXX for gathered Israel but now, for the first time (5:11), *ekklesia* is used of the Christian assembly rather than a Jewish synagogue.

Israel needs the gifts of repentance and the Spirit (5:17-42)

The apostles—freed from incarceration by an angel (cf. 5:19-24)—continued their ministry in the temple precincts until they were discovered and arrested once more (5:25-26). The high priest (5:28) forbad all of them (not just Peter and John, Acts 4) to preach in the 'name' (5:28). Interestingly, it seems that the High Priest cannot bring himself to utter the personal name of Jesus! At the same time, the high Priest wants to absolve the council from the guilt of the death of Jesus (5:28).

Peter replies on behalf of the unified apostolate (5:29): God must be obeyed, not men. The apostolic witness given before the authorities is that the God of their fathers had raised Jesus. Jesus was rejected as accursed by Israel (5:30) but the God of Israel has resurrected Jesus to the point of authority and power as Prince, exalted ruler (5:31; cf. 3:15, 'pioneer', 'leader') and Saviour. So, Peter concludes, Israel needs the gifts of repentance and the Spirit and without these gifts the Sanhedrin will never understand. The witness of the apostles was affirmed by the Holy Spirit in their midst working his ministry of conviction on their hearers (5:32).

Stephen is a deacon full of the Spirit (Acts 6-7)

After perhaps five or six years, the church in Jerusalem is still vibrant and active as God is causing it to grow (6:1). But there is factionalism in the group with an open dispute between the Hebrews (Aramaic speaking Christian Jews who would have been able to speak Greek) and the Hellenists (Greek speaking Christians, probably non-Palestinian Jews).

The apostles needed to give themselves fully to ministry so they could not be diverted by the disgruntled or burdened by a crushing administrative load. Led by the apostles, the wisdom of the congregation (6:5) was to choose and appoint seven men with Greek names to attend to the problem. The congregation presented their choice to the apostles then prayed and congregationally laid hands on those appointed (6:6). The seven were of good standing, full of the Spirit and wisdom—evidently mature in the faith and theologically astute. The narrative singles out Stephen at the head of the list, adding a comment on his spirituality. Both Stephen and Philip (second on the list) are important for subsequent narratives. Nicolas, a proselyte of Antioch, is also chosen indicating the diversity of the congregation and the place of Antioch in the later narrative. Acts 6 does not call the seven appointees deacons however, as the verb indicates, they did perform this function (6:2–3). The Spirit attests the required personal standing of those who are to be chosen as 'deacons'.

The name Stephen means 'crown' and, indeed, to Stephen—who is faithful unto death—God gives the crown of life (cf. Revelation 2:10). The emphatic, repeated word that describes Stephen is (a permanent state of being) 'full' (6:3,5; 7:55; cf. 6:10) of the Spirit and wisdom. The Spirit controlled Stephen's life in all its dimensions and the Spirit was the source of his spiritual power. The spread of the divine word through Stephen continued the fulfilment of the divine purpose. Accordingly, Stephen is not simply consigned to tables because the planned division of labour breaks down in the face of Stephen's power in the Spirit. Human plans to progress the mission were not God's plans! Philip's ministry shows the same surprising shift. The narrative reports the progress of the word,[171] emphasising the Spirit's control of the mission.

Stephen entered a life of full ministry in the vein of Pentecost with wonders and signs (6:8). He witnessed vigorously in synagogue disputes, particularly in Greek-speaking synagogues including that of the Freedmen (that is, former slaves). Stephen's powerful witness before the leaders of Israel forms the early climax of Acts. He disturbed the synagogue audiences when he spoke but they were not able to match the power and wisdom of his arguments.

As they had done with Jesus—and for much the same reasons—the Jews decided to kill Stephen using, almost precisely, the same false charges. The Jews accuse Stephen of attacking the foundation of Jewish life: temple and Torah, God and Moses (cf. the charges against Jesus, Mark 14:58; 15:29; Matthew 26:61; 27:40). Significantly, the people now sided with the

---

171 6:7; 9:31; 12:24; 16:5; 19:20; 28:30–31.

accusers (6:12) even though earlier they had sided with the apostles (4:21; 5:26). Stephen had not only preached the inconsistencies of the oral law, rather, the thrust of the charges was that Stephen had preached the end of the Mosaic age. The end of the law era (cf. against Moses, 6:11) had arrived with the impending destruction of the temple (cf. against God, 6:11). False witnesses said that Stephen spoke against Moses but, like Moses, Stephen's face shone (6:15; Exodus 34:29-35). False accusers also said that Stephen spoke against God but God had given to Stephen the fullness of the Spirit, which his speech demonstrated.

Stephen's opponents—the Sadducees—accused Stephen not only of challenging them and their ideology, but they also said that Stephen challenged the place of the temple which was the institution that guaranteed the Sadducees' power. Moses' glory had come to his face from outside but Stephen glowed from the inner spiritual radiance of his soul (6:15) which was the product of a transformed Christian character.

Acts 7 includes Stephen's speech and his death. Like Jesus, Stephen rejected the temple as 'made with hands' (*cheiropoietois*, 7:48; cf. Mark 14:58; John 2:19-21). According to Stephen, Israel had failed to recognise the preparatory character of its religious institutions. The Spirit heightened the effect of Stephen's preaching which included the accusation that Israel had killed God's messengers including Jesus (7:51-52). The vision granted to Stephen at the climax of his speech (7:55-56) attested conclusively to God's presence through the Spirit. Full of the Holy Spirit (7:55), Stephen could bear witness to the present reality of Jesus Christ at the right hand of God. Stephen looks with prophetic vision through the open heavens at Jesus, now the glorified Son of Man, standing in the heavens with God where Daniel saw that he would be (Daniel 7:13). Jesus had affirmed that he would sit in heaven at the right hand of God (Matthew 26:64) and, having been given a kingdom and dominion, Jesus would be there in vindication of his saints. Then the Sanhedrin inflicted its punishment of death (7:57-60).

Missionary expansion empowered by the Spirit (8:1-3)

The persecution following the death of Stephen scattered the church out of Jerusalem but the Apostles remained in Jerusalem as the centre for the new Israel. Philip is one of the deacons chosen because he is full of the Holy Spirit (6:3). After Stephen's death, Philip's ministry (8:4-40) is the beginning of general missionary activity extending to Phoenicia, Cyprus and Antioch (11:19). The Jews probably expelled Hellenists from Jerusalem because they presumed them to be anti-temple compared with the presumably pro-temple Hebrews. Martin Hengel may be right in suggesting that the expelled Christian Hellenists had correctly claimed that Jesus the Messiah superseded Moses and that the gospel had taken the place of the exodus and Sinai, that is, that the new covenant had superseded the Mosaic covenant (cf. Paul's view in his letters to the Romans, Galatians, and 1 Corinthians).[172]

The Spirit at work in Christ-like ministry in Samaria (8:4–25)

The narrative about Philip begins with him being chosen as one of the seven to wait at tables (6:5). Philip was evidently among those scattered by persecution (8:1–4) with 8:4 representing the first significant fulfilment of Jesus' command to be witnesses beyond Jerusalem and Judea to Samaria and to the end of the earth (1:8). Philip goes with the Christian dispersion to Samaria—the old capital of Northern Israel under the divided kingdom—proclaiming Christ and continuing the ministry of Jesus: working signs (8:6,13); and preaching the kingdom (8:12). Clear evidences of the work of the Spirit attended his Christ-like ministry including exorcisms and healings (8:6–8). Phillip attracted great crowds with spectacular results (8:8). Before Phillip's ministry in Samaria, Simon had been practicing magic in the city and was hailed for the divine powers that he appeared to demonstrate (8:9–11). Luke uses a different word for Simon's wonders (*mageia*, 8:9) to contrast magic with Christian signs and wonders. Simon had boastfully accepted acclamations from the people (8:9) but his influence ceased when Philip came preaching the advent of the kingdom through the exaltation of Jesus. The city now gave heed (*proseichon*, 8:6) to Philip but they had formerly listened eagerly (same verb, *proseichon*, 8:11) to Simon! Even Simon believed and received baptism (8:13).

Peter and John came from Jerusalem—the focal point from which all mission must be commenced—to extend the hand of fellowship to the new believers of the old Northern kingdom who had received the word of God! Jerusalem is the verifying and unifying element in world mission so when a new development in the spread of the gospel occurred in Samaria, Jerusalem (the home of the apostles as witnesses of the risen Lord) must know (cf. 8:14). After the laying on of hands by the apostles (8:14–17), the Samaritans

---

172 Hengel, 1979, 72–73.

received the Spirit which, so far, God had withheld from them. Acts 8 is unique in presenting a body of baptised believers who remained without the promised Spirit for a significant time (the time it took the apostles to arrive after the evangelisation was well under way).

8:16 is the critical verse. For emphasis, *oudepo* (not yet) begins the clause at the beginning of the verse and the participle baptised is modified by *monon* (only). Luke is pointing to a highly unusual situation. In Acts, the laying on of hands does not always accompany baptism but the laying on of hands is elsewhere associated with receiving the Spirit (9:17; 19:6). The withholding of the Spirit from the Samaritans during Philip's ministry does not point to a defect in Philip's ministry since the genuine belief of the Samaritans presumably indicated activity of the Spirit (8:12,14).

For the first time (cf. John 4), post-ascension ministry had reached Samaria (cf. the intention of 1:8). The Samaritans' reception of the Holy Spirit (8:17) from the hands of the apostles bridged the spiritual gap between Samaritans and the first, Jewish Christians. The Spirit was the confirming agent who descended on the Samaritans when they submitted to the Jerusalem apostles thereby forcing the two separated Israelite bodies to unite. Heterodox Samaria was restored to Jerusalem orthodoxy as the focal point of new covenant faith but without the former emphasis on the temple (cf. John 4:20-21,41ff). The laying on of hands incorporated Samaria into Christian fellowship, symbolising the re-establishment of fellowship between Jerusalem and Samaria which had been ruptured since the Northern exile of 722 BC. The bestowal of the Spirit in this special circumstance documented the incorporation of the believing North into the restored Israel.

Simon does not receive the Spirit, instead, his heart returns to evil as he seeks to buy the capacity to confer the gift of the Spirit (8:18-20). Simon regarded the Spirit as a power mechanism associated with the laying on of hands and hence a marketable commodity. Simon had genuinely believed and accepted baptism but he could not give up his old infatuation. Simon's conversion parallels the conversion of the Samaritans, emphasising that: conversions are not the product of mere intellectual persuasion (cf. 5:14; 13:12; 16:34; 18:8); conversion must be accompanied by receiving the gift of the Spirit; and the gifts (or gift as in Spirit) of God are not traffickable (8:20). So Simon, who relied on the art of persuasion and the appearance of special gifting, could not have a part in any Christian ministry (8:21-24). God's gift of the Spirit was not for sale! Simon—identified in later Christian tradition as an arch-heretic—apparently humbles himself and repents, as commanded by Peter, and requests prayer.

The Samaritan episode does not illustrate special power inherent in the apostolic laying on of hands, rather, it shows that the apostles—representative of the continuing Israel who first received the Spirit—must confirm each new stage in the extension of the church in the mission of Israel. Jerusalem is the mother church because it is the home of the birth of the new Israel and the home of the apostles who are witnesses of the risen Lord. The Samaritan event illustrates that the church had reached a decisive stage in her mission.

Any mission must begin in Jerusalem and move from Jerusalem (1:8) for the new and decisive event of salvation took place in Jerusalem. Jesus' departure (cf. *exodus*, Luke 9:31) and ascension (*analempsis*, Luke 9:51) occurred in or near Jerusalem, and Jerusalem is the latter point for world pilgrimage (Isaiah 2:2-4). The Lukan view is that Jerusalem, apostles and Spirit belong together in the picture of the early church—so the apostles should be involved in any extension of the church beyond Jerusalem and Judea, and the Spirit should appear as the confirming agent.

The Spirit directs Philip to the Ethiopian treasurer (8:26-39)

After his work at Samaria, Philip is directed by the Spirit (8:29) to a chariot on the Gaza road where he finds an Ethiopian eunuch reading from Isaiah. The eunuch invites Phillip up into his chariot and inquires about the meaning of Isaiah's text. Philip explains that Isaiah was writing about Jesus. The Ethiopian eunuch is returning south to his country but when they came across some water the eunuch presumes to ask Philip to baptise him (8:36-38), expecting a positive response even though his physical condition disqualified him from entering the assembly of the Lord under the Mosaic covenant (Deuteronomy 23:1). The predicted restoration of Israel indicates that the new people of God will include outcasts (Isaiah 56:3-5,8).[173] In this new era, nothing should prevent the emasculated gentile's baptism. So Philip baptises him. The Spirit initiated and concluded this encounter (8:29,39) but the account does not say whether the eunuch received the Spirit, nevertheless, after the Spirit snatched Philip away the eunuch went on his way rejoicing which probably indicates reception of the Spirit (cf. 13:52). After the divinely arranged meeting, Philip finds himself north at Ashdod and he

---

173 cf. Pao, 2000, 141.

continues to preach while he travels in his Spirit-directed mission until he comes to Caesarea (8:40).

Saul is filled with the Spirit for Gentile ministry (9:1-19a)

The conversion of Saul is reported in 9:1-30.[174] Ananias' vision is in the form of a typical prophetic call (9:10-16). The Lord (Jesus) instructed Ananias to go to a particular place and seek a particular individual, indicating with the attention seeking 'for behold' (9:11) that something surprising is to follow. Saul is praying and has seen Ananias coming to heal him. Ananias knows Saul's reputation and his reasons for coming to Damascus and is, understandably, reluctant (9:13-14). But the Lord overcomes Ananias' reserve by announcing the very different future in store for Saul who is now a chosen instrument (9:15-16). Saul is chosen to be Christ's messenger to the nations, to take up the ministry that the apostles as a whole should have exercised—and, in this sense, chosen out of due time (cf. 1 Corinthians 15:8). Saul receives the Spirit (9:17) and, for the first time in Acts, there is reference to a Gentile mission (9:15). Saul is chosen not only to take the name of Jesus in a suffering ministry before Gentiles and kings in the wider world but also to take the name of Jesus to the children of Israel who are not forgotten.

Ananias exactly fulfils Saul's vision (9:17-19a; cf. 9:12)—entering the house where Saul is residing and laying his hands on the man who had violently laid hands on Christians (cf. 8:3; 9:2),[175] and restoring Saul's sight. With his first words (in Aramaic, as is evident from the transliteration *Saoul*, 9:17), Ananias enacts the changed identity of Saul who is no longer 'this man' (9:13) but is now a 'brother' member of the Christian community. Ananias says that he has come so that Saul may receive his sight and be full (*pleroo*, 9:17; not filled with, which would use the Greek verb *pimplemi*) of the Spirit as a continuing endowment for ministry. Ananias is not referring to a gift for an occasion, rather, Saul is commissioned by the Spirit for ministry then filled with the Holy Spirit and then he is baptised. The

---

174 An introduction (9:1-2) is followed by: the bright light which is symbolic of being turned by the Spirit from darkness to light (9:3-4); the epiphany of Christ and Saul's response (9:5-9); the appearance of the Lord to Ananias (9:10-16); Ananias mediates the gift of power to heal and baptises Saul (9:17-19a); and the persecutor becomes the persecuted witness (9:19b-30).

175 Clark, 2002, 161.

restoration of sight occurs so it is reasonable to assume that the reception of the Spirit has also occurred, perhaps connected with his baptism (9:18).

After preaching in Damascus, Saul spent seven years in Arabia (the Transjordanian region). By the good offices of Barnabas—who appears to be open to new developments—Saul is brought to the apostles in Jerusalem (9:27). Saul cannot claim spiritual equality with the Jerusalem apostles since he does not meet the requirements of 1:21ff., however, Barnabas says that Saul has also seen the Lord (clarifying 9:3-6 which is not clear on this detail).

Pauline apostleship rests on the threefold recitation of the Damascus Road story (Acts 9, 22, 26) together with Paul's claim to have the Spirit and be under the special direction of the Spirit. Saul freely moved about and spoke openly in Jerusalem but, following an attempt on his life by Greek Jews, he was sent by the Christian community to Tarsus (9:28-30). But even though Saul is now the nominated apostle to the Gentiles—equipped by the Spirit for this apostolic ministry—neither Saul nor his early mentor Barnabas will be the one to open the missionary door to the Gentiles, rather, the strongly Jewish Peter of the twelve original apostles will do this. Luke's narrative continually shows Paul to be strongly directed by the Spirit and—with Barnabas' important role as a Jerusalem envoy—the narrative distinguishes Paul and Barnabas as an apostolic pair who, though not of the original twelve (cf. 9:27; 15:2), are nevertheless closely related to Jerusalem.

Opposition to Saul in Jerusalem required his return to his home city, Tarsus. Indeed, the increasing focus on circumcision and Torah in Jerusalem would cause difficulties for the Pauline mission there, including a long-term imprisonment. Even so, Saul continued to see Jerusalem as the salvation history centre of the Christian world (cf. 21:17-26; Romans 15:25-33).

The comfort of the Paraclete multiplying the church (9:31-43)

A bridge in the narrative returns to Peter and the penetration of the gospel into Judea but not yet to the Gentiles. This is a time of stable church growth with the abatement of persecution (9:31). The church is developing a distinctive life-style—walking in the fear of the Lord—and is being strengthened by the activity of the Paraclete (*paraklesis*, 9:31). The Holy Spirit is multiplying the church. However, Peter declares in the healing of

Aeneas that the source of all the blessings bestowed by Pentecost on the church is Jesus Christ (9:34).

The Spirit directs Peter to table fellowship with Gentiles (10:1-43)

Divine intervention involving a Jerusalem Apostle initiates the movement of the gospel to the Gentiles. By divine guidance (10:15), Peter proceeded from Joppa to Caesarea—with Jewish witnesses, for this visit had great potential for damage and division within the Jewish Christian community (cf. 10:45). Evidently, Peter and the rest of the apostles had great reservations about a Gentile mission as the visit to Cornelius occurred perhaps ten years after the death of Christ. Peter did not intend to lead a mission to the Gentiles but he was emboldened by the vision to enter a Gentile home. God had overruled so that the church would go beyond the boundaries of Judaism to open the mandate of the Abrahamic covenant to the whole world.

For Peter, movement to the Gentiles would violate his commitment to God and render him unfit in God's eyes. Peter's speech at Cornelius' house (10:34b-43)—the first direct Christian address to Gentiles—repeats the concepts of Luke's Nazareth manifesto (cf. Luke 4:16-30). Since it is evident that God had brought both sides (Jews and Gentiles) together, Peter opens the door to the Gentiles by recalling the biblical truth that God was the God of all humankind. Indeed, the central issue in the Cornelius narrative was not the preaching of the gospel but the table fellowship of Peter with the Gentiles. This was the substance of the later Jerusalem complaint (11:3). For Peter, the Spirit had given divine confirmation in this first stage of ministry to the Gentiles that table fellowship with Gentiles is now permitted (10:19-20). It was on this basis that Peter went to be with the Gentiles. The three men visiting from Cornelius probably recognised that the request for Peter to visit the house of a Gentile would offend and therefore prefaced their request with a statement of Cornelius' virtues (10:22). But the virtues of the case did not persuade Peter, rather, the Spirit's prior direction (10:19) impels Peter to go.

Peter's summary of Jesus' ministry (10:35-38) appears to be modelled on Luke 4:16-30 for, in both passages: the word *dektos* (acceptable, 10:35; cf. Luke 10:35)—rarely used elsewhere—is used; the message is 'sent' by God (10:36; cf. Luke 4:18); the 'he is Lord of all' content of the message is, like the angels' message to the shepherds (Luke 2:14), the essential universality of the gospel (10:36; cf. Luke 4:26-27) envisaging the reception of the Gentiles; 'preaching peace' (10:36; cf. Isaiah 52:7) interprets *euangelisasthai ptochois* (to evangelise the poor, Luke 4:18); the proclamation of the gospel begins in Galilee (10:37; cf. Luke 4:14-16); Nazareth is mentioned (10:38; cf. Luke 4:16), the only other references to Nazareth occurring in the infancy narratives; Jesus' rejection is described (10:39; cf. Luke 4:28-29); and the Holy Spirit is a special endowment of Jesus as the Messiah, the Anointed One (10:38; cf. Luke 4:14,18). Luke understood the work of the Spirit as the power operative and effective in the spread of the gospel.

Peter then draws attention to the Gentile mission as he completes the summary of the gospel from Jesus' infancy to his resurrection (10:39-43). The Jewish emphasis in the narrative makes it clear that salvation is of the Jews but for the entire world and that Cornelius needs to hear this account of the ministry of Jesus Messiah—including healings, exorcisms, and benefactions from Galilee to Jerusalem; from birth to death and resurrection. The universal message of the gospel is that Jesus is Lord of all (10:36), the judge of the living and the dead (10:42). This universal message of the gospel anticipates the general resurrection and the last judgement. The message of Jesus is now a faith for the world: there is salvation for whoever believe in Jesus' name (10:35,43).

The Spirit falls on Gentiles (10:44-48)

The Spirit interrupts Peter's sermon by being 'poured out' on the Gentiles prior to their baptism (10:44-45), indicating that God's choice necessarily precedes community endorsement. The Spirit 'fell on them' (10:44), reflecting relatively common Old Testament imagery of the Spirit (in Isaiah 32:15 and 44:3-4, the future action of the Spirit on Israel brings spiritual life and growth like the vivifying effect of God pouring out water on parched earth; cf. Ezekiel 39:29; Zechariah 12:10; Joel 2:28-32). The Spirit is not some kind of a liquid, rather, poured out indicates the copious nature of the gift. The experience of the Spirit will be rich, vivifying and transforming.

A Gentile Pentecost-like reception of the Spirit[176] (including speech in tongues, 10:46; cf. 2:6-11; perhaps the tongues spoken at Caesarea, like Pentecost, were foreign languages) interrupts Peter. As the Spirit fell on

---

176 While Acts 10 cannot reproduce Pentecost—which was the gift of the Spirit to bring into being the new Israel including the admission of the Gentiles—nevertheless, a manner of receiving the Spirit like Pentecost is reproduced in Acts 10.

the Gentile audience—without any associated rite or institution—the Spirit endorsed, by his holy presence, the word preached by the apostle (cf. 10:44,45,47). God had initially poured out the eschatological gift on Jews (2:38) but now the same gift was also poured on Gentiles, and circumcised Jews had witnessed it (10:45)! The action completes the divine orchestration of proceedings from Peter's vision in Joppa to its conclusion and, like the beginning action in Joppa, Peter really only played a minor role. This outpouring was God's acceptance of the Gentiles. They could not now be called common or unclean for 'they received the Spirit just as we have' (10:47; cf. 11:15,17; 15:8). So Peter does not raise the issue of circumcision when he approached Christian baptism (10:48) and, asking the Jewish witnesses whether anyone could object to the identifying mark of baptism, no objections were raised. Presumably, these Jewish witnesses baptised the Gentiles.

This important section speaks of both water baptism and the reception of the Spirit. The purpose of Peter's visit was to declare the message whereby Cornelius' household will be saved (11:14). But the Cornelius episode of reception of the Spirit followed by baptism seems to reverse the order of 2:38. Evidently, 2:38 does not say when or how the Spirit will come with regard to baptism, simply that there is a connection between the two. The water baptism that followed in Caesarea is the public affirmation of the baptism of the Spirit already received and indicated that regeneration had, with repentance and faith in Jesus, already occurred.

Peter tells Jerusalem that the Spirit fell on Gentiles (11:1-18)

Peter must now justify himself, in Jerusalem, to the critical Christian body in Judea because the step taken at Caesarea was a turning point in the proclamation of the gospel as it raised questions pertaining to the basis of Christian fellowship between Jews and Gentiles. Israel must understand that these conversions attested the outworking of the new covenant and the rejection, by the cross, of the Mosaic Covenant. The affront in Jerusalem of Peter eating with uncircumcised Gentiles is narrated directly (11:3). This covenant transgressing abandonment of 'Jewishness' is the substance of Acts 11. The Gentiles may have exercised faith in Jesus but did this make them members of the covenant people?[177]

---

177 Johnson, 1992, 200.

The men who criticise Peter in Acts 11 must have been the apostles and church members in Jerusalem. In his explanation, Peter makes it clear that he was an orthodox Jew who did not intend to defile himself. But Peter ate with Gentiles—a religious sin of the worst kind—and that called Peter's Jewishness and, in their judgement initially, his salvation into question. But God had sovereignly intervened in a vision and with instruction by the Holy Spirit, and then the Spirit fell on the new Gentile converts while he was still preaching. Peter was convinced that the Gentiles at Caesarea had received the same gift that the disciples received at Pentecost, namely, the Holy Spirit. The rules for Jewish orthodoxy were changing! With all their religious and national inhibitions, only divine intervention could have got a Gentile mission off the ground!

The affront taken by the Jerusalem congregation infers deference to the Mosaic covenant by Jewish Christians after the cross, which would have informed their attitude to Gentile Christians. Peter's experience at Caesarea should have definitively addressed any difference between Jewish and Gentile Christians under Jesus' new covenant. But Paul will later take issue with Peter's continuing religiously superior attitude to Gentile believers at Antioch (Galatians 2:11-14). Paul's letters to the Galatian and Roman churches point to the demise of the Mosaic covenant following the death of Christ.[178] Indeed, the advent of the new covenant (cf. Luke 22:20; cf. 2 Corinthians 3:6) renders the nationalistic identification of circumcision to have no religious significance (cf. 1 Peter 2:4-10).

In Acts the phrase 'be baptised with the Holy Spirit' is only used twice (1:5; 11:16), referring to unique one-time events, namely: the Pentecost events in Jerusalem and Caesarea. Whereas there are no other commands to be baptised in the Spirit, there are continual prayers for the filling of the Spirit. Peter relates the coming of the Spirit at Caesarea to the prophetic promise given by John the Baptist (11:15-16), namely: John had baptised with water but the one coming after him would baptise in the Holy Spirit.

Peter's explanation convinced the meeting of circumcised Jewish Christians to recognise that, now, uncircumcised Gentile believers also shared in the blessings of eternal life. The ministry to Israel remained primary (cf.

---

[178] The Epistle to the Galatians—addressing a similar problem caused by Peter—repudiates the Jewish covenant and offers in its place an understanding of the significance of the new covenant. I have written about this in my commentaries on Romans (2005) and Galatians (2006).

'also', 11:18) but it was evident that God had granted to the Gentiles repentance that leads to life and the Jerusalem church now agreed that if Gentiles received the same Spirit as they did then God must have granted them entry into his new covenant through repentance and forgiveness. The gift of the Spirit was the down payment on the future completeness of resurrected life for both Jewish and Gentile believers.

A ministry by Israel brought into being a Gentile church in Caesarea but a key question about whether there could be table fellowship between Jewish and Gentile Christians remained unresolved for Peter and other Jewish Christians. Pertinent to this question is the fact that the Gentile Caesarean experience and the Jewish Pentecost experience are parallel events because both relate: the outpouring of the Spirit (2:17–18,33; 10:45); Spirit baptism (1:5; 11:16); the gift of the Spirit for ministry (2:38; 11:17); and speaking in other tongues (2:4; 10:46).

Pentecost is not repeatable as a once and for all event in redemptive history. The coming of the Spirit at Pentecost is the evidence of the enthronement of Christ just as the resurrection is evidence of the efficacy of the atonement. Baptism and Spirit are related together on seven important occasions in the New Testament, five of which clearly refer to Pentecost in virtually identical language with respect to the role of the Spirit (Matthew 3:11; Mark 1:8; John 1:33; Acts 1:5; 11:16). In each of these, Christ is the baptiser and the Spirit is the medium in which baptism takes place.

The Spirit is central to continuity in salvation history (11:19–30)

Antioch in northern Syria was the third largest city in the Roman Empire—after Rome and Alexandria—and the seat of the Roman provincial administration in Syria. The church at Antioch was formed by Christians who had been scattered in the aftermath of Stephen's death, that is, not by direct evangelisation from Jerusalem but by diaspora Jews proclaiming the gospel to Jews (11:19). But the Antioch church would also be the sponsor of missionary activity to the Roman world. Gentile Christians from Cyprus and Cyrene penetrated the church at Antioch and this was accompanied by great blessing as they preached Jesus to Hellenists (Greek speaking Jews, 11:20; some texts read Hellenes, that is, Greeks) who then believed and turned to the Lord. When news of what had happened reached Jerusalem (11:22), the apostles appropriately sent Barnabas to ensure continuity between the restored Israel in Jerusalem and the rapidly growing church at

Antioch (11:23). Indeed, Barnabas had come from a dispersion, Cypriot family (cf. 11:20) and was full of the Holy Spirit and faith (11:24) as Stephen had been (6:5). Barnabas saw the potential of this work of God (11:23). Full of the Holy Spirit, Barnabas departed from fruitful ministry at Antioch, for a time, to travel to Tarsus to seek Paul so that they could return together to ministry in Antioch.

Luke recognised in Paul and Barnabas an apostolic pair: both are described as being full of or filled with the Holy Spirit and, whereas both are distinguished from the original twelve (9:27; 15:2), Luke is nevertheless concerned to show their close relationship with the Jerusalem church long before the confirming commissioning to apostolic evangelisation at Antioch (13:1ff). Paul and Barnabas are commissioned for a specific apostolic ministry to the Gentile world. Luke neither created the idea of the Jerusalem twelve apostles nor did he seek to exclude the apostleship of Paul. Evidence that Luke sees both Paul and Barnabas as apostles of the Lord—not simply as emissaries of a local congregation—includes: Paul's call, received at his conversion, is to be a universal witness of the gospel (9:15; cf. 13:1–4; 22:1ff.; 26:1ff); both are called, specifically, by the Spirit (13:1–4); both are described as being filled with or full of the Holy Spirit (9:17; 11:24). Ultimately, it is the Spirit who sends Paul and Barnabas out on their first missionary journey, probably speaking through prophets (13:1,4).

But Paul never makes a claim to have the Spirit in any greater measure than any other church member, rather, he stresses that the one Spirit is at work in the entire body of Christ (1 Corinthians 12:3). However there are moments when Paul, as an apostle, claims specifically to possess the Spirit of the Lord. To the pneumatics in the Corinthian congregation, Paul says—not with any doubt in his mind but, rather, with a certainty that is underlined by his touch of sarcasm—'I think I also have the Spirit of God' (1 Corinthians 7:40). Paul's proclamation of the word of the cross has been accompanied by demonstration of the Spirit's power (1 Corinthians 2:4,13; cf. 1 Thessalonians 1:5; Romans 15:17–19). Paul knows that the reason he is an apostle is because he has seen the Lord (1 Corinthians 9:1; 15:8). Paucity of references to the Damascus Road experience perhaps attests the difficulty Paul had in convincing those who challenged his authority that his vision was an objective call. It appears that Paul is forced to employ the 'pneumatic' argument even to the point where he must engage in folly, boasting over the signs and marks of a true apostle (cf. 2 Corinthians 12:12 in the context of 11:1–12:13).

Thus Paul appeals to his readers that they are, themselves, his workmanship in the Lord (1 Corinthians 9:1)—a letter written not with ink but by the Spirit of the Living God (2 Corinthians 3:3). Paul not only claims the gift of tongues, which some Christians prized inordinately, but also other special experiences of the Spirit together with the Spirit-worked signs of an apostle. But his own evaluation of these experiences and signs is different from that of his opponents.

The pneumatic, charismatic nature of Paul's apostolate is clear from the list of ministerial gifts of the Spirit (1 Corinthians 12:28). Paul's apostolic office is called a charism, a concrete gift of grace (Romans 1:5; cf. 1 Corinthians 3:10). Nevertheless, in Paul's thinking the connection between the apostolate and the Spirit in no way stands in tension with the origins of his office in the encounter with the risen Lord. Whereas Paul's commission and authority comes from the Lord, the power and ongoing certification of Paul's ministry was from the Spirit who is the Spirit of the Lord (2 Corinthians 3:17). Indeed, Paul's claim to speak the Spirit's words is a claim to speak the words of the *martus* (cf. 14:3; 26:16). So there is no tension in Paul between the two essential elements of his apostolate, that is, between official (dominical) authority and charism (certification) by the power of the Spirit. The assumption that Paul and Luke have different views on the apostolate—in particular, the link between the apostle and the Spirit—is not correct.

There is no tension in Paul or Luke between apostle and charisma. The Spirit confirms the choice of an apostle by equipping and directing him, and performing signs through him that attest the power of the gospel. But in Acts the link between apostle and Spirit does not serve an apologetic purpose as it does in Paul's letters. Rather, in Acts the link between apostle and Spirit serves to develop a central theme of the universality of the gospel. Every decisive step in the extension of the church from Jerusalem to Rome is marked by the Spirit's guidance as he works through the apostles who represent the risen Lord himself. The justification of the Gentile mission is the narrative of the Spirit at work.[179] The apostles do not authenticate the Spirit, rather, the Spirit authenticates the apostles as they represent the Lord in the movement of the church to ever widening circles.

---

[179] Wilson, 1973, 241.

While it is the whole people of God as the Israel of the last times that possess the Spirit, it is the apostles as the original witnesses of the Lord who are led to grasp the significance of the universality of the gospel and the Abrahamic mission of Israel. Historically, it may have been the Hellenists in Antioch who were the first real missionaries of the church but it was the apostles led by the Spirit who had to confirm the Gentile mission. Continuity in salvation history is one of Luke's major themes in Acts, developed in three ways: continuity between the acts of God and his people in the Old Testament, and the acts of God and new Israel in the last times (Jervell rightly identifies continuity in salvation history in Acts in terms of the fulfilment of the promises once given to Israel);[180] continuity between the ministry of Jesus and the ministry of the apostles, demonstrated by the activity of the Spirit; and continuity between the original apostolic ministry of the twelve in Jerusalem and the apostolic ministry to the Gentile world.

The Spirit is central to this continuity in salvation history, indeed: the Spirit is called the Spirit of Jesus (16:7); and the presence and work of the Spirit in the word the apostles proclaim and the mighty works they do confirm the apostles' identity both as the Israel of the end-time and as the authorised witnesses of the risen Lord. By the Spirit's power, the words and deeds of the apostles represent the continuation of the ministry of Jesus himself. To speak and act in the Spirit is the same as speaking and acting in the name of Jesus. Paul is not a second-class apostle—even if his apostolate rests, historically, on later foundations—because Paul possesses the Spirit and the Spirit confirms Paul's work.

The prophet Agabus, from Judea (cf. 21:10), is present in the church at Antioch. Through the Spirit (11:28)—that is, depending on a divine gift—Agabus predicted a worldwide famine in a divine pronouncement following which the Antioch disciples arranged a collection for the church in Jerusalem (11:29). This collection became the norm by which Diaspora churches, probably until AD 70, recognised the theological primacy of Jerusalem. Barnabas and Saul were chosen to deliver this act of church fellowship.

The Spirit sends Barnabas and Saul out on mission (13:1-12)

The *ekklesia* (church, 13:1) in Antioch is equipped with prophets and teachers who, together, provide insight into the Scriptures. As the church in Antioch is worshipping (13:2), she is willing to surrender its best candidates

---

180 Jervell, 1972, 53.

when the Spirit's message leads them to send Barnabas and Saul on mission (13:3). Barnabas and Saul had already proved themselves in the congregation as prophets and teachers (13:1). Thus the ground-breaking mission to the Roman Empire is directed by the Spirit (13:4) just as Jesus' ministry had been directed by the Spirit (Luke 4:1,14).

In Cyprus, Barnabas and Saul (nominated as Paul by Luke from the first mention of the filling of the Spirit at the start of this Gentile mission, 13:9) go to the synagogue to preach their first mission sermon (13:5). Going first to the Jewish synagogue will be the missionary pattern for Paul's journeys. At Paphos—the seat of government—a Jewish sorcerer named Bar Jesus (also called Elymas, 13:6,8), a Jewish opponent described as 'a son of the devil' (13:10), demonically opposed their ministry to the Roman proconsul Sergius Paulus. Then the Holy Spirit, superintending the mission, enabled the first breakthrough in this Gentile ministry in the court of the proconsul (13:9ff) by thrusting Paul forward in opposition to the magician. Paul speaks with prophetic power as he confronts this opponent of the gospel and convinces the proconsul to believe with words attended by exodus type signs and wonders (13:11–12). The 'hand of the Lord' that wrought the victories over Pharaoh was with Paul (cf. Exodus 15:6; cf. Acts 4:30), eliciting belief from the proconsul. From this point on, Paul is the dominant partner in the team ('Paul and his companions', 13:13).

Gentile acceptance and Jewish persecution concluded the ministry conducted by Paul and Barnabas in Pisidian Antioch. So Paul and Barnabas shake the dust off their feet as they leave (13:51)—thereby declaring Pisidian Antioch to be pagan territory—as they move on to Iconium. However, the new disciples are filled with joy because of the ever-present fullness (Greek imperfect *eplerounto*, 13:52) of the Holy Spirit. Paul and Barnabas had offered God's message of salvation openly to the Gentiles and they had responded and now God himself was present with them by his Spirit.

The stern words of 13:46 do not preclude further apostolic ministry to the Jews nor do they mean an exclusive ministry by Paul to Gentiles in future but they emphasise that Jewish audiences must understand the universal character of salvation.

The Spirit convinces the Council at Jerusalem (Acts 15)

After returning to Antioch (14:26) on the completion of the first missionary journey, Paul and Barnabas attended the Jerusalem conference which was held to discuss Pharisaic insistence on circumcision for Gentile converts. But God's treatment of the Gentiles on equal terms with Jews—giving the Holy Spirit to both Jewish and Gentile believers—convinced Peter and his fellow Jews (10:47; 11:15-18; 15:8-9) that Gentiles and Jews were saved in the same manner regardless of old covenant circumcision by the grace of Jesus Christ.

Peter's aforementioned belief set the stage for James, the Jerusalem leader (12:17), who spoke last (15:13-21). James' speech is the literary centre-point and the high point of Acts 15 which is focussed on the problem of how the Gentile converts were related to Israel, on whom the church was being built, that is: could Gentile converts continue as redeemed without a change to Jewish lifestyle? James argued that the salvation of the Gentiles is not a new idea initiated by Peter but is part of God's predetermined plan (cf. 15:14-17; cf. Amos 9:11-12), so the Gentiles should not be troubled by requiring them to undergo further ceremonial law in order to gain covenant acceptance. Luke's narration has this statement by James terminating the issue as it represents the unanimous consensus of the church. Therefore, Jewish harassment of Gentiles who turn to God must stop—but Gentile converts should also be instructed to abstain from certain practices (benefiting from anything offered to idols, sexual immorality, eating meat of strangled animals that still retain their blood, and eating blood). These decrees were regarded by the apostles and elders as having been reached by the work of the Holy Spirit (15:28) and were thus to be distributed through subsequent missionary activity.

The Spirit directs movement of the mission to Europe (16:6-10)

After Acts 15, the apostles virtually disappear from view as new ventures appear and Paul becomes the apostle to the nations—the legitimate heir to Jerusalem—in missionary activity. Paul and Silas begin the second missionary journey under the direction of the Spirit who forbad them, in some discernible way, from preaching the word in Asia (the Roman province of that name, 16:6). The missionaries proceeded west and north to Troas (16:8) which was the city on route to Europe through Phrygian Galatia.[181]

---

181 Hemer, 1989, 120.

They had proceeded by the direction of the 'spirit of Jesus' (16:7; cf. Romans 8:9; Galatians 4:6; Philippians 1:19), a unique phrase that indicates Jesus' control of their missionary activities. The Spirit is sent from the Father and acts on behalf of Father and Son, under the control of both. This intervention of the Holy Spirit marks the important juncture of the movement of the gospel to Europe. Luke comments that in European Corinth after the Macedonian call, Paul is compelled by the Spirit (18:5) to testify that Jesus is the Christ. Later, similarly purposed in the Spirit, Paul heads for Jerusalem in order to minister in European Rome (19:21).

Apollos must understand the work of the Spirit (18:24-28)

Luke narrates the arrival of Apollos in Ephesus, from Alexandria (18:24-28). Apollos' understanding of Christianity was defective in that whereas he was able to teach accurately about Jesus with great eloquence (18:24) he nevertheless only understood the baptism of John, that is, he had not received Christian baptism even though he had probably received the Spirit (18:25 appears to refer to the Holy Spirit and possibly Spirit-baptism) as a clear sign of his conversion (cf. 19:1-7). Recognising not only Apollos' potential from his synagogue presentations but also his need of instruction, Priscilla and Aquila took him aside and redressed his shortcomings (18:26). Apollos' accurate knowledge of the 'way of the Lord' (18:25) required integration in the wider 'way of God' (18:26), that is, the divine purpose into which the life of Jesus fitted and an understanding of the work of the Spirit.

Receiving the Spirit is the essence of life in Christ (19:1-7)

Apollos' encounter with Aquila and Priscilla (18:24-28) is contrasted with Paul's encounter with the Ephesian disciples who, like Apollos, had only received John's baptism. But the Ephesian 'disciples'—unlike Apollos—had neither received nor heard of the Holy Spirit and, hence, were not Christians (19:1-2). These Ephesian disciples needed to be shown the true significance of John's baptism, that is, as preparation for the coming of Jesus Christ (19:4). Paul therefore instructs these 'disciples' more carefully what John himself would have taught with conversion in view.

For Apollos, the baptism of John that he received had been completed by his knowledge of Christ as the fulfilment. The term 'disciples' is usually positively evaluated but perhaps Luke's use of the word in 19:1 is loose or ironic. Paul does not question these disciples about previous instruction but his diagnostic question about the Holy Spirit centres on their baptism.

Since their first baptism had not been in accordance with Christian instruction they are re-baptised. Paul lays hands on them as an act of incorporative fellowship and they receive the Spirit as part of their conversion-initiation which is evidenced by them speaking in tongues and prophesying (19:5-7). The narrative shows further the Spirit correcting theological practice in the early church. John's baptism towards purification of old covenant Israel—in preparation for the coming of Christ Jesus—is no longer relevant and misses the new covenant vitality imparted by Jesus' life-giving Spirit.

The Spirit appoints elders and directs mission plans (20:13-28)

The Spirit now decides Paul's further mission plans for, by divine mandate, he must see Rome. Paul's travel decision is 'in/by the Spirit' (19:21), that is, prompted by the Spirit or under the Spirit's sovereign control. Arriving at Miletus from Troas (20:13-16), anxious to reach Jerusalem for Pentecost, Paul sent for the elders of the Ephesian church. Paul's speech to the Ephesian elders: recalls his ministry to them, including his integrity and consequent suffering (20:18b-21); speaks of his impending departure (20:22-25), the Spirit directing the future of his ministry (20:23; cf. 21:4,11); declares the comprehensive nature of his ministry among them (20:26-27); and, finally, admonishes the Ephesian elders to exercise careful oversight of the church after the model for ministry that Paul had presented among them (20:28-35). Paul ignores the warning from prophets at Tyre (21:4) because he understands that, for him, suffering was unavoidable (cf. 21:13).

The Holy Spirit is the life of Christ in his church throughout the Acts narrative. So the Holy Spirit directs and empowers the testimony to Christ in mission including under persecution.[182] A new covenant missionary would be inept without the filling of the Spirit in addition to the general work of the Spirit in regeneration (13:9). The Holy Spirit guides the decisions of church meetings (11:28; 13:2; 15:28). And the Holy Spirit appoints and fills overseers (elders, deacons, bishops—6:3,5; 9:17; 20:28) in the church, indeed, Holy Spirit charisms are necessary for the church to minister as the body of Christ (2:17-18).

---

182 1:8; 4:8,31; 5:32; 6:10; 7:55; 8:29,39; 9:31; 10:19; 11:12,24; 13:4; 16:6,7; 18:5; 19:21; 20:23; 21:11.

The Spirit prepares Paul for future imprisonment (21:10-11)

Agabus was a member of a prophetic group that came down to Antioch from Jerusalem and predicted, through the Spirit, a severe famine throughout the entire (Roman) world, which happened (11:27-28). This same prophet came down from Judea to Caesarea when Paul was on his way to Jerusalem and, taking Paul's belt, he bound his own hands and feet to indicate that the Holy Spirit was revealing that the Jews in Jerusalem will bind Paul and hand him over to the Gentiles (21:11). It is argued that this revelation was not genuine prophecy since Paul was not handed over to the Romans by the Jews in Jerusalem but, rather, rescued from a Jewish mob and then imprisoned by the Romans. But Paul verified the prophecy (28:17) because—regardless of the details—the Jerusalem Jews did deprive Paul of his freedom thereby handing him over to the Romans. In Caesarea, Paul was urged to avoid Agabus' prediction (21:12-14) but this does not militate against the accuracy of the prophecy. Indeed, Agabus' prophecy confirmed earlier advice given to Paul at Tyre by disciples who were speaking 'through the Spirit' when they warned him not to go up to Jerusalem (21:4; cf.20:22f).

The Spirit inspires all Scripture (Acts 28)

After a succession of imprisonments and examinations in Jerusalem followed by a convict sea voyage (21:15-28:15), Paul is now in Rome in chains because of the hope of Israel. Discussions with Roman Jews were inconclusive (28:21-22,24-25,29). Paul's last word to the Roman Jews (28:25a) introduced scripture quoted from Isaiah as inspired by the Holy Spirit. In general terms, the Holy Spirit inspires all scripture (2 Peter 1:20-21; cf. 2 Timothy 3:16) so all words attributed to the Spirit must be in accord with the canon of revealed scripture. However, the distinctive nature of this introductory formula serves to emphasise the importance of the quotation as Paul applies the prophetic words condemning national Israel (Isaiah 6:9-10, a passage that leads on to national exile and the emergence of a faithful remnant) to contemporary Jews. This final thrust by the apostle contains the rationale for his ministry for, just as in Isaiah's time, Israel is now undergoing a permanent exile for breaching covenant. God had drawn a line under national Israel for persistent and wilful provocations culminating in the execution of Jesus. The Roman Jews leave Paul's house arrest with this prediction for their national future!

This important Old Testament quotation indicates, at the end of Acts, the completely unrepentant position of national Israel. The audience left after this quotation, indicating Paul's conclusion on Israel at the end of Luke's two-volume work, that is: national Israel has refused to hear thereby enabling salvation of the Gentiles. However, Paul's hope is that Jews—including Roman Jews—would be provoked to jealousy (Romans 11:11) and thereby also find salvation. By AD 70 the hope for the nation is extinguished but the apostle makes it clear that there will always be access for Jews who discard institutionalism and Mosaic covenant to obtain membership of the new covenant through faith in Christ into new Israel (Romans 11:17–24).

Romans

Spirit of holiness as the sphere of encountering Jesus (1:1-7)

The new covenant, which is basic to the total theology of Paul, fundamentally concerns the mission of Israel to its world and the incorporation of Gentiles as equal partners with Israel. Paul's theology in Romans is an exposition of his missionary undertaking with regard to the behavioural obligation for Gentiles who converted to Christianity, namely, Mosaic Law minus particular Jewish applications. Basic to Jewish law was the constitution of the Ten Commandments which—devoid of ceremonial law—set the framework for social, civic, criminal and ceremonial formation of the Israelite State. The Ten Commandments remain the required expression of what it means to be truly human in God's world.

The gospel is primarily a message to the world about God's lordship and intentions. The Spirit's work of applying the basic question 'who rules the world?' to the individual should result in personal recognition of God's claims.[183] Israel's rejection of Jesus' ministry led, at Pentecost, to the formation of an alternative Israel through whose witness the march to total world transformation would continue. The essence of the gospel always concerned the final full demonstration of the rule of God in the advent of the new creation. Transformed through inclusion in Christ, we are to look forward and communally witness to the final outcome of our transformation, namely: the fullness of our final salvation under kingdom of God rule in the new creation (1:16).

Paul's argument is that Jesus' resurrection decisively transformed the personal mode of Jesus' existence—as the last Adam, by the Holy Spirit—so that Jesus becomes a life-giving Spirit. The Spirit raised up Jesus as the firstfruits and dwells in him so completely in such a way as to be instrumental in the resurrection of the full harvest. By virtue of the functional identity of the Spirit and Christ, effected redemptively-historically in his resurrection, Christ is the communicator of life. The change in Christ's person is commensurate with the transformation to be expected by the rest of the harvest. The risen Jesus has a new status given to him by God, namely, God declared that Jesus is the Son of God with power according to the Spirit of holiness

---

[183] cf. Wright, Romans, 1994, 427. Over-individualization in the presentation of the gospel loses sight of the primary message of the Bible which is the people of God in submission to divine leadership as the new world society.

by the resurrection of the dead (1:1–4). This does not refer to religious or ethical transformation in Jesus by the resurrection, rather, the change was bodily and psychical such that Christ's resurrection is nothing less than the counterpart of creation (1 Corinthians 15:45), the beginning of the new and final spiritual and heavenly world order, the dawn of the new creation.

Paul details the place of Jesus Christ in the divine plan for humanity. 'Concerning his Son' (1:3) defines the content of the gospel, including: the significance of the incarnation, with the divine Son born of the seed of David; and the messianic role of the historical person, with the addition of 'Christ' to 'Jesus', and also being a descendant of David. Jesus' Jewish identity formed the basis of Paul's theology of his apostleship to the Gentiles. Jewish messianic expectations and the gospel virtually coalesce.

'Becoming from the seed of David' (1:3) suggests that pre-existence and deity are combined in the incarnation with human Davidic descent. Nevertheless, Jesus lived within the constraints of human limitations, 'according to the flesh' (1:3; 'flesh' in its normal Pauline pejorative sense means human existence characterised by weakness and mortality—but not, in this verse, sin). The Jesus of the incarnation lived not only within all the limitations of the old Adamic era but Jesus also shared our human situation in the sphere of the flesh (*kata sarka*, cf. John 1:14). The division in 1:3–4 between two modes of presence (flesh and Spirit) implies that the goal for which Christ was born of the seed of David is messianic restoration of Israel which was completed by becoming Son of God in power. Indeed, Jesus is enthroned as Messiah king in the full power of his office from his resurrection.

Horisthentos (declared, 1:4) points to the significance of the apposition of 'His Son Jesus Christ our Lord' (1:3). Lord is the term used for Yahweh in the Old Testament. As the Son is divine in both 1:3 and 1:4, the contrast in these verses is not two aeons but, rather, two natures.[184] Most commentators agree that *kata pneuma hagiosunes* (Spirit of holiness) has the same meaning as *pneuma hagion* (Holy Spirit), the former couplet being a Semitic periphrasis (cf. Psalm 51:11; Isaiah 63:11) for the latter. But why should a Semitism be used if 'Holy Spirit' was intended? More probably, 'spirit of holiness' points to what will be the sphere of encounter in which the powerful effects of the ministry of the risen Jesus will be experienced.

Kata pneuma does not primarily have the resurrection in view rather— as with *kata sarka*—*kata pneuma* refers to the condition originating from

---

184 cf. Gaffin (1978, 109) referring to the present and coming eons.

divine action, that is, Christ being appointed to his position of power means the continued possibility of encounter with Christ through the Spirit who manifests the transforming divine nature to believers. Christ's power in his post-resurrection condition has to do with, and is according to (*kata*), the Spirit and his work. Believers may now experience the risen presence of Christ as we are equipped with the power of the Spirit (cf. 15:19) by whom Christ exercises his lordship among his people. Holiness is the communication of the divine nature and the implications which stem from communication with the risen Christ as Lord.

1:3–4 thus refer to two stages in the life of the Son of God—one coming after the other—that is, two spheres of existence, 'flesh' and 'Spirit', in which the Son of God could be encountered. The new-aeon perspective on the Son is that Jesus is declared (1:4), as a result of the resurrection, to be what he always had been: the divine Son. However, Jesus the Son is no longer limited by his earthly life but transcended to embody both perfected humanity and deity in one person. Raised up, Jesus is the source of power for resurrection and redemption, the transition from wrath to grace. His death was a dying to sin and the resultant condition of his resurrection is 'Son of God in power' in a great transition from wrath to grace. The exaltation and enthronement of Christ resulted in a change of status justifying the adjective 'powerful', normally taken to refer to the saving power of the vindicated Christ.

But 'powerful' seems to denote even more. Taking perfected humanity to the right hand of God, after his death Jesus was invested as Israel's Messiah with kingly authority and power thereby fulfilling messianic predictions (Psalms 2:7–12; 72:1–2,8–12,17; 89:20,22–23,25–27; Isaiah 11:1,4,10; 42:1; Daniel 7:13–14) by his resurrection as Son of Man.[185] By the resurrection of Christ, the kingdom of Christ over the universe had come into being whereby what was envisioned for human nature (Genesis 1:26) came to be in Christ. Humankind had been created with the purpose of bringing order to the world but this task belongs to Jesus because Jesus is the only person who has ever properly expressed humanity. By his resurrection, Jesus is revealed to be the Lord of the world—humanity as it was intended to be.[186] True humanity in obedience to God will finally rule the world (cf. 1

---

185 Wright, 2003, 564–5.
186 Wright, 334.

Corinthians 15:20-28). Until then, the Creator and covenant God is over the Messiah, and the Messiah is over the world.[187]

Thus 1:3-4 do not contrast two natures but, rather, point to two successive modes of incarnate existence moving from humiliation to exaltation providing a capsule summary of the gospel (cf. Philippians 2:6-11; 1 Timothy 3:16; 1 Peter 3:18). Christ the eternal Son of God became incarnate in the present evil age, suffering death and humiliation as the incarnate Son of God. Christ by God through the Spirit was raised up to be the source for others of eschatological power and life as the life-giving Spirit. Only by his resurrection was his death a dying to sin. And by his resurrection, believers look forward to the divine adoption as the redemption of the body (8:23).

For Christ and believers there is an essential tie between the Spirit and the eschatological world (1:4-6). Paul expresses a compressed overview of history with the Spirit's role in the act of resurrection of believers.[188] The Spirit conditions the resurrection life emerging from Christ's resurrection with an analogy between the resurrection of Jesus and that of believers. The Jesus who rose from the grave is now equipped with new status and new qualities (cf. 1:1-4)—a constructed adjustment for the future heavenly environment wrought by God in him.

The Messiah's eschatological coming unfolds in two episodes—the already and the still to come—but the age to come is already present. There is an organic connection between the resurrection of Christ and the bodily resurrection of believers at the second coming. For believers, the resurrection constitutes a new womb out of which believers issue as sons of God (8:23) who therefore neither marry nor are given in marriage (Luke 20:35-36). The resurrection means entry into a higher world with a newly structured life and new potencies because the Messiah is over all the world.[189]

The kingdom of Christ lasts until the Second Coming when all authority will again be handed to the Father (1 Corinthians 15:24-28), therefore, Christ's kingship spans the post-cross gospel age. So Israel's king through the Spirit is exercising Israel's ministry to the wider world now—a ministry that was impossible for Israel because of her disobedience throughout the Old Testament. Through the Spirit, Jesus communicates the power of his

---

187 Wright, 336.
188 Vos, 1994, (vs.4-6) 83, 155ff, 209.
189 Vos, 336.

risen divine-human life and draws his people from the world into fellowship as the true Israel (Acts 1–2) who witness to the world.

True circumcision is of the heart, by the Spirit (2:25–29)

Circumcision was the seal of God's eternal covenant with Israel—the outward mark of covenant relationship and, hence, the passport to salvation.[190] But Paul defines with clarity who is the true Jew, under covenant, with a climax at 2:28–29. The outward mark (circumcision) on its own could not be used to define the true Jew living in covenant relationship with the Lord God. The Old Testament always assumed that true circumcision for the Jew was a matter of the heart, effected by the Spirit (cf. Jeremiah 9:25–26; Deuteronomy 10:16; 30:6). Physical circumcision, the mark of the covenant, did not ever save; rather, it was always circumcision of the heart that saved. In the post-cross situation, the saved Jew must come to the Messiah through the cross and resurrection (10:8–9). And just as we are saved by a personal work of the Spirit, likewise, we serve God in the newness of our personal relationship with Christ and our heavenly Father through the Spirit (7:6). Written statutes with consequent penalties are true enough but the written word cannot produce the family relationship that compels and empowers obedience.

The Spirit pours the love of God into our hearts (Romans 5)

The gift of the Spirit is the ground of all hope (5:5) for the new age prophesied by Joel has come (Joel 2:28–29). Through the Spirit, God's love for us is shed abroad in our hearts (5:6–10; cf. 8:28a). Believers shall be saved from the wrath of judgement through Christ—in particular, through his resurrection life (5:9,10)—thereby enabling the Jewish injunction to love God with the whole being (the 'Shema', Deuteronomy 6:4–6, the basic Jewish confession of faith) a reality for all who are in Christ. By the Spirit, God has created a people that in response to their redemption will love him from the heart. The flooding of the heart by the Spirit with love for God, however, does not completely overcome our sinful will (cf. Romans 6–7). By the Spirit, those who are God's people by faith are the true covenant people who inherit all the covenant blessings.

---

190 Chae, 1997, 124.

New life in the Spirit (Romans 8)

There is new freedom for those who are in Christ (8:1-4).[191] 8:1-2 connect with 7:6; and 7:7-25 is a development of 7:5. The crucial change to life in the new covenant is registered in 8:1. To meet the situation described in Romans 7, *pneuma* (Spirit) becomes the focus of discussion (8:1-17)—not about the Spirit himself but what he does. In a passage dealing primarily with the work of the Spirit, Paul begins by talking about Christ whose complete work enabled the gift of the Spirit. 'Now' is the eschatological marker of the new age which moves from no 'condemnation' (8:1) to no 'separation' (8:39, thus Romans 8 is about assurance from beginning to end).

In Christ Jesus, now risen to a new estate, a radical change from a sin-dominated existence is possible. 8:2-4 sketches the solution to the dilemma of 7:7-25—that is, to 'the law of sin and death' (8:2, cf. 7:13-24)—which describes present post-cross Jewish life under Mosaic Law (which leads to death by highlighting transgressions). 8:3-4 lays bare the issues of Romans 7 and points to the solution of 3:21-26. 8:5-11 discuss more fully the alternative of the two forces, flesh and Spirit, representing two covenant eras now. The dialogue about Jewish concerns ends at 8:11.

8:12-17 is about general Christian experience, that is, being led by the Spirit under the new covenant thereby evidencing that the believer is a child of God. A survey of the present in the light of the Christian's future reveals that we may suffer now but this suffering is not to be compared with the glory which is to come (8:18-30) for, indeed, all creation is waiting for the unveiling of the Sons of God (8:19-22). 8:23-25 is about our longing for the fullness of salvation, the redemption of the body. The Spirit of God (that is, 'from' God) enables us to pray through the infirmities of the present (8:26-27). God's elective love glorifies us (8:28-30). The hymn-like ending (8:31-39) returns to the no 'condemnation' of 8:1. Final salvation is attributed to the love of God and connected with the confident assertion of the conquest over suffering (cf. 5:1-11).

---

191 8:1-11 continues the argument of Romans 7, as indicated by the Greek connective ara (therefore, 8:1). The second person addressee of 'set you free' (note NASB 8:2) refers to the Jews.

Flesh verses Spirit in the new covenant (8:1-11)

Based on the argument of previous chapters, and following 7:25a, Paul begins Romans 8 with an emphatic 'therefore now'. In the new covenant era there is 'no punishment' (*katakrima*, what follows condemnation; 8:1) arising from the final judgment. This resolves issues raised in Romans 7 but only for those who live in union with Christ and are thus free from the inward controlling power of sin. 'In Christ' refers to being incorporated by the Spirit into the sphere of power and authority of Israel's risen Messiah; living in a conscious relationship with him. The conclusion of 'no punishment' or freedom from the operation of divine wrath forms the basis for Paul's discussion of the two forces—flesh and Spirit (8:1-17)—in which *pneuma* (Spirit) is the focus of discussion.

The better Greek alternative, *se* (thou, 8:2; that is, the representative Jew)—replaced in many translations by *me*—indicates that Paul is continuing the discussion of Romans 7 with the representative Jew, however, 8:1-11 is addressed to the Jew who has now experienced transformation in Christ (this passage is, therefore, applicable to all Christians). There is no longer a place for a national decision (cf. Romans 10-11), that is, the Jewish nation post-cross is a secular state in a secular world.

8:2-4 raise the issue of the operative new covenant 'law' (2 Corinthians 3:6). The distinction between Paul's ministry at Corinth and that of Jewish Christian infiltrators was their insistence on the framework of a continuing Mosaic covenant for Gentiles who became Christians. But the age of the old covenant institutions and sacrificial atonement had ended. Now, atonement for sin is only found in the operation of the new covenant.

Hence Paul's approach to the 'law' of the new covenant (8:2) whereby the Spirit is the life-giver. This approach to 'law' is meant to pose a covenant difference (cf. 6:14) between Jewish and Christian communities. 'Law' in 'the law of the Spirit of life in Christ Jesus' most probably refers to the Torah fulfilled through the Spirit by faith inaugurated by Christ's death and resurrection. In the new covenant, the Torah points to Christ—that is, the Torah is fully expressed in the Law of Christ (Galatians 6:2; cf. 1 Corinthians 9:21). The Spirit initiates entry into the new covenant and communicates the eschatological, risen life of Christ thereby conforming the believer's will to the will of God. The express change in the New Testament is that the divine law is established by the inward work of the Spirit and the obedience produced by faith (1:5; cf. 3:31). Hence the Law of Christ endorses the Decalogue which is God's universal creation-demand on humanity. So in the New Testament era, the 'law of sin and death' refers to the black letter Mosaic Law which traditional Jews still considered to be operative. But Jews are now free from the controlling power of black letter law and, in its place, they are now offered the regulative influence of the Spirit who is able to give them life and peace in the new covenant.

There are two sides of the Trinitarian saving transaction. On one side, God sent Jesus in the likeness of sinful flesh so that sin may be condemned in Jesus' flesh (8:3). On the other side, God works through the Spirit to supply risen power for moral action so that the requirements of the law of Christ may be fulfilled (8:4). It was impossible for the law to effect salvation and impart life because of human weakness, nevertheless, God in Christ effects salvation and gives life according to the Spirit by bringing the Jewish age to an end (8:3). 'Sent his Son' (8:3) implies the pre-existence of Christ as the only begotten Son who, 'in the likeness of sinful flesh', assumed true humanity. But as Son of God there was also an unlikeness to sinful flesh. The Greek word *homoioma* (likeness, 8:3) reveals that Jesus shared fully with humanity but did not share the sinfulness of humanity. Indeed, the power of sin was broken by the Son of God in his life, death and resurrection. Hence, in the sphere in which sin reigned—that is, in the flesh—Jesus condemned sin. 'Flesh' is a force beckoning all towards this-world orientation as a result of the fall.

Interwoven in this contrast between Spirit and flesh is Jesus—representing total humanity—who condemned sin by taking on physical flesh and showing how the law could be fulfilled by a true human who did not sin. Israel's repeated, intentional, national sin constantly put her outside the old covenant. But flesh and Spirit in Romans 7–8 represent covenant contrasts: flesh points to a lapsed covenant still being enforced by Judaism; Spirit points to life in the new covenant. The source of sin is not physical flesh as a product of creation, rather, the sin of the first man Adam is imputed to all. And there is still a connection between the past legitimate role of Torah as a means of sanctification and Christian experience (8:1–11), indeed, the fulfilment of the law is only possible by Christ in us through the Spirit. Through the Spirit, the effects of the 'law of sin' (7:23) can be countered. So in the new covenant age the Jew can, in Christ, fulfil the righteous requirement (*dikaioma*, 8:4) of God by the motivation of the Spirit who enlightens understanding of God's word and enables obedience—though not always perfect—to God's moral will. The life of obedience, produced by faith following identification with Christ's death, is constantly walking in the Spirit (8:4) as opposed to following the beckoning of the flesh (cf. 8:1).

To walk according to the Spirit is to: serve Christ by the imparted power of his resurrection given through the Spirit (cf. Galatians 5:16); be led by the Spirit (Galatians 5:18), that is, towards the final goal; be guided in our serving by the Spirit's empowering and revealing presence. The opposite of walking according to the Spirit is walking according to the flesh, that is, yielding to temptations that appeal to fallen human nature. But now, by the gift of the Spirit, we are able to resist such temptations.

The argument continues (cf. *gar*, for, 8:5) by posing alternatives for determination of human choices. Either the Spirit determines the new mindset and directs our thoughts so that we walk in the rule of the Spirit which is liberty, or the rule of sin continues to lead us into bondage through the flesh. We are only flesh—directed by fallen human impulses—if we have no contact with the Spirit of God.

The Spirit is to be the guide and inward controlling power in all conduct, indeed, there is no possibility of a Christian life without the Spirit's power. The continuing opposition of Spirit and flesh is not primarily anthropological but, rather, two dominating powers in the realms of salvation history (8:6-8).[192] Death is the penalty for a life dominated by flesh (8:6a). But life directed by the Spirit—controlled by the values of the new era—is all-encompassing wellbeing since we now think as the Spirit thinks (8:6b). The power of Christ through the Spirit brings life and peace with God. To choose to be dominated by the value system of the rebellious world is idolatrous subjection to sinful human inclinations (8:7). The solution to being directed by flesh is not to change the law but, rather, to change the mindset by the indwelling Spirit under the new covenant. Jews must therefore live eschatologically, that is, they must turn away from the barrenness of their past toward the appointed Messiah.

The one reality of the Spirit as the basis for new life is described in three ways (8:9-10). First, if the Spirit of God lives in you then you have the Spirit of Christ; that is, Christ is in you. By the resurrection and ascension, Christ (as Last Adam and second man) so permanently and completely possesses the Spirit that the two (Christ and the Spirit) are equated as one in giving

---

192 Flesh (sinful human nature) and Spirit are mutually exclusive. Flesh is the human power of this age—Spirit is the power of the age to come (cf. Gaffin, 1978, 106-109).

eschatological life to the church. By virtue of Christ's resurrection, the work of the Spirit of life in Christ Jesus is that Christ permanently resides in us; that is, the Spirit from God inwardly reveals the presence of God in Christ (8:9a).[193] The indwelling Spirit of (from) God brings about divine transformation in regeneration thereby establishing God's new covenant ownership of the believer.

Secondly, the Spirit of Christ dwells as God's presence in new covenant Israel (8:9b; cf. Ezekiel 37:26–28), that is, the Spirit of Christ is the necessary medium of the indwelling presence of God in his people. Using 'spirit of Christ' (8:9b) in place of 'spirit of God' (8:9a) does not change the meaning but refers not only to the particular New Testament indwelling presence of God but also the interrelationship of God the Father and God the Son. To belong to Christ is to have the Spirit of God communicating the presence of Christ within, thereby completing the Trinitarian arrangement.

Thirdly, the internal presence of Christ through the Spirit unites believers to Christ as members of his body. Changing from the indwelling 'Spirit of God' to 'spirit of Christ' clarifies the connection between Old and New Testament presentations of the Spirit. The Holy Spirit—the Spirit of God—mediates to our spirit the work of Christ, the risen life of Christ, and the exaltation of Christ (8:10). The Holy Spirit is, therefore, the Spirit of Christ in relation to his new covenant people in the same way that the Holy Spirit mediated the work and words of God to Old Testament believers. By changing from Spirit of Christ to Christ in you (8:10), Paul specifies that the Spirit communicates Christ as the life-giving Spirit in believers in this life 'because of' (causal, *dia dikaiosunen*) God's righteous action in Christ.[194]

---

193 Turner, 1998, 135 (quoting Fee, 1994, 898).

194 The function of the Spirit post-resurrection is decisively extended. To be in Christ and in the Spirit are not interchangeable, that is, in Christ has a larger forensic application and speaks of one's destiny to share in Christ's glorified state. Neither 2 Corinthians 3:17 nor 1 Corinthians 15:45 identify Christ with the Holy Spirit. Indeed, the Spirit of Christ in believers develops Christ in them, ultimately transforming them into the image of the heavenly man at the resurrection (8:29; 1 Corinthians 15:49; Philippians 3:21). Until then, the Spirit is a down payment for the future (*arrabon*, money given in purchase as a pledge with the full amount to be paid later, 2 Corinthians 1:22). Thus the Spirit not only constitutes the earthly make-up of the future life but present possession of the Spirit also anticipates the heavenly fullness which is to be received later. Between the saving moment of new creation and the consummation of salvation in future resurrection, Paul anticipates a dynamic process of transformation into the image of Christ (2 Corinthians 3:17,18).

New life has come to believers through the death of Christ and his resurrection by the Spirit. In the same way that God had used the Spirit in the resurrection of Jesus, God would also use the Spirit in the future resurrection of believers.

For the Christian, to possess the Spirit is to possess Christ as the life-giving Spirit himself. The Spirit and Christ are virtually interchangeable (8:9–10; cf. the economic Trinity refers to the functional operation of each person of the Trinity while recognising their personal distinctions) but there is also interaction between the Spirit and Christ. The Spirit of God lives in you is equivalent to Christ as the indwelling Spirit in you (8:9). To be in the Spirit means to be in Christ. The Spirit—as the inner power moulding and controlling spiritual development—communicates the experience of the indwelling Christ.

A Christian anthropology understands that the body—that is, the continuing person—though destined to be resurrected, is nonetheless now dead through sin as part of the fallen world (8:10). So the body is not capable of reflecting Christ's risen life apart from the operation of the Holy Spirit affirming and communicating the divine action of God in Christ's death. God raised Jesus from the dead through the Spirit[195] and God will also make alive the mortal bodies of believers through the indwelling Spirit (8:11). The Spirit assures believers of their future bodily resurrection to immortality in God's great renewal of full redemption. This full redemption, including the resurrection of the body, has not yet occurred so the body is still oppressed by the power of the sinful world however the presence of the Spirit gives the life of Christ to bodies of death as the guarantee of future bodily resurrection.[196] Hence the contrast that the Christian feels between life in the present world and life in Christ through the Spirit.

The Spirit of God who raised Jesus dwells in believers and believers are in Christ, hence Christ (that is, the Spirit of Christ) is in believers. What the Father had done for the Son, raising him from the dead, he will also do for believers by making alive their mortal bodies through his Spirit who indwells them. God's Spirit dwelling within believers gives life to their mortal bodies, that is, God raises believers from the dead as he raised the human Jesus. God raises Jesus from the dead in his representative capacity

---

195 Gaffin (1978, 63) notes that the unstated understanding that God had raised Jesus through the Spirit is fundamental to the argument in 8:9–11.
196 Ferguson, 1996, 179.

as Messiah thereby guaranteeing that Christ's resurrection will be repeated in others. God raised Jesus through the Spirit of God who is present within believers so the Spirit of God will accomplish for believers what he has already accomplished for Jesus. Note Paul's present tense 'dwells'. The body is able to be resurrected but still belongs to this present sinful age. So whereas the body is dead, even now the Spirit who is life is preparing believers for the eventual climactic transformation of the body at Christ's return. The final transformation is the Spirit raising believers, as he had raised Jesus, giving resurrection new life to mortal bodies. In a context where Paul appears to be instructing Jewish Christians under severe Jewish influence (8:9–11), the Spirit is spoken of as the self-revealing Christ in us—reproducing Christ's sonship in us through the Spirit.

The Christian resurrection—like Jesus' resurrection by the power of the Spirit—will be bodily. Being Christian and having the Spirit is clearly one and the same thing for no one can belong to Christ as the new covenant Lord unless he possesses the Spirit of Christ (8:9; cf.1 Corinthians 12:1–3). Indeed, Christ: transforms us to be true servants of God through the Spirit; and indwells his people by the Holy Spirit thereby revealing himself and his will to us, enabling us to obey him, and influencing us from within.[197]

The unity of believers with the resurrection of Christ represents a past and a future as the believer has been raised from the dead and is yet to be raised. The resurrection of Jesus is refracted in a two-fold pattern: first, resurrection of the inner man is past; and, secondly, physical resurrection of the outer man is future. Or resurrection is invisible (6:14) or visible. From the inside, resurrection has already taken place; from his mental and physical outside, resurrection is still outstanding.

The Spirit as personal

The resurrection body will be immortal (cf. 2:7; 2 Timothy 1:10) with power and glory and the personal presence of the Spirit. Paul's use of 'in Christ' often parallels with 'in the Spirit' such that the two phrases are equivalent and personal (8:9–11). The functional identity of the Spirit and Christ is effected redemptively-historically in Jesus' resurrection. Hence Christ, through the Spirit, is the communicator of life.[198]

---

197 cf. Fatehi, 2000, 233.
198 Gaffin, 1978, 70ff.

The glory of the Father through the Spirit raised Jesus (cf. 6:4) and God will make alive the mortal body of believers through the Spirit (8:11)—and, indeed, the Spirit is already at work in believers because the present life of the believer is with the Spirit and also in the dead body of sin (8:10).[199] The somatic evidence of the future resurrection, even more than had been experienced so far, will disclose the full dimensions of the Spirit's work in the believer.

Just as Israel's God raised Christ Jesus from the dead by the Spirit in Christ's representative capacity as Messiah, likewise, the divine Spirit will make alive the mortal body of all who are in Christ on the last day (8:11). The body is able to be resurrected through the Spirit but, nevertheless, still belongs to this present sinful age. The body is dead but even now the Spirit—who is life—is preparing believers for eventual heavenly transformation of the body at Christ's return as he gives them new spiritual life in mortal bodies. Both Jews and Jewish Christians would have been at home with 'spirit of God' (*ruach Yahweh*) but unbelieving Jews could not accept the functional, relational indwelling equivalence of 'in Christ' and 'in the Spirit'.[200]

God, through the divine Spirit dwelling within, gives life to the mortal bodies of believers (8:11) just as he raised Jesus' human nature from the dead. The instrument through whom God raised Jesus is present within believers. The resurrected and ascended Christ—the last Adam, the second man—has come to possess the life of the Spirit permanently and completely.

The experience of Holy Spirit baptism took place when believers were incorporated into the one body of Christ (cf.1 Corinthians 1:13) bringing righteousness in Christ, renewal of life, and deliverance from the guilt and corruption of sin. Believers all share an experience in the gift of the Spirit with which he baptised the church at Pentecost (cf. 6:3f; Galatians 2:20; Ephesians 2:5f; Colossians 2:12f; 3:1-3). Holy Spirit baptism is being incorporated into the church, the body of Christ. All believers drink one Spirit (1 Corinthians 12:13) so baptism in the Spirit is not a second blessing, indeed, there cannot be an un-Spirit-baptised Christian. The Spirit creates a

---

199 Gaffin, 1978, 66–68.

200 To be 'in Christ' is to live in conscious intercourse and fellowship with him (Gaffin, 1978, 73). Whereas 'in Christ' and 'in the Spirit' are functionally equivalent, they are not interchangeable since to be in Christ is determined by the believer's destiny to share in Christ's glorified state.

capacity in believers to receive the gift of faith—his principal blessing—giving a new heart, the intimate human centre, thereby changing the whole of sin-controlled man.

Led by the Spirit as sons indwelt by the Spirit (8:12-17)

8:12-17 amplifies the work of the Spirit in believers generally (cf. brothers, 8:12). The logical conclusion of 8:1-11 is that believers have an obligation to live differently (8:12). The Spirit brings about a progressive dying to the deeds of the body, that is, the believer is continually dying with Christ to the old Adamic life (8:13) and receiving—through the Spirit—his resurrection power (cf. 8:10-11) so that God's lordship is manifested in believers' wills and actions.

The Spirit is both the source of resurrection and also the substratum of resurrection-life, that is, the life of the coming aeon. The Spirit is both creator and sustainer: producing life and continuing life.[201] But the Spirit is not given simply to assure Christians of ultimate attainment, rather, the indwelling Spirit must attest itself by activity commenced in Christian life prior to the eschatological permanent indwelling. The proof for the eternal, heavenly state—according to Paul—is that God has given the earnest of the Spirit, that is, the promise of the Spirit (8:15-16; 2 Corinthians 1:22; and Ephesians 1:13-14). The Spirit indwelling the human believer is a provisional instalment for later heavenly fullness (cf. 8:23).

The Spirit of Adoption (8:14) is the crowning blessing of the gospel as adoption in Christ not only brings personal relationship and status, but also a future. Believers are heirs with Christ provided they follow in his path of suffering before glory (8:17), indeed, the Spirit assures us of our adoption by continually bearing inner witness to the presence of God (8:16). Christians who pray 'Abba father' may have confidence because they are using Jesus' prayer language of filial intimacy (8:15; Galatians 4:1-7), which is evidence of adoption. Christians pray as a child of the Father rather than address God as a slave because the Spirit bears witness with our spirits that we are children of God (8:16). Believers must, if led by the Spirit of God, show evidence that they are children of God or otherwise face the penalty of eternal death (8:13-17). But it is by the inner power of Christ through the Spirit that we can overcome sin. Indeed, Christians who are led by the

---

201 The Spirit is not the source of resurrection, rather, the Spirit is the agent of resurrection.

Spirit—not Israel, as was the case in the Old Testament—are now sons of God.

The Greek word *gar* (for) connecting 8:13-14 makes it plain that 8:14 is expounding 8:13, hence, new life (8:13) will occur under the indwelling and leading of the Spirit (8:14). The gift of sonship—formerly the privilege of Israel—is evidenced by transformation (8:14) resulting from reception of the gift of the Spirit of Sonship (8:15). The Spirit (of God) foreshadows and assures believers about final adoption into sonship (and joint heirship with Christ, 8:18,23), thereby affirming their sonship and eternal future.

Prospective adoption into full sonship—the great blessing of the transformation—assures believers of eternal life in the Father's presence. The believer's knowledge of sonship provides assurance, in conjunction with demonstration of new life springing from within, that establishes something of the future in the now (8:23). Past tense denotes the fact of the Romans' reception of adoption (8:15b) but continual present tense denotes the Spirit's inner witness, constantly confirming the believer's cry of '*Abba* Father' (8:15c,16).[202]

Glad obedience is due to receiving the firstfruits of the Spirit. God's Spirit *himself* (8:16) bears witness with our spirit of the new situation, that is, God's Spirit acts on the human spirit enabling reception of spiritual knowledge—the divine presence assures us of our new and true identity. Concluding the argument of 8:14-17, Paul refers to participation in Jesus' sufferings (8:17) establishing a connection between Jesus and the suffering believer.

We have the eschatological firstfruits of the Spirit (8:23-30)

The reception of the Spirit is the firstfruits of eschatological consummation (*aparche*, 8:23). The gifts of the Spirit are a down payment pledge (2 Corinthians 1:22; 5:5; Ephesians 1:14) of the full inheritance of heavenly adoption as sons where the redemption of the body will mean being fully Spirit controlled. So the church's possession of the Spirit is now partial and anticipatory and yet both what is now, and what is yet to be, belong to us. To have the Spirit is not only to have the guarantee of final redemption but also to possess the One who is definitive of that final condition, namely, the

---

202 The cry 'Abba Father', attributed to believers (8:15; Galatians 4:6), is the personal activity of the Spirit himself (cf. Gaffin, 1978, 71). The Spirit does not groan for believers but through them.

Spirit of Christ. The hope we have is confidence in a future reality and this hope will not be disappointed because God has already poured the Holy Spirit into our hearts (5:5). Already the Spirit enables us to experience an overflow from the heavenly world, an outpouring of divine love.

8:26a refers to the Spirit groaning as he intercedes for the believer, in addition to the groaning of creation (8:22) and the groaning of Christians (8:23). The groaning by the Spirit, who has been given to Christians as firstfruits, is evidence of the divine presence and gives us a new assurance of our relationship to the Father. The ascending sequence of groanings—from creation to Christians to the activity of the Spirit in adoption—points to eschatological resurrection and redemption of the body. Unutterable groanings uttered by the Spirit is probably not a reference to the personal gift of tongues, rather, the Spirit himself groans because we are unable to totally overcome our sinful human condition. So the Spirit's intercession is on behalf of (and in) all believers because each believer dwells in a weak, unredeemed body.

8:28-30 reinforce what believers 'know' to be true, namely, what God will do as a result of the Spirit's intercession. 'We know'—taking God as the true subject of 8:28 and 'all things' as the totally embrace sphere in which God works—that God is working through the Spirit for our ultimate good in respect of all things, including Christian sufferings (8:18-25).

To be in Christ—or in the Spirit—is to live in conscious earthly intercourse and fellowship with Christ. Note the new creation work of the Spirit (8:11; cf. Philippians 3:21) has already begun in believers, towards ultimate transformation by the Spirit into the image of the heavenly man at the resurrection (8:29; 1 Corinthians 15:49; Philippians 3:21).[203] Until the ultimate transformation, the experience of the Spirit is *arrabon* (pledge); between the initial moment of new creation and its consummation in future resurrection, Paul anticipates a dynamic process of transformation into the image of Christ (cf. 2 Corinthians 3:17,18).

Resurrection: the goal of the Spirit's activity in the believer

In his resurrection, Jesus is passive—so Christ's resurrection by God is Christ's vindication, as Christ is the firstborn in resurrection among many brethren (8:29). The goal of the Spirit's activity is to transform believers (the many brethren) into the full likeness of Christ. This transformation is

---

203 Transformation occurs from God, in Christ, through the Spirit (8:11).

effected through the Spirit's work of sanctification. The Spirit transforms those who have distorted God's image in the shame of sin so that they now bear the image of God in glory, that is, they become partakers of the divine nature (2 Peter 1:4). Sanctification makes us fully human: what we were created to be (cf. 1 Corinthians 15:49), bearing the image of Christ who is the man from heaven (1 Corinthians 15:49; 2 Corinthians 3:18). The predestined goal of the Parousia is conformity to God's image in the Son so that Jesus might be the firstborn among many brothers. This is the end in view, for heavenly adoption is the resurrection of the body (8:23; 1 Corinthians 15:49; Philippians 3:21).

Christ's resurrection is the pivotal focus of Paul's soteriology because the resurrection constitutes Christ as the life-giving Spirit for those who are joined to him in the new age. Others are also brought in. So Christ is the firstborn among many brothers (paraphrase of 8:29). Those who are predestined by God to resurrection with Christ (defined as adoption, Ephesians 1:5) are called into fellowship with the resurrected Christ (1 Corinthians 1:9); that is, those whom God called he has already raised with Christ (defined as justification, 8:30) and those whom he has already raised (with Christ) these he will raise with Christ (defined as glorification, 2 Corinthians 4:14).[204] The last resurrection of believers is bodily but must also be a somatic transformation—not a simple return to what was lost in death but also endowed with new powers. The transformed body is richer not just because of the removal of sin-caused defects. We do not merely receive back the body in the resurrection, we also bear the image of Christ which he obtained in his own resurrection (1 Corinthians 15:45-49).

To be in Christ and in the Spirit are not interchangeable as in Christ has a larger forensic application: being in Christ is determined by the destiny of believers to share in Christ's glorified state. Even dead believers in the intermediate period before the resurrection are dead in Christ so the dead are thus never separated from Christ (1 Thessalonians 4:16)—and the living will also be changed. For Christ, resurrection is entering a new phase of sonship and a new phase for the soul—entry into a new world constructed

---

204 Vos (1994, 163-171) points to the intimate connection between the Spirit and eschatology which is clear in the Old Testament and emphasized by Paul in Romans 8 (cf. 1 Corinthians 15). In the New Testament, the transcendental and supernatural Spirit is intimately associated with Christ.

on a superabundantly dynamic plane. For the believer, the resurrection new aeon means an unprecedented sense as sons of God.

In Christ, by the Spirit (Romans 9-11)

Two phrases—'in Christ' and 'by the Holy Spirit'—highlight a distinction (9:1; cf. 8:16): 'in Christ' has in mind our union with the heavenly Christ; 'in (or, more accurately, by) the Spirit' refers to our consciousness of this heavenly presence in us. Paul is confident that what he is saying about Israel is true because Paul is in Christ and the Holy Spirit is revealing the truth (bearing witness) to Paul's spirit (9:1).

Romans 9-11 emanates from Paul's agony over Israel's position, induced by his conscience moved by the Holy Spirit. The preamble (9:6-29) issues into justification for the admission of the Gentiles into the New Israel (9:30-33) while Israel remains outside the blessing because of her inability to accept Christ crucified and risen as the cornerstone of New Israel. Paul argues that faith in Christ ends the pursuit of righteousness by Mosaic Law (10:1-4) so Israel must take action to redress her situation which is marked by rejection of God's Messiah, Jesus Christ (10:4-5). Israel's blindness to Christ (9:25) will enable the full number of Gentiles to be freely accepted into new Israel. The partial disobedience of contemporary national Israel has opened the future course of the gospel to all. When the full count of Gentiles comes into the kingdom then all Israel that is to be saved will have been saved with the Gentiles to be grafted into the olive tree also complete (9:26). Then the saving work of God is completed. Salvation must come by the acceptance of the crucified Christ as Israel's Messiah. No other way is possible. Paul is not proposing Israel's salvation as a nation.

Bearing the imprint of the Spirit of Christ at work (Romans 14-15)

Gentile Christians were indifferent to Jewish food laws (which, post cross, were simply a cultural decision). But the Gentiles are not to offend unnecessarily. 14:17 is a comment (*gar*, for) on 14:15-16 where Paul is addressing the 'strong'. Membership in the kingdom of God—which exhibits righteousness (evidence of divine acceptance), peace (the resulting condition), joy (the inner attitude), and hope (the future expectation)—is the product of the inner working of the Holy Spirit in the believer (14:16-18). In this text, righteousness is the conduct that indicates the inworking of the Holy Spirit to make and keep believers right with God.

Righteousness is not something that we may do or not do but conduct which bears the imprint of the Spirit of Christ at work within. Christian peace and joy will be reflected in Christian relationships empowered by the Spirit (15:13).[205] We should strive in differences to emulate the selflessness of Christ in our dealings with others. Paul's desire is that the hope awakened by the gospel of God—which establishes peace, the inner consciousness of our Christian oneness and acceptance by God—may be fervent and alive by the work of the Spirit bringing right relationships together in the Body of Christ.

Paul repeats his obligation to serve the gospel and refers to his ministry as a servant of Christ (15:16,25–27). Paul's gospel ministry of grace is from God to the Gentiles. Gentile Christians are Paul's apostolic offering acceptable to God through the Holy Spirit (15:16); though it is possible that the genitive is subjective, that is, the offering is the collection that the Gentiles offer along with their glorying of God for the gospel (15:9) through their obedience of faith (cf. 15:18). With the visit to Jerusalem in view, Paul uses priestly language analogous to the language of temple sacrifices and offerings, perhaps from conviction that the journey to Jerusalem is symbolic evidence that his Gentile ministry is the work of the power of the Spirit—the high point of his call and a supreme act of worship. The Gentiles coming into Israel is the fulfilment of true Israel's eschatological hope (Isaiah 66:20).

In reviewing his ministry, Paul asserts that Christ has been the active agent in word and deed through the power of the Spirit using Paul as an agent (15:18–19). The power of signs and wonders (5:19) further specifies the work of Christ (5:18) through him—what was done in word and deed was done through the power of the Spirit making clear that Christ was working in and through the signs and wonders reported. Paul is not making Christ and the Spirit equivalent for the Spirit does not work only on behalf of Christ. But Christ is present in believers in and through the Spirit's agency.

Paul urges prayer support from the Roman believers through 'the Lord Jesus Christ' and the 'love of the Spirit' (15:30)—love for what the Spirit has produced, or Christian love for Christ induced by the person of the Spirit dwelling within. This represents a powerful synthesis (cf. 'in one Spirit we were all baptised into one body', 1 Corinthians 12:13). It is now not merely

---

205 Gaffin (1978, 68–69) points to the close connection in Paul between Spirit and power (cf. 1:4; 8:11; 15:13,19; 1Corinthians 2:4,5).

baptism in the Spirit but baptism in one Spirit into one body, that is, into Christ (1 Corinthians 12:12). Not only is the rite of baptism an experience of the Spirit but it is also a share in the action of God whereby the convert comes to share in the risen life of Christ and becomes a member of Christ.

1 Corinthians

Paul's controversy in 1 and 2 Corinthians is with those who consider themselves to be *pneumatikoi* (Spirit people) as they seem to be advocating mere human wisdom to solve community problems. But Paul indicates in these two letters that the operation of true life in the Spirit will remedy community problems. Paul begins the first letter with thanks for the community and their giftedness but the letters proceed with direction towards correction of personal and community life in the Spirit.

God's grace has been given for the church at Pentecost in response to the death and resurrection of Christ Jesus, who enriched the church with every kind of spiritual (Spirit) gifting (1:4-7). Note that 'grace', not 'Spirit', is the term that Paul uses. The gifts in their abundance are exercised through all *logos* and *gnosis* (word and wisdom, 1:5) but the problem is that the Corinthians are boasting in them. But gifts must be realised and used in the light of waiting for the return of Christ (1:7).

The Spirit's persuasive power (2:4)

In the first use of Spirit in the letter (2:4), Paul refers to the Spirit's persuasive power. Rejecting the method of Greek rhetoric, Paul preaches the gospel of Christ crucified—depending on the Spirit to produce results, avoiding the use of human dynamics or persuasion to produce belief. The content of the gospel had come to Paul by revelation through the Spirit. Revelation involves an unveiling of God's mystery (2:16) whereby the Spirit reveals what had previously been hidden, indeed, what is still hidden without the Spirit. The Spirit is the sole communicator of salvation life awakening faith (2:4f; 1 Thessalonians 1:5; 2 Corinthians 3:3 with 1 Corinthians 3:5 and 2 Corinthians 4:13).

Paul did not rely on crafted word power or rhetoric, rather, Paul uses the adjective *peithois* and the genitive *sophias* together to define and limit his *logois* (in persuasive words of wisdom, 2:4). *Ho logos mou kai to kerugma mou* (my message and my preaching, 2:4) is an hendiadys referring to Paul's preaching and the content of his preaching. The content that Paul preaches is Christ crucified (2:2)—and Paul's preaching is by the Spirit and power, that is, the Spirit was present so there was power that produced faith that rested in God. Paul's use of *kerugma* (factual proclamation) made *logos* more specific, showing that his persuasive power was not rhetoric or word craft.

Paul continually reminds the Corinthians that the evidence of their changed lives was powerful proof not of their wisdom but of the Spirit's work. Using Paul as a divine agent in his 'weak' (non-rhetorical) preaching, God's wisdom—that is, the gospel of divine wisdom (1:21)—showed human wisdom to be foolishness (1:18-25). So the Corinthians' faith in response to Paul's preaching is to be in the power of God alone, not in human wisdom from which they must be disarmed (2 Corinthians 2:5). The preaching of the gospel needed human instruments like Paul who had been totally stripped of self-reliance.

'However' (2:6) indicates a major transition as Paul begins to test (cf. 2:6–4:21) his foundational conclusions (1:10–2:5), providing criteria by which true wisdom can be assessed. The crux of the matter is that the Corinthians had come to faith through the wisdom of the cross but now they were espousing human wisdom.

God's wisdom revealed through his Spirit (2:6-16)

Paul now defines divine wisdom. By the cross, the aeons of the old and new ages overlap. The rulers of this age—the wise, wellborn and powerful of the age—were responsible for the crucifixion (2:8). But these rulers are impermanent representatives of the achievements of the present world order; their fame is measured by the standards of human rebellion and unbelief. These rulers exemplified the best that the age had to offer but Paul disqualified their human wisdom for they did not understand the gospel. Their failure was not only moral but also epistemological for the Christ event was the place where all of God's mysteries converged. This is the epistemological difference between believers and unbelievers. They belong to two totally different worlds.

The subject of 2:6-16 is 'we' (as opposed to 'I' in 2:1-5; 3:1-2), that is, all who have the mind of Christ (2:6). Having denied the place of secular wisdom in the formation or preaching of the gospel, Paul now defines (cf. 'we speak', 2:6a) the proclamation of the gospel as wisdom preaching.[206] 2:6a and 2:6b set the direction in the chiastic sequence so that: 2:7-9 expand on 2:6b; and 2:10-16 expand on 2:6a—thus 2:6-16 is an enlargement of 1:18–2:5.[207] God's wisdom is granted to believers (2:6,7,9), that is, instead of the perspective of the world (1:18–2:5) now we have the divine perspective

---

206 Sandnes, 1991, 90-91.

207 Stuhlmacher, 1987, 328-347.

(2:6-16) from God's hidden wisdom. There is a significant shift of *sophia* (wisdom) from the worldly frame which depicts the cross as foolishness (1:17-25) to the divine viewpoint that the death of Christ is the profundity of wisdom (2:6-7). Paul's message was foolish from the world's perspective but not from God's perspective. This is an indictment on some at Corinth (cf. 1 Corinthians 3-4).

Sophia theou (wisdom of God) with the dative *kletois* (to the called, 1:24) and *hemin* (for us, 1:30) makes it clear that salvation rests on divine initiative. The wisdom of God is not, ultimately, cognitive or merely intellectual although a body of knowledge is integral (cf. Romans 6:17; 2 Timothy 1:13). The controlling reference or ultimate demonstration for the body of knowledge in divine wisdom is Christ's crucifixion. Hence Paul's decision to know only Christ's death while he is preaching among the Corinthians (2:2) because this divine wisdom (the cross) is soteriological. Paul is not arguing in 1 Corinthians 2 that there is a deeper, reserved or esoteric truth for the initiates. Those who take this view of Paul ignore 1:18-2:5. Wisdom in 1 Corinthians 2 is the gospel of the cross, and the role of the Spirit is to work through the preacher and apply this wisdom message to the listener. The 'we' subject of 1 Corinthians 2 seems to refer not only to Christian preaching in general but also to Paul's situation as paradigmatic—for Paul seeks to communicate with simplicity the divine wisdom of the cross in rhetorically disposed Corinth.

Paul's gospel presents divine wisdom that is not derivable from this world and therefore his presentation does not echo this world's methods. Response to Paul's gospel involves reception by the mind and reflection in conduct but only the *teleioi* (mature, that is, perfect or fit for the purpose; 2:6)—that is, those who are open to the work of the Spirit—will respond. The mature recognise their imperfection which characterises human need. The opposite of *teleioi* is *psuchikos* (natural or sensual; 2:14, cf. 3:1ff). The mature grasp things from God's perspective with the cross in the centre. There is no other message, no deeper Christian *sophia* that Paul saves for the elite. The single *kerugma* for all is the *sophia* of Christ crucified. The *teleioi* (the mature) have received the Spirit (2:12,15) which produces Spirit-directed preaching of the wisdom of God. This knowledge of God from the Spirit confirms the deity of the Spirit. This maturity, though not exhibited by some (3:1-2), is expected from the whole Christian congregation.

Thus Paul's gospel is not wisdom of this age and is therefore not recognisable as wisdom from the standpoint of this age. Two kinds of wisdom control Paul's thought (1:18ff), that is, the wisdom of two ages. The wisdom of the cross is not human wisdom of this age but the wisdom of the new age now breaking in, revealed through the Spirit. Divine revelation given in the preaching of the cross is required to understand the secret, hidden wisdom of Christ crucified. The background for 2:6 is the contrast between inter-testamental Judaism and Paul's comprehensive framework which encompasses history from creation to consummation, accenting its eschatological goal.

The wisdom of the old age is represented by rulers of this age (2:6-8) who represent power structures of this age and shape the present world order. But they will not leave a valid legacy because they have not seen that the eternal wisdom of God is revealed in the death of Christ. The human rulers' non-perception of the significance of the cross (1:18-25) is by God's design (cf. 1:21) for the wisdom in Paul's preaching remains hidden in mystery (2:7), beyond human understanding, except by revelation in the Spirit to the elect (cf. Daniel 2:27-28). The hidden mystery is revealed in Christ. The rulers of this age in which Paul wrote 1 Corinthians included the Sanhedrin who were the chiefs in Jewish society—a class of human power brokers who held social, political, and economic influence—and were responsible for the crucifixion. In the crucifixion, they were fulfilling God's will. But working through the Sanhedrin and controlling them were the demonic figures who are the real rulers of this age. These earthly powers and demonic controllers will pass away, indeed, the manifestation of God's hidden purpose in Jesus Christ crucified was an indication of the certainty of their defeat.

God foreordained the hiddenness of divine wisdom for the believers' glory, which will be revealed when they are finally presented in the divine image (2 Corinthians 3:18). None of the rulers perceived the power or supreme worth of Christ crucified even though this act provides the key to all human history (2:7-8). All of God's mysteries (past, present and future) converged in the Christ-event but still remain hidden for unbelievers (cf. the Greek perfect participle, 2:7). Indeed, God's mysteries will remain hidden if worldly standards or worldly impressiveness, like Corinth's oratorical display, control the appreciation of values.[208] The word of the cross—the

---

208 Sigurd, 2002, 689-709.

mystery of God's intention marked out before creation but now revealed in Jesus' death—draws one of two responses because its truth can only be discerned by the Spirit.

The paradox was that the rulers of this age—who exemplified the most that this age had to offer—sent the Lord of glory to the cross. Christ came to radiate the supreme manifestation of divine glory in our world but the world substituted poverty. Even so, Paul indicates that the new age has broken in as he apocalyptically applies allusions from the Old Testament (2:6–9; cf. Isaiah 64:4; 65:17).

God's purposes in salvation cannot be understood by human reason or the devices of the leaders of this age. Understanding the hidden wisdom—God's plan of salvation—requires revelation for God's plan is beyond human fabrication or expectation but conceived by God long ago for those who would return his love. A sequence of biblical allusions indicates the character of eschatological glory that awaits believers (2:9). The revelation of divine glory (the cross) could not fit into the world's understanding so when the world saw this glory it did not register because it clashed with their preconceptions. Thus people are dependent on divine illumination, for God can only be known by his self-revelation by the work of the Holy Spirit. By the Spirit, the mature understand the cross as God's revealed love (2:11). So the Spirit is the key not only to Paul's preaching but also to the conversion of the Corinthians. God's wisdom (2:9) was communicated through the Spirit who is the channel of revelation (2:10–3:4). The Spirit searches all things including the deep recesses of the divine mind so the Spirit can reveal the divine mind to believers. Hence the Spirit must be God.[209] The wisdom of the cross is the full declaration of the divine purpose which is gradually communicated by the Spirit as the Christian matures.

As divine disclosure of God's plan is required to understand God's hidden wisdom, it cannot be ascertained by human inquiry. Only the divine can fully understand and communicate the divine. So the Spirit's revelatory activity (2:10a) is set in opposition to human wisdom of this age (2:5–16). A word play on *pneuma* (Spirit, 2:11) alongside an anthropological use of *pneuma* (the innermost self, the knower and willer in self-awareness) compares the unique self-knowledge of God with the unique self-knowledge we have of ourselves—accordingly, the Spirit knows the hidden depths of God as Father and Son, and this knowledge is given to believers as an indwelling

---

[209] cf. Cole, 2007, 71.

presence. The things of God (2:11) are God's eschatological wisdom-gospel while the spirit of the world (2:12) means humanity in rebellion against God.

The Spirit is the principle of self-knowledge in the Godhead (2:11). The Spirit is the Spirit of God and thus himself God. There is a total human incapacity to know the divine mind revealed through Scripture without personal illumination from the Spirit who personally communicates with the human spirit. As Fee puts it:

> *The Spirit is at once both fully God and distinct from the Father. The closest kind of intimate interior relationship exists between the Father and the Spirit, so close that the only proper analogy for it is that of the human spirit, the interior expression of personality.*[210]

The Spirit is the means of communicating God's thoughts to us (2:12–13). We can only know God as the Spirit communicates him by God's self-revelation. From God, through the Spirit (2:12), come the free gifts of God: a personal understanding and faith response to God's eschatological wisdom-gospel of Christ; and knowledge of the important things that God gives us in Christ. No amount of human ingenuity, technique, ability, effort, or knowledge can open the Scriptures but with the illumination of the Spirit all these natural giftings will be used. The things given (*ta charismata*, 2:12)—the spiritual gift of insight—can only come through the inner transforming work of the Spirit which gives new illumination into the gospel of salvation, our need for salvation, and our increasing awareness of the truth and relevance of the Bible. As Cole states:

> *if from Scripture we find that the Spirit is principally involved in our knowing God, then why not with our knowing God through the Scripture?*[211]

The alternative to such Spirit-control is control by the spirit of the world which leaves humanity in rebellion against God.

The Spirit's revelatory role involves the apostle (2:13) with Paul featured in the 'we' that includes all believers (cf. 2:10,12). So speaking what 'we know' (cf. 2:12) is the Spirit's activity such that Paul's words evaluate spiritual things by divine revelation—not clever human fabrications but

---

210 Fee, 1994, 101. Fee is referring to relationships in the 'essential Trinity' as opposed to activities and functions in the administration of the plan of salvation.

211 Cole, 2007, 266.

what the Spirit teaches. All previous accusatives relating to content are picked up in 'we speak of these things' (2:13). Paul's words are not humanly fabricated but taught by the Spirit, embracing both form and content (*logos* and *sophia*, 2:13; cf. 2:4). True wisdom will not depend on profound speech, rather, true wisdom depends on the knowledge of God and his intentions for the world conveyed by the Spirit. The Spirit explains spiritual things to spiritual people because they have been previously taught and moved by the Spirit and therefore have the ability to understand (*pneumatikois*, 2 Corinthians 2:13; cf. 1 Corinthians 2:15). Whereas the natural man is blind to God's saving work, truly spiritual people illuminated by the Spirit will recognise true wisdom in the cross.

Only two responses to the word of revelation are possible—acceptance or rejection—there is no middle ground (2:14–16). The inclusion of both *psuchikos* (natural, the ordinary person, the unbeliever living on the human level; 2:14) and *pneumatikos* (spiritual; 2:14) covers all readers. The unspiritual are incapable of understanding God's wisdom so their response to the cross reveals who they are. They cannot receive the baptism of the Spirit. The contrast between *psuchikos* and *pneumatikos* may have been a distinctively Corinthian issue.[212] Indeed, Paul indicates that each human being has a divinely created *pneumatikos* nature within that is open to spiritual communication of divine truth. Within the believer, there is an unqualified antithesis between the natural and the spiritual man (2:14f), between the flesh and the Spirit (Romans 8:5; Galatians 5:16ff). Unbelievers are fleshly (fallibly human, cf. 3:1), so for them there is a total cognitive inability to understand the gospel because the Spirit is required to produce discernment. So unbelievers will naturally reject the gospel as foolish. 'Fleshly' hearers who live life without the Spirit cannot understand Christ crucified so they will not believe because they are not able to.

The discernment produced by the Spirit (2:15) can discover all things, that is, the totality of revelation (cf. 2:10)—everything that God wants us to know about ourselves and our world! To have the Spirit of God is to have the Spirit of Christ (Romans 8:9) and, hence, the mind of Christ or Christ's own understanding of his saving significance revealed through the Spirit.[213] So believers who rely on the wisdom of God are subject to judgment by no

---

212 Davis, 1984, 116.
213 Fee, 1994, 109.

one other than God (2:15b). So worldly Corinth cannot judge Paul's ministry of gospel proclamation.

Paul's astounding conclusion to the argument begun at 1:18 is that 'we have the mind of Christ' (2:16). This human impossibility (cf. Isaiah 40:13) can only be produced by a Spirit-filled understanding of the word of the cross. This Spirit-filled understanding of the cross is the essential element to bring about the unity for which Paul pleaded (1:10). The long discussion about wisdom (1:17–2:16) is not a digression from the issue of division in Corinth (1:10–13) for the wisdom they were pursuing was a product of the human psyche which had stripped the gospel of real power and led to divisions. If the Corinthians think spiritually then there will be no divisions. Believers could achieve this because, having the Spirit of discernment, they have the mind of Christ. By the action of the Holy Spirit, they are able to think as Christ thinks. In Christ, the plan of God has come to 'crucial expression' but Christ not only reveals God's wisdom but he also reflects the source of God's wisdom. Having the 'mind of Christ' means that the mind of God has been revealed to the believer.[214] The mind is not merely cognitive but directive of the total personality (cf. Romans 12:1–2) therefore if we have the mind of Christ—that is, Christ's own understanding of his saving work—then there has been a total transformation of our thinking and acting. If Corinthians have the mind of Christ revealing the hidden wisdom of God in the cross then they will present their bodies as a living sacrifice! For Paul, having the mind of Christ means prophetic revelation into understanding the Scriptures. The wisdom which the world craves but cannot see is in the understanding of the cross. So 'we have the mind of Christ' summarises, as a thanksgiving, Paul's message for the Corinthians' situation (2:16).[215]

The congregation is the temple for God's Spirit (3:1-4)

The argument of 2:6–16 is now applied to Corinth. There is no middle ground between the two classes of people in humanity, namely: believers and unbelievers (cf. 2:14–16); or converted and unconverted (3:1–3); or those with and those without the Spirit. There is no middle ground in the

---

214 Fatehi, 2000, 188 (quoting Davis, 1984, 92f).
215 Sandnes, 1991, 115.

adjectives carnal, fleshy or worldly. Those without the Spirit are not merely worldly Christians but, rather, they are not Christians because they are bound up in behaviour that confirms their identity. 'Worldly Christians' are characterised by jealousy, strife (3:3; cf. Galatians 5:20), deeds of the flesh, and deeds of darkness (Romans 13:12). True Christians (2:6) are mature (cf. 1:24,30). 'Infants in Christ' (3:1) does not refer to a regressive Christian state that is puerile, infantile or retarded (cf. Hebrews 5:12ff), indeed, Paul is not addressing the Corinthians as mature Christians because they don't fit that description.[216]

Paul continues to address the problem of dissension to all of the Corinthian church, not just a faction. The gospel of the wisdom of the cross exalts the humble and builds up the congregation (1:18–2:16). Spiritual Christians would appreciate God's modus operandi so if Corinthian believers had presuppositional difficulties with Paul's preaching, the problem was theirs. Paul addressed the Corinthian congregation as infants in Christ because of the regressive state of spiritual affairs in their church. The congregation behaved like they were unconverted (*psuchikoi*, 2:14)—maintaining worldly values—rather than Spirit-possessed Christians (*teleioi/pneumatikoi*). Paul is not demanding academic theological progress, rather, Paul is exhorting the Corinthians to adjust their thought patterns (3:1–3).[217] They were still operating from limited human perspectives (3:3) characterised by distressing non-Christian divisions.[218] Indeed, Corinthian Christians were acting as if they were unbelievers therefore Paul treats them as immature babes and *sarkinoi* (Christians who are maintaining their old world point of view).

Sarkinoi (fleshly, 3:1) emphasises the physical side of human existence absent of the spiritual.[219] The text progresses from *psuchikoi* (totally devoid of the Spirit—living on the purely human, unredeemed level; 2:14) to *sarkinoi* (not showing the presence of the Spirit). Paul regularly uses children (*teknon*) to reflect his apostolic relationship with converts but he uses the pejorative *nepioi* (babes) of the Corinthian congregation because of their

---

216 Gaffin Jr, 1979, 35.
217 Fee, 1987,122.
218 The combination of 'jealousy and strife' (3:3; cf. Galatians 5:20) is a non-Christian attitude opposed to the Spirit and his fruits (cf. Gaffin, 1979, 35).
219 Thiselton, 2000, 292-3.

infantile behaviour. They are adults of the wrong kind who think that they are full grown spiritual but this is an unreal self-assessment.

Paul is not promoting progress into a deeper form of teaching, rather, they must abandon their puerile practices and thereby progress from milk to solid food. Perhaps the Corinthians accused Paul of feeding them with milk as opposed to solid food but Paul's gospel of Christ is both milk and solid food (2:6–16). The milk is the good news of salvation and the solid food is the understanding that the entire Christian life is predicated on the reality of the cross. But the fundamental contrast in Paul's mind is not between two diets, rather, the fundamental contrast is between the true food of the gospel and the synthetic wisdom substitutes that the Corinthians preferred.

3:16 sums up the application of Paul's rebuke (3:1–4). The church was arguing over the force of personalities—Paul and Apollos—but the congregation is a sacred group that does not belong to personalities, rather, the congregation belongs to Jesus as the new temple. The congregation is the place where the deity resides, that is, the corporate place where the action of the Holy Spirit constitutes the Body of Christ. So the gathered congregation is the temple where God's presence is encountered, a local manifestation of the divine presence, irrespective of whether the people of God have or do not have a building. Accordingly, 3:16–17 is a stern warning about the responsibility of leadership in the congregation because wrong attitudes to internal divisions, or action against the gathered people of God, will have eternal effects. The warning is that factional leaders in Corinth have potentially put themselves in the path to final judgement.

The Spirit is with the assembled congregation (5:1–13)

In the matter of sexual immorality, the issue is whether they will pay attention to Paul or continue to follow the worldly wise thinkers at Corinth. The emphatic 'I on the other hand' (*ego men*, 5:3) indicates that Paul is taking decisive action in contrast to Corinthian neglect. The absent Paul is, nevertheless, present with them personally in the shared Spirit.[220] Paul's letter will act for him to speak a word of judgement on the offender (*kekrika*, 5:3) and the congregation must share Paul's judgement as his letter is read to them.

---

220 Fee, 1994, 121.

The discipline is to be carried out when they are assembled (5:4) since the whole church bears responsibility. Christian morality in secular Corinth would have been considered culturally restrictive. Perhaps the offending member was a high profile member of the church against whom some in the congregation were reluctant to take action. But when they are assembled the Spirit is among them—that is, the power of Jesus as Lord is among them—and since Paul shares the same Spirit (cf. the emphatic 'my Spirit'; 5:4), Paul will also be present (though absent) in the gathered congregation. Where moral virtue is absent, the Spirit's direction is also absent. The fleshly body is marked by weakness and dishonour, but the spiritual body is characterised by incorruption and power.

Paul states that the sinner must be expelled for his own sake—perhaps the spirit of the sinner will yet be saved in the day of the Lord Jesus (5:5). There is also a holiness motive, that is, that the church may be sanctified as a covenant community exercising corporate responsibility. The man under review must be excluded because, in Old Testament terms: he is guilty of heinous covenant disloyalty; while he remains the church is implicated in his sin; and the community is the temple of the Holy Spirit. Paul's New Testament approach to dealing with the covenant-breaker in the community is to both expel the sinner and yet still seek the salvation of the sinner.

Paul makes a clear call for congregational purity. In Christ the Corinthian believers had moved from the old to the new leaven (5:6-8), that is, Christ had accomplished their exodus deliverance. Christ freed them from what bound them to the past (the old leaven) and brought them to a continuing new life in the pursuit of holiness. To celebrate the feast continually (present tense, 5:8) banishes the leaven so that they walk in newness of life by the power of the Spirit in them. The Spirit within foreshadows the new creation—with its new heaven and new earth that Christ founded—in which the leaven of the old life is banished.

The Spirit is the covenant God with us (6:1-11)

Taking issue with regard to lawsuits between believers (6:1-8), Paul points out that the Corinthian believers had been set apart (sanctified, 6:11) for the production of Christian holiness. Now freed from the wrath of God, the Corinthian believers are in right relationship with God—they are members in right standing of the new covenant (justified)[221] through the power

---

221 Fee, 1994, 127-132.

(in the name) of Christ. Their right standing is because of total surrender to Christ in his death and resurrected life, mediated by the Spirit from God. The great change from their past lives is that, through the Spirit empowering them for life in the present, the benefits of Christ's saving work had been supplied and are now being progressively applied (6:11). Christ's sacrifice, applied through the Spirit in the name of Christ (that is, by Christ's authority), had made them: clean (washed in rebirth); sanctified, that is, progressively changed into Christ-likeness; justified, that is, declared right with God (the divine passives point to the Spirit's act in conversion).[222] God had raised the Lord and will also raise the Corinthian believers by his power (6:14).

Paul likens the relationship between Christ and the believer to the physical union of marital sexual intercourse (6:17), that is, to be joined to the Lord is to be one Spirit with him. *Soma*—used of a sexual union with a harlot (6:16)—is replaced by *pneuma* as the medium of intimate union between the power of the exalted Christ (the Spirit of Christ) and the Christian (the human spirit; cf. Romans 8:16).

Paul quotes the Corinthian belief that sin had no connection with the body: 'every sin which a man commits is outside the body', that is, the body has no connection with sin (6:18). But Paul argues that sexual sin affects the physical body (6:12–13), indeed, fornication stands in a category by itself. In the sexual act, the immoral person perverts the faculty that is meant to be the instrument of the most intimate bodily communication in union between persons—he sins against his own unique power of bodily communication. The nub of the dispute between Paul and the Corinthians concerns the value to be placed upon our present bodies. For the Corinthians, the fact that the body was soon to be done away with rendered it of no moral significance; but for Paul, the body is the sphere of the Lord's communication given expression through the Body of Christ (6:12–20).

The Spirit remains, primarily, the power of God—however much the Spirit may manifest the character of Christ. Christ has an ontological relation to God which appears to be without the Spirit. But the Spirit in the essential Trinity, administering the plan of salvation, is the Spirit of Christ revealing Christ and the Spirit of God revealing the mind of God (2:10).

---

222 Gaffin (1978,72) argues that in three Pauline references to the Spirit (12:4ff; 2 Corinthians 13:14; and Ephesians 4:4ff) with a common triadic structure, the Holy Spirit is correlated with the Father and thus viewed as person.

The exalted Christ appears before God as firstborn Son of a new family of resurrected humanity, that is, the first instalment of a new relationship between God and man. To humanity, Christ appears through the Spirit giving life, not just the first instalment of that new relationship but as the one who makes the relationship possible for others.[223]

The body is destined for resurrection, hence its importance. Accordingly, sinful sexual behaviour: denies the work of the cross with regard to resurrection; severs the relationship with Christ's body; contravenes the Scriptures; and rejects the presence of the Holy Spirit.[224] The body is the self in communication and therefore must be preserved from misuse. Paul refers to biblical precedents—Joseph in Genesis 39 as opposed to Judah in Genesis 38—in making a comparative judgment concerning the lasting and irreversible personal effects of the sinful sexual act (6:18). Sexual sin is also against the ongoing wellbeing of the body,[225] since believers in both Old and New Testaments are not their own (6:19b). The Corinthian disdain for the physical body (as of no heavenly use) is wrong. Indeed, Christians are doubly owned, by creation and redemption: bought by Christ (6:20) to become a temple for God's presence mediated by the Spirit. God, through his Spirit, inhabits the body as a divine owner. The nature of God's presence through the Spirit in the believers should be clear from what they do to glorify God in (*en*, 6:20) their physical body. 'Bought with a price' is a reference to the slave market (6:20) because, by purchase, Yahweh has acquired a people for himself. Relationship with God comes through Christ's death and by God's gift of the Spirit who presents Christ so that the believer is in Christ. God is the initiator. When this relationship is established, believers belong to a new master who is resident in them.[226]

---

223 There is a distinction between the economic Trinity and the essential Trinity regarding the roles within the Godhead in administering the plan of salvation (Cole, 2007, 171–173).

224 Sandnes, 2002, 193.

225 Rosner, 1994, 144.

226 Fatehi (2000, 211) points to Ezekiel 37:27 where God's dwelling in the midst of his people is God giving his Spirit and requiring from them new obedience.

Excursus: The Temple as Spirit's Presence

The temple motif is Paul's soteriological understanding of the Spirit's presence in the life of the individual believer. God not only dwells in the midst of his people by the Spirit but also has taken residence in the lives of his people individually—from conversion—as the life-giving Spirit. Thus God's presence has returned to his people not only corporately as they gather for worship but also individually. Through the Spirit, God's promise that he would be personally present with his people is fulfilled. Those who have experienced decisive spiritual change will know God directly and respond to him positively, desiring to keep the covenant stipulations. In Christ the Corinthian believers are the temple of God (3:16–17; 6:19) and therefore they are not their own but, rather, they are holy.

Paul moves from the idea of the new covenant presence of the Spirit to the concept of the church as the temple of God. This corresponds with the expectations of the new covenant (cf. Jeremiah 31:31–34), namely, that the new covenant cannot be broken and is everlasting.[227] God will make an everlasting covenant of peace with them and set his sanctuary, his dwelling place, in their midst. He will be their God and they shall be his people (Jeremiah 31:33; cf. 31:1; 32:38; Ezekiel 37:27) and the nations will know that the Lord sanctifies Israel when his sanctuary is in their midst forever. God himself will dwell in the midst of his people (Ezekiel 37:26ff). The promise of the Spirit poured out on his people serves as the permanent witness and seal of the covenant of peace, the eternal covenant (Ezekiel 36; 39:29). In the old covenant, the Spirit conveyed God's presence on earth (cf. Joel 2:28–29; Zechariah 12:10; Isaiah 32:15; 44:1ff; Ezekiel 39:29)—and as the Spirit is poured out in the new covenant, the covenant relationship of believers is ratified and sealed (cf. Acts 8:4–17; 10:44–48; 19:6; cf. Ephesians 1:13; 4:30).

So Paul's reference to the Corinthians being sealed in the Spirit is confirmation of their covenant relationship (2 Corinthians 1:22; 5:5). In Christ, the people of the new covenant have already become the eschatological temple of God's presence by virtue of the presence of the Spirit. As the temple of God, we display and communicate the presence of God on earth for we are now being filled with glory by the transforming work of the Spirit (2 Corinthians 3:18). The glory of God seen in the new covenant people of God is the face of Christ (2 Corinthians 4:6). The wonder of the gospel is

---

[227] cf. Jeremiah 32:40 and Ezekiel 37:24–28 (a summary of the prior passage of restoration, Ezekiel 36:25ff).

that, wherever the Spirit resides, all are free to enter the holy of holies with unveiled face (2 Corinthians 3:17). The Spirit frees us from hard-heartedness that—in the past—required the veiling of God's glory from his people. So Paul's preaching was not persuasive words of wisdom but demonstration of the Spirit and power so that their faith would not rest on the wisdom of men but on the power of God (2:4ff). In other words, as an apostle of Christ, Paul was called upon to exercise the new covenant ministry of the Spirit that abounded in glory for the people of God.

Paul relies on the Spirit in all his communication (7:1-16)

The sexual relationship in marriage involves giving authority over the body to another person (7:4). Accordingly, if a man gives his body into the possession of a prostitute then he is mastered or possessed by her. But believers have already given authority over their bodies to Christ in spiritual union so they cannot give their bodies to anyone else. In Christian marriage (7:1-7), the mutual self-giving of husband and wife to each other is taken up into the lordship of Christ in which all of the Christian's bodily activity takes place (Romans 12:1-2). The pattern of self-giving in marriage is basic, like Christ giving himself for believers (Romans 14:7-9). Thus Paul warns the Corinthians against fornication.

Paul draws a distinction between what he thinks and what the Lord says (7:12,25,40) but, even when he is expressing a personal opinion, Paul relies on the Spirit for what he says (7:40). This reliance on the Spirit is—as Fee highlighted[228]—explicit at 7:40 but arguably implicit at 7:12,25. Paul's communication with Christ by the Spirit meant that his wise decisions in ministry (recorded in Scripture) reflected the mind of Christ. The Spirit within Paul did not guarantee every word of Paul, nevertheless, Paul's life is guided by the Spirit.

The Spirit enables a true confession about Jesus (12:1-3)

A new item appears (*peri de*, 12:1) in Paul's discussion about the problems associated with worship at Corinth with regard to their identification and use of spiritual things. The Corinthians have mistaken views about spiritual things which Paul will correct (rather than instruct about) in 1 Corinthians 12-14. Corinth regarded speaking with tongues as the prime or only endowment of the Spirit, however—whereas Paul finds a place in

---

[228] Fee, 1994, 139-40.

Christian expression for tongues (14:5,18)—Paul defines circumstances when tongues may be used. Continuing the earlier theme about issues affecting Christian fellowship in the self-directed Christian life (1 Corinthians 8–11), 1 Corinthians 12–14 revolve around the misuse of tongues (principally) and prophecy but also call for recognition of a diversity of gifts. The key is 13:1 where tongues and angels are linked. The Corinthians considered themselves like angels already, that is, truly spiritual and therefore without any need for sex in the present (a relationship involving the body, 1 Corinthians 7) or a body in the future (1 Corinthians 15). They also considered themselves to have truly angelic speech experiences through the Spirit. But Paul reveals that the gift of the Spirit is primarily to enable believers to live in human weakness for Christ through divine power.

Pneumatikon (12:1) may refer to either spiritual things or spiritual people (Thisleton suggests that *pneumatikon* denotes what comes from the Spirit in the normal course of Christian experience; cf. 15:44).[229] The translation 'spiritual men' (12:1) is unlikely as it does not account for the probable intended ambiguity. The argument in 1 Corinthians 12–14 has to do with spirituality (cf. the neuter 'spiritual things' in 14:1) as a result of illumination by the Holy Spirit who is the source of all spiritual gifts. Spiritual activity is the issue, but there is an emphasis on tongues and then on prophecy.[230]

Various derivatives of *pneumatikos* (spiritual) are used often by Paul in 1 Corinthians, hence this word group was probably well understood in Corinth. Paul teaches that all gifts should be understood and used correctly[231]—indeed, the summary of 1 Corinthians 12–14 could be: 'You all have spiritual gifts, but seek the best'.[232] In this way, Paul corrects the Corinthian confusion about the pre-eminence of a couple of the more unusual spiritual gifts.

The Gentile past of Corinthian believers was characterised by being compulsively drawn to idols (12:2) and perhaps consequently drawn to being

---

[229] Thisleton (2000, 393–395) agrees with Fee (1994, 153), suggesting that 'the things of the Spirit' intends both possibilities.

[230] Hill (1967, 266) states that it is likely that the Corinthians believed in many spirits giving varied gifts—but Paul believed that there were many gifts but one source, that is, God through the Spirit (as in the Old Testament).

[231] cf. 12:4–11,27–30; 13:1–3.

[232] A development of 12:2–3, expanding 12:1.

'carried away' at pagan shrines by manufactured, demonstrative ecstatic utterance on behalf of a god that was incapable of responding. Through the work of the Spirit, Corinthian believers have transitioned from being Gentiles to being members of the new covenant (12:2) and consequently numbered among the people of God, that is, the restored Israel (cf. Romans 11:7). The transition is from dumb idols in a pagan temple to the emphasised expressiveness (*lalon*, 12:3) of the Holy Spirit in his work of personal spiritual regeneration.

Then Paul identifies his own revelation to the Corinthians, namely, no one can say that Jesus is Lord apart from through the Holy Spirit (12:3). This is not a casual aside. The experience of Jesus as Lord (cf. Romans 8:9)—that is, being in the new covenant where Jesus is the covenant Lord—depends on being in the Spirit, indeed, the Holy Spirit is the active agent in inspired Christian articulation. So Paul moderates the Corinthian emphasis on tongues and prophecy by showing that they are only part of a wider view of the distribution of gifts (12:4–11), that is, tongues is not the essential (basic) gift of regeneration nor is tongues the down payment (firstfruits) of the eternal resurrected life. All Christians are regenerated through the Spirit—which is the essence of the new covenant—and therefore all Christians are 'spirituals' who possess spiritual gifts. Indeed, particular gifts don't distinguish levels of spirituality among members of the congregation.

Christian, Spirit-led speech cannot call Jesus cursed. Many explanations have been offered for *Anathema Iesous* (12:3) such as contemporary pagan temple ejaculation or a cry of faith that Jesus crucified had become a curse (Galatians 3:13). But Jesus is now Lord. The relationship between 12:3 and 12:1–2 is signified by *dio* (therefore, 12:3). Paul does not want the Corinthians to be ignorant of spiritual gifts but their previous lives included temple attendance so Paul clarifies the difference between the Spirit-gifted believer and the unbeliever (12:3). The believer confesses appropriately that his or her life is totally yielded to Jesus as Lord because of the empowering and prompting of the Spirit—but the unbeliever blasphemes. This contrast between the believer and the unbeliever makes it clear that 'Jesus is accursed' (12:3) is a curse statement (that is, it is not well-meaning recognition that Jesus took our curse in his death). Alternatively, 'Jesus is accursed' may have been a Jewish response that Paul had uttered in his pre-conversion rabbinic days.[233] In any case, 12:3 states that Christian giftedness is the out-

---

233 Bassler, 1982, 418.

come of possessing Christ through the Spirit. The distinction between the Spirit-filled Christian and the unbeliever is recognition of the lordship of Christ through the Spirit's empowering presence resulting in a life of service under that lordship.

Many gifts expressing unity in the one Spirit (12:4–6)

There is one Spirit and many gifts (12:4,11). Paul's emphasis is the harmonious balance in the diversity of gifts expressed across the congregation coming from the same Spirit, the same Lord, and the same God (a Trinitarian formula; 12:4-6).[234] Such gifts—as opposed to the singular gift of the Spirit in regeneration—characterise true believers. Paul accepts without comment that spiritual gifts will be present in Corinth's factionally divided congregation, indeed, Paul promotes gifts for edification. And the diversity of gifts within a church congregation is rooted in the diversity in unity of the Trinitarian Godhead, with the Father as the bestower of grace. Charismata, divine gifts, are for service in ministry as the concrete expression of *charis* (divine gift of the Spirit) is expressed in service within the church. The distribution of gifts and gifting by the Spirit is designed to result in the unity of the Spirit in the congregation (12:4).

There are different allotments of charismata (divine gifts) resulting in differing ministries of service (*diakoniai*, 12:5) and different ways of effectual workings (*energmata*, 12:6). Charismata[235] are displayed gifts, ministries and workings. These gifts are not only effectual but are all demonstrations of divine grace.

Whereas 12:4-6 defines the gifts, 12:8-10 makes it clear that spiritual gifts are to function in churches. Spiritual gifts are how God, by the power of his Spirit, uses Christians as instruments in his service (cf. 7:7 where celibacy and marriage are gifts). As the Spirit is the promise of the Father (Luke 24:49; Acts 1:4; cf. 2:33) so God is the giver of the gifts (1 Corinthians 12–14) but the expression of the gifts is the manifestation of the Spirit (12:7,11). The Spirit divides the gifts among the congregation as he wills for service or edification in the church (12:4-6; 14:12,26). The diversities

---

[234] Carson (1987, 21–22) suggests that 12:4-6 is not referring to natural propensities or potential within a person.

[235] Turner (792) believes that 'charismata' is not derived from charis (grace) but, rather, means 'thing given' or 'gift'.

of gifts, differences of ministries, and diversities of activities (12:4-6)[236] are through Jesus (12:12-26) but ultimately from God as author—or, put another way, the survey is of three categories of spiritual gifts or charismata of the Spirit enabled by the Lord as the workings of God (12:27-30).[237]

The change of terminology from *pneumatika* to *charismata* (12:4) signifies that Christian gifts are linked with the Spirit. *Pneumatika*, apparently a contentious word, is not picked up again until the issue of gifts has been thoroughly discussed (14:1). These revelatory manifestations (*phanerosis*, 12:7) of the Spirit are not given by the Spirit (of Christ, Romans 8:9-11) but by God communicating himself through the Spirit (12:6). The role of the Spirit is manifestation and distribution—in word or deed—of gifts from God through but not by the Spirit (12:4-6,11). Gifts from God through the Spirit honouring the Lord represent an incipiently Trinitarian linkage. Attributes and abilities possessed prior to conversion may, by the addition of God's grace, become harnessed for Christian service as true *charismata* for common advantage (*sumpheron*, 12:7) to provide for the welfare and growth of the congregation. The gifts are meant to provide evidence of God in action in the vitality of congregational life. Through the Spirit, God establishes diversity such that each member is a recipient of some gift of the Spirit for the common good (12:7).

The gifts are given—passive, indicating that their author is God, that is, they are expressions of Christ's ministry through the Spirit—for congregational unity and edification, not merely for personal encouragement in Christian service (though that will undoubtedly happen in exercising the gifts). The list of gifts may not be exhaustive. When Christian offices appeared later, the potential bearers were not assessed in terms of the gifts they possessed but in terms of Christian maturity and wisdom.[238]

Different manifestations of one Spirit for all (12:7-11)

Hekasto (12:7) refers to the variety in distribution or reception of the nine gifts listed (12:8-10). This list is representative, not exhaustive.[239] Some gifts require habituation and development so they are not necessarily

---

236 cf. Smit, 1991, 211-29.
237 cf. Smit, 1991, 218.
238 cf. Hays, 1997, 250-2.
239 cf. 12:27-28; Romans 12:6-8; Ephesians 4:11.

spontaneous (cf. prophecy and evaluation of what is of the Spirit).[240] The sequence in the list of gifts (12:8–10) is arranged by changing the pronoun from *allos* (another of the same kind; 12:8,9b,10abcde) to *heteros* (another of a different kind; 12:9a) at the third and eighth items in the list (faith and tongues). Ranking is not the issue since the order varies in different lists (12:28–31). The first two items (word of wisdom, word of knowledge) and the last two items (tongues and interpretation) in the list are word or language items. In between, the items appear to be an outworking of the third item (faith)—as a supernatural endowment—in healings, miracles, prophecy and discernment of spirits.

The gift of uttering wisdom in the church is not cleverness but, rather, the wisdom of God declared through the Spirit—that is, insight into the profundity of the message of Christ crucified (2:6–16). Communicating wisdom to the common advantage heads this list (12:8–10) but is not included in the later list (12:28–30). The word forms in the list (12:8–10) suggest operation in a specific situation but where these gifts require development it would appear that they are not given in the moment of their use but for such a moment.[241] Siegfried Schatzman suggests that, since *sophia* is God's saving deed through the crucified Christ (1:18–2:5), the word of wisdom would be a communication of God's redemptive purposes at the right time under the right circumstances.[242] The word of knowledge is difficult to delimit as Paul couples all knowledge with all mysteries (revelation furthering knowledge, 13:2). So a word of knowledge includes God-given insight into previous revelation or Christian tradition.

In this list, faith is given to another person (*hetero*, 12:9), signifying a special gift of faith to specific people—with some special exhibition—as distinct from the faith that all believers possess. *Charismata* (gifts, plural) of healings (plural) emphasise diversity, all given by God, perhaps including: gradual or sudden; through the use of medication or advice; physical or mental; through various people; in co-operation individually or institutionally; various kinds; various occasions; or administered to others. Effective deeds of powers (12:10) are divine interventions through people sometimes in the form of supernatural acts. Since 'powers' is plural, the range is wide

---

240 cf. Thiselton, 2000, 936.
241 cf. Thiselton, 2000, 943.
242 cf .Schatzman , 1982, 218.

including the effective preaching of the gospel or extraordinary Christian dedication.

Prophecy (12:10) is spoken under inspiration of the Spirit for edification, including teaching and doctrine. Prophecy will cease at Jesus' return (13:10) but now requires careful explanation and application. During the formation of the canon, prophecy may have included the ability to receive and expound on divine communication other than through existing Scripture. Wayne Grudem states that Paul's definition of prophecy is broad and could include any speech activity that is helpful to hearers.[243] Prophecy should be regulated (14:29-33; cf. 1 Thessalonians 5:20-21); is a gift (cf. Acts 2) available to all in the new age; is a spontaneous—that is, not prepared, not a sermon (cf. 1 Corinthians 14)—Spirit-inspired message for edification or encouragement, or in response to pastoral needs of the congregation. As an inclusion in this list, prophecy cannot be given a special status above other gifts. Some were called prophets probably because they were frequent speakers but the gift was potentially available to all. To discern spirits is to evaluate a prophecy (14:29), discerning whether what is spoken is from the Holy Spirit.

Kinds of tongues (plural) indicate variety (12:10). These are Spirit inspired, controlled, inarticulate utterances of different kinds addressed by believers to God (14:2). Tongues must be regulated in the congregational setting (cf. 14:2-5) and cannot be endorsed by the assembly without being interpreted. Tongues are unintelligible (14:2b,5,7-9,11,19) to unbelievers (14:23b)[244] but are a sign to them (14:22) and can be interpreted by those who have the gift of interpretation (12:10). Tongues are signs to the individual (14:4; cf. 14:18) and may be in such exalted language as to be associated with angelic speech (13:1). The Holy Spirit makes deep, inarticulate intercession for us beyond the limits of consciousness (Romans 8:26)—hence, the work of the Spirit must play a part in the understanding of the Spirit phenomenon of tongues.[245] Unlike prophecy, tongues are directed towards God (14:2,14,28) as a Spirit-motivated utterance (12:11). As tongues ought to be used for private devotion, they are not specifically a gift for the

---

243 Grudem, 1982, 219.

244 Gaffin (1979, 76-77) suggests that the preceding phrase (since you are zealous of spirits, 14:12a), referring to spiritual gifts, makes it likely that the phrase 'my spirit prays' (14:14) refers to the work of the Holy Spirit through the believer.

245 cf. Thiselton, 2000, 985.

assembly and will edify the congregation only if interpreted. Paul did not expect all to speak in tongues (12:30) but wished that they would, however even more Paul wished that they would all prophesy (14:5). Theissen argues that tongues articulate what is hidden in the personality, making 'unconscious depth dimensions of life accessible'.[246] The interpreter of tongues (12:10), either the speaker or another, is given the power to provide intelligible articulation of tongues-speech.[247]

The church as the Body of Christ is the place where the Spirit is present and working in the distribution of his gifts. Consider the list of gifts alongside the ministry of Christ in the gospels. Will not the exercise of these gifts in the local congregation display the life of Christ in contemporary society? The variety of gifts (12:4–11) function in one body as organically interactive parts (12:12)—distributed by the one Spirit representing God and Christ. So there is no ground for human boasting about the various ways in which the Spirit is working through members of the one body because all members necessarily share in the one Spirit. Finally, the gifts are graces, divine manifestations, and 'events' given not for individual aggrandisement but for the common good of the congregation as the Spirit pleases to edify and build up the church. The gifts may be spontaneously expressed but are habitual dispositions of character 'shaped and nourished by the Holy Spirit' for the benefit of the church at the moment of God's choice.[248]

Gifts of the Spirit

The phrase 'gifts of the Spirit' is not Pauline, rather, the gifts are from God through the Spirit—as the creator of the body of Christ—to members of the body. Nevertheless, the association of gift language and Spirit activity makes the title 'gifts of the Spirit' appropriate as they were given at the time of incorporation into the unity of Christ's body. As members of one body, we all share in the work of Christ in redemption and the gifts of the Spirit are dependent on this basic gift of salvation in Christ (even so, gifts such as prophesy were also present in the Old Testament; 1 Samuel 10:7;10–13; 19:23f).

---

246 Thiessen, 1987, 276–341.

247 Thiselton, 2000, 1988.

248 Thiselton, 2000, 943. However, in an illuminating unpublished paper, D.W.B. Robinson (Sydney, March 1972) suggested that the gifts were natural endowments and temperaments extended with the lordship of God through Christ.

The church exists by God's grace. Any capacity of the believer is by God's grace and to function in his service is a gift. Spiritual gifts comprise all the ways that God by the power of his Spirit uses Christians as instruments in his service. Paul qualifies *charisma* (gift) at times with *pneumatikon* (spiritual) which indicates that *charisma* is not necessarily 'spiritual' but may also be a 'natural' gift brought under the lordship of Christ. Paul refers to gifts as: the Spirit's *charismata* (12:4); manifestations (*phaneros*, 12:7) of the Spirit; unqualified *charismata* (12:9,31); and *charismata* confined to healings (12:28).

The activities of God are called *energmata* (12:6) but *energmata* also refers to the Spirit's manifestations of power in miracles (12:10) and, indeed, the Spirit energises (*energei*, 12:11) all things as God does (cf. 12:6). The activities of the people of God associated with the Lord are called *diakoniai* (services, 12:5) and, in another list, *diakoniai* is a *charisma* (Romans 12:6-7; but the Spirit is not mentioned in Romans 12).

Charisma is a distinctively Pauline word—it is only used once outside of Paul's letters in the New Testament (1 Peter 4:10) and it is used rarely in other Greek literature. The noun derives from *charis* (grace) and denotes a concrete expression of grace like what could be seen in the ministry of Jesus. Every gift is a manifestation of grace. As the Church continues to exist by God's grace, therefore the church is charismatic displaying the fruits of the Spirit which are also gifts. The Christian life is to be a charismatic life of serving as a charismatic gift. The bestowal of gifts is expressly Trinitarian (12:4-6; cf. Ephesians 4:4-6) in that the gifts are the Spirit's, the Father's and Christ's for the churches (cf. Romans 1:11). The ministerial purpose of gifts is for service within the church (12:4ff). Approximately half of the references to *charisma* in the New Testament show a variety of ways that God's grace is evidenced among his people in: eternal life (Romans 5:15,16); special privileges to Israel (Romans 11:29); celibacy and marriage (7:7); and deliverance from deadly peril (2 Corinthians 1:10-11).

God's grace finds expression in *charismata* (1:4-7; cf. with reference to the Spirit, 12:4,9,28,30,31) including gifts of healings, pointing to specific instances of healing within the community (12:9,28,30). The list of gifts (12:8-10) are manifestations of the Spirit, so the community is urged to seek greater *charismata* (12:31)—especially faith, hope and love—necessarily in the context of love.

When Paul resumes this argument, *charisma* is replaced with *pneumatica* (Spirit manifestations, 14:1; cf. 12:4–11) when referring to the community gathered for worship. Concrete expressions of grace are manifestations of the Spirit's empowering in the community. *Charisma* in Paul's letter to Timothy probably refers to giftedness in the Spirit for ministry (1 Timothy 4:14; 2 Timothy 1:6). So when *charisma* refers to Spirit activity in the New Testament, it refers to specific visible ways in which the Spirit manifests himself in the believing community to build them up and meet their various needs as the eschatological people of God. There is no tension between gift (Spirit) and office (role) within the church in the New Testament.

Charisma emphasises God's graciousness and *pneumatika* (12:1; 14:1) refers to the Spirit nature of the activity to which *charismata* bear witness. *Pneumatika* at 12:1 is neuter, perhaps indicating a reference to spirit matters rather than spiritual gifts. *Pneumata* (spirit) is used in relation to the discerning of spirits (12:10) and the spirits of the prophets (14:32). The human spirit is the place where the Spirit of God works. *Dorea* (gift, Ephesians 4:7) precedes another list of gifts (Ephesians 4:11) which are not described as *charismata*.

Paul and Corinth are at odds about true spirituality (14:36–37) and tongues is part of the problem. Perhaps tongues, emphasised as the language of angels (13:1), could have denoted—for the 'spirituals' among the Corinthians—the present realisation of heavenly existence, with only the sloughing off of the body being required for full realisation. But Paul argues for diversity. If the community is truly to be of the one Spirit (12:4–30) then gifts are worthless if there is no love, furthermore, love demands intelligible utterances (14:1–25) and order (14:26–40) so that the community is built up (14:1–19,26–33) and outsiders are converted (14:20–25). Various lists of *charismata* and forms of service are provided (12:8–10,28,29–30; 13:1–3,8; 14:6,26) which are not alike in every respect (cf. 12:28,29–30).

The diverse list of Spirit activities (12:8–10)—representative but probably not exhaustive of the manifestations of the Spirit in the congregation at Corinth—should stop the Corinthians from having a lopsided emphasis on a particular gift. Some classify this list in order of value, descending from gifts of instruction (wisdom and knowledge) to gifts of supernatural power (faith, healings and miracles) to gifts of inspired utterance (prophecy, discerning spirits, tongues, interpretation of tongues). Discerning of spirits does not fit easily in this arrangement. However, as demonstrated previously, the gifts of faith and tongues are introduced with a different word (*hetero*, a different other) perhaps indicating Paul's groupings in the list.

Words (*logos*) of wisdom (*sophia*) and knowledge (*gnosis*)—highly esteemed in Corinth—head the list of gifts (12:8) but the wisdom and knowledge in evidence among the Corinthians was worldly and defective. Wisdom is God's plan to rescue humanity from sin through the death and resurrection of Jesus (1 Corinthians 2). On entering the new covenant, believers become new creatures who—at the return of Christ—enter the new creation. So the gift of knowledge is outside of human experience in understanding and communicating the mind of God as it is revealed in Scripture.

The last seven items—concluding with tongues and interpretation—are visible gifts with a supernatural endowment that are manifestations of the Spirit's presence in the congregation. These seven gifts sometimes display extraordinary phenomena. Faith is a special gift beyond saving faith. Healings refer to special, episodic instances. Prophecy was available to all from Pentecost but its practice at Corinth required ordering (14:29–32). Post-Pentecost, prophecy is the revealed and recognised application of biblical revelation to particular circumstances. Discernment of spirits is attached to evaluation of prophecy, judging whether the prophecy is from the Spirit or from other spirits (14:29; cf. 1 Thessalonians 5:20–21 in which discerning also follows prophecy). Tongues and interpretation follow (12:10; cf. 14:26–29). Are these earthly languages (cf. Acts 2:5–11), angelic languages (13:1) or unconscious groans of the Spirit that language cannot express (cf. Romans 8:26)? The mystery continues!

Baptised by one Spirit into one body of Christ (12:12–31)

Union with Christ as the life-giving Spirit is incorporation into his body, the church—involving experiential participation in Christ's death, resurrection and ascension.[249] Through the Spirit the body of Christ exhibits unity in diversity (12:12–14) as the Spirit is the self-revealing Christ in us,

---

249 Gaffin (1979, 29–30) argues that the church is Christ's Spirit-baptised body (cf. Romans 6:3ff; Galatians 2:20; Ephesians 2:5; Colossians 2:12ff; 3:1–3). Gaffin (1979, 31) also notes that all believers, from the time of their incorporation into the body of Christ, share in the gift of the Spirit (14:13). 14:13a does not convey an instrumental force of the Spirit as the creator of the Body of Christ but, rather, the necessary share of the living Spirit—which is Christ—for members of one body. Indeed, the one body of Christ have all been made to drink of the one Spirit.

reproducing Christ's sonship in us. Through the Spirit we receive fellowship with Christ himself. In the body of Christ, the diversity of spiritual gifts function within a defined Christian context (such as the Corinthians' assembly) to meet the needs of that diverse group of related Christians. The spiritual gifts of the Spirit of Christ that are exercised in a congregation bind the church to Christ. So at Corinth the congregation are the body of Christ and not merely a body of Christians; a locus through the Spirit of Christ's activity in the world. The Corinthians need this understanding of the genesis of community.

The Pentecost experience relates to all believers (12:13). Paul says that the church as the body of Christ (12:23-27) is the place where the Spirit is expressing unity in diversity in the harmonious function of the body, necessarily sharing in the one Spirit (12:13). The Spirit is not the creator of the body of Christ but the gift granted to all by virtue of being in Christ's body (cf. Romans 8:9; 6:17). So the focus of 12:13 is unity. All in the one body have been baptised with the Spirit, that is, the whole church—if it is the church—has been baptised in the Spirit.

When were all baptised in the Spirit? The answer is provided by the preposition *eis* (into) which indicates that experience of Spirit Baptism takes place at the time of being incorporated into the body of Christ, that is, the time of saving inclusion in the covenant community. Salvation is being united to Christ—the life-giving Spirit—and being joined into his body, the church. Along with salvation there is forgiveness of sins, the imputed righteousness of Christ, renewal of life, and deliverance from the guilt and corruption of sin. Union with Christ means that we share what took place in the work of Christ. Those who are incorporated into Christ's body share experientially in the Spirit with whom he baptises the church (12:13a), which means involvement in the death, resurrection and ascension of Christ.[250] The union of the church with Christ also means union in the eternal design of redemption (Ephesians 1:4) and in its once and for all historical accomplishment on the cross. Those who are baptised with the Spirit are not only members of one body on whom the Spirit has been poured out but they have also been made to drink of the one Spirit (12:13) in Holy Spirit baptism. Indeed, one cannot be a Christian without Spirit baptism (cf. Romans 8:9). By virtue of incorporation in Christ's body, all Christians share in the thirst-quenching gift of the Spirit (cf. John 7:37-39).

---

250 Romans 6:3; Galatians 2:20; Ephesians 2:5; Colossians 2:12; 3:1-3.

Since the gifts have a common origin—worked by one Spirit (12:12) and yet given to individuals—the diversity does not mean disunity. The confluence of the gifts of the Spirit is apportioned so as to bring the presence of Christ in the group (12:12, explained and clarified in 12:13).[251] The life-giving Spirit initiates unity in Christ in the salvation process so that we are all connected or incorporated into Christ's body which is the church. Union with Christ means that we share what took place in the work of Christ, that is, an experiential share in the Spirit with which he baptised the church (12:13a). Union with Christ means involvement in his death, resurrection and ascension.[252] Those who are baptised with the Spirit are therefore members of the one body on which the Spirit has been poured out (12:13a).

If the Spirit directs the body of Christ then the Spirit's power enables members of the body to function charismatically in harmony and thereby grow together towards the full stature of Christ.[253] *Gar* (for, 12:12) indicates that 12:12-14 is an explanation of the diversity introduced at 12:4. The metaphor of body imagery was a common Greco-Roman political analogy to explain unity in diversity (12:15-20) and Paul's emphasis is diversity within the unity from the one Spirit. Paradoxically, it is the seemingly weaker—less presentable, less honourable—parts of the body that are valuable, indispensable and more honoured (12:22-24). The seemingly weaker parts cannot be disregarded. Evidently, while ever the more spectacular gifts were favoured and other gifts were depreciated by some of the Corinthian congregation, they did not understand that all the gifts distributed across the body formed part of their necessary unity as Christ's body.

But the gift of the Spirit is the exalted Christ himself present and fully working in the church, present in the church in all his fullness. So the Spirit is always related to the body of Christ (12:13a). Any theology of the Spirit must be focussed on the body of Christ where the Spirit is present in his diverse working. The Spirit is not the creator of the body but the gift granted to believers who are the body.[254] 'All' are baptised in the Spirit and all have a vital function in the body even if seemingly insignificant (12:22-24). Hence, experience of Holy Spirit baptism takes place at salvation, at the

---

251 Chiu, 2007, 263.
252 Romans 6:3; Galatians 2:20; Ephesians 2:5; Colossians 2:12, 3:1-3; cf. Acts 2:32.
253 1 Corinthians 12 with Ephesians 4:1-16; cf. Galatians 6:1ff; Romans 15:5.
254 cf. 12:13a, where 'all' is the point; 6:17, where to be joined to the Lord is to have one Spirit with him; Romans 8:9, where to belong to Christ is to have the Spirit.

time of incorporation into the Alpha and Omega, when we are united to Christ and thereby incorporated into Christ's body. Such incorporation brings righteousness in Christ, renewal of life, and deliverance from the guilt and corruption of sin. This once event baptism of the Spirit should be distinguished from the repeat or continuous filling of the Spirit (cf. Ephesians 5:18). As all (not some) were made to drink (12:13), baptism in the Spirit is probably not a second blessing. That is, there cannot be an un-Spirit-baptised Christian. Being spiritually baptised into one Christ is a foretaste of eschatological life in Christ (cf. Romans 8:23) accompanied by special gifting within the congregation.

The Spirit has produced in them a common Christian experience of conversion and regeneration which is the basis of their unity. Fee notes that the point is not to indicate how they began the common Christian life but, rather, to explain how the many are one body through the baptism of the Spirit.[255] I have suggested that the Baptist's reference to an impending baptism in the Spirit and fire—by the mightier one to come—refers to two outcomes which are consequent to a personal reaction to the cross: acceptance by faith (baptism in Spirit); or rejection by unbelief (baptism in fire, cf. Mark 10:38; Luke 12:49–52).[256] Our attitude to the cross will either bring us blessing and conversion/regeneration, or rejection. To be baptised in the Spirit is to be incorporated into the death of Christ and there is no other way into the kingdom. By virtue of incorporation into Christ's body, all Christians share the gift of the Spirit (cf John 7:37–39). The gift of the Spirit: individually applies redemption by integration into the once and for all work of Christ; is the spiritual power that redirects lives; and transforms the believer's experience through salvation, forgiveness of sins, the imputed righteousness of Christ, deliverance from guilt and corruption, and renewal of life in the new covenant.

Baptism in the Spirit is, therefore, conversion/regeneration and not a triumphalist experience for it is baptism into Christ's death with the grace, then, of new life. By this founding baptism in the Spirit, we enter into the new community in which the new relationship in Christ begins by which we progress to final glorification. As all are given to drink (past tense) one

---

255 Fee, 1987, 603.
256 cf. Dumbrell, 2008, 42. The baptiser is not identified but seems to be Christ (cf. Cole, 2007, 214).

Spirit, so all—from different social backgrounds such as Jews and Greeks—are members of the one body of Christ (12:13b).

Paul does not assert that we receive the Spirit by water baptism for it is not baptism that makes us one body but the Spirit. The baptismal candidate is clothed with Christ, not the Spirit.[257] Paul subordinates water baptism to the preaching of the gospel (1:13-17) and the reception of the gospel is linked with the Spirit (1:13-25; 12:13; Galatians 3:2-4) but life in the Spirit is not just one experience of baptism upon entry into the body of Christ. Whereas Pentecost documents the rebirth of every believer, the filling of the Spirit (Ephesians 5:18) is not the same as the baptism of the Spirit for we are to be filled with the Spirit over and over again. Being filled with the Spirit overflows into Spirit-worked obedience to Christ expressed in ordinary relationships. Believers are to be strengthened in the inner man through his Spirit (Ephesians 3:16,17).

The body metaphor (12:12-26) presupposes Paul's concern that some members of the Corinthian congregation have used their gifts to distinguish themselves from the rest of the congregation. But all members contribute to the function of the whole, indeed, the weaker parts are equally necessary (12:15-20) so any ranking of members within the body by their gifts is absolutely excluded. The conclusion that the body is not one member but many (12:14) is worked out in 12:15-20, dealing with the charismata which are specific gifts by divine grace to be exercised within the congregation (but excluding, at this point, the specific endowments of prophecies and tongues; cf. 1 Corinthians 14). The fruits of the Spirit are intended for all but the individual capacities of believers, brought by conversion within the controlling power of the Spirit in the Body of Christ, are distributed throughout the congregation. So individualism in the Body of Christ is absurd. Diversity in the one body is God's intention (12:18) with each member there by divine placement. There could be no body (unity) without diversity (12:19). The interconnection of members means that sharing experiences is inevitable (12:26). A balanced recognition and contribution of gifts is necessary if the congregation is to function as a body (12:20 with 12:12; 12:21 with 12:14). Members are both interrelated and interdependent (12:21-26). Despite their differences, they need each other. There can be no hierarchy among members (12:21), rather, the Body of Christ is a harmony.

---

257 Fee, 1994, 862-864.

Another list combining persons and gifts (12:27–31; cf. 12:8–10) gives apostolic leadership first place as a foundational gift—a factor that was not recognised by some of the Corinthian congregation. The gifts in this list represent ministries or functions, not persons, including 'helpful actions' and 'administrations' (12:28). The Corinthian enthusiasts may not have esteemed these less obviously 'supernatural' gifts. Tongues, the problem in Corinth because this gift was not always used to build up (*oikodomeo*, 14:4,17), comes last. A concluding series of rhetorical questions underline the point of the chapter, namely, that it is not possible for one member to exercise all the necessary functions in the Body of Christ.

12:27–31 concludes the argument that there are diversities of gifts but the same Spirit (12:4) by tying together 12:4–11 and 12:12–26, with application to the church at Corinth. God is responsible for the diversity (12:28; cf. 12:8–10). The ranked list (first, second, third, then, 12:28) of persons includes *charismata* at the fourth (miracles) and fifth (healings) items (cf. the fifth and fourth items in the previous list, 12:8–10). These two items are not mentioned again in the New Testament. The list (12:27–31) represents a range of services in the church with the first three being vital ministries for the founding and growth of the local assembly. Fee suggests that 'apostles' are plural because, in addition to Paul's ministry to Corinth, there are others in other churches who exercise the same ministry. Richard Gaffin makes the important point that congregational use of gifts does not relate to presumed personality strengths but, rather, to the manner in which God will use us.[258]

Apostles in the New Testament[259] are part of the foundational task in the initial spread of the gospel. Some say that apostles apply only derivatively today (cf. Acts 8, 10, 11, 19), that is, the Apostolate was temporary for New Testament times and not applicable from then until Christ returns. Apostles are the cornerstone in the church but do not supplement Christ's work, rather, apostles bear witness to the work of Christ. Whereas apostles and prophets are separate groups, there may be overlap since prophets—like apostles, according to cessationists—belong to the foundation of the church. In New Testament times prophecy had a revelatory, covenantal contribution in which God was revealing himself to his covenant people as Redeemer and Saviour. Redemption was completed by Christ's death

---

258 Gaffin, 1979, 54.
259 cf. Gaffin, 1979, 91–93.

so there could be no more covenantal, historically-redemptive revelation. There is now no place for private, localised revelations. But in New Testament times, prophecy was still operating in an open canon where inspiration was a prerequisite (but not a sufficient condition) of canonisation of inspired writings as Scripture (cf. Paul's lost letter to the Corinthians is not included in the canon of Scripture). Furthermore, not all can be apostles (or prophets or teachers or workers of miracles, 12:29) since the body requires diversity in unity.

Did Paul intend these ministry gifts to be ranked by significance? The first three items are numbered and therefore appear to be ranked but the remaining items are not numbered. The gift of tongues is listed last not because it is least but because it is the problem, that is, tongues is included at the end to emphasise diversity. All of these gifts are needed in the congregation for the work of the gospel. Even so, Paul is yet to mention the greatest gift (love, 1 Corinthians 13).

The final two of the seven rhetorical questions (12:29–30) indicate that, to preserve diversity, not everybody in Corinth will speak in tongues. Furthermore, the Corinthians are to be zealous for the greater gifts (12:31, perhaps the first three enumerated in the list) and aspire to the gift that is beyond the list—the gift that surpasses and enables all the gifts. They are to seek (imperative verb; 14:1,39) prophecy but they must also seek (12:31; cf. 1 Corinthians 13) the more excellent way. Love is not in a list of gifts because it does not rank with the gifts discussed and is not part of the diversity, rather, love is the command from Jesus for all. Love is the greatest gift, the greatest way of life, the fruit of the Spirit (Galatians 5:22). The Corinthians were concerned about influence and spirituality but had forgotten the gift which makes every other gift effective.

All gifts depend on the Spirit (12:11) and the Spirit produces unity in the congregation. Without the collaboration of members there can be no unity in diversity (12:12–26), that is, there will only be cliques and factions. The solution (1 Corinthians 14) to the problems of division in the Corinthian congregation can only be reached through the greatest gift of the Spirit (1 Corinthians 13) without which the lesser gifts cannot be exercised.

Tongues is a gift of the Spirit but is not the priority (14:1–40)

Paul's answer to the imperative to seek a more excellent way (12:31a) is found in the structure of worship (1 Corinthians 14) and general principles referring to Christian congregational gathering. Thiselton argues that 14:1-25 is a congregational application of 13:1-13,[260] which is supported by the imperative to pursue love (14:1), suggesting that 1 Corinthians 14 is controlled by the aims of *agape* (selfless consideration for others, 14:1). Nevertheless, the Greek particle *de* (14:1) expresses a hesitation. The Corinthian congregation is to seek love as their continual aim (14:1)—and also spiritual gifts such as tongues and prophecy because these revelatory gifts are from the same Spirit, that is, from the same God. Chiu points out that the mention of love and spiritual (gifts) together indicates their compatibility (14:1).[261] But the spiritual gift of tongues (14:2)[262] apparently came first in Corinth's list even though tongues do not edify the church unless interpreted. Hence Paul prefers prophecy in worship (14:3; cf. 14:2-25) because the results of prophecy are edification, comfort and consolation (14:3).

Tongues (14:6-19) cannot be understood without interpretation so they are not addressed to the congregation but, rather, tongues are private prayer and praise to God. But prophecy—based on divine revelation—is integral to the growth of the church as a revelatory gift, that is, the word of God to the church. The gift of tongues is put to good use when accompanied by interpretation (12:13-19). The tongues speaker is to pray for interpretation (12:13) for that helps the church. Since tongues are not framed by the mind, when the human spirit prays there is no benefit for the congregation (12:14-15). The gift of tongues is a particular, individual reception of the Holy Spirit by the speaker (my Spirit = the Spirit given to me; 12:12,14). However, the tongues speaker is to pray or sing not only through the Spirit but also with the mind (12:15) so that there will be congregational benefit from what would otherwise be obscure or incomprehensible. With tongues

---

260 Thiselton, 2000, 1074.

261 Chiu, 2007, 284.

262 Gaffin (1979, 76) argues that 'spirit' in 14:2,14,15 is the Holy Spirit. Likewise, 14:12a refers to the Holy Spirit (cf. NEB, eager for the gifts of the Spirit). Since prophets are to control prophetic gifts of the Spirit, then 14:2 refers to the Holy Spirit. So whereas in prophecy the Spirit uses the voice of the prophet, the Spirit does not use tongues. Gaffin (1979, 77-78) points out that Paul associates prophecy with intelligible speech, which involves the mind (cf. 14:19, NEB). Tongues must be inspired as they can be interpreted.

in view, Paul stresses the pre-eminence of prophecy because prophecy builds up as tongues may not (12:20–25).

14:26–40 demonstrate the need for unity within diversity (cf. 12:4–31). Paul rebukes the disorder in Corinthian church meetings particularly in regard to the use of spiritual gifts and then gives norms for the use of spiritual gifts in corporate worship (12:26), including: principles for tongue speakers and prophets in the assembly (14:27–33a); and the contribution of women at church gatherings (14:33b–35). The Spirits of the prophets are subject to the prophet (14:32), that is, the prophetic gift given by the Spirit to each prophet is subject to the control of the prophet.[263] Turner cogently argues that 14:37–38—which sums up the whole argument from 12:1 by dealing with what builds the congregation up in worship—refers to pretensions to prophecy and spiritual gifts.[264] True members of the Body of Christ will recognise that Paul's message is a command from the Lord for Paul writes as an apostle with the Lord's authority; any spiritual person should recognise that Paul's writing is of the Spirit. So, with regard to prophecy and tongues (14:39–40; cf. 14:1): the congregation, as a whole, are to seek to prophesy; and tongues as a spiritual gift may be exercised in the congregation when interpreted. 'All things' (14:40) probably refers to spiritual gifts (14:12–14), summing up the teaching on spiritual gifts (cf. 12:1) with a call to order.

The last Adam—a life-giving Spirit (15:1–58)

At the resurrection of Christ, the personal mode of Jesus' existence as the last Adam was so decisively transformed by the Holy Spirit that he became a life-giving Spirit (15:12–20,45). The Spirit who raised him up as the firstfruits dwells in him so completely and in such a way that Jesus will be instrumental in the resurrection of the full harvest. Only by virtue of the functional identity of the Spirit and Christ, effected redemptively-historically in his resurrection, is Christ the communicator of life. The change in Christ's person is commensurate with the transformation to be expected and experienced by the rest of the harvest. The living and dead undergo a change at the Parousia. What is mortal will then be swallowed up by life with a different body to the former body. We are changed and our earthly

---

263 cf. Gaffin, 1979, 77–78 (NEB 'It is for prophets to control prophetic inspiration').

264 Turner, Vox Evangelica, suggests that it was reasonable to suppose that there was no sharp distinction between apostolic prophecy and prophets' prophesying.

bodies are done away with but the substance of this present world will abide (cf. 7:31).

The Spirit in the resurrection of Christ and believers

Paul says that believers have already been raised (cf. Romans 6:3ff; Galatians 2:19ff; Ephesians 2:5f; Colossians 2:12-13). Does the reference to the verb *sunegeiro* (raise with; Ephesians 2:6; Colossians 2:12; 3:1) refer to what took place in the historical experience of Christ or does it also apply to what has happened in the life of the believer? In view of Christ's identity as firstfruits, there is solidarity with believers in Christ's emergence from the tomb—but it seems that Paul is also referring to an experience of believers (cf. united in Christ's death and resurrection, where 'being dead' is not just solidarity with Christ but actual spiritual deadness; Romans 6:5). Enlivening and resurrection took place when believers were transformed from spiritual deadness to, at least in the initial experience, ethical renewal.

The Resurrection simply means becoming a new creation both now and at the end in the supreme crisis. The certainty of the believer's resurrection lies in the justification of Christ, and the Spirit is the efficacious principle in the transformation. Resurrection comes out of justification. Christ's resurrection was the de facto declaration of God in regard to his being just. Our trespasses were the cause of Christ's death (Romans 4:25) but God suspended the forces of death operating on Jesus and raised him from the dead thereby securing by the resurrection of our bodies our final justification (Romans 8:23). The resurrection of Jesus indicates the advent of the new creation and *Pneumatikos* soteriology, that is, transformation by the Spirit. There is a change in Jesus' resurrection with new status and new qualities— but Jesus is changeless with regard to religious or ethical properties. At the Parousia, living and dead believers undergo this resurrection change by the Spirit but are also then fully led by the Spirit.

The resurrection is the pivotal focus of Paul's soteriology with a focus on the life-giving Spirit and the inauguration of the new age in which Christ is the first born among many brothers. Redemption is defined as resurrection with Christ but there are different facets of this single act. We are now raised with Christ, being united to Christ as resurrected and—at the Parousia—what is mortal in us will be swallowed up by life producing a different body. We are changed and our earthly bodies are done away with but the substance of the present world will abide (cf. 7:31).

For Christ, according to Paul, resurrection is entering both a new phase of sonship and a new phase for the state of the soul. Likewise for the believer, resurrection means entry into both a new world constructed upon a superabundantly dynamic plane and a new aeon in an unprecedented sense as sons of God. For the believer, all of life is preparation for the crowning grace of resurrection. The resurrection constitutes a new womb out of which believers emerge as sons of God—sons through resurrection who no longer marry nor are given in marriage (Luke 20:35–36). Resurrection means entry into a higher world, a newly structured life with new potencies. There is an analogy between the *anastasis* (resurrection) and the cosmological *palingenesia* (regeneration, Matthew 19:28). Paul shows that the sum total of earthly Christian experience leads to regeneration via resurrection. Being raised with Christ, the likeness of the Saviour's bodily resurrection will be produced in the Christian (Romans 6:5). And, even now, believers are to reckon themselves alive unto God in the resurrection life of Christ Jesus the Lord (Romans 6:11). The vision of the glorified Christ transforms believers into the same image from glory to glory.

The unity of believers with the resurrection of Christ is both past and future. The believer has been raised from the dead and is also yet to be raised (Romans 6:5). Resurrection of the believer's inner man has already happened but resurrection of the outer man is still in the future. So the believer's resurrection occurs in two parts, both invisible and visible—both past and future—the hidden, inward resurrection of saved humanity from sin has taken place; the exposed, outward mental and physical heavenly resurrection is still to come.

The Spirit in the believers' future resurrection

The living and dead will undergo change at the Parousia. The bodies of dead believers, whilst possessing the Spirit, exist in a condition of un-pneumatic life with a bodily resurrection change to come (15:42–49).

Paul views Christ's resurrection as his redemption. Christ experienced death as the wages of sin, separation from life, judgement under the wrath of God, and alienation from the face of the Father (Romans 6:10; 2 Corinthians 5:21; Galatians 3:13). He died to the sin under whose domain he had come (Romans 6:10) but he was raised, delivered, justified, or saved from this death through the resurrection (1 Timothy 3:16) by God through the power of the Spirit. Deliverance from death was the salvation of Jesus as the last Adam and hence the transition from wrath to grace. Paul describes the application of redemption to the believer in terms which explicate the meaning of Christ's resurrection. The application of redemption to us is rooted in the application of redemption to Christ. Through the power of the Spirit, as per the promise of the Father, Christ was redeemed and delivered as his justification thereby becoming the Last Adam.

The Spirit's raising of Jesus is Jesus' justification (1 Timothy 3:16), sanctification (Romans 6:9-10) and glorification (15:42-44). In his death, Jesus was made to be sin but he was declared by resurrection to be righteous—as our representative. Jesus did not see decay because he was God's Holy One (Acts 2:27). Even so, he died in our place as the condemned one and was raised as the justified one. The resurrection could also be seen as Christ's adoption for he was declared to be the Son of God in power through the Spirit of holiness by his resurrection from the dead (Romans 1:4). Romans 1:3-4 is not about two natures (flesh and spirit) but, rather, two aeons of existence for in his death Christ came under the dominion of sin but in his resurrection Christ was delivered from the dominion of sin. Therefore, Christ's resurrection was his sanctification and also his glorification (cf. 15:42-44; Philippians 3:21). Believers in Christ share all that has been accomplished in Christ's justification, adoption, sanctification and glorification through his resurrection conveyed immediately and eschatologically through the Spirit's ministry. Christ becomes our covenant partner as the Holy Spirit binds us to him. Justification, adoption, sanctification and glorification are distinct categories of the application of redemption. We enter with Christ in the oneness of a mysterious union analogous to becoming one flesh in marriage (Ephesians 5:30-32).

The Spirit is the efficacious agent for the new resurrection body

The relationship between the present earthly body and the resurrection body is analogous to the sowing of a seed which emerges as a different plant—organically identical but changed in the transformation (15:35-38). Paul's analogy is somewhat constrained because in agriculture the seed is not destroyed, rather, the seed grows into a plant. Nevertheless, there is continuity albeit with final transformation and Paul's argument is that what happens after the seed as a result of the death-resurrection transformation is what matters. The seed represents our earthly bodies which come before the transformation into heavenly bodies. So death means a necessary change to advance what God has determined.

The resurrection of Christ is fundamental. Jesus 'was raised' (John 21:24) by God, that is, Jesus did not contribute to his own resurrection. God's resurrection (the active agent) worked on Jesus (the passive recipient) so that God may work resurrection on others also with the outcome that believers become sons of the resurrection in a higher world. In the justification of Christ by his resurrection lies the certainty of the believer's resurrection. The pneumatic theology of 1 Corinthians is that resurrection will bring about vast change in the body with real continuity residing with the Pneuma (Spirit) and not the body (flesh), indeed, the Spirit is the efficacious principle of all transformation.

Applying the seed analogy (15:35-41), Paul now contrasts two bodies successively, namely, the pre-eschatological body and the eschatological body (15:42-49). The pre-eschatological body is characterised as *psuchikon* (natural, 15:44) and the eschatological body as *pneumatikon* (spiritual, 15:44). But Paul's eschatological body is not immaterial or ethereal or without physical density, rather, Paul uses *pneumatikon* to describe the final heavenly resurrection state of the believer as being ruled by *Pneuma*. The psychical (*soma psuchikon*) body—in order of time and inward redemption—precedes the spiritual (*soma pneumatikon*) body.

The transformation for the believer at the resurrection is a physical and moral change (15:42). The Corinthians have failed to reckon with the fact that the corruptible body disappears after death, being transformed by an inner ethical change which frees the body from sin (15:43). But this truly spiritual state in the era fully controlled by Spirit must wait until the Parousia. For now, the present 'natural body' is appropriate to its earthly sphere (15:44). The contrast that Paul raises is between *soma psuchikon* and *soma pneumatikon*—between the primordial body (the first Adam, 15:45) and the consummation body (the last Adam, 15:45). Indeed, in the cosmos, *to pneumatikon* (the spiritual, 15:46) is not first, rather, *to psuchikon* (the spiritual, 15:46) precedes *to pneumatikon*. So the second man from heaven (15:47) does not refer to the original provenience of Christ from heaven.

Up to 15:43, Paul's argument compares the body of sin (cf. Romans 6:6) and the body of the resurrection. But from 15:44, Paul substitutes the normal body of the new creation for the body of sin. Why? Geerhardus Vos argues that, from the outset, God had made provision for a higher kind of body with a higher stage of existence.[265] The world of creation points toward the world to come. On the principle of typology, the first Adam of the garden prefigures the last Adam and hence the psychical body (cf. Genesis 1) precedes the pneumatic body (cf. Romans 5:14). Even so, the fact that Adam was brought into being by God with the breath of God (Spirit) in his nostrils as a 'living being' (Genesis 2:7) prefigures Paul's description of the last Adam made as a 'living Spirit' (15:45). The distinction between 'living being' and 'living Spirit' underlines the proposition that the resurrection life is spiritual and that the Spirit is the author of the miracle of Christ's resurrection. The heavenly world is the pneumatic world in Paul (cf. humanity blessed in the heavenly realms with every spiritual blessings; 10:3,4; Ephesians 1:3). For Christians, the Spirit's action becomes evident in the ethical-religious sphere so that the body made of Spirit is a body reflecting the new creation of the Spirit. In the new creation under the new covenant the *pneumatikoi* are those who live by the Spirit.

Thus 15:42–49 contrasts the new eschatological creation begun at Christ's resurrection (distinguished as spiritual) with the old order (deemed as psychical). The body of the present order—set over against the final resurrection order—is characterised by corruption, dishonour and weakness (15:42–44ff) associated with the *sarx* (flesh, 15:50) and this *sarx* is contrasted with the Spirit. Thus, in Paul, *psuchikos* (15:44,46) is synonymous with *sarkikos* and *sarkinos* (carnal, cf. 2:14; 3:1,3). *Sarx* describes the self-maintaining impetus of the present evil age, focusing on the inertia and weakness of the old aeon, in antithesis to the Spirit as the power of the age to come (Hebrews 6:5).

So Christ's resurrection is integral to his subsequent mode of existence (15:45,47–49). What Christ is and continues to be—received at the resurrection—is exalted, heavenly existence as a life-giving Spirit. Hence Christ's resurrection is the indispensable foundation for believers to share in the resurrection life. Jesus became the last Adam by his transition to becoming a living Spirit at the resurrection. The risen Christ—with the personal mode of Jesus' existence totally transformed—is the model spiritual man (15:45).[266] By virtue of the functional identity of the Spirit and Christ effected historically-redemptively in the resurrection, the heavenly Christ becomes the communicator of the new life through the Spirit. Hence, the

---

265 Vos, 1994, 169.
266 Gaffin, 1978, 89.

resurrection is the counterpart of creation, cosmic in scope. There is a new world order, the dawn of new creation, the start of the new eschatological age with the resurrection of Christ. This final order is pneumatic and its atmosphere is spiritual. The eschatological resurrection state is that in which the *Pneuma* rules.

The distinction (15:44) between *psuchikos* (natural, subject to death) and *pneumatikos* (spiritual, controlled by the Spirit) points to the future age of the new creation of the Spirit. *Psuchikos* occurs only in 1 Corinthians and *pneumatikos* occurs fifteen times in 1 Corinthians.[267] At Corinth, those who regarded themselves as possessing heavenly blessing considered themselves to be *pneumatikoi* (3:1; 12:1; 14:37), that is, they claimed to possess superior spiritual wisdom. But Paul involves those who consider themselves to be spiritual as being sown in *psuchikos*, that is, ordinary human existence subject to ordinary human restrictions and prone to sin as Adamic existence always has been. In this sense, 'spiritual'—that is, totally ruled by the Spirit—only relates to the age to come.

15:45 points back to the analogy in 15:22 (inclusion in Israel's Messiah, which was necessary for redemption). Jesus was the representative of the new, true humanity—as the last Adam—just as the first Adam represented fallen humanity. Indeed the eschatological prospect held out to the first Adam, which he forfeited by his disobedience, was realised by the last Adam.[268]

The distinction between the contrasting concepts of natural versus spiritual and death versus resurrection—in terms of Adam and Christ (15:45,22)—is not a Christological aside but an anthropological assertion with reference to the nature of the resurrection body. All in Adam are subject to death and decay. All in Christ (the last Adam by his incarnation), through incorporation into him, will become through his life-giving capacity what he became by resurrection: a living Spirit. There is direct connection from the beginning of creation (Genesis 2:7) between the concepts of the spiritual body (the body into whom the Lord God breathes his Spirit) and the natural body (the body formed by the Lord God). Indeed, a 'first' Adam presupposes a 'second' Adam. This had always been the divine purpose, that is, God in his wisdom had from the beginning made provision for a higher body. The created form of the first Adam and his separation

---

267 Lincoln, 1981, 40.
268 Lincoln, 1981, 43.

from the outside world in the Garden of Eden necessarily pointed forward to a higher form. The first Adam prefigured the last: the world of creation points forward to the world to come. The assumption underlying Genesis 2 is that the heavenly world is a pneumatic world. The eschatological state is a pneumatic state, that is, the highest form of life is in the world of heaven which is made possible by the action of the Spirit in resurrection life. Paul is the first to ascribe to the Spirit a dominating place and pervasive uniform activity along with the Father and the Son in providing for the Christian state at every point from regeneration to glorification.

No inference could be drawn from the abnormal body of sin, that is, the abnormal body could not be correlated with the eschatological body even though the world of creation points forward to the end. Hence, 15:44b ('there is a natural body, and there is a spiritual body') is an argument, not an assertion—that is, if there exists one type of body then God's intention produces the other kind also. The physical body of the first Adam, damaged by sin, prefigures the spiritual body of the second Adam conceived without sin. The world that now is prefigures the world to come. The Garden in Eden (Genesis 2), as the repose of God, prefigures the ideal world of the end (Revelation 22:1–5). The divine assumption underlying Genesis 2 points to the heavenly world as a pneumatic world. Richard Gaffin argues that from the outset God had made provision for a higher kind of body within a higher stage of existence generally.[269]

In the inter-testamentary period, Jewish speculation over Adam's role restored honour and glory for Israel and not for man in general. But Paul states that inclusion in Israel's Messiah (the last Adam) provides for redemption to life for all humanity (15:45,22). So the eschatological prospect held out to the first Adam, which he forfeited by his disobedience, has been realised by the last Adam in his resurrection body.[270] The first man became a living soul (15:45) with an appropriate body but the last Adam had, by resurrection, a higher quality of life which enabled him to become a life-giving spirit. Paul does not suppose that believers will be like Christ as life-giving spirits for Christ is uniquely the source of the new spiritual bodily life. The first Adam was a living soul but that was not the end of the human story for the natural must give way to the spiritual (15:46) in the purposes of God.

---

269 Gaffin, 1978, 169.
270 Lincoln, 1981, 49.

Paul has moved from (firstly) the Spirit's constitutive role as God in action in the resurrected life to (secondly) his role in the act of resurrection—rather than the reverse[271]—so 15:46 is a compressed overview of history. The spiritual body, of the Spirit, in the new creation is appropriate for the pneumatic order of the final world age. The Spirit conditions the resurrected life, hence the eschatological aspect of the Spirit's role in the resurrection is dominant dating from Christ's resurrection. Indeed, the Messiah's coming is one eschatological coming unfolding in two episodes—one already and one still to come, but the age to come is already present. There is an organic connection between the resurrection of Christ and the bodily resurrection of believers (the second coming) when believers will have bodies reflecting the final new creation of the Spirit.

The first man was of the earth (15:47)—and therefore earthy—but the second man was of heaven and therefore heavenly, belonging to a new spiritual order of existence. In this present era there is a physical or natural order of existence which has to be reckoned with as part of the tension of living in this age for the future. Paul still focusses on Christ's humanity (15:47) for, as the life-giving second Adam, Christ is the source and model for the new eschatological humanity. Jewish tradition says that Adam is, by a general resurrection, to be returned to Paradise with full eschatological glory which will be shared with the righteous in the age to come. The promise in this Jewish tradition is, according to Paul, accomplished by Christ in his inauguration of the new age.

The representative character of both Adam and Christ is discussed further in 15:48-49. Christ is the prototype for the resurrection body of believers just as Adam determined the bodily fate of earthly humanity (15:48). Believers who share dust with Adam will also certainly share the glory of the heavenly man (15:49). While complete conformity to the image of Christ will not occur until the believer is clothed with the heavenly body, the process of transformation has nevertheless begun now (cf. 2 Corinthians 3:18). Paul's exhortation—let us bear (rather than we shall bear) the likeness of the man from heaven (15:49)—is based on present incorporation into Christ and presumes ongoing change.

The necessary deduction from the previous argument is an assertion—repeated in the synonymous parallelism of two lines—that flesh and blood (the perishable) cannot inherit the kingdom (15:50), that is, the physical

---

271 Vos, 1994, 169-170.

body cannot inherit heavenly existence. Joachin Jeremias argued for synthetic parallelism between the two lines, namely: the first line is concerned about the living, those who will be alive at the Parousia; the second line is concerned with those who had died prior to the Parousia; and this distinction is repeated throughout 15:51–54.[272] This plausible view depends on the meaning of 'corruption', however, which cannot be narrowly identified with death (as argued by Jeremias). Flesh and blood (15:50) undoubtedly refers to those who are now alive but the mystery (15:51), previously concealed, is that not all will die (sleep) but all will be transformed at the Parousia so that they are raised incorruptible (15:52).

It follows that corruption is the present material state of humanity and, consequently, in its present constitution humankind cannot enter the new world (15:53). So when the herald of the new age sounds, then we—all Christians, dead or alive—will be instantaneously transformed. The defeat of death (death was generated by sin, and sin was generated by law; 15:55–56) will be marked by this instantaneous transformation from corruption to incorruption, from mortality to immortality (15:53–54). Vos suggests that *pantes ou* (all not, 15:51) may be understood as *ou pantes* (not all),[273] carrying the sense: 'it is not true of all but only of some that we shall all sleep, but true of all that we shall all be changed'. This reading has Paul affirming transformation for both groups (those previously dead and those currently alive at the Parousia), a pneumatic transformation where the dead are raised incorruptible (15:52). Sin's sting, the knowledge that the wages of sin is death, has thus been nullified in the victory of the cross. So sin's power has gone along with the law whose positive demands, used by sin, provided content for sin's perversity. So the question of 15:35 has been answered.

The glorified existence of Christ in heaven has all the merit of the cross laid up forever (15:55–57). The last resurrection of believers is bodily but there must also be a somatic transformation—not a simple return to what was lost in death—with the organism endowed with new powers, even richer than removal of sin-caused defects. To the restored normal (pre-death life) there are added faculties and qualities because we do not merely receive the heavenly body, rather, we also bear the image of Christ (15:45–49) which he obtained in his own resurrection.

---

272 Jeremias, 1955, 151–156.
273 Vos, 1994, 212

Hence Paul's doxology of gratitude (15:57) and strong word of exhortation for vacillating Corinth to stand firm (15:58) and continue in the labour that builds up the body, secure in the certainty of the future for believers (cf. 15:1-2). If they have believed they will not have laboured in vain. The Christian hope of life in the new world depends on the certainty of the resurrection (15:1-34). Whatever shape our present world may be or become, the certainty of the resurrection generates for believers knowledge of the certainty of new creation with a bodily resurrection awaiting us.

The Spirit is the instrumental cause of eternal resurrection

The Spirit of Christ is the seal and fruit of his righteousness. In Christ, the fountain of justification springs up for all believers. Through the resurrection, the Spirit is closely identified with Christ for—in the resurrection—the Spirit imparted to Christ his own life-giving power. The Spirit is thus the instrumental cause of the resurrection act and following life. Up to the resurrection, the Spirit was the Spirit of God but in the resurrection the Spirit imparted life-giving power thus becoming the instrumental cause of the resurrection act and the following eschatological pneumatic state of the believer's life. Hence the Spirit in the post Pentecost New Testament operates alongside the Father and the Son.

Following Jesus' earthly ministry, the Spirit is the application and extension of Jesus living in the church (cf. 'I' am with you = Spirit = Christ as the life-giving Spirit who is now active in the new covenant community; Matthew 28:20). The initial possession of the Spirit of God by believers is an initial enjoyment of adoption (Romans 8:15), to be fully and openly received at the resurrection of the body. The resurrection of the dead through man (that is, Jesus; 15:21b)—and Christ, making all alive (15:22b)—explains the significance of Christ as the firstfruits. Only those who belong to Christ, who are united with the second Adam, shall be resurrected so that Christ's resurrection is the firstfruits or representative beginning of the resurrection of believers. The change in Christ's person is real, commensurate with the transformation to be expected and experienced by the rest of the harvest. The risen Jesus has a new status with new heavenly qualities imparted to him by God, indeed, Jesus is declared to be the Son of God with power according to the Spirit of Holiness by the resurrection of the dead (Romans 1:1-4). This is not religious or ethical transformation which Jesus had to undergo through resurrection, rather, the change in Jesus in his resurrection was bodily and psychical.

At the resurrection, believers who possess the Spirit will undergo resurrection change in which what is mortal will be swallowed up by life. We will be changed as the earthly body (the form of this world) is done away with but the substance of this present world will abide (cf. 7:31; 2 Corinthians 5:1–5; Philippians 3:21). The gift of the Spirit is the down payment and pledge of the inheritance to be received by believers at Christ's return, that is, the church's present possession of the Spirit is anticipatory of the eschatological and full heavenly possession of the gift. But this covenant gift of the eternal life-giving Spirit in the new covenant community is no longer restricted to Israel but now includes Israel and the nations for the Spirit has been poured out on all flesh (Acts 2:17). The Spirit, as the blessing of Abraham, has come to the Gentiles (Galatians 3:14) thereby fulfilling the primary function of Pentecost which is mission.

2 Corinthians 5 states 'if our earthly body were (subjunctive) dissolved, we have a building from God' (2 Corinthians 5:1) meaning that, sometime after death, we will have a new body—but we are not told when. 'We have' is not an imaginative projection but, rather, states the place (heaven) where the body will be received and be at home. *Oikia* (house, 2 Corinthians 5:1) references permanence as opposed to what had been under construction, that is, an eternal heavenly body in contrast to a frail earthly body. So the resurrection body is from heaven (that is, from God) and heaven is the source of the *Pneuma* by which the resurrection body is formed.

Paul did not expect to receive the new body at death but, rather, at the Parousia when the *oikia* will be *ependusasthai* (put on over, 2 Corinthians 5:2). The exegesis of 5:2,4 cannot lead to the concept of reception of the new body at death, rather, we are unclothed at death and then at the Parousia we are clothed anew. Paul's groaning is unintelligible if he is thinking of being clothed anew at death. 'This very thing' (2 Corinthians 5:5) refers to being clothed anew. Paul declares himself to be of good courage because he is confident that immediately after death he will be with the Lord (5:6–8). With certainty, but uncertainty about the details—after this tent body is dissolved, the believer will at some time be put in possession of an eternal body—Paul knew that after death he would be at home with the Lord. Death will mean absence from the earthly body but presence with the Lord, eventually in the new glorified body.

Immediately preceding 2 Corinthians 5, Paul refers to an eternal weight of glory that is to be enjoyed in the body—just as affliction had been borne in the body (2 Corinthians 4:17-18). This eternal weight of glory is for our permanent house (*gar*, for, continuing the thought of the previous verse; 2 Corinthians 5:1). Then, in a further continuation (*kai gar*, also for), Paul adds that we groan because we long to be clothed upon. The affliction had been borne in the body and the reward will also be in the body (2 Corinthians 5:1). The house will be a manifestation of the glory, indeed, without a body glory could not exist. The further continuation in the next *kai gar* (in this respect, emphasising the consequential for, 2 Corinthians 5:4) forms the basis for the conviction 'we know' in 2 Corinthians 5:1. This view of God's plan for our bodies is not subjective. Paul knows what will be because he possesses the Spirit (2 Corinthians 5:5), indeed, the ardency and eagerness of Paul's desire rests on the Spirit's witness to him. The Christian is sure to obtain a new body (*ei ge kai ekdusamenoi*, if indeed having been clothed; 2 Corinthians 5:3), indeed, 'this very thing' (2 Corinthians 5:5) refers to the groaning issuing from the heart for the heavenly body.

Paul says that the whole of creation is waiting for the revealing of the sons of God, that is, the open demonstration of their adoption as sons with all the privileges of sonship (Romans 8:19). Paul also says that now our life is hidden with Christ in God but when Christ appears in glory then the believers' glory will also be manifest (Colossians 3:4). The believer's life was first hid with Christ because it was a disembodied life but at the last day it will be manifested because it is clothed upon with the eschatological body (cf. Philippians 3:20-21). Paul said to the Corinthians that the Lord Jesus will raise him up and present (reveal) him with the Corinthians (2 Corinthians 4:14)—and, in order to be 'presented', Paul and the Corinthians will need a glorious body like Christ's resurrected body. Indeed, all believers will be made manifest in resurrected bodies before the judgement seat of Christ.

Resurrection change worked on believers by the Spirit

Living and dead believers will undergo change at the Parousia (15:51-53; 1 Thessalonians 4:15-17; 2 Corinthians 5:1-5; Philippians 3:20-21). At the Parousia, after the raising of dead believers, believers who are alive shall also be raised and caught up in the air with them to meet the Lord (1 Thessalonians 4:15). This resurrection for the dead is guaranteed by the *Pneuma* which had underlain their being in Christ between death and resurrection. Believers who are alive at the time of the Parousia share in the same activity of the Spirit so they will also be changed and clothed with resurrection bodies. The change worked on believers by the Spirit will be eternally effective as mortal (the earthly body) will be swallowed up (*katapothe*, drunk down so as to disappear; 2 Corinthians 5:4) in life. The resurrection body no longer has the nature of a tabernacle, rather, believers will then have solid bodies to be possessed and used in heaven forever (2 Corinthians 5:1).

In 15:51–53 and Philippians 3:20–21, the old (corruptible) body is changed into a new body whereas 2 Corinthians 5:1–5 speaks of the old (unclothed) and new (clothed) bodies side by side. In Philippians, the identical body of our humiliation is changed (*metaschematismei*, Philippians 3:21) but in 1 Corinthians we ourselves are changed (15:51). Indeed, flesh and blood cannot inherit the kingdom (15:50) but this does not mean that there is no continuity between the old (corruptible) body and the new (resurrection) body. Paul says 'we shall be changed' (15:51) for the corruptible must put on incorruption. So the principle of continuity pertains.

Paul supposes an analogy between the resurrection of Jesus and that of believers. In the resurrection, God wrought in Jesus a constructed adjustment for the future heavenly environment. Jesus had been determined (declared effectually) the Son of God with power according to the Spirit of holiness by the resurrection from the dead (Romans 1:4). Likewise, the constitution of the second Adam (15:45–49) cannot be described in purely physical terms as the psychical side of our Lord's human nature was also affected by the resurrection. Paul speaks of believers as 'raised with Christ' which must mean changed with Christ. Does Paul have a term to designate this change?

Paul saw the resurrection as a pneumatic transformation because dead believers shall be raised incorruptible (15:52). But the 'dead in Christ' (1 Thessalonians 4:16) are not dead, indeed, they are living as they wait for the saviour to change their lowly body (Philippians 3:20:21). So the change is not making alive. For Christ, the resurrection secured not only a new phase of sonship but also a new phase for the soul. Likewise for the believer, the change fits us for entry into a new world—a new aeon—in an unprecedented sense as sons of God. All of previous life for the believer has been a preparation for this crowning grace of the resurrection where the likeness of the Saviour's resurrection is to be produced in the Christian (Romans 6:5).

Believers are to sow in the Spirit (Galatians 6:7–9) because they will be presented to Christ in a sanctified condition at his coming with the saints (1 Thessalonians 3:13; 5:23). The destiny for all who are 'in Christ' is sharing in Jesus' glorified state. Even dead believers—in the intermediate period between falling asleep and the Parousia—before the resurrection, are dead in Christ (1 Thessalonians 4:6). The dead are thus never separated from Christ, that is, they are in Christ. The living are directed towards acting in the likeness of Jesus (Galatians 6:7–9), indicating that there is a connection between the future life of the Christian and his conduct on earth (cf. Philippians 3:10,11).

Resurrection of Christ and believers by the Spirit under God

The unity between Christ and believers is presented most graphically in the description of Christ, by virtue of his resurrection, as the 'firstfruits (*aparche*) of those who are asleep' (15:20,23). The Old Testament provides the sense of the word 'firstfruits', namely, the first portion representing the total harvest or entire flock for which recognition and thanksgiving would be given to God. Even better than an Old Testament annual harvest, the resurrection of Christ signals the dawn of the new creation. And the 'firstfruits' has more than a temporal meaning because firstfruits indicates that the initial quantity (Christ) is inseparable from the whole, that is, firstfruits carries the idea of representation and organic unity and not simply temporal priority. Hence 'firstfruits' makes the connection between the bodily resurrection of Jesus and the later resurrection of believers, that is, the resurrection of Jesus is the representative beginning of the bodily resurrection of all believers who are asleep. So Jesus' resurrection is a pledge or actual beginning of a general resurrection event in which the Spirit, under God, is the agent. Jesus' resurrection and the general resurrection of all believers are, therefore, two episodes of the same event with a temporal distinction (cf. the movement from the firstfruits of the dough to the whole lump—or from the root to the branches—both indicating organic union, Romans 11:16). Similarly, Epaentus is called the firstfruits of Asia to Christ (Romans 16:5) because he is the beginning of an organic union of those who will respond to the preaching of the gospel in Asia (cf. 16:15).

The reason (*gar*, for; 15:21) for this graphic description of organic connection between Christ (as firstfruits) and believers (15:20) is that the resurrection of the dead comes to man through a man, that is (*gar*, for; 15:22), in Christ all shall be made alive (cf. Romans 5). Christ is the firstfruits of those who sleep because he was raised as the second Adam. But it is only as they are raised in Christ (the second Adam) that believers are raised. Jesus was delivered up for our trespasses and raised for our justification (Romans 4:25)—even so, the heavenly transformation of death for life declares the final removal of condemnation with the heavenly result of bearing the image of the resurrected Christ (in both body and soul) and reckoning ourselves alive unto God as sons (Romans 6:11).[274]

Life in the Spirit even in the dead body of sin

Unity of believers with the resurrection of Christ is both past and future. The believer is one whose inner man has already been raised from the dead but the outer—mental and physical—man is yet to be raised. Paul draws two conclusions from the solidarity of the Spirit with believers (Roman 8:9-11). First, with regard to the believer's present, God makes alive the mortal body of believers through the Spirit who dwells in them and raised Jesus from the dead (Romans 8:11). The instrument employed by the Father in the resurrection of Jesus (that is, the Holy Spirit), who will be employed by God in the future resurrection of believers, is already at work in believers. What the Father did for Christ, he will do for those in whom Christ dwells (Romans 8:10) so that the present experience of the believer is life in the Spirit even in the dead body of sin. Secondly, the Spirits work in the future resurrection is no less definite. The somatic evidence of the future resurrection, even more than has been experienced so far, will disclose the full dimensions of the Spirit's work in the believer beyond what has already been experienced.

---

[274] Vos, 1994, 157

2 Corinthians

The Spirit guarantees sonship and integrity (1:22)

Paul's integrity had been called into question by the Corinthian church for changes in his travel plans which initially included returning to Corinth after travelling to Macedonia. Instead, Paul returned to Ephesus. In his defence, Paul turns the Corinthians' reflection from his ministry to them—the results of his ministry—and to God, who continues to fulfil promises for Paul and his co-workers to confirm them in Christ (1:20-21). God moved Paul and Corinth into faith in Christ; God confirmed and authorised (anointed, 1:21) Paul through the Spirit (1:22; cf. Ephesians 1:13); and God gave the Spirit as a sign of his ownership, protection (the seal, 1:22), and assurance of completion with regard to the new covenant community (of which they were but a portion). The text of Paul's letter emphasises the common possession of the Spirit (sealed us, 1:22; that is, both Paul and the Corinthians) as a first pledge of full reception. This first instalment of the Holy Spirit gives partial insight into the permanency of the full life in the Spirit to come. The Spirit testifies to their hearts by creating a new heart and a capacity to receive him. God had anointed and sealed the church and is now establishing it and protecting it with reference to Christ by the work of the Spirit. Mutual reception of the Spirit accounts not only for Paul's integrity but also for the Corinthians' Christian existence in Christ. Their experience of the Spirit is real but partial, since it is a treasure experienced in earthen vessels (4:7).

So Paul offered reasons for his change in travel plans (1:15-16) but then argues that his fidelity rests on the character of God who provides the Spirit who guarantees Paul's sonship and thus also guarantees the integrity of his conduct (1:21-22). Indeed, Paul gives thanks to God for the triumphal progress of the gospel brought about by God through apostolic proclamation (2:14-17).

God engraves Christ on human hearts by the Spirit (3:1-3)

A controversy had been engendered by a group of itinerant Jewish preachers who—coming to Corinth after Paul's initial ministry—had challenged Paul's authority and slighted his demeanour and delivery. These 'false apostles' (11:13) or 'superlative apostles' (11:5; 12:11) who engendered controversy among the Corinthians with regard to Paul, were probably Hebrew

Israelites (11:22–23a) who came to Corinth with letters of recommendation (3:1). Presumably also, like Paul, they were Greek speaking Jews. Paul complains that these Jewish preachers had trespassed into his territory (10:12–16), perhaps referring to the arrangement agreed at the Jerusalem Council (Acts 15). So the Jewish preachers were probably from Jerusalem, but these 'ministers of righteousness' (11:15) were only concerned with expounding the Jewish old covenant connection (cf. 3:1–11). This narrow connection with the law and the Mosaic Covenant (3:6–7) suggests that the Jewish preachers in Corinth were Judaizers.

The Corinthians did not deny Paul's apostleship (11:1) but the Jewish preachers were attempting to discredit Paul by claiming that he lacked the proper epistolary credentials—perhaps a letter from Jerusalem authorising his ministry—and he did not conduct himself in the fashion of an accredited minister of the gospel, in particular, Paul did not ask for financial remuneration. Instead, Paul presented his sufferings connected with the cross as a mark of his apostleship. Perhaps the objection of the Jewish preachers was Paul's gospel of an inglorious suffering Messiah. Paul did not take up the particular issues of circumcision and law keeping in his letters to the Corinthians, perhaps indicating that by this time the Judaizers were attacking on a broader front.[275] It is not clear who these 'false apostles' in Corinth were but 2 Corinthians 3 gives some clues about them.

The sufficiency of an apostle was derived from his call to new covenant ministry, which is analogous to Moses' call under the old covenant (3:1–3). So the apostle does not need letters of introduction—either to the Corinthians or from them—to establish his legitimacy. Paul developed the analogy of his ministry with the ministry of Moses who delivered the old covenant to Israel (Exodus 34). The similarity is that just like Moses' ministry delivered the old covenant so Paul's ministry delivers the new covenant (cf. Jeremiah 31:31–34). The issue of the chapter is what ministry promotes the glory of God. What constitutes the true glory?[276] There were specific obligations imposed on the Hebrews in the Sinai covenant and this historical Judaism seems to have been the content of the ministry of the Judaizing false apostles in Corinth. These false apostles probably saw the Christian era as a continuation or consummation of the Jewish era, that is, the Mosaic covenant was—for the false apostles—the continuing covenant. These

---

275 Barnett, 1997, 32–40.
276 Young and Ford, 1987, 1–16.

false apostles incorporated Jesus into their schemata as the fulfilment of the Mosaic covenant.

But the existence of the Corinthian church is a testimony to Paul's new covenant apostolic ministry (1 Corinthians 9:2), indeed—as the founding missionary—no other recommendation was possible or necessary. As recipients of the grace of Christ working through Paul's ministry, the Corinthians themselves were Paul's letter of recommendation which had already been written in 'our' (Paul and his fellow new covenant ministers) hearts (3:2). Their changed lives were sufficient epistolary recommendation to themselves of Paul's widely known ministry. The letter was written on the heart by the Spirit in their regeneration and ongoing sanctification (3:3). This work of the Spirit conforms with the divine promise of the new covenant (Jeremiah 31:33; cf. Ezekiel 11:19; 36:27). The letter written on their hearts attests inward progressive transformation and the author of this transformation is not merely an eminent person but Christ himself.

In the new covenant, God pours out the Spirit on hard-hearted Israel so that they observe his statutes and ordinances (3:3b; cf. Ezekiel 36:27). Accordingly, Christ writes his epistolary commendation of his apostle on the believers' hearts by means of the Spirit.[277] The contrast between Paul's new covenant ministry and the ministry of the Mosaic covenant is that whereas the Mosaic covenant involved external communication on stone tablets,[278] new covenant ministry transforms the deep resources of the inward being. Through Paul's ministry, by the work of the Spirit, God engraves his letter of Christ on tablets which are human hearts. This new covenant letter is not objectively written on stone tablets, rather—as promised in Jeremiah 31:33-34—the new covenant is written on sensitive human hearts. Thus new covenant ministry is very different from the Judaizers' message to observe Mosaic law (an external ministry with no spiritual results since the Mosaic covenant is now defunct).

Covenant without the Spirit must kill (3:4-6)

Paul's confidence and sufficiency are both defined by and based on the work of the Spirit through his ministry (3:4-6). He claims no credit for himself nor does he rely on his background or heritage, rather, Paul trusts the message that he has received through Christ from God. God had

---

277 Fatehi, 2000, 290.
278 Exodus 24:12; 31:18; 32:15; 34:1; Deuteronomy 9:10.

qualified Paul (3:6)—perhaps a reference to his conversion and call—but God had not qualified the false apostles who were ministering in Corinth while Paul was writing this letter.

The basis of Paul's confidence is that the operation of the new covenant prophesied by Jeremiah is proceeding, hence Paul's sequential introduction of the related new covenant passages from Ezekiel and Jeremiah (3:6; Ezekiel 36:25-27; Jeremiah 31:31-34). The conversion and new life of the Corinthians was evidence that the new age has arrived, that is, the age when experience derived from the heart of flesh replaced experience generated by Israel's national heart of stone. For the law written in the hearts (Jeremiah 31:33) is the new inner obedience to God's statutes enabled by the Spirit. Ezekiel affirms that the Spirit will bring about a change of heart in Israel at the time of the eschatological restoration of God's people (Ezekiel 36:25-27). In Ezekiel, Israel's forgiveness is pictured in the priestly terms of God cleansing the people from their uncleanness and idolatry (Ezekiel 36:25,29). As a servant of the new covenant, Paul emphasises that the work of the Spirit transforms the heart so that obedience to the law is possible (3:1-18). Thus Paul's apostolic ministry of the Spirit (3:6b) is a fulfilment of Ezekiel's prophecy (Ezekiel 11:19; 36:25-7), that is, Paul's role is to be a servant of the new covenant.

The contrast in experience between letter and Spirit was possible and, indeed, occurred in both covenants. There is abundant evidence in the Old Testament—such as in the Psalms and Proverbs—that Old Testament saints put the old covenant into valid internalised operation in the heart as distinct from national Israel's cumulative disobedience. Equating the Old Testament era with letter (or Law) and the New Testament era with Spirit (or heart) misconceives the unitary biblical view of salvation by grace. The problem for national Israel in the Old Testament was that national experience was always external, that is, merely letter. But the national experience does not tell the complete story of the piety of saints within Israel.

Furthermore, the present tense 'kills' (referring to letter, 3:6) implies that Paul is referring to the difference between two current bases for ministry operating in Corinth (cf. 3:1-3)—the ministry of the Spirit and the Judaizing preaching of the letter. Paul's gospel, applied in regeneration through the Spirit, was producing changed lives but the continued application of the Mosaic covenant by Jewish-Christian missionaries 'killed' since covenant forgiveness through sacrifice was withdrawn from Israel by their rejection of the cross (John 19:15). Indeed, throughout the history of Israel, the old covenant ministry to Israel had not produced significant national change. In Corinth post-cross, the new covenant Christian gospel was now being supplemented by formalistic and legal demands as Judaizers required full obedience to what they regarded as the continuing Mosaic covenant structure. Thus the nature of the contrast is not between the Mosaic age and Paul's own age but, rather, the contrast is between Paul's new covenant ministry and attempts by the Judaizers to continue the Mosaic age into the post-cross era. Paul's unexpressed presupposition is that the age of the old covenant ceased with the death of Christ. With the rending of the temple veil (Mark 15:38) at the death of Jesus, the Jewish era had passed away and Jewish institutions had been divinely discarded. This point is never made explicitly by Paul but this is what Paul understood (cf. Galatians). After the death of Jesus, only the new covenant gospel applied by the Spirit could give life.

The Judaistic and Christian communities were different. It wasn't just whether the Messiah had come (Christian) or was coming (Judaistic), more than that, the coming of the Messiah meant the end of the age of Judaism. The Epistle to the Hebrews attests the dilemma which confronted Christian Jews until AD 70, namely, old covenant temple worship—with all its institutional attractions including sacrifices, priesthood, altar and worship structures—continued to function after the death of Christ. Hebrews counters the continuing attraction of the old covenant temple system by pointing to the institutions of the new covenant age which replicated and replaced the institutions of the old covenant.

So Paul is not writing about a formal letter/Spirit clash that is characteristic, respectively, of the old and new ages. Rather, Paul is referring not only to the case of national Israel without the Spirit in the time of the operation of the old covenant but also to the present possibility in his own time for those who pursue the operation of the old covenant without the Spirit post-cross. So the Jewish-Christian emissaries in Corinth who resisted Christian rejection of old covenant cultus were, in fact, preaching another Jesus—another Spirit—another gospel (11:4). Indeed, Paul's use of Abraham as the paradigm believer in Galatians 3 and Romans 4 indicates that salvation was by grace through faith in God's promises in both testaments. We must assume that the dispenser of grace in personal salvation in the Old Testament was the Spirit (cf. John 3:10; Isaiah 63:11). The Exodus national rescue had been an expression of divine grace (Exodus 20:1ff). The law, delivered within the context of the grace of national rescue, was therefore a call to a new way of national life. Of course, for Israel, the gift of the law had also meant the exposure of sin (Galatians 3:19).

It is usually suggested that the distinction between national Israel and the new Christian movement is that the latter is wholly dependent upon the leading of the Spirit while the former virtually untouched by it. The comparison is said to be between two corporate bodies: unredeemed national Israel and the new people of God. The Israel of the Old Testament (unredeemed national Israel) was a mixed faith grouping, that is, in Old Testament Israel there were both believers and unbelievers. But a Christian body (such as the Corinthian congregation) is—at least ostensibly—believing.

Under the old covenant, the law was required to be in the hearts of each person individually (as it was under the new covenant) and also in the heart of the nation corporately (cf. Deuteronomy 6:4-6; 11:18). The law was in the heart of believing Old Testament individuals (Isaiah 51:7; Psalms 37:31; 40:8). Indeed, the Spirit must have put the law in the hearts of Old Testament believers! To know righteousness in the Old Testament, to understand the true nature of the covenant relationship, was to have the law in the heart (Isaiah 51:7). And there was no possibility of national obedience for national Israel unless the law was in the national heart, indeed, having the law in the heart was God's call both nationally and individually (Deuteronomy 10:16).

Foreshadowing the return of Israel after exile, God undertakes to circumcise the national heart (Deuteronomy 30:6). God's circumcision will produce ideal love from the heart and ideal obedience (Deuteronomy 30:8). So Jeremiah, demanding repentance from the men of Judah and Jerusalem, announces God's message to them to circumcise their hearts (Jeremiah 4:4). Thus the emphasis on inward circumcision is not confined to the New Testament, that is, the inwardness of the covenant relationship is a Bible-wide expectation.

The demand for a pure, clean, contrite heart is unequivocally Old Testament[279] and return to Yahweh is always the result of a change of heart.[280] The problem in assessing the difference between Old and New Testaments with regard to covenant relationships is the fact that the Old Testament is

---

279 cf. Psalms 51:10,17; 73:1,13; Proverbs 22:11; Isaiah 57:15.
280 Jeremiah 3:10; cf. 9:25–26; Ezekiel 44:7,9.

dealing with the history of a failed covenant entity, namely, national Israel. So the experience of individual believers, which ought to be the basis of comparison with new covenant Christians, is submerged except in a few highly personalised Old Testament books. And whereas there were individual believing saints, the nation broke its covenant experience with the rebellion of the golden calf.

So whereas the Old Testament emphasis is the history of a nation, the New Testament emphasis is the birth of the church which is—in effect—the same nation. Whereas the old covenant was between the nation and God, the use of the second person singular in the delivery of the Ten Words (Exodus 20:1–17) indicates that the covenant must be kept by individuals. In both Testaments the emphasis is corporate, upon the role of Israel in the Old and the restored Israel in the New. And the role of both national Israel (Old Testament) and the new Israel (New Testament) is evangelist to the world.

But these corporate covenants (Sinai and New) can only be compared with regard to their efficacy in the lives of individuals. Throughout the Bible, salvation always involves faith in God's commitment of himself and God commits himself by imposition, by covenant, and by affirming his promise. The newness of the New Testament does not consist in a new basis of salvation, indeed, salvation in both Testaments is predicated on the work of the cross (cf. Revelation 13:8; 17:8; Romans 3:25). Nor is the work of the Spirit in regeneration new in the New Testament since this is something that Nicodemus, the teacher of Israel, should have known (John 3:10). And the fruit of salvation in both Testaments is to love God with the whole heart.

But Paul draws a distinction between the results of his own new covenant ministry and old covenant ministry (Mosaic ministry, 3:1–6). Paul does not contrast the character of the ministries, rather, he contrasts what each ministry had to offer. Whereas both Moses and Paul offered life, Moses' offer was first corporate to Israel and then individual through the second person singular in the Ten Words—but Paul's offer was first to the individual and then corporate in its effect. Both ministries offered life in God's presence but the new covenant was designed to speak to the new situation in which Christ had been rejected by the nation of Israel (Matthew 21:43), so the new covenant introduced a new phase in salvation history. Inaugurated by the death of Christ, conveying a breadth of spiritual gifts beyond the fundamental spiritual gift of new life evidenced in the Old Testament, the new covenant was designed to bring in a new age prefatory to the final blessing of a sin-free society conveyed by the Parousia. But the comparison that Paul is making in 3:1–18 concerns two reactions to differing covenant ministries in the new covenant era, not the ministries of Moses (old) and Paul (new) in their proper contexts. The comparison concludes climactically with the glorious transformation of new covenant ministry (3:18).

The glory of Spirit-filled covenant commitment (3:7–11)

Paul contrasts the two covenants (3:7–11) before discussing the reasons for the necessity of the new covenant (3:12–18). The letter kills but the Spirit gives life (3:6), that is, covenant without the Spirit must kill since it is the Spirit alone who can give life. But covenant without the Spirit was the position of national Israel in the Old Testament from Sinai onwards. In his ministry following that of John the Baptist, Jesus had come to offer Israel covenant renewal and the end of its exile. But national Israel's practice of covenant of the letter only—without Spirit-filled commitment—had killed, so Jesus finally said to national Israel: 'the kingdom of God will be taken away from you and given to a people that produces the fruits of the kingdom' (Matthew 21:43).

The potential of the covenant—that is, life within the covenant—was realised in Old Testament Israel prior to the death of Christ by individual believers who are described by Isaiah as remnant Israel. All Israel was nominally included by birth within the covenant but this nominal inclusion was actualised in the Old Testament by regeneration through the Spirit. But now post-cross the Mosaic covenant letter ministry without the Spirit was still being offered by Jewish Christians at Corinth. Even though this ministry was now being offered in association with the new covenant, this Mosaic ministry must kill just like national Israel's corporate experience of covenant without the Spirit in the Old Testament attested death. There could be no offer of life attached to the now defunct Mosaic covenant. So Paul, in claiming to be a minister of the new covenant, is taking aim at those who are still ministers of the old in the new era. There is little other evidence to construct the content of the gospel of the false apostles but this much can be deduced from 2 Corinthians 3, namely: the comparison between letter and Spirit is between external demand and Spirit-produced obedience to the law.

The argument of 3:1–18 is continually moving toward its climax (3:18). The two covenants are both accompanied by divine glory though in different manifestations. But the new covenant is superior because there are superior results in the ministry of the new covenant (3:7–11). The difference in glory between the two covenants is examined with reference to the circumstances surrounding Israel's reception of the old covenant (3:7–11; Exodus 34:29–35).

Paul remarks that the ministration of death written and graven on stones (old covenant) came with (or in) glory (3:7a). Glory is the radiant outward manifestation or personal inward awareness of the divine presence. This glory could be seen on the shining face of Moses (Exodus 34:29–35), indicating that the old covenant minister had undergone a personal transformation as a result of direct covenant communication with God on Sinai. Judged by the reaction of the crowd who were overcome by awe as they saw Jesus (Mark 9:15), the parallel to the shining face of Moses is Jesus' face glowing as he came down from the Mount of Transfiguration. The crowd were amazed and ran to meet Jesus. But when Aaron and all Israel saw Moses' face, they were afraid to come near him (Exodus 34:30).

The second giving of the covenant (Exodus 34) was also inaugurated in glory but it was a ministry of death (3:7a). When Moses broke the tablets coming down from Sinai (Exodus 32:19), he broke the covenant. A further covenant was initiated at Exodus 34:10 (cf. the verb *bara*). The subject of *bara* in the Old Testament is always God and *bara* is always used to record something new and unprecedented coming into existence. So the covenant of Exodus 34 is not a renewal of Sinai (Exodus 19–24) but a totally new divine intervention in Israel's history.

God had declared Israel to be stiff-necked (Exodus 33:5) and had refused to accompany them to Canaan so God transferred the promise of his presence with all Israel (Exodus 3:14–17) to a promise to be present only with Moses (Exodus 33:14). God's revelation for Israel would now come through Moses, that is, the second conclusion of the covenant with Israel came through Moses. Accordingly, Moses alone (cf. Exodus 24:1) ascended the mount (note the sustained use of the second person singular throughout the giving of the second covenant in Exodus 34). Moses now assumes the role of Israel's mediator (contrary to the position in Exodus 20 when the entire nation before the mount heard the Ten Commandments). From this point on throughout the Old Testament revelation the presence of God would come to Israel indirectly through mediators, judges, kings, prophets and wise men. But Israelites were not able to gaze for a long period (*atenizo*,[281] attentive and prolonged visual observation of a subject; 3:7,13) on the glory of God's vessel, Moses, through whom the revelation came. The repeat of *atenizo* with regard to Israel's encounter with Moses indicates the significance of the word.

The Greek participle *katargoumenen* (normally translated 'fading', 3:7c) is present, passive or middle and modifies *doksa* (glory, 3:7). But the point is not that the glory on Moses' face was fading. Indeed, elsewhere in the New Testament *katargeo* means to abolish or render inactive. But what is rendered inactive? Moses is cast in the unique role of covenant mediator, so the point is that the covenant revelation itself—communicated in the reflection on Moses' face—was not going to endure. Even in the delivery of the Mosaic covenant it was evident that Israel's constant unfaithfulness would mean that this covenant was destined to be replaced.

The whole of 3:7 is referring to Moses' time, that is, 3:7d is not (as NRSV supposes) a reference to Paul's time. Paul is not concerned about the question of 'fading glory' on Moses' face, rather, Paul is demonstrating that the glory evoked by the reception of the old covenant ministry was always destined to be replaced by the glory associated with Jesus' new covenant ministry. Moreover, says Paul, if a covenant attached to a limited history of Israel was revealed with glory then how much more glory will be associated with the ministry of the new perpetual covenant given through the Spirit (3:8)?

If the ministry which led to condemnation and covenant exclusion came in glory, the inference is that the ministry which leads to life within the new covenant (that is, the ministry of the Spirit offering righteousness) abounds in much more glory (3:9). Not only does glory characterise new covenant ministry but glory is also seen in the lives of those who have been transformed by new covenant ministry (3:18). Paul's argument with regard to the Mosaic covenant is that the initial ministry of the old covenant came with glory but led to condemnation for the nation (3:9a). Old covenant ministry could not communicate glory because of Israel's unbelief but new covenant ministry will communicate glory, indeed, will abound in glory (3:9b) because new covenant ministry is attended by the life giving Spirit bringing life out of death for all who will receive.

---

281 cf. Spicq, 1994, 227.

Israel's national death was not due to the reception of the law, rather, Israel's national death was due to disobedience when the will of God had been plainly revealed. Clearly, Israel's national death was due to the mere external letter reception of the covenant by national Israel. The covenant provisions never became an inward determiner of Israel's national life, that is, the law was never kept nationally because it was never lodged by the Spirit in the national heart. But even under the old covenant God did not demand perfect obedience from either the nation or individuals. And perfect obedience is not Paul's point in 3:4–18. But God did demand absolute commitment and customary obedience—that is, the national disposition should have been to keep the law—and, in the case of transgression, there was the provision for sacrifice with heart-felt confession (even for premeditated sin) and genuine repentance.

In contrast to lifeless post-cross old covenant ministry, Paul's ministry brings life since it is a ministry which has its source in the Spirit and offers the Spirit who is the source of life (3:8). Paul is not obsessed with the superiority of the new covenant over the old, although that is implied, but he is concerned with the consequences of the ministry of the new covenant which affirm his apostleship. The old covenant was written with the finger of God (3:7) but it remained—for national Israel—external, simply engraved on stone.

The point of comparison between the ministry of the old covenant—which led, in the case of the nation, to death—and the ministry of the Spirit in the operation of the new covenant, is their respective glory (3:8). The basis of this comparison is provided in 3:9 and 3:14–18, that is, the contrast is between death and Spirit. In creation, humans are merely inanimate (dead) dust sculptures prior to receiving the breath (Spirit) of God (cf. Genesis 2:7). The dry bones in Ezekiel's vision (Ezekiel 37) are mere (dead) skeletons until God's reviving (Spirit) breath enters them so that dry bones live. Accordingly the future 'will be' (glorious, 3:8) does not refer to the Parousia, rather, 'will be' refers to revival when the Spirit gives life where there was death as there is movement from the (temporary) old covenant to the (eternal) new covenant. 3:9 continues this lesser to greater argument. The ministry of the old covenant led to condemnation because it was not accepted by the nation. Even so, the inauguration of the old covenant was attended by divine power. Then Paul continues his traditional Jewish *qal wahomer* (how much greater) argument: how much more, then, does the ministry of the new covenant—which led to acceptance with God (righteousness) and the gift of the Spirit—abound in glory? The results of Christian ministry are in eternal relationships, hence the glory of Christian ministry exceeds by far the glory of Mosaic ministry.

3:10 begins with *kai* (and, even) intensifying the argument of the previous three verses and providing the reason for the comparatively greater (*perisseuei*, surpassing, 3:9b) glory of Christian ministry. Indeed, the ministry of the new covenant abounds (3:10) in comparison to post-cross law ministry, for the result of the law—when it is separated from the Spirit—is to kill. So the theological outcome of post-cross old covenant ministry must be condemnation (3:9a); and the ministry result of post-cross old covenant ministry must be death (3:7). The old covenant is no longer invested with glory (*ou dedoksastai*, does not stand glorified; 3:10), that is, no glory is attached to old covenant ministry now even though it had previously been partly glorified (*dedoksasmenon*, 3:10, taken as a pluperfect) for the former revelation and vehicle of God's glory (the old covenant) is no longer the means through which God is revealing his glory.

After Exodus 34:10, the Sinai Covenant was a nationalistic instrument bound up with the mission of Israel to the world. However, now not only had Israel's covenant ceased (with the death of Christ) but also her commission to be God's witness to the world had been withdrawn by Jesus (Matthew 21:43). The covenant history of Israel (2 Corinthians 3) indicates that national Israel was never an example for the world to follow. But now the replacement for national Israel, the true Israel, has been brought into being at Pentecost (Acts 2) and in Corinth through Paul's gospel.

Free full covenant fellowship by the Spirit (3:16–17)

Paul takes up the significance of his gospel ministry for the redemption of Israelites (not national Israel, 3:16) and then turns to the ministry of the Spirit to all within the new covenant (3:17–18). Paul begins and ends his argument (3:7–18) by drawing a contrast between Israel's hard heartedness first revealed by her sin with the golden calf (3:7,13–14), and the eschatological work of the Spirit among Jews and Gentiles (3:8,15–18). 3:16 (referring to anyone who turns to the Lord) paraphrases Exodus 34:34a (referring to Moses). Moses veiled himself after speaking for Yahweh to the people (Exodus 34:33) and he removed the veil when speaking with the Lord (Exodus 34:34a). The Exodus contrast is between stiff-necked Israel and the transformation wrought by the glory of God's presence in Moses. Moses is the prototype of the remnant within Israel who are in the new covenant.

3:16 seems to be primarily referring to the salvation of Israelites but the subject is indefinite. The subjunctive (this is probably repeatable, that is, the veil can be taken away; 3:16) is constative (this is general, not referring to a specific instance). If Israel turned to Christ—the Lord of the new covenant—her hardened condition would be reversed and she would enter into the new covenant. Israel must return to confess Christ as Messiah and Lord, indeed, already individual Israelites are confessing Christ when the veil on their hearts is taken away. Moses' experience in the tent (Exodus 34:33ff.) is the current experience of the Christian Israelite with the Spirit (3:16-17). Those who accept the new covenant are in direct continuity with Sinai and the revelation of Yahweh given to national Israel. The intimacy of full covenant fellowship which Moses experienced then as a representative Israelite is now possible for all Israel through the Spirit, that is, Christ is made available to new covenant believers by the Spirit (3:17) and new covenant believers in the presence of the Spirit are free from the external compulsion of law-keeping because they have an inner desire to be holy.

The Spirit in the New Testament does not refer to the Christ as he is in himself but as he communicates his life, his will, his very presence to his people. There is an economic sense in which the risen Lord is actually present and active through the Spirit (cf. 1 Corinthians 15:45) but the Spirit retains the primary ontological characteristic as the Spirit of God. Paul at times may refer to God's or Christ's present activity through the Spirit (1 Corinthians 3:16; 6:19-20; Ephesians 2:18,22) but the Spirit remains the Spirit of God and was an extension of his personality. The Yahweh of the Sinai covenant is now encountered through the Spirit of Christ (3:17) and there is freedom in that encounter. New covenant believers are free from the letter of the old covenant, free from external law, free from the restraints which Judaism seeks to impose on Christian converts in Corinth, and free from the veil of hard heartedness (3:16b,17b,18).

However, freedom 'from' is also freedom 'for'. The glory which Moses experienced is available in the new covenant through the Spirit who presents Christ. Yahweh is no longer a remote mountain top experience for he now dwells through the Spirit in the heart of each new covenant believer. The logical conclusion is that all within the new domain of the Spirit (Jew and Gentile alike) are being transformed (3:18). With unveiled face—that is, with unrestricted access—all Christian believers now behold the glory of God revealed in the gospel of Jesus Christ. When the gospel is preached, all are being transformed indirectly by the reflection of God's glory through the Spirit into the 'same image'. We are being incorporated into Christ who is the image of God (4:4), indeed, this is the goal which God always had in mind for humanity (Genesis 1:26).

In the Old Testament the Spirit does not refer to God as he is in himself but God as he communicates his power, his life, his very presence. We cannot identify God and Christ with the Spirit—they are always greater than revelatory or redemptive acts through the Spirit. Paul does not identify Christ as the one who bestows the Spirit on others, rather, God is the one who gives the Spirit.[282] Christ is Lord but never in relation to the Spirit. The Lord is the Spirit because he became a life-giving Spirit by his resurrection (3:17), hence Christ and Spirit are identified not ontologically but in their redemptive activity. The oneness of the Spirit and the last Adam is a function of dynamic identity emerging from the resurrection. Christ's resurrection transformed his humanity, a change which is analogous to the transformation experienced by believers, and the consequence of the resurrection and dynamic oneness with the Spirit is that Christ is actually present with new Israel through the Spirit as the extension of Christ's personality. So the Spirit experienced redemptively by Christians is the presence of the heavenly resurrected Christ whose own resurrection was his human redemption. His resurrection was not evidential in regard to his divinity but critical in regard to his humanity.

Where the Spirit prevails, the Yahweh of the Sinai Covenant is encountered in the risen Lord who is the Spirit (3:17). When the veil is removed in direct covenant relation, there is freedom for new Israel to serve God, freedom to be a light to the nations—a freedom which national Israel never possessed.

New covenant transformation by the Spirit (3:18)

So Jewish and Gentile believers (we all, 3:18) alike now participate in glory at the hands of the Spirit of the new covenant as we are being transformed each day for ministry. The participle *katoptrizomenoi* (3:18) could

---

[282] 1:21f; 5:5; 1 Corinthians 2:12; Galatians 3:5; 4:6; Ephesians 1:17; 1 Thessalonians 4:8; cf. the divine passive at Romans 5:5; 1 Corinthians 12:3; Acts 1:5; 11:16.

be translated 'beholding' then 'reflecting' since it is the transformation for ministry—like Moses in the Tent—which is in mind.[283] This transformation is the glory of God in Paul's ministry. Paul anticipates a dynamic process of transformation into the image of Christ but, until the resurrection, believers live in a body of death (Romans 8:10,13) as they share solidarity with Adam.

The 'same image' (3:18; cf. Genesis 1:27) suggests a total inner and outer transformation by the Spirit, that is, the new covenant minister becomes the glory image of the heavenly Christ (4:4). For believers, the whole person is involved in the same dimension of change for this same image and glory (3:18) is, specifically, the divine radiance of God being visibly revealed in the face (that is, the person) of Jesus Christ (3:18-4:6). The glory of Christ's heavenly existence is seen in believers who are beholding the glory of Jesus, and the consequent change in believers is conformity through the Spirit to the image of God's Son who is the very image of God (4:4; cf. Romans 8:29). Paul's gospel that he preached is that Christ, the resurrected Lord, is the glory of God (cf. 4:5). At the Parousia, our Lord Jesus Christ will bring about the final change for believers into the full glory of God in Christ (1 Corinthians 15:50; cf. Philippians 3:21). For Corinthian believers before the Parousia, the indwelling Spirit was their encounter with the concrete and real presence of the glory of God in Christ.

However, 3:17-18 does not mean that the formation of the new body is already happening as Paul also says: 'we faint not, though our outward man is decaying yet our inward man is being renewed day by day' (4:16). So 3:18 speaks of a transformation by which as in a mirror the believers behold the glory of the Lord. Moses had a visible, bodily glory but for Paul the transformation is an inward glory of Spirit illumination through the gospel (4:4). Paul communicates this knowledge of the glory of God in his preaching but actual transformation of the body could only come about through putting aside mortal flesh at the Parousia. The point is that the Spirit of Christ in believers develops Christ in them (3:17; 1 Corinthians 15:45) and the Spirit will ultimately transform us into the image of the heavenly man at the final resurrection (1 Corinthians 15:49; Romans 8:29; Philippians 3:21).

---

[283] Young and Ford, 1987, 90 (for the translation of the participle *katoptrizomenoi*).

The Spirit reveals divine treasure through clay jars (4:1–18)

God is the author of the illumination which had transformed Paul (3:6). God had shone (past tense definite; cf. Genesis 1:3-4; Isaiah 9:2) this inward revelation not only to Paul by the Spirit but also through Paul by his preaching to the Corinthians—giving them the light of the knowledge of the glory of God in the person of Christ (3:6). The outward human reality is that Paul is simply an unprepossessing pot of common clay (4:7); a totally unfit, expendable container. Yet the Spirit communicates through Paul the divine treasure of gospel ministry (4:7), indeed, this treasure is contained in his expendable container.

The pattern of polemic commendation begun in 4:1 is rounded off in 4:13-15. Apostolic sufferings are not to be ashamed of but, rather, they reveal God's glory and provide impetus for the continued ministry of preaching the gospel. Gospel preaching through suffering depends on divine power working within, which is the Spirit's ministry in the new covenant. The source of the power referred to in 4:7-13 has been identified (4:14), that is, faith communicated through the Spirit (4:13) provides assurance that the success of the apostolic ministry is because of Jesus' resurrection. Paul's ministry induces a grace theology of abundance which causes great thanksgiving to God with even greater glory given to God for new covenant ministry, thereby enabling even greater ministry.

Heavenly expectation and guarantee of the Spirit (5:1–5)

5:1 is not just about the future, as 'we have' (5:1b) must somehow mean present spiritual reception of the future secure possession of the Parousia new body. Spiritually—though disembodied—we are with Christ at death and conscious of the future, spiritual body which is totally (thankfully) controlled by the Spirit at the Parousia of Jesus. So believers have confidence that the heavenly house is firmly ours, for future possession, when the earthly body dies and we are spiritually with Christ. The resurrection spiritual body that is controlled by the Spirit is received at the second coming for occupancy in the eternal new age. This final reality (5:4) has been constructed for us by God (5:5) and now, before the final reality, God has given us the guarantee of the Spirit as assurance of our eternal future (4:16). So the gift of the Spirit draws attention to the great renewal which is already taking place within us and will continue after death until the final transformation when—at the second coming of Christ—we will be further clothed with a body that is completely controlled by the Spirit. So the gift of the Spirit to believers at regeneration (as a pledge) leads to spiritual growth throughout our human life-time and then to the full possession of spiritual life in the resurrection body at the Parousia. Having been given the Spirit of adoption as sons, our progressive renewal is then consummated at the Parousia as adopted sons (Romans 8:23).

The tent metaphor (5:1a) emphasising the provisional nature of the earthly age is contrasted with the 'building (*oikodome*) from God' (5:1b). Elsewhere in the New Testament, *oikodome* refers to a building under construction (cf. Ephesians 2:21) so the '*oikodome* from God' in 5:1b refers to the immense unseen present changes taking place in us towards the ideal possession at death of the eternal house in the heavens. The present earthly body, the temporary dwelling of the Spirit, is dismantled at death; but, at death, our person will look forward to the bodily structure fit for eternity, to be completed at the Parousia in the new age.[284]

The house (*oikian*, 5:1c) arising from the '*oikodome* from God' is divinely wrought—not made with human hands—to be a permanent end-time spiritual body, that is, the resurrection/transformation body at the Parousia (cf. 1 Corinthians 15:47–49). This *oikian* (5:1c) is an eternal habitation, that is, belonging to the age to come in which the believer bodily receives the full benefits of eternal salvation and will then be totally controlled by the Spirit. But even in this present age the final transformation has begun so that we look toward complete fulfilment at the Parousia. The Spirit mediates Christ's resurrection life to his people both in their pre-heavenly and heavenly states. So the building (5:1b) now begun in us—not built by human hands (cf. Colossians 2:11; Acts 7:48; 17:24; Hebrews 9:11,24)—is a spiritual, heavenly reality. So the basic contrast in 5:1 is permanence versus impermanence through transformation.

Gar (for, 5:2) indicates that 5:2 elaborates 5:1. Paul's experience is that affliction, rejection and suffering has not only drawn him to the resurrection power of God but also—in 'this' tent, 5:2 referring to 5:1—he has been made to groan in longing for his heavenly home, that is, longing for the completion of the building that is already in progress. Paul's use of the clothing metaphor (putting on over, 5:2) indicates how the transformation at the Parousia will take place. 'Putting on over' (clothed, 5:2) implies an action beyond death but also applies to believers who are living at the time

---

284 cf. Young and Ford, 1987, 132.

of the Parousia as they will be immediately transformed with no period of disembodiment.

Meyer points out that 5:1–10 present three stages: this life; the disembodiment of the dead; and the two-stage consummation at the end-time resurrection.[285] Death will be the end of mortal sinful humanity (the 'flesh', cf. Romans 6:23)—death will be a putting off—leaving the human spirit to be 'added to' by the completion of bodily transformation at Christ's return (1 Corinthians 15:42,51–54). Harris suggests that the doubly compounded Greek verb meaning 'putting on over' (*ependusashai*, 5:2) stresses continuity in the process of moving from the earthly tent to the final heavenly building.[286] At death, the earthly body is put off and we are in a spiritual relationship with Christ, to be consummated in our spiritual body at the Parousia. At the Parousia, we put on by transformation the complete, final resurrection physical body. For believers who are alive at the Parousia, the spiritual body will be 'put on over' the physical body and replace it.

The aside in 5:3 sums up the argument so far, reinforcing 5:2.[287] A full bodily existence is the final intention (the matter of an intermediate state—while it may be implied by the total argument—is not the issue here). As the single compound verb *ekdusamenoi* (having put off this body, 5:3)[288] is used of unclothed (5:3), this may suggest that Paul's object throughout is longing for the resurrection body (to be received at the second coming). This suggests that 'naked' (5:3), though capable of a variety of meanings, means in this context the bodiless state which ensues upon death. Now the believer is clothed with Christ (the verb is used several times for putting on Christ; cf. Romans 13:14; Galatians 3:27). Conversion, putting on Christ, is necessary for expectation of an eternal future. Before the judgement seat, believers will not be found to be unsaved and therefore disembodied (that is, naked) before Christ the final judge. Indeed, those who are disembodied (who have not put on Christ) will be rejected at the last judgement. Nevertheless, the process of being disembodied at death is to be welcomed since to die is to be with Christ (Philippians 1:21) and this is far better than the present life. So 5:3 is a strong statement of Paul's assurance of embodiment

---

285 cf. Meyer, 1986, 378.
286 Harris, 1971, 44–45.
287 Thrall, 1994, 356.
288 Vos, 1994, 190–191. Vos proposes that Paul has in mind a longish period of being unclothed before the Parousia.

by transformation and a rejection of the view that disembodiment is the ideal future state.

5:4 amplifies 5:2 after the parenthesis of 5:3. Paul expresses natural horror at the prospect of death because death will in fact unclothe him of his present body (5:4a). But the final state is being further clothed (5:4b)—that is, fully justified at the final transformation when salvation is complete, death swallowed up by eternal life—when Christian experience will be complete for eternal life in the eschaton. Paul might have been expected to use 'immortality' at the conclusion of the argument to match the preceding 'what is mortal' (5:4b) but, instead, his contrasting noun to 'mortal' is 'life'. Thus he draws attention to the body and not just the spirit. When this transformation is complete, mortality will then have been swallowed up in (eternal) life (cf. Isaiah 25:8).

This final reality (5:4) has been constructed for us by God (5:5) and now, before the final reality, God has given us the guarantee of the Spirit as assurance of our eternal future (4:16). So the gift of the Spirit draws attention to the great renewal which is already taking place within us and will continue after death until the final transformation when—at the second coming of Christ—we will be further clothed with a body that is completely controlled by the Spirit. So the gift of the Spirit to believers at regeneration (as a pledge) leads to spiritual growth throughout our human life-time and then to the full possession of spiritual life in the resurrection body at the Parousia. Having been given the Spirit of adoption as sons, our progressive renewal is then consummated at the Parousia as adopted sons (Romans 8:23).[289]

New creation—the sovereign activity of the Spirit (5:17)

For those who have been raised with Christ to new life in Christ, the old life according to the flesh has passed away and we have become new creatures in Christ. Regeneration is the inauguration of our new life (new creation) by the sovereign and secret activity of God through the Spirit. Regeneration (*palingenesia*, cf. Matthew 19:28) also refers to the final resurrection. Regeneration is also used alongside *anakainosis* (renewal, Titus 3:5; cf. Romans 12:2) where the regeneration is the washing or baptism or renewal

---

[289] cf. Harris, 2005, 394.

of the Spirit in effecting rebirth. There is a response to transformation from outside consequent to transformation within by the work of the Spirit.

Regeneration (*anagennesas*, 1 Peter 1:3) is causally rooted in the resurrection of Christ. We are born again: not of our own will, but by God's decision (John 1:12); from above, not from below; of the Spirit, not of the flesh (John 3:3,5–6); of God, not of man (1 John 2:29; 3:9; 4:7; 5:1,4,18); by God's choice through his word, not by our own energies or will (James 1:18). We are flesh so regeneration occurs outside of human ability (John 3:3–10), indeed, Jesus' explanation of rebirth was a complete mystery to Nicodemus. In John, flesh (*sarx*) is human weakness or frailty—but in Paul, flesh (*sarx*) is human nature debilitated by sin. In both John and Paul, *sarx* refers to man apart from God. We all need rebirth to worship in the Spirit (John 4:23–24).

What is rebirth? Rebirth conveys intellectual illumination as the kingdom of God is now visible in our world so we know the truth (1 John 2:20) without teachers (1 John 2:27). Rebirth involves an anointing with the Spirit thereby granting knowledge of the Lord without human mediation. Rebirth liberates the will from bondage to self-interest and sin. Rebirth cleanses (Titus 3:5) and sanctifies. Desires are renewed as regeneration changes our attitude to the world so we understand that the world is in rebellion (1 John 5:19), in the darkness of sin (John 1:5; 12:46). In regeneration we are cleansed by the expulsive power of a new affection so that we become careful to do the Lord's will which is now possible by the indwelling Spirit's transforming power. We move from total depravity—totally affected by the power of sin in all our parts—to openness to the work of the Spirit within. Regeneration takes place by the word of God applied by a direct creative act through the Spirit (1 Peter 1:23; James 1:18; John 15:3). This new birth to faith by glad reception of the word takes place within.

Finally, regeneration will mean the eschatological renewal of all things—that is, a new creation and general resurrection of all believers through the power of the Holy Spirit (cf. Romans 8:11). This regeneration is an act of God's absolute sovereignty to be effected, as was the initial creation, by the word of God (cf. 1 Thessalonians 4:16).

All faith is trust in another (cf. Ephesians 2:1–10) so the power to save is not in our faith but in the God who gives faith, indeed, faith and repentance are inseparable gifts of the Spirit. We repent—that is, we recognise our offence against God and turn away from our sin—when we believe in the gospel (Mark 1:15). Belief cannot exist apart from repentance. The marks of a changed (repentant) life will be obedience in changed attitudes to self, others and God.

Repentance is a gift of the ascended Christ to us conveyed through the Spirit (Acts 5:31). God brings us to himself by revelation through his word illumined by the Spirit. A right view of God as holy and merciful is the only foundation for genuine evangelical repentance. God's holiness grounds the necessity of repentance—God's grace and mercy provide for the possibility of repentance. Faith and repentance, as expressions of regeneration, belong to the whole of Christian experience (not just the initial rebirth). The entire process of sanctification is regeneration coming into its own with faith and repentance becoming more dominant characteristics of our life in the Spirit.

Ministry credentials formed by the Holy Spirit (6:1-10)

Paul commends to Corinth the character of his ministerial activities (6:6-7a) adopted in the context of trials (6:4-5). Paul lists qualities developed through the work of the Spirit which have carried him through crises. These eight qualities or virtues, beginning with the same preposition *en*, are Paul's credentials in the new era:[290] first, purity of life and motive; second, knowledge or understanding of and insight into God's truth; third and fourth, forbearance and kindness, that is, patience and its fruit which is love (cf. the juxtaposition of forbearance and kindness as fruits of the Spirit in Galatians 5:22, and the conjunction of forbearance and suffering as the outworking of Christian love in 1 Corinthians 13:4); fifth, the somewhat surprising mention of the Holy Spirit as the list turns from internal attributes to manifest ministry activities; sixth, unfeigned love expressed in Christian conduct; seventh, the ministry of proclamation or the word of truth (the gospel, the word of the cross); and, eighth, the Spirit manifesting the power of God through the results of Paul's ministry. The manifest presence of the Holy Spirit impacting character is a necessary credential of the new covenant minister of God.

Paul's exposition of the new covenant (2:14ff) commences with his role followed by the nature of the covenant (3:1-18), then Christian ministry and assurance (4:1-5:10). The exposition concludes with the central aim of the Christian calling (6:14-7:1) in the new covenant which is worship

---

[290] cf. Grabbe, 2000, 124.

(6:17a–c). Not only the new covenant minister, with a specific calling from God, but all new covenant people are to have their characters formed by the living presence of the Spirit. Like ancient Israel coming out of Egypt, worship was the goal of the new 'exodus' of the new Israel who are committed to serve under God's kingship and to be God's dwelling place on earth. Central to 6:14–7:1 is the notion controlling the whole section from 2:14–7:1, namely, that Christian worship as the temple of the living God (6:16) is the personal and corporate aim of God's salvation. As the temple of God (1 Corinthians 3:16–17; 6:19; cf. Leviticus 26: 11–12; Ezekiel 36:26–27), those who are in Christ have the Spirit—they know God directly as king and respond to him positively, they desire to keep the covenant stipulations—so they are not their own but are holy, belonging to God. Indeed, the whole church ministers the presence of God in the world as the new covenant temple of God.

The new covenant emphasis on the presence of the Spirit is congruent with the church as the temple of the living God (6:16), that is, the church is God alive in the world in his people. This corresponds with expectations of the unbreakable and everlasting new covenant (cf. Jeremiah 31:31–34). In Christ, the people of the new covenant have already become the eschatological temple in which God is present by the Spirit. Believers, like the consecrated tabernacle of Exodus 40, are being filled with glory now (3:18) by the transforming work of the Spirit whereby the glory of God is now seen in the face (person) of Christ (4:6). The wonder of the gospel is that all may now enter the holy of holies with unveiled faces. This is the freedom which exists wherever the Spirit resides (3:17) for the Spirit frees new covenant sons and daughters of God from the hard heartedness that had necessitated the veiling of God's glory from his people in the past.

A different gospel confers a different spirit (11:1–33)

The Greek construction of 11:4 makes it clear that 'if' refers to a situation which has occurred. When Paul came to Corinth, he preached the gospel and those who believed received the Spirit. But these Corinthian believers are now in danger because they had also tolerated a false gospel introduced by itinerant, unsolicited missionaries who had come without divine authorisation. The itinerants' heretical teaching proposed the acceptance of another Jesus, another Spirit, and another gospel. A different interpretation of the ministry of Jesus might nationalise him and tie him into the Mosaic covenant, thereby making him out to be exclusively for the Jews. Another gospel might pronounce that admission into the Mosaic covenant is necessary for conversion to Christianity. Another spirit might concentrate on the spectacular and neglect the Holy Spirit's ministry of confirming the message of the gospel and strengthening the convert to faithfully exhibit Christ in the conduct of his Christian life.

If these suppositions are accurate, Paul's conflict in Corinth would have been with Judaizing Christians (like Galatia where the Judaizers' different covenantal understanding required teaching the Mosaic Law to Gentile converts). The issues of circumcision, food laws, the Jewish law and liberty are not emphasised in Paul's letters to the Corinthians—but we do know that Paul's opponents were proud of their Jewish heritage (11:22). His opponents were also skilled rhetoricians (11:6) which could indicate a Hellenistic-Jewish background (sophistic but also Mosaic, cf. 2 Corinthians 3). Paul's approach was strength through weakness, but the Corinthians had 'readily submitted' to a new gospel which emphasised power and present glory leading to a kind of Christian triumphalism. This new 'gospel' thoroughly deprecated Paul's gospel of a crucified Christ.

The communion of the Spirit (13:14)

In his final greetings, Paul calls the Corinthian congregation to comfort each other and to live at peace with each other. These attributes of Christian community will be cemented by their experience of God's love and peace with them (13:11). Does the Spirit create Christian community or is the Spirit a partner in Christian community? Communion with the Spirit carries the blessings of the gospel in the context of the church of Christ (13:14) as the Spirit is our fellowship partner (cf. Philippians 2:1). In the old covenant, God was immanent among his people in the Spirit. In the new covenant, the consummation of this immanence is God's personal presence in the Lord Jesus Christ by the Holy Spirit. The relationship in the Spirit is more intimate than mere divine influence (cf. Romans 8:11; 1 Corinthians 3:16; 6:19). The believer is being shaped relationally in communion with the Holy Spirit according to the pattern that has always existed within inner-trinitarian relationships. At the same time, the body is being customised in communion with the Holy Spirit for the future dominion of the Spirit. The anticipated future state of glory will even surpass the present amazing state of grace (cf. Romans 8:18–23; 2 Corinthians 4:17–18; 1 John 3:1–3) in the final, radical work of the Spirit at the Parousia.

Galatians

We receive the blessing of God—the Spirit—by faith (3:1-14)

3:1-5 take up the important question of the Galatians' experience of the Spirit in the light of Paul's insistence on the revelatory character of his gospel. The Spirit is the internal blessing of the new age. The consequence of the new covenant assertion of justification by faith (2:14-17) is clear: if Galatian gentile Christians have received the Spirit—that is, the fulfilment of all the Abrahamic promises—by faith, it follows that participation in the promises is based on faith in Christ alone and not on the Mosaic Law added 430 years after Abraham's acceptance by God (3:1-14). Paul's gospel of grace cannot be supplemented under any circumstances. Paul's argument exposes the error of those who demand a place for the Mosaic law as well as, or instead of, the gospel. By grace through faith is the only way to become legitimate sons of Abraham and thereby share the blessing attached to God's promises. This has been the plan of salvation from the beginning. The law was never to be the condition for entering covenant relationship with God, rather, the law was provided only for Israel as the means of responding to covenant prior to the advent of Christ. But now, post-cross, Jewish and Gentile believers are to live in Christ through the Spirit (not under the Mosaic law).

The Galatians are 'foolish' (3:1) if they exchange the new covenant in Christ for an old, defunct Jewish covenant. The Spirit conveys to believers (3:5) the Trinitarian effect of Christ crucified (2:16-21). The Galatians were fascinated by the Judaizers—as though they had an evil eye (*baskaino*, 3:1) cast at them—but their experience in the Spirit should have prevented them from succumbing to this bewitching influence (3:2). Paul had clearly preached to them: the significance of the cross; the implication of the Messiah's crucifixion as a common criminal; and that Christ's death had superseded all forms of legal righteousness. And when they believed the gospel they also received the Spirit which fully endorsed Paul's message of the fully operative cross covenant. God has accepted them, admitted them into the new covenant (that is, justified them), and adopted them as sons (4:6; cf. 4:28-29). Indeed, when they heard Paul and believed the gospel, God then (at that time, before they knew anything about Moses' law) gave to them his own Spirit. So they belong to the body of Christ independent of the yoke of the Torah.

Paul therefore asks the one question that really matters, because receiving the Spirit was the mark of a true Christian as this signified covenant acceptance (3:2). By faith—not by observing the Mosaic law—the Galatians received the Spirit at the beginning of their Christian life (cf. 1 Corinthians 6:11). The Galatians' reception of the Spirit (3:1-5) and Abraham's experience of justification (3:6-9) are parallel because Abraham (like the Galatians) was justified when he believed God's promise. Neither Abraham's justification nor the Galatians' reception of the Spirit had anything to do with Mosaic law.

Progress in faith, like the beginning of new life in regeneration, is also a gift of the Spirit. Flesh (*sarx*, 3:3)—describing autonomous human nature in its fallenness, that is, unredeemed humanity—is absurdly presented as the alternative to the Spirit as a source of strength. But if effort in the flesh is sufficient then the totality of their experience of suffering (*pascho*, 3:4) for their faith was in vain. The Galatians should consider what they will lose if they rely on flesh as opposed to living by faith in the Spirit, for to live in the flesh is 'to live according to the values and desires of life in the present aeon that stand in absolute contradiction to God and his ways'.[291] Indeed, by definition, miracles cannot be produced by *sarx* for flesh can only produce cause and effect; but miracles happen when God is present by his Spirit. This is another parallel between God's activity among the Galatians and his dealings with Abraham, that is, the sign of God's continuous activity in supplying the Spirit and working miracles (3:5) is correlated with the unforeseen miracle of reckoning righteousness to Abraham (3:6). Therefore (*oun*, 3:5) builds on the expected answer to Paul's question of how the Galatians received the Spirit (3:2), namely, that the ground for the continued presence of the Spirit must be the same as their initial acceptance into the covenant (that is, faith).

Abraham's faith is accounted to him for righteousness (3:6; Genesis 15:6), that is, because of his faith Abraham is in right relationship with God and the evidence for this right relationship is inclusion in a covenant relationship with God (Gen 15:18). 'Just as' (3:6) indicates that the Galatians, likewise, are included by faith in covenant relationship with God. A shared faith in God's promises links Abraham and the Galatians, making the Galatians Abraham's spiritual descendants. Faith, not circumcision, was Abraham's means of entry to a covenant relationship and faith is also the means

---

291 Fee, 1994, 385.

of entry into new covenant relationship. Those who by grace believe in Jesus as Messiah and Lord are members of the new covenant. Those Galatians who rely on faith alone (3:9) are within the same covenant of promise and therefore enjoy the same blessings as Abraham (Genesis 12:3; 18:18). Like Abraham, all who live by faith are fully convinced that God is able to do what he has promised (Romans 4:21).

From the beginning of biblical redemption with Abraham, internal faith—not external Mosaic law keeping—had been the only way of being accepted by God. Paul parallels the bestowal of the Spirit and crediting with righteousness (3:14) as both follow believing God's promises. Thus there is no distinction in the path of salvation for Jews or Gentiles, that is, the common denominator is faith (*pistis* 3:5,6,7,8,9). 'By faith' is, therefore, the answer to Paul's question (3:5) about how Gentiles receive blessing (that is, the gift of the Spirit; 3:14).

The Spirit of Jesus in us cries out 'Abba, Father' (4:1-7)

Fatehi suggests that Paul defines believers' new identity as sonship in Christ and incorporation into Christ (3:26-29).[292] Furthermore, God sends the much needed Spirit of His Son for the disciple's life—as a son of God—in this new age (4:6). By 'putting on' through baptism (3:27), Spirit baptism covers the disciple with a new nature in Christ over the old 'Adamic' nature which we still possess until death. So the Christian has two natures: the old flesh-directed nature and the new Spirit-directed nature. Fatehi points to the contradiction between Romans 8:15 (where the believer, by the Spirit of sonship in Christ, cries 'Abba, Father') and 4:6 (where the Spirit of his Son, in the believer's heart, cries 'Abba').[293] This contradiction is resolved by recognising that, in both cases, the risen Christ himself is present and active crying Abba to his Father through his Spirit within the believer. Christ is the source as well as the pattern of the believer's sonship through the Spirit.

Paul clarifies the relationship between faith, Mosaic law and filial relationship with God (cf. 3:23-29) with an analogy (4:1-7) of a son growing up in a patrician household—regulated as a minor by guardians and administrators (4:1-2). Guardians (*epitropoi*, 4:2) and stewards (*oikonomoi*, 4:2) could include state officials. Until he reaches adulthood, the son is little different from a slave even though he is the heir. This analogy contrasts

---

292 Fatehi, 2000, 218.
293 Fatehi, 2000, 219-220.

Jewish pre-Christian experience under the law with new-found Christian freedom. James Scott has argued that the sonship referred to is Israel's pre-exodus Old Testament experience (when a child; cf. Hosea 11:1)[294] and the 'fullness of time' (4:4) is the divinely decreed time limit fixed for the bondage.[295] Accordingly, 4:1-2 refers to Israel's Egypt experience (in slavery in Egypt though heir of the world through the promises to Abraham) and the deliverance from Egypt was symbolic of the freedom achieved by Christ's death and resurrection.

The Mosaic Law is now a type of general elementary teaching (*stoicheia*, the material world; 4:2).[296] Contamination from contact with the fallenness of the elements of the world has placed Jews (national Israel)—having ignored their mandate for separateness from their world—in bondage. Gentiles were in similar bondage to elemental materialism (*stoicheia*, 4:9) but their bondage was expressed in worship of pagan deities. Remarkably, after the cross, Paul equates Jewish 'law service' with pagan polytheism.

The fullness of time fixed in God's purposes for redemption in Christ corresponds—in the analogy being drawn with the date ordained to Abraham (4:2; Genesis 15:13)—to Israel's deliverance from Egyptian bondage. There is a parallel between Israel's bondage in Egypt and the later bondage for national Israel under Mosaic Law. In Paul's analogy, 'so with us' (4:3) probably applies to Jews. 'God sent his Son' (4:4) suggests pre-existence but the conjunction of being sent 'in the fullness of time' (4:4-5) with 'God sent the Spirit of his Son into our hearts' (4:6) makes the coming of Jesus an eschatological event bringing in a new age, a new creation.[297] Jesus was a truly representative human being (4:4): born of a woman, a reference to the virgin birth; and born under the law, that is, under the curse of the law (cf. 3:23) and under the Sinai Covenant. Jesus was an Israelite and therefore obliged to keep the Sinai covenant and, indeed, Jesus fulfilled all the requirements of the Sinai covenant thereby absorbing its curse in his death on the cross. The divine aim was salvation (4:5; cf. 3:26-29) with the biblical model being Israel's exodus, that is, movement from being Pharaoh's slaves to becoming God's sons by adoption. Accordingly, Jews now need to be 'redeemed from under the law' (4:5).

---

294 Scott, 1992, 129.
295 Scott, 1992 (140, 147, 161-162).
296 Thielman, 1989, 82-83.
297 Cho, 2005, 63-4.

Receiving the gift of adoptive sonship (4:6), the Galatians simultaneously received the Spirit of 'his Son'—that is, the Spirit who is the indwelling Son. The indwelling Spirit of the Son not only confirms the filial relationship with God but is also the means of conforming them, inwardly and progressively, to the image of the Son by mediating Christ's presence and power. The 'adoption as sons' was instantaneous but the conformity to the image of the Son is a gradual process 'from one degree of glory to another; for this comes from the Lord (that is, through) the Spirit' (cf. 2 Corinthians 3:18). Sonship was provided by Christ's death but actualised by the risen Christ's indwelling presence communicated through the Spirit. And the reception of Christ in the Spirit makes them children who are progressively being formed to respond as obedient sons like Jesus. So the Galatians ('your hearts', 4:6) naturally (by their new nature) utter the Spirit-inspired cry of deepest familial intimacy in prayer and worship, addressing God as Father (Abba, 4:6).

'So that' (*hoste*, 4:7) sums up the argument (4:1–7): the Galatians are not slaves or strangers from the commonwealth of Israel, on the contrary, they are sons and heirs of God—members of Abraham's family of believers.

The promise to Abraham is the gift of the Spirit (4:21–5:1)

Two sons of Abraham—Ishmael and Isaac—represent two covenants: Sinai (Judaism); and Christ (the new covenant). Sarah, the biological mother of the Jews (as Abraham's wife), now becomes mother of all who receive Christ in the Spirit through promise under the new covenant (as the mother of a miracle, 4:23). Hagar, the slave woman who is the biological mother of non-Jews (Arabs, 4:25), is now the mother of all who are still in slavery to the defunct covenant of Mosaic law for those who live according to a defunct law-code are living by cause-and-effect *sarx* (4:29). And just as Ishmael (born according to *sarx*, 4:29) persecuted Isaac (born according to the Spirit as a miraculous event), likewise, the Judaizers (Hagar's descendants) persecute those who have been miraculously brought into new covenant relationship by the baptism of the Spirit (Sarah's descendants).

The conclusion is that the Galatians, regardless of their biological or religious descent, are now children of the new covenant promise that was realised at Pentecost. Isaac, the marvellously born child of promise, is the brother (4:28) of all who are divinely born according to the Spirit

(4:29)—children of promise (4:28), not children of Mosaic law. Thus Paul again links the promise given to Abraham with the gift of the Spirit (cf. 3:14).

The Spirit is the guarantee of our final justification (5:2-6)

Our state of being—that is, liberty in the Spirit or bondage to striving by flesh (5:1; cf. 2 Corinthians 3:17)—is determined by whether our religious mother is Sarah or Hagar. Any attempt to secure covenant acceptance by keeping the Sinai covenant law (such as a requirement for circumcision, 5:2,4) is a rejection of the gospel of grace and therefore a movement from liberty to bondage. Post-cross, the yoke of slavery is the Mosaic Covenant and its law (5:1) which would have to be followed in its entirety (5:3) if the Galatians accepted one aspect of the Mosaic Covenant (circumcision) as a requirement for continuing acceptance by God in the new covenant. And surrender to a Judaistic Christianity would result in loss of salvation because those who seek justification under the Mosaic Covenant cut themselves off from the grace of Christ (5:2,4).

The Spirit gifts believers with the awareness that we wait for the hope of final justification, that is, acceptance by God (5:5) through inclusion in his covenant. Initial justification (righteousness) comes through the death of Jesus, by which the ungodly are reconciled to God. This initial justification in Christ is being confirmed by our continual walking in step with Christ in and through the Spirit. The reception of the Spirit is the guarantee of our final justification at the last judgment. Through the Spirit, believers—who have already been accepted into the new covenant in Christ—wait with eager expectation for this declaration of acquittal at the final judgment.

Freedom in the Spirit is the basis of the moral life (5:16-25)

Freedom in the Spirit—that is, Christ present day by day in the Spirit—is the basis of the moral life (cf. the present imperative *peripateite*, walk by the Spirit; 5:16). Paul commands the Galatians to continue to walk by the Spirit, that is, to let their conduct be motivated by the Spirit's dictation which the believer recognises by its appeal to scripture. Discrimination comes with a cleansed conscience, a desire to do the will of God, and spiritual strength given to resist the disposition of the flesh.

It may seem that Paul's emphasis on human predisposition to sin stemming from the flesh (5:16) indicates a new topic in his letter to the Galatians. But Paul connects 'flesh' with 'law' (cf. 3:3-5; 4:21-31) so Torah and circumcision as a means to covenant acceptance are still in Paul's mind in this section of the letter with a pericope commencing with his indicative imperative command to 'walk by the Spirit' (cf. the inclusive encouragement 'let us walk by the Spirit' at the end of the pericope; 5:25). Paul evokes commitment to follow the directions set by the Spirit, for the Spirit is the power of the new era. The Spirit overcomes the power of the old age, that is, the flesh with which Christians still must battle. Believers who submit to the leading of the Spirit will normally repudiate the demands of their fallen nature (5:16b) which can easily be recognised by their non-Christian character or selfish gratification. In 5:16-25, believers are active as they do the walking (5:16,25) but they are passive with regard to producing the fruit which is the work of the Spirit (5:22).

5:17 presupposes that the advice of 5:16 has not yet been taken. The reality when life is still lived under the domination of natural impulses and desires (the flesh)—the reality when Christians seek covenant acceptance through submission to Mosaic law—is total lack of power to overcome sin (cf. Romans 7:14-25) because the law is unable to deal with human fallenness. The Christian believer is not necessarily stuck in the continual domination of flesh over Spirit but acceptance of Mosaic law as a means to covenant acceptance will fuel the corrupting power of sin in the flesh. Life under a defunct Mosaic Covenant will not benefit from the Spirit's presence for the Spirit is the blessing of the new covenant. 5:17 presupposes life directed by the flesh working through Mosaic law disconnected from the power of God in the Spirit and, even though the law itself is good, proud human effort represents opposition from the flesh which prevents conduct that expresses the will of God through law. For believers who are 'in Christ' (and thus, through the Spirit, under his lordship), behaviour is determined and defined by Christ. Living in sin means that life is controlled by the sin principle or the destructive power of sin. 5:17 makes it clear that Christian experience will involve struggle because sinful desires remain with us until the end of life but, because of the gift of Christ in the Spirit, sinful desires do not need to be dominant.

There is a fixed antithesis between 'flesh' and Spirit in Paul's teaching (5:17). But there seems to be no direct association of flesh with sin in either Old or New Testament. The source of sin is not in the flesh—a product of creation—but in the act of the first man Adam, then imputed to all (Romans 5:16). In both testaments, the Spirit is the exterminator of sin in the flesh. The inertia and lack of power of flesh can only be overcome by the Spirit of God.

5:18–23 provide the choice between law-led or Spirit-led life. The Judaizers influenced the Galatians to rely on Torah to direct moral choice but the Torah was never a life style to be done, rather, Torah was given to Israel to indicate what God's will operative in human life would produce. In the Old Testament, believers were always aware of divine power being evidenced in a life that loved the law (cf. Psalm 119:97). If the Spirit directs believers then—under the new covenant—they are the New Israel. But New Israel are not regulated by the Mosaic Covenant, as the Judaizers required, since that covenant has been invalid since the death of Christ.

Christianity involves direction through the power of the new covenant, that is, by the Spirit of Christ (5:18). In Christ there is no obligation to the Mosaic Law but there is obligation to the law of Christ which is fulfilled by love for neighbour (5:14). The 'works of the flesh' (5:19–21)—the episodic and disordered way in which sin manifests itself—need no special revelation. Those who gave themselves over to such practices, typically condemned by Judaism as associated with pagan temples, do not show the fruit of new covenant transformation and therefore are not members of the kingdom of God. The opposite to 'works of the flesh' is life directed by the Spirit which is characterised by harmonious and orderly behaviour.

Excursus: The ethics of life in the Spirit under the new covenant

The ethics of new covenant life start with a renewed mind in a life led by the Spirit devoted to righteous conduct (5:18).[298] The Spirit brings freedom for service in Christ so that sin is no longer the ruling drive, indeed, the Spirit changes our nature so that the purpose of ethics is the glory of God (1 Corinthians 10:31). The pattern of ethics is Christ Jesus (1 Corinthians 4:16–17; 11:1; Ephesians 4:20) and the undergirding principle of ethics is love because love reflects the character of God and fulfils the command of Christ (5:13–14; 1 Corinthians 8:2–3; 13:4–7; Romans 13:8–10). The reception of the Spirit and the power of the Spirit (cf. 5:13–6:10) are the key to ethical life. Believers are set apart to be his holy people in the world (cf. 1 Thessalonians 4:3–8) so that life in the Spirit involves both abstinence and putting to death their former way of life.[299] Life in the flesh—that is, life

---

298 cf. Romans 12:1–2; Colossians 1:9; Ephesians 1:17.
299 Romans 6:1–18; 8:12–13; Colossians 3:5–11.

before and outside of Christ—is life without God. Holiness or holy living requires the indwelling Holy Spirit to produce in believers the life of Christ but unholy living grieves the Holy Spirit of God (Ephesians 4:30). Walking in the Spirit produces the fruit of the Spirit which is the reproduction of the life of Christ in the believer by the Spirit (Romans 8:9-11). The fruit of the Spirit (5:22-23) covers attitudes, virtues and behaviour but the list does not include rules designed to regulate behaviour.

The fruit of the Spirit is the way of life operating from a central principle of inner direction by the Spirit in all the required choices which life demands. Life in the Spirit is both passive (that is, being led by the Spirit) and active (that is, walking in the Spirit). The manifestations of 'the fruit of the Spirit' are clear indications that the Spirit is the inner motivating source of our life, as opposed to human effort. All of the fruit except the last, that is, 'self-control'—the pre-eminent Greek virtue—have to do with relationships. The grouping is somewhat Trinitarian with three groups of three fruits: first, dispositions of the mind (love, joy, peace); secondly, qualities affecting human relations (patience, kindness, goodness); and thirdly, principles that guide conduct (faithfulness, gentleness, self-control).

The first fruit mentioned is love, the key virtue of the new covenant. Joy is not included in the Galatians list but is associated with righteousness (Romans 14:17) and is the result of God-directed healthy relationships arising from the assurance of covenant-acceptance. Peace is peace with God, the wellbeing that issues from divine acceptance which then flows into 'the peace of God'. Peace, the perfection of relationships, and hope are grouped together (Romans 14:17; 15:13). Patience is evenness of temper, the opposite of fits of rage. Kindness, goodness, and faithfulness are qualities of keeping commitments in relationships. Gentleness is the opposite of selfish ambition and self-control is the opposite of self-indulgence. The emphasis in this list is on the first and last members—love and self-control—the positive and negative sides of the same virtue. A Hellenistic list would have given much greater prominence to self-control but Paul's list emphasises the outgoing virtues. While all of these are produced without reference to law as such, they nevertheless fulfil and do not contravene the law (5:23).

In the light of being in Christ and having crucified the flesh (5:24), sharing in the Spirit-life (5:25) means dying to self-direction and self-centredness, and ending the tyranny—though, in this life, not all of the struggle—of the flesh. The Spirit is the source of this new life but the indicative-imperative is repeated when Paul calls on the Galatians to walk in the Spirit (5:16,25) and thereby reflect the transformation of new covenant life in Christ in their life-style with the Spirit setting the direction and providing the content.

The Spirit enables us to fulfil Christ's law of love (6:1-10)

Those who are 'spiritual' (6:1)—that is, those who in Christ by the Spirit live by and in conformity to the inward leading of the Spirit—are to bear the burdens of others and thereby fulfil the law of Christ (6:2). We cannot fulfil Christ's manner of life explicated in the law of love (5:14; cf. Matthew 22:39) unless the Spirit is in our hearts directing us toward the Father's love in the filial dependence of Jesus Christ. Our manner of life as believers led by the Spirit is Christ in us who bore all the burdens of the sinful race and, indeed, his love for others fulfilled all the law.

The peroration of the epistle (6:7-10) reviews the main topics discussed with intention to arouse the emotions of the Galatians. There is both a warning (with an explication) and an appeal. God will not, finally, be treated with contempt (*mukterizetai*, 6:7) by mankind's attempt to ignore the cause and effect relationships of justice. If we sow to the flesh (6:8; cf. 5:16-21) then we will reap destruction. But if by grace alone, open to the activity and leading of the Spirit of God, we sow to the Spirit then we will reap final blessing (6:8). And the final blessing is nothing less than eternal life, that is, we will be transformed by the Spirit at the Parousia so that we will be fully under the control of the Spirit and then all will be life without the decay of mortal bodies susceptible to sin. If we labour (work hard) in well-doing (6:9)—that is, if we earnestly seek the Spirit within and trust God to produce the fruit of the Spirit—the final blessing will be great, even everlasting life. So we are to use the great opportunities we have to put the law of Christ into action (6:10), with particular concern for opportunities to help those within the household of faith.

Ephesians

Three concerns dominate Paul's letter to the Ephesians. The first concern is the merger of Jew and Gentile into one new man. This theme emerges at the end of the thanksgiving (1:3-14)—in which Paul blesses God for what he has done in salvation through Christ—and the prayer following the blessing (1:15-23). God is the cause and initiator of salvation (1:3-6). Historically, the work of Christ effected our salvation (1:7-12) and the Holy Spirit personally applies the work of God in Christ to the believer (1:13-14). Continued thanksgivings emerge (2:11-22; 3:1-13) with the Spirit providing access to the Father through Christ. Unity in the Spirit between Jew and Gentile is the focus of exhortation in Ephesians 4-6. The second concern dominating Paul's letter to the Ephesians is Christ's victory over the powers for the sake of the church, with the Spirit playing a key role in our participation in that victory (3:10,16; 6:17-18). Paul brings the first and second concerns together in Ephesians 3 where Jew and Gentile believers become one people (3:6). Together they confront principalities and powers as they become aware of the present and ultimate defeat of the powers in Christ. The Spirit underlies their adoption (1:5,13; 2:18; cf. Romans 8:15-16; Galatians 4:5-6) and makes known the mystery of God's will (3:5). The third concern dominating Paul's letter to the Ephesians is the maintenance of the unity of the Spirit (Ephesians 4-6) by the way that they live out the life of Christ in their corporate relationship including in their worship (5:1-20) and in their Christian households (5:21-6:9). All three concerns are brought into focus in the concluding peroration (6:10-20) about the weapons and armour provided by Christ and the Spirit enabling the Ephesians to stand as one people in their ongoing conflict with the powers.

Blessings are released in us through the Spirit (1:3-14)

The opening words of the blessing (blessed be the God and Father of our Lord Jesus Christ, 1:3) serve as a sub-title for the entire letter as well as a topic sentence for the blessing. The letter is about God who effected our salvation—that is, gave us every kind of blessing through Christ by the Spirit's activity (spiritual blessing)—in the heavenly realm where Christ is now seated at God's right hand above the powers for the sake of the church. The mention of the Christian inheritance to be effected in heavenly places is unique to Ephesians. Our blessing of God is in response to his prior blessing of us through Christ and the Spirit. The use of *pneumatikos* (spiritual,

1:3), rather than the genitive of Spirit, indicates that the emphasis is on the nature of the blessing rather than the source of the blessing. Even so, the Spirit is the present means whereby God appropriates to believing communities the blessings that flow from the redemptive work of Christ. The Spirit's blessings for which Paul thanks God are: marking us in love to be blameless before him (1:4); marking us out for adoption as his own children (1:5); lavishing grace on us in Christ (1:6); and effecting adoption for us historically in Christ, who procured our redemption (1:7). Jew and Gentile have received these blessings as one people by having received the Spirit as down payment on our final redemption (1:13). So all the blessings are made known to us and realised in us through the Spirit.

1:3-14 is one long Greek sentence, with the series of relative pronouns all referring to the blessings that we have received in Christ. The theme of the epistle is summarised at the beginning of the blessing, namely, God's eternal blessing to us in Christ in redemption and the gift of the Spirit for faith expressed in righteous Christian living (1:3-4). God is blessed by our recognition of divine blessing on us. Through the Spirit, God gives us every blessing—in the hidden, inner life—required for the onset and maintenance of the Christian life. Blessing is the equipment needed in our lives for accomplishing God's purpose. So the peace and wellbeing of accomplishment emanates from God. We are blessed because we are part of the new humanity begun in Christ, just as we had been part of the old humanity in Adam when we were outside of Christ. These blessings take place for us in the heavenlies where Christ is now seated, head over all the spirit powers for the sake of the church.[300] We are already the recipients of all the blessings of God in Christ through the Spirit. These blessings have come to Jews first (1:11-12) and then to Gentiles (1:13-14).

Election is, primarily, a corporate term signifying inclusion in the true Israel in the Old Testament or in Christ in the New Testament (1:4-6). All we are together, as a corpus, is determined by the grace of God's prior choice and the continued purpose of God's love. However, since corporate fellowships are comprised of individuals, individual election in Christ is also included. Election encompasses from before the foundation, so the decisions which shaped the beginning and end of our universe—and the eternal future—were taken before creation, enacted solely by God, and stem entirely from his love.

---

300 Fee, 1994, 668.

The initiation of choice comes from the Father; the implementation of the choice comes through Christ; and the personal application of the choice is by the Spirit (1:13). When the Ephesians believed the gospel, they were sealed to mark God's authentication of belonging to him (1:13). The purpose of election is for service, that is, to give glory to God by living changed and holy lives as those who belong to God (cf. 1:12). We bear witness to our election so that all the world may come to a saving knowledge of God. At the beginning of this eschatological age, Gentile Ephesians who have heard the truth of the gospel have also been authenticated (sealed) by God as God's own possession through the impartation of the Holy Spirit—like the day of Pentecost—promised as part of the new covenant (Ezekiel 36:26-27; 37:14; Joel 2:28-30).

By giving them (the Ephesians, the Gentiles) the Holy Spirit of promise—that is, promised to Israel but given to all at Pentecost—God has sealed the Gentiles as his own possession thereby signifying the certainty of their final redemption. Indeed, God guaranteed the final inheritance for Jew and Gentile believers alike since the Spirit is God's *arrabon* (guarantee, 3:14) of the inheritance. Thus, with a subtle shift of pronouns, Paul moves from we (Jews) having obtained the inheritance (1:11-12) to you (Gentiles) having been sealed by the promised Holy Spirit (1:13) to the Spirit as God's down payment on our (Jew and Gentile together) final inheritance. The seal is the sign of ownership and the Spirit (not baptism) is the seal or mark of that ownership.

The Greek aorist tense for sealed (1:13) does not refer to subsequent reception of the Spirit, rather, the reference is to two sides of the one conversion experience—in particular, this is a corporate reference to the reception of the Spirit by these Gentiles. The Spirit is the crucial element of the new covenant with Israel so, as a down payment, the Spirit is the present possession of what has been promised to come in the final redemption (*eis apolutrosin*, 1:14) of those belonging to God as his possession.

The Spirit is an *arrabon* (guarantee, 1:14; 2 Corinthians 1:22; 5:5), that is: a pledge or down payment; the initial gift of salvation; a guarantee for the believer that the final instalment of salvation and glory is assured. In this sense, his indwelling is provisional but belongs to the same order of reality as the consummation. The fullness of the Spirit belongs to the future age, not now, but his intimate presence—which belongs in all its fullness to the end-time—is giving us something of the future in the present. His indwelling in every believer is a prophecy of his eschatological fullness. The Spirit's presence as life in our body of death heightens the tension within us between the now and the not yet, so any assumption that the fullness of the Spirit relieves the conflicts of this life misunderstands New Testament teaching. The Spirit's presence tends to maximise rather than minimise the contrast between the present and the future.

God grants the Spirit of wisdom and revelation (1:15-23)

1:15-23 is a thanksgiving prayer (again, as with the blessing, in one long sentence) that affirms the present position of Christ (and believers with Christ, 2:6) at God's right hand as head over the powers for the sake of the church. Paul begins with what has been reported to him—that is, their faith in the Lord Jesus and their love for the saints (1:15). The thanksgiving prayer (1:16ff.) is for God to grant the Spirit of wisdom and revelation (cf. 1 Corinthians 12:8; a Messianic gift, Isaiah 11:2) manifested in the cross (1:8; cf. 1 Corinthians 2:8) by which they will come to a more experiential knowledge (*epignosis*, 1:17) of God. This relational knowledge of God will evolve into a better understanding of their own existence in the light of what God has done for them. Paul wants them to understand the certainty of their eschatological future secured by God's power working in Christ through the Spirit (1:18-19). The ultimate concern is that the recipients might receive the wisdom and revelation they need but the issue here is the penultimate concern which is the Spirit as source of wisdom and understanding (cf. 1 Corinthians 2:10-13).

The first two items following the Spirit's enlightenment form a pair (1:18) which is then paired with a third item (3:19). The first two items (hope of his calling, riches of the glory) are in apposition to each other as two sides of the same eschatological coin. The third item (his power toward us) brings them back into the present in terms of the Spirit's work on their behalf. The Spirit's revelation will cause them to understand how sure their hope is (first item), a hope which is grounded in the experience of God's call. God himself has an inheritance (second item) to be realised in the future when the saints are brought to rest in the place of his glory. Paul now prays that—as a result of the first two items—they will understand how surpassingly great is God's power (third item). The Spirit will reveal to them a fuller understanding of God and what he has done in Christ for them including the power available to them in the inner person through the Spirit communicating the indwelling Christ to them. Paul's thanksgiving prayer report (1:15-19) is followed by a theological affirmation (1:20-23) focusing on the second major topic of the epistle, namely, victory over the powers. Paul celebrates the greatness of the power of the enthroned Christ as head of all things for the church.

Common life in Christ through the Spirit (2:1-22)

Believers who were dead in sins (2:5), even morally depraved (2:3), have been saved (2:5,8) and raised with Christ to sit with him in the heavenlies (2:6). Gaffin makes the point that being raised with Christ is not regeneration,[301] rather, when God makes believers existentially alive with Christ—when believers are transformed from wrath to grace—we are also seated in the heavenlies, that is, we have been joined to the risen Christ (cf. 2:5f; Romans 6:3ff; Galatians 2:19ff). It follows that justification, adoption, sanctification and glorification are not separate distinct acts for believers but different aspects of the one act of incorporation into the resurrected Christ (cf. 1 Corinthians 1:30). 2:1-10 is the only major section of the letter in which the Spirit is not directly mentioned but Paul presumes the Spirit's involvement in the themes addressed.

In the light of Christ's position of authority over the powers, the Ephesians share in his resurrection triumph (2:11-12). Gentile believers, as full members of the new covenant, become one body with Jewish believers (2:16) who are bonded together as God's temple (2:21). 2:11-13 present the 'before' and 2:14-18 the 'after' of the bonding of Gentile and Jewish believers. 2:14-16 describe how reconciliation is brought about, that is, Christ destroyed the enmity between Jew and Gentile by the cross. The result is that Jews and Gentiles reconciled by Jesus' death form together, in one Spirit, the new humanity in Christ (2:18) with equal access together to the Father. This makes the church a fellowship of believers—not an institution but a sharing of a common life in Christ through the Spirit built on the foundation of the apostles and prophets with Christ as the cornerstone. Jews and Gentiles in Christ are now fellow citizens, members of God's household (2:19). The household is also a building (2:20) which is the Spirit-Temple (2:21-22) replacing the Jewish Jerusalem temple as the point of Christian access to God. Through the work of Christ, in the present ministry of the Spirit in the one body, we have access to the Father.

---

301 Gaffin, 1978, 128-129.

The new covenant church (2:11ff) is the new temple (2:19ff) resulting from God's great building work between the resurrection and the return of Christ (cf. 1 Peter 2:4-8). Apostles supplement Christ's work not by doing more atoning or redemptive work but by bearing witness. The unity of Jew and Gentile believers occurs because both have been built on the cornerstone, Christ, and on the foundation of the apostles and prophets (2:20). God is making great additions to the church between the resurrection and the return of Christ. The apostles and (New Testament) prophets did not lay the foundation, for Christ himself is the corner stone—nevertheless, the apostolic message was foundational for the existence of the church.[302] 2:20-22 refer to the functions (not the offices) of apostles and prophets within the local church which is God's temple (the universal church finding expression through the local church). God is in the midst of his people when they are assembled as a local church. The Spirit is building them into a habitation of God which means that God by his Spirit abides among them. The church is becoming, through the presence and work of the Spirit (2:22), a holy temple in the Lord.

The Trinitarian aspect appears again in 2:18-22. Through the death of the Lord Jesus Christ, the church comes into existence by the Spirit who presents Christ in them and grows them into a holy temple. So the church becomes the habitation of God by his Spirit. The people of God are constituted on the basis of the new covenant effected by Christ and actualised by the Holy Spirit. It is God's presence through the Spirit that marks the new covenant Church out as Christ's body characteristically including Gentiles as well as Jews.

The mystery revealed by the Spirit (3:1-21)

Paul speaks of his own role in the proclamation of God's mystery (*musterion*, 3:3) of Christ, made known by revelation (3:3-4) in all its fullness (3:8; 16-19). The mystery—which follows on from the previous description of one household of God and one temple of God formed by both Jewish and Gentile believers (2:1-22)—is that Gentile believers are co-heirs in the covenant promises with Jewish believers and consequently Jews and Gentiles form one people of God (3:2-9). This mystery is now being made known by the church to principalities and powers (3:10). God in Christ is forming

---

302 Fee, 1994, 67-8. The foundational ministries positioned on Christ as cornerstone are consecutive but overlapping (4:11; 1 Corinthians 12:28).

one new humanity through the Spirit's revelation (cf. 1 Corinthians 12:13). God has revealed this mystery—that the Gentiles are now fellow heirs in the same body (3:6)—by the Spirit (3:5).

The mystery proclaimed by Paul of one new humanity in Christ is legitimised by the Spirit's revelation to the holy apostles and prophets, the foundational ministries (3:5). As an apostle, Paul was responsible for founding churches. As a prophet, Paul understood what God had done in Christ on behalf of the Gentiles. So Paul includes himself in the circle to whom this revelation had come. Paul uses the adjective holy to describe the apostles and prophets but also ascribes to himself the position of the least of all the saints (3:8). Paul was made a minister of this mystery (3:7) and empowered to communicate it by the Holy Spirit (cf. 4:7). God is the author of the grace (3:7), the Spirit is the power at work (3:5,20), and the body of Christ is the result (4:11).

Paul recommences his prayer (3:14-21) with an urgency for his readers to know the unknowable love of Christ (3:17-19) and so to be filled with all the fullness of God himself (3:19). The prayer concludes with a praise-benediction extolling the power of God who will succeed in his plan through Christ according to the power of the Spirit (3:20-21) even though we are still flesh. What makes the prayer achievable is the strengthening of believers in their inner person through the power of the Spirit (3:16).

The Spirit functions in the 'inner person' (a uniquely Pauline expression) to: elaborate or explain; preside over moral decisions; give content with power through extraordinary manifestation of God's presence; and thereby preserve the unity of the body of Christ. The inner person is the seat of our moral being, not our interior consciousness. So to be strengthened with power through the Spirit in the inner person is to have Christ dwell in our hearts by faith (3:17) thereby enabling the Christian congregation to live the life of Christ together (3:18) so that God produces in us a congregational character that evidences the fruit of the Spirit (3:20-21).

The gifts and graces of unity in the Spirit (4:1-16)

Paul's third major concern is that the Ephesian church maintains the unity produced by the Spirit (cf. 2:18-22). Paul reminds them of their calling to Christ (4:1) and then exhorts them to display five graces—lowliness, gentleness, longsuffering, love and peace (4:2-3)—the latter four having been elsewhere identified by Paul as fruit of the Spirit (cf. Galatians

5:22-23). There is a Trinitarian base for Paul's exhortation (3:4-6) which stems from their common possession of the Spirit. They possess one Spirit and they are one body and they have one hope. The intimate presence of God and Christ in the church by the one Spirit should be evident in graces that maintain unity and forge a bond of peace between the members of the one body of Christ.

The church is an amalgam of believers, each having a different measure of Christ's gift. The gifts of the Spirit are distributed for the work of ministry and for building up the body of Christ (4:12) so that we grow into the unity of faith in Christ. The necessary expression of this unity as one body—of one Spirit, one Lord, one faith, one baptism, and one Father (4:4-6)—is then applied not only to the Ephesians' corporate life as a church but also within their Christian households as God's people in the world (4:17-6:9). Recreated after the image of God in true knowledge, righteousness and holiness (4:24; Colossians 3:10), the congregation is being ethically transformed from glory to glory by the Spirit of the Lord (2 Corinthians 3:18).

Communion with the Spirit can be grieved or spoilt (4:30)

The Spirit—along with the resurrection of Christ—is the key element in Paul's theological framework for by the resurrection of Christ with the gift of the Spirit, God has set the future in motion in believers leading towards the final consummation of salvation. But believers already share God-likeness in Christ (cf. 5:1-2). 4:17-29 describe the changes that should follow inner renewal,[303] indeed, continued dependence on the work of the Spirit must bring about these changes. Renewal of the mind by the Spirit (4:23) is one of the priorities of the Christian life with the outcome of a life of holiness (4:24).

The Spirit seals Christians as a guarantee of their future inheritance as children of God. This sealing involves a sensitive relationship between Christians and the Spirit since the Spirit can be grieved (4:30; cf. Isaiah 63:10), that is, our relationship with the Spirit can become strained by behaviour and attitudes which are not led by the Spirit (4:25ff.). Christians are sealed by the Holy Spirit for the day of redemption so grieving this relationship with the Spirit threatens assurance of salvation. Grieving the Spirit weakens eschatological prospects. In the Old Testament, the Israelites

---

[303] Brown, 2002, 122-123. External teaching must point to the needed openness to the internal work of the Spirit (5:23-24).

grieved the Spirit of God in their rebellion (Isaiah 63:10)—that is, they grieved God's presence with Israel. Believers are instructed to clothe themselves with the new self, created according to the likeness of God in true righteousness and holiness (4:24). Failure to live according to this new self (particularised by Paul in 4:25ff) grieves God's presence in us and grieves the Spirit's personal relationship with us. The Spirit is the agent who is to bring about in believers the life of righteousness and holiness. The Spirit works personally in those who bear the imprint (seal) of the divine nature. Communion with the Spirit can be spoilt. The Holy Spirit is not merely a presence but a person present for the verb 'grieve' is to cause sorrow, pain or distress which only a person can experience. The Spirit is the agent who will bring about the changes to be made for our heavenly transformation. Hence Paul's clear command: do not grieve the Spirit (4:30).

Paul has just warned the Ephesians to give no place to the devil (4:27) and now he urges them not to grieve the Holy Spirit who is the divine personality present and active in believers. The Spirit changes our dispositions toward self, other people and the world but the Spirit is operating in a context in which there are other influences on our spirit within the deep recesses of personality. The Greek present tense of the verb (*didote*, 4:27) suggests that there are Ephesians who are already giving place to the devil so the relationship with the Spirit would already be under stress. This is a call to give up what we are already doing that grieves our relationship with the Spirit of God. Paul is not referring to some offence aimed directly at the Spirit but at believers committing the sort of sins mentioned (4:25-29) by which, disrupting the communal life, they are disrupting and opposing the work of the Spirit in building up the church.

Isaiah records that the children of Israel had grieved the Holy Spirit in the exodus wilderness trek with the consequence that God fought against them and gave them up to their self-will (Isaiah 63:10). The Ephesians are reminded that, when they believed, they were sealed with the promised Holy Spirit as a mark of the genuine nature of their faith (4:30; 1:13). The Spirit had put his mark on them because they belonged to God, because they were God's precious possession, because they were specifically loved by God. The seal of the Spirit will also protect believers through the testings, battles and sufferings of the end-time until he takes complete possession of them in the eschaton.

Paul's mention of the sealing of the Spirit was a reminder to the Ephesians of their baptism in the Spirit and indwelling gift of the Spirit. The sealing was the pledge, guarantee or first instalment of the full and final redemption to come. We do not belong to ourselves and we cannot do with our personality or body what we want because we are under divine control. The Spirit is the power of the age to come, given ahead of time in history, but the portion of the Spirit that we receive is still only the beginning and guarantee of the full salvation of the eschaton. The present possession of the Holy Spirit vouches for our full salvation inheritance—'for the redemption of the possession' (RSV), 'until we acquire possession of it' (NEB) (4:30)—until God has redeemed what is his own. Redemption is always God's work so the Spirit in our possession as believers is a down payment vouching for God's future full redemption. Let us praise him for that expectation!

If they had grieved the Spirit how could they restore the relationship? This is why Paul is writing. They grieved the Spirit so their connection with God now needs strengthening and, hence, they should now plead for forgiveness. They must understand that the most precious thing in life is the presence of the Spirit in their lives. God will halt the drift toward godlessness if they maintain the channels of blessing through repentance, enabling the free flow of God's blessing.

The only place where Paul uses the full title 'the Holy Spirit of God' is 4:30. Sealed by the Spirit, believers are equipped with the glory of God to express the ultimate purpose of all that God has done for us and for our salvation. So we bear fruit for righteousness (Philippians 1:11) for the glory of God (cf. 3:14–21)—and we come to know his love, and are filled with all the fullness of God.

Paul has warned the Ephesians to give no place to the devil (4:27) and has urged them not to grieve the Holy Spirit. Now Paul urges the Christians not to express hostility in their actions because hostility destroys human relationships (4:31). Instead, they are to be Christ-like in their kindness and in their willingness to forgive (4:32). They are to nurture their relationships with each other even as they are to nurture their relationship with God through the Spirit.

We are called to be like God (5:1–2) for to be unlike God is to grieve the Holy Spirit. Covenant people take their character from God and we grieve God when our talk or actions damage relationships in the body of Christ. Paul exhorts believers not to quench the Spirit (1 Thessalonians 5:19) and not to disregard God who gives the Spirit (1 Thessalonians 4:8). Stephen spoke of the Jewish leaders as always resisting the Holy Spirit (Acts 7:51). All Christian behaviour depends on the Spirit's activity in the believer and being filled with all the fullness of God will impact community life in praise, hymns, spiritual songs and always giving thanks (5:19–20).

The fruit of the Spirit is walking in love (5:9,18)

There is a stark contrast between a redeemed being who is fully alive because of the indwelling Holy Spirit, and a human that is mere flesh because the breath of the life-giving Spirit is not in him. Ever since the fall (Genesis 3), the human potential for perverse sin has been actualised in behaviour that yields anti-fruits that cannot sustain life, namely: fornication, uncleanness, covetousness, filthiness, foolish talking, and coarse jokes (5:3–4; cf. 5:11). The unfaithfulness of sexual sin destroys relational peace, fractures unity, and ends in death. The practice of the perversity of sexual sins deforms the human being to the extent that the human who was made in the image of God transmogrifies into sin that bears no relationship to God: the person who commits fornication becomes 'fornicator'; the person who talks and thinks dirty becomes 'unclean'; and the person who is bent by the desire to have something (or someone) that belongs to someone else becomes 'covetous' (5:5). The transmogrified individual is clearly not related to the heavenly Father, that is, the family resemblance to God is no longer evident. Indeed, the image of God in which the person was originally made is being overtaken by cancerous, lethal, foreign, anti-life sins.

This dark, transmogrifying path was the state of the Ephesians before they received the gospel. But now the Ephesians are free to walk as humans in the light, imitating God as God's dear children (5:8,1). They are walking in the light, indicating that they are truly alive; for the dead can only be in a state (of darkness), they cannot move. Those who are alive by the revival of the Spirit are not only in a state of light in the Lord Jesus Christ (cf. John 8:12) but they also walk as children of light, that is, their walk bears the family resemblance to God and Christ (their elder brother). There is a parallelism between walking as children of light and walking in love, that is, when we walk as children of light we are walking in love for that is how the Son of God walked as he loved us and gave himself for us (5:8,2). Parenthetically, there is congruence between walking as children of light and evidencing the fruit of the Spirit. So the fruit of the Spirit is action in life which bears resemblance to God's character—namely, goodness, righteousness and truth (5:9)—and these actions are consistent with God's core attribute which is love (cf. 1 John 4:8,16).

Already the Ephesians are in the state of light in the Lord (5:8). Already the Ephesians are sealed by the Holy Spirit for the day of redemption (4:30; 1:13). Already the Ephesians are in the new covenant (1:1). The regenerating work of the Spirit has already woken them from the terminal sleep of sin and they have already arisen from the dead with Christ by the power of the Spirit (5:14). But again, for the third time, Paul emphasises that being alive in Christ is not just a state of being but also walking (5:15,8,2)—that is, exhibiting the life of Christ in action—as children resembling the holiness of our heavenly Father and, therefore, with actions that are entirely distinctive from the evil of days governed by humans who reject God's gospel of life in Christ by the Spirit. So Paul then reminds the Ephesians that in order to act out being children of God in an age of dissipation they will need to be (present continuous, ongoing, always again) filled with the Spirit (5:18). The Ephesians can only walk as those who are alive if they are constantly being filled with the life-giving Spirit. In order to walk bearing the family likeness of the image of God in an evil age, the Ephesians will need to be constantly (over and over again) filled with the Spirit. Selfless giving like Christ should be the hallmark of God-like love in the new creation community but this is only possible if we are constantly being filled with the Spirit. Being filled with the Spirit will be evidenced in: worship that is lively and unified (5:19-20); Christians who are submitted to each other towards unity (5:21); and avoidance of the profligate fragmenting pleasures of the present age (5:17-18).

The human spirit is intoxicated when the believer is filled with the Holy Spirit. Mockers on the Day of Pentecost said that the apostles were 'full of new wine' (Acts 2:13) because they were amazed and perplexed by the exhilaration of being 'filled with the Holy Spirit' (Acts 2:4). There is a boldness in uninhibited prophetic utterance that may accompany being filled with the Spirit.[304] When Stephen was full of the Holy Spirit, regardless of his dire personal circumstance in the flesh, he saw the glory of God in heaven (Acts 7:55; cf. Revelation 1:10ff). Simon, the Samaritan sorcerer, described the

---

304 Acts 4:31; 13:9-11; cf. Numbers 11:25-29; 1 Samuel 10:6-10; 2 Chronicles 20:14, 24:20.

evident effect of the personal presence of the Holy Spirit as 'this power'.[305] When the Holy Spirit fell on Cornelius' household, and later on the Ephesians, they spoke with tongues and magnified God like the Apostles on the Day of Pentecost (Acts 10:44-49; 11:15; 19:6). After a period of persecution, the disciples are filled with joy and with the Holy Spirit (Acts 13:52). Ezekiel describes his experience of the Spirit as lifting him up.[306] Indeed, when the Holy Spirit is poured upon us from on high there is an intoxication of life yielding a fully fruiting field of goodness, righteousness and truth (Isaiah 32:15). But as an intoxicating beverage, alcohol is a poor substitute for the Holy Spirit as—instead of yielding life in abundance—alcoholic intoxication dissipates life (cf. Proverbs 23:29-35).

Empowered by the Spirit to withstand the devil (6:10-20)

The Ephesians are to be empowered in the Lord and put on God's armour to withstand the devil (6:10-12) in their part of the ongoing war against the powers over which Christ has been appointed as head over all things (cf. 1:22). The armour provided for the Christian to hold his ground is through redemption in Christ (truth, righteousness, gospel of peace, faith and salvation; 6:13-17a) and the empowerment of the Spirit (word of God and prayer; 6:17b-20). The Christian will need to pray in the Spirit (6:17-20). How the believer is to take his stand is signified in four participial phrases which modify 'stand therefore' (6:14), namely: having girded your waist; having put on the breastplate; having shod your feet; and taking the shield (6:14-16). When he comes to the final piece of armour, faith, Paul commences a new sentence. There are two critical pieces of defensive equipment: the helmet of salvation; and the sword of the Spirit, that is, the sword that is given by the Spirit and belongs to the Spirit. Word (*rhema*, 6:17) refers to the message inspired by the Spirit so the sword of the Spirit will be the gospel proclamation of Christ. Conduct this warfare praying in the Spirit continually (6:18) since the victory will come by the Spirit's empowering of our prayers. Christ's triumph on the cross has provided the power so the victory is assured but the grim struggle continues. Paul asks for prayer for himself that he will promote the gospel even as a prisoner (6:19-20).

---

305 Acts 8:19; cf. Judges 3:10; 6:34; 14:6,19; 15:14.
306 Ezekiel 3:14; 8:3; 11:1,24; 43:5; cf. 2 Corinthians 12:1-4; Revelation 17:3; 21:10.

Philippians

Common fellowship and mutual love in the shared Spirit of Christ

Paul prays for deliverance by the Spirit of Jesus Christ (1:19). This genitive expression attributing the Spirit to Jesus is unique in the Bible. Paul expects to get help in his particular circumstance—whatever that circumstance may be, Paul does not elaborate—from the Spirit, that is, Paul's deliverance will come when Christ is exalted in him whether by life or by death (1:21), for all is for the sake of Christ and for the progress of the gospel (1:12). Paul is in chains, evidently in some sort of custody, but this is not an issue because the chains are in and for Christ (1:13). Fatehi suggests that Paul is appealing to the promise from Jesus, recorded in the Synoptic tradition, that the Spirit will speak through the disciples when they are brought to trial for Jesus' sake (Matthew 10:18-20; Mark 13:9-11).[307] Accordingly, Paul had provided a witness for Christ before the Praetorian Guard (1:13).

Paul hopes that the Philippian believers are standing firm in the Spirit and thus striving together with one mind (1:27). If 'spirit' is read instead of Spirit, then spirit and mind would be virtually synonymous.[308] Indeed, their common fellowship and mutual love is brought into being by the shared Spirit of and from Christ (2:1). In communion together in Christ they experience the Spirit and then worship God through the Spirit (3:3),[309] sharing the common power of the life of Christ through the Spirit. Their common bond is worship or service (*latreuo*, 3:3, could mean either worship or service).[310] The relationship between believers—indeed, the relationship between the Philippians and Paul—is not by ritual or an external rite such as circumcision, rather, their community (*koinonia*, 2:1) is brought about because they worship and serve together in the Spirit of God. True service is engendered by the inward work of the Spirit of God so they may boast in the effective work of Christ through them but they must not trust in their own efforts in the flesh. Being justified by God's grace alone they are to place no confidence in human achievements including, for Paul, his former righteousness under the law (3:4-6).

---

307 Fatehi, 2000, 226.
308 Gaffin, 1979, 74.
309 Gaffin, 1979, 74.
310 Fee, 1994, 752.

Paul realised that there was no gain in all his human achievements or triumphs (3:7), indeed, it was better to lose his whole world (all things, 3:8) than miss out on knowing Christ in life and death and resurrection (3:10–11). God had given Paul righteousness—that is, covenant acceptance—through faith in Christ (3:9) and this was far better than the righteousness that he was trying to achieve for himself through the defunct law code. So Christ himself is the goal and Paul is found to be in Christ through the Spirit of Jesus Christ (1:19). To know Christ personally through prayer and the supply of the Spirit of Jesus Christ is to participate now in the gospel of Jesus' life, death and resurrection (3:10–11): to know in our life and ministry the power of Jesus' resurrection; to experience the tribulations of bearing witness to Jesus with him, having fellowship (*koinonia*, 3:10) with Jesus in his sufferings; to die in the will of the Father, being conformed to Jesus' death; and to be clothed by the Spirit with all the saints in our glorious resurrection bodies at the Parousia. Believers form a colony of the age to come in the present age because they are aware that they belong in heaven (3:20). So believers look forward to the refashioning of their 'lowly' mortal bodies to the likeness of Christ's heavenly bodily (3:21). When Christ bestows the likeness of his glory-image on his people, he will be fulfilling the mandate of dominion given to humanity in Adam at creation (cf. 'have dominion over … fill the earth and subdue it'; Genesis 1:26,28).

Colossians

Love in the Spirit (1:8)

Paul had not visited the church at Colossae and yet he had heard through Epaphras of the love which characterised the Colossian church. They loved all the saints (1:4). This love had been implanted in them and was fostered in them by the gift of the indwelling Spirit (1:8). The Colossians had been delivered from the kingdom of darkness into the kingdom of the Son of God's love (1:13). Paul's desire for all believers who have not seen his face in the flesh is, in part, that their hearts would be knit together in love (2:2). Paul describes elements of character befitting those who have been effectually called by God—that is, raised with Christ by the Spirit (3:1) and destined for glory (3:4)—as clothes which are to be 'put on' (3:12,14). But the most important item of clothing to be put on, as those who are holy and beloved by God, is love (3:14).

Love and the Spirit are often juxtaposed in the New Testament. The love of God poured into our hearts by the Holy Spirit who is given to believers (Romans 5:5) is the inexhaustible source of love within the Colossians for all the saints (1:4). The Colossians' love in the Spirit is universal (for all, 1:4), like God's love (cf. John 3:16), and not limited by personal preference. Paul's résumé of ministry credentials includes a recommendation by the Holy Spirit followed by a recommendation by sincere love (2 Corinthians 6:6). Love in the Spirit was the recommendation that Paul received from Epaphras's declaration about the Colossians (1:8). In a Trinitarian benediction, Paul invokes the grace of the Lord Jesus, and the love of God, and the communion of the Holy Spirit (2 Corinthians 3:14; cf. Philippians 2:1). Paul tells the Colossians that the mystery is Christ in the believer (Jew and Gentile) and that, by the Holy Spirit, the hearts of believers are knitted together in love (2:2; 1:8,27). The fruit of the Spirit is, primarily, love (Galatians 5:22); and this fruit is evident in the Colossians as declared by Epaphras (1:8). The Spirit that God has given us is a Spirit of power and of love and of a sound mind (2 Timothy 1:7). The Colossians have been delivered from the power of darkness and have been conveyed into the kingdom of the Son of the Father's love (1:13) and now their community is characterised by love in the Spirit (1:8). As the believer's soul is purified by obeying the truth through the Spirit—that is, as revealed by the Spirit and empowered by the Spirit—the consequential action should be sincere and fervent love with a pure heart for brothers and sisters in the family of God (1 Peter 1:22). The Colossians are to put to death every impure passion engaged in by sons of disobedience (3:6) for the sins of passion are a deadly flesh substitute for the bond of perfection (3:14) which is the love of God expressed in pure lives as children of God remade in his image.

1 Thessalonians

The powerful presence of the Spirit in ministry (1:5-6)

The Thessalonian church suffered much affliction from pagan Thessalonians when they believed the gospel (1:6-7; 2:13-16; 3:2-4) just like the churches in Judea suffered at the hands of other Judeans (2:14). The conversion of the Thessalonians was not merely a response to Paul's words accurately conveying the gospel, much more, the Thessalonians were converted because of word accompanied by the powerful presence of the Holy Spirit (1:5). The conversion of the Thessalonians confirms their election (1:4). Paul's association of Spirit and power establishes a virtual synonymy of Spirit and power in his inspired ministry, that is, the blessing in his ministry was because his proclamation was accompanied by the Spirit's power.

Paul was not a purveyor of empty words but the work of God confirmed the words Paul preached and verified that God was present by the conviction and conversion brought about by the Spirit (cf. John 16:8). The powerful presence of the Spirit may or may not have been with accompanying signs and wonders (cf. Acts 15:12; 19:11; Romans 15:18-19; 2 Corinthians 12:12; Galatians 3:1-5) but the outcome of God's powerful presence was the effectual conversion of the Thessalonians even though this conversion was accompanied by suffering. Despite the distress of persecution, there was evident joy among them emanating from the presence of the Holy Spirit bearing testimony to the significance for their ultimate future (cf. Acts 13:52; Psalm 51:12). Indeed, joy is a fruit of the Spirit (Galatians 5:22) and associated with life in the Spirit (Romans 14:17; 15:13). For Paul, coming to Christ always involves the experience of the Spirit. Salvation is, then, the activity of the triune God. This is Paul's economic, soteriological Trinitarianism: salvation is always initiated by God's love, historically made available by the atonement of Christ, and presently applied through the powerful work of the Spirit. The coming (1:5) of the Spirit's presence to the Thessalonians means that divine power and human weakness co-exist in the overlap of times when God through Christ made an historical entry into the world and Christ by the Spirit enters the life of the new believer.

Relationship with God in the Spirit is intimate (4:8)

In a context of encouragement, Paul reminds the Thessalonians of their conversion (4:7) and the gift of God's Holy Spirit to them (4:8). Their relationship with God is intimate because of the indwelling Spirit so they must refrain from sexual immorality for the Spirit within them indicates whose they are and how they should behave. This is the first of the matters—often a subject in Paul's prayer—where their faith is deficient (cf. 3:10). Paul's prayer is, ultimately, that the Thessalonians will be blameless as followers of Christ at the coming of the Lord (3:12-13). Paul had already instructed them about behaviour that pleased God and the majority are living faithfully (4:1) but not all. In addressing the matter of sexual immorality (4:3-8), Paul calls the Thessalonians to holiness (*hagiasmos*, 4:3) arguing that indulgence in sexual sin is a rejection of the Holy Spirit and likewise a rejection of God who has given the Holy Spirit to them. Indeed, the ongoing work of the Spirit of God reproduces the divine life in converts. So the Spirit is the divine companion by whose power we live out holiness, that is, the Spirit is the power for the practice of Christian ethics. The Spirit gives the power to resist impure desires. So the Spirit is not only the key to conversion but also the power for the Christian to engage in truly Christian behaviour.[311]

Do not quench the Spirit (5:19-22)

The commandment 'do not quench—do not put out the flame of—the Spirit' (5:19) may be the first attestation of the charismatic nature of early Christian communities. The Spirit inspired prophecy and the Thessalonians must not despise these prophetic utterances (5:20) but they should subject the prophecies to proper evaluation (5:21). This advice would be appropriate for any Christian community (cf. Romans 12). Paul declares five imperatives in two sets (5:19-20 and 5:21-22): the first set contains two negative imperatives in a form of parallelism, with the second item specifying the first with regard to what they must not do with regard to the charismata; and the second set contains three positive imperatives specifying what they should do with regard to the charismata, the first spelling out the general rule followed by further specificity in the remaining two. Their worship needs adjustment but not elimination of charismata. They are to test all things but not quench the Spirit in doing so.

---

311 Fee, 1994, 53.

The collocation of Spirit and fire makes the use of 'quench'—most likely referring to charismatic manifestations—apposite. So 'do not put out the Spirit's fire' means, in this context, do not quench the manifestation of the Spirit through the charismata.[312] Specifically, do not despise spontaneous prophetic utterance in the community. Perhaps Paul is referring to an incident in the Thessalonian congregation where they had rejected an inspired utterance but, whilst not rejecting the charismata, they must also test the spirits (cf. 1 John 4:1) using the criteria of the apostolic teaching of Christ. The implication is that they are to keep away from evil forms of prophecy which are not of the Spirit. They are not to be gullible or naive. Indeed, Paul's next letter to the Thessalonians indicates that there has been confusion caused by a spirit (not the Holy Spirit, not a genuine exercise of the charismata) prophesying that the day of the Lord had already come (2 Thessalonians 2:2).[313] Testing this spirit should mean that they abstain from the misrepresentation of Paul's teaching about the timing of the Day of the Lord. So they are not to be alarmed by teaching coming from other sources on the coming of the Day of the Lord, even a purportedly prophetic utterance attributed to the Spirit.[314]

---

312 Fee, 1994, 59.
313 Gaffin, 1979, 71.
314 Fee, 1994, 71–75.

2 Thessalonians

God chooses, the Lord loves, the Spirit sanctifies (2:13)

Paul gives thanks for the eternal destiny of the Thessalonians (2:13–14) and then gives an exhortation to stand firm in the apostolic teaching delivered to them (2:15). This is followed by a prayer that God and Christ would encourage and firmly establish the Thessalonian believers (2:16–17). God's people are loved by the Lord for through Jesus' death God has elected them for salvation through the sanctifying work of the Spirit that effects conversion.[315] So God chose them, the Lord loved and saved them, and the Spirit sanctified them.[316] All three members of the Trinity are mentioned in the salvation of the Thessalonians.

---

315 Fee, 1994, 79.

316 cf. Romans 15:16; 1 Corinthians 6:11; 1 Peter 1:2.

1 Timothy

Christ's justification (resurrection) in the Spirit (3:16)

3:16 presents six parallel lines controlled with passive verbs with Christ the implied subject. The poetic exposé of the mystery of godliness contrasts the earthly and heavenly orders (cf. flesh, Spirit, angels, Gentiles, world, glory). Christ's manifestation in the flesh is set over against his justification in the Spirit. The justification (vindication) refers to Christ's resurrection, that is, by resurrection Christ enters into a state of being justified thereby introducing the heavenly order or new age. Christ's resurrection (justification) removes condemnation and eradicates the state of death[317] thereby annulling the sentence of condemnation (cf. Romans 4:25). So Christ was delivered up for our sins and then raised as a life-giving Spirit (1 Corinthians 15:45) for our justification. The first *dia* in Romans 4:25 ('because of' our offences) is retrospective to Christ's earthly life and the second *dia* ('because of' our justification) is prospective of his eternal standing as a life-giving Spirit. The end is resurrection out of which flows justification.

Christ's death identified him with us in our transgressions and Christ's resurrection on account of our justification identifies his righteousness—which he had established by his obedience unto death—with us. Solidarity with Christ's resurrection is the appointed means of our justification. Justifying faith is based primarily and directly on Christ's resurrection (cf. Romans 10:9; 8:33–34). Christ identified with his people when he was made sin for us (2 Corinthians 5:21), that is, born under the law to redeem those under the law (Galatians 4:4–5). Christ bore our sin (1 Peter 2:24) and therefore became cursed (Galatians 3:13) because he was subject to the condemnation of the law (Galatians 4:4). Death was the penalty for the condemnation of the transgressions he bore (Hebrews 9:15). Resurrection is the removal of condemnation and the eradication of the state of death, the effective removal of the verdict of condemnation. So when God declares Christ to be just (3:16), the supreme consequence of sin had reached its justification (cf. Romans 8:3–4). Paul is concerned with the Adamic signification of Christ's resurrection. Justifying faith was worthless if Christ had not been raised (1 Corinthians 15:14,17) for an unjustified Christ means an unjustified believer. The supreme fruit of Christ's justification was the

---

[317] Gaffin, 1998, 122.

Spirit who bears in himself the efficacious principle of a transformation to come, that is, the final resurrection. In Christ's resurrection God declared himself just.

Wherever justification is mentioned, underlying justification is resurrection or existential union with Christ resurrected. Justification and sanctification are not sequences but different facets of the single act of being raised or incorporated with Christ. Justifying righteousness (the obedience, blood and death of Christ, Romans 5) and the justifying act (resurrection, Romans 4:25) should not be confused. The justifying aspect of being raised with Christ does not rest on the believer's subjective enlivening and being joined to Christ but on the resurrection, that is, the justified (resurrection-approved) righteousness of Christ reckoned to him. Thus not justification by faith but union with the resurrected Christ by faith is the central motif of Paul's applied soteriology.

Adoption in Christ is bestowed through faith (Galatians 3:26) by the Spirit (Romans 8:15) and juxtaposed in the text with being baptised into Christ and putting on Christ (Galatians 3:27). Justification, adoption, sanctification and glorification are future as well as present for the believer.[318] The future aspect of justification (cf. Galatians 5:5) and adoption (Romans 8:23) expects the redemption of our bodies.

The Spirit warns about false doctrine (4:1–4)

The Spirit has explicitly indicated a dire apostasy in the latter days (4:1), but there is little detail (cf. Revelation 2–3). Paul is warning Christians that the Spirit has revealed that church history will be characterised by unremitting warfare with evil and controversy over false doctrine (4:1–3). The context suggests that Paul has in mind heresies that invoke a spirit of bondage—forbidding marriage as unspiritual; forbidding certain foods, perhaps with a view to the old covenant; slavery to rules, obsession with the small things of the Christian life—resulting in a spirit of fear, that is, a wrong fear of God. There is a right fear of God which we neglect to our peril but there is a craven fear of God that is nothing more than a torment. The torment fear is the outcome of regarding God as an exacting taskmaster who is constantly watching to discover faults and blemishes and to punish accordingly. Commitment to performance and Christian works may also lead to thinking of God as a far away, stern lawgiver.

---

318 On the significance and application of justification, cf. Vos, 1994, 42–61.

Baptism in the Spirit or being (again and again) filled with the Spirit does not impose a dichotomy between spiritual and unspiritual with regard to creation. The Spirit of God hovered over the face of the waters in creation (Genesis 1:2)—that is, the Spirit of God was intimately involved in the creation process—which resulted in a world that God judged to be good.[319] And when God created man and reviewed everything that he had made, his judgment was that it was very good (Genesis 1:31). The creation account clearly states that God made food in creation for consumption and therefore so-called 'spiritual' rules that forbid certain foods are not of the Spirit. This is in accord with the Council of Jerusalem which concluded that 'it seemed good to the Holy Spirit, and to us' (Acts 15:28) not to insist on Old Testament food rules but still to consider (with regard to eating habits) the importance of affirming life and abstaining from participation in idolatrous contemporary culture. So it is not more spiritual to live by or impose food rules and, consequently, believers filled with the Spirit can enjoy food without a guilty conscience.

Likewise, the flesh creation of man was given life when the breath or Spirit of God entered his nostrils (Genesis 1:7). And enjoyment of the relationship between man and woman as humans in marriage was also God's idea as he created the difference between male and female—indeed, God joins two flesh into one (Matthew 19:4-6; Genesis 2:23-25) and Jesus celebrates the marriage union (John 2:1-11). Scripture does not ever suggest that the flesh union in marriage is less spiritual than abstinence from sexual relationships. But Scripture consistently describes sexual union outside of God-ordained marriage as sins that are inconsistent with eternal glory (1 Corinthians 6:9; Revelation 22:15) because they are flesh lusts against the Spirit (Galatians 5:16-19). This was also affirmed in the Council of Jerusalem which concluded that 'it seemed good to the Holy Spirit, and to us' not to impose abstinence from marriage but, rather, to impose abstinence from sexual immorality (Acts 15:28-29). So it is not more spiritual to abstain from marriage and, consequently, believers filled with the Spirit can enjoy the marriage union without a guilty conscience.

---

319 Genesis 1:10,12,18,21,25.

2 Timothy

A Spirit of power and of love and of a sound mind (1:6-7)

The *charisma* (gift, 1:6) of God which Timothy is ordered to fan into flame is probably the gift of the Spirit of God, given the context of the next verse which states that God has given us a Spirit of power and of love and of a sound mind (1:7; cf. 1:14). This gift of the indwelling Spirit came originally when Paul laid hands on Timothy (1:6). Paul has also given to Timothy a good deposit of sound gospel teaching which Timothy must keep alive in himself and in his ministry by the presence of the indwelling Spirit (2 Timothy 1:14). Timothy has been called to be a next generation leader in the church: under Paul's tutelage as a spiritual father;[320] to continue ministry in churches that Paul had founded;[321] as a fellow worker (Romans 16:21) and fellow preacher (2 Corinthians 1:19); and as the co-author in some of Paul's letters.[322] And just as Paul was dependent on the gift of the Spirit for his new covenant apostolic ministry,[323] likewise, Timothy is dependent on the gift of the Spirit for his new covenant pastoral ministry.

In the kingdom of God, leadership ministries have always been dependent on the gift of the Spirit.[324] The young leader Joshua was full of the Spirit of wisdom because Moses had laid hands on him (Deuteronomy 34:9; cf. 2 Timothy 1:6). The disciples must not commence their ministry in the name of Jesus until they have been baptised with the Holy Spirit (Acts 1:4-5). When the early church was looking for leaders who would assist the apostles in practical service, these servant leaders were required to be full of the Holy Spirit (Acts 6:3). Barnabas was sent by the church in Jerusalem to minister in Antioch because he was full of the Holy Spirit (Acts 11:24). In the church, all ministries are dependent on the gifts of the Spirit (1 Corinthians 12).

---

320 1 Timothy 1:2,18; 2 Timothy 1:2.

321 Acts 17:14-15; 18:5; 19:22; 1 Corinthians 4:17; 16:10; Philippians 2:19; 1 Thessalonians 3:2,6.

322 2 Corinthians 1:1; Philippians 1:1; Colossians 1:1; 1 Thessalonians 1:1; 2 Thessalonians 1:1; Philemon 1.

323 Acts 19:17; 1 Corinthians 2:4; 2:10,12,13; 7:40; 2 Corinthians 3:3,6; Ephesians 3:5; Philippians 1:19; 1 Thessalonians 1:5.

324 Genesis 41:38; Exodus 28:3; 31:3; 35:3; Numbers 11:17,25; 27:18; Judges 3:10; 6:34; 11:29; 13:25; 1 Samuel 10:6; 11:13.

Excursus: Sanctification occurs by agency of the Spirit

The cross was not Christ's sanctification because Christ's obedience precluded Jesus from having the depravity that requires moral restoration (Romans 6:1ff). Nevertheless, Christ died to sin and lives to God (Romans 6:10), that is, Christ's former life in a sinful world is in stark contrast to his present life to God. Christ is then the pattern for believers. Once saved in identification with Christ's death and resurrection, believers can't continue in sin because they have died to sin and have been freed from sin (Romans 6:7). Paul refers to sanctification not as a progressive act but as a definite act occurring at the inception of the Christian life[325] by the agency of the Spirit.[326] But the believer must also undergo continual transformation and engage faithfully in the continuing struggle with sin.[327] Sanctification means deliverance from the power of the flesh. Christ was made sin (2 Corinthians 5:21) so Christ was subject to the power of sin, that is: subject to the dominion of the flesh; and exposed to the world's suffering and weakness.

Believers have been raised with Christ by the Spirit and by virtue of this involvement they are dead to sin and alive to God (Romans 6:11), that is, alive from the dead (Romans 6:13). Freedom from the dominion and power of sin comes with being raised with Christ so sanctification is defined in terms of resurrection. Sanctification of the individual believer involves deliverance from the old age.[328]

Excursus: Glorification of the believer's body by the Spirit

The pneumatic transformation Christ received at the resurrection was the final definitive investiture of his person with glory. Glorification is the predestined goal, signifying conformity to the image of the resurrected Christ.[329] Christ will transform the body of the believer by the Spirit so that it will be in conformity to the body of the resurrected Christ (2 Corinthians 3:18). The resurrection of Christ is the resurrection of the last Adam and—in accordance with the nomenclature identifying Christ with Adam—this

---

325 Acts 20:32; 26:18; 1Corinthians 1:2; 6:11; Ephesians 5:26; 2 Timothy 2:21; 1 Thessalonians 4:3–4; 2 Thessalonians 2:13.
326 Gaffin, 1978, 124.
327 Romans 7:14–25; Galatians 5:13–26.
328 Romans 12:2; 1 Corinthians 3:18; 1 Timothy 6:17; 2 Timothy 4:10; cf. Galatians 1:4; Titus 2:12.
329 Romans 8:29f; Philippians 3:21; cf. 1 Corinthians 15:49.

resurrection of the last Adam involves significant solidarity with those for whom he purchased redemption.

Titus

Christian initiation is one activity of the Spirit (3:5)

Salvation—necessarily accompanied by the baptism of the Spirit—is described as washing of regeneration and renewing by the Holy Spirit (3:5). Christian initiation is thus presented as one activity of the Holy Spirit (cf. Ezekiel 36:25-27)[330] which is entirely necessary because, before the washing and renewing, every believer was a vile distortion (3:3) of God's intention to create a being like him (Genesis 1:26-27). But we are saved by God's mercy in the provision of Jesus Christ made available to us by the activity of the Holy Spirit (3:4-5). The lavish gift of the Holy Spirit (3:6) creates the new people of God who are now ready for every good work (3:1,8). This lavish gift of the Spirit is not dependent on any right thing that we might have done, indeed, the opposite is the case. But just as the breath of God gave life to the Adamic clay jar, in the same way, the renewing of the Holy Spirit brings us into the certain hope of our inheritance which is eternal life (3:7).

---

330 Fee, 1994, 81-2.

Hebrews

The witness of signs and wonders and gifts of the Spirit (2:4)

God himself (2:4) is still (Greek present tense participle) confirming the testimony of the superiority of the Son (Hebrews 1) by continued significant acts of power. Signs and wonders was the standard combination used for the events of the Exodus and then for miraculous events attesting Jesus' resurrection (cf. Mark 16:20). 'Miracles' is the more general term. Signs point beyond themselves to what is signified. Wonders amaze or excite to awe. Miracles, in this context, indicate the irruption of the supernatural into the world. The charismatic distributions of the Spirit (2:4) in the church—as the body of Christ in the world—put the seal on the word received by the whole congregation through the apostles as they signify that Jesus is now seated at the right hand of God (1:3).

The Holy Spirit speaks through Scripture (3:7-11)

Cole notes that a Psalm ascribed to David is introduced as 'what the Holy Spirit says' (3:7-11). There is a double agency in the writing of Scripture. First there is inspiration through divine control of human authorship but, secondly, people are also involved. Cole comments, 'Scripture is indeed God-breathed, but there is a human story to it as well'.[331] The appeal attributing authorship of the quote to the Holy Spirit gives weight to the warning about unbelief (3:12) and emphasises the importance of listening to the Holy Spirit today. Not only is the Holy Spirit the author of all Scripture (2 Timothy 3:16) but this inscripturated word of God is also the sword of the Spirit (Ephesians 6:17), indeed, this living and powerful word of God (the sword of the Spirit) speaks to the inner man with surgical precision (4:12).

Partaking of the heavenly gift of the Holy Spirit (6:4-6)

The people of God in both Testaments had experienced the indwelling gift of the Spirit as enlightenment in the present age with the prophetic promise of a renewed paradise (6:4-5). Enlightenment (6:4) could refer to Israel's experience,[332] indeed, Psalm 36:9 speaks of God as a fountain of light through which his people see light. Israel had eaten the bread of heaven (Psalm 78:24; 105:40) and thus tasted of the heavenly gift (6:4). There

---

331 Cole, 2007, 263.
332 cf. Psalm 43:3; 44:3; 78:14; 105:39.

are particular instances of what seems to be regeneration reported in the Old Testament, clearly the work of the Holy Spirit. There are also individual instances of the reception of the Holy Spirit, such as Bezalel (Exodus 35:30–31) and the elders of Israel (Numbers 11:27ff). The leading of the nation at the exodus (Isaiah 63:14) was by the Holy Spirit. Israel also had the good word of God and her history demonstrates the miraculous powers of the coming age. They had the goodness of the word of God continually. They had tasted again and again of the powers of the age to come, particularly in their exodus wilderness experience but also as prophets revealed God's saving and purifying activity throughout their national history.

Throughout the letter, the author is demanding more commitment from Jewish Christians. They have assumed the Christian faith and are believers (6:9–10), but there is a coalescence of faith in Christ with the retention of overlapping Jewish principles of faith. They are now being asked to make a break with their former allegiance. This is notwithstanding the pressure of the still existing Jewish temple in Jerusalem with Jewish atonement still being conveyed. However, these Jewish Christians are now being encouraged to view Christ as the mediator of a new covenant (9:15). They are to take the new and living way (10:20) which his death has provided, and go out to Jesus beyond the camp bearing his reproach (13:13) to become citizens of a lasting city (13:14). The continuing Old Testament covenant sacrifices being conducted in the Jerusalem Temple post-cross were only a symbol (9:9–10) for a new age regulated by a new covenant has arrived where, by the death of Jesus, the way into the heavenly holy of holies has been disclosed. The continuance of Jewish sacrifice relating to food and drink—and various washings—were now only cultural regulations that had been imposed until 'the time of reformation' which has now come in the death of Jesus. The blood of bulls and goats, once a vital element in a sacrificial system instituted by divine command, was needlessly perpetuated in a sacrificial system after the cross until AD 70. But this sacrificial system could never possibly take away sins. The application of blood as an indication of what sacrifice involved was valid up to the death of Jesus but after Jesus' death the continuing sacrificial system was merely cultural. Jewish Christians are now being confronted as God's people on the move again to the Promised Land.

They are warned (6:6) that a foundation that has once been laid cannot be laid again. This foundation is based on repentance, not in a concept of future messianic fulfilment. The Messiah has come, and the national response that is now required is a complete change of thinking. The Hebrew believers are to endorse the uniqueness of the revelation in Jesus, requiring—in the case of Jewish readers—a radical change of heart and mind, the redirection of the whole personality and the soul, a total change of life direction which ought to be complete and final. The outcome will be a life guided by faith towards God in Christ.

Faith towards God through Christ is the positive act of trust and self-commitment that follows and balances the negative act of repentance and renunciation. These are the two complementary faces of one coin. Faith is a turning towards God for newness of life in Christ, first evident by the impetus of the Holy Spirit in repentance and then belief in the gospel (Mark 1:15). Christian faith always presupposes repentance and repentance always presupposes prior faith, the inward enlightenment of the human spirit through the Holy Spirit.

The pilgrims to whom the author writes must seek to avoid Israel's unfaithfulness as demonstrated specifically in the exodus wilderness. Wilderness Israel had decided to terminate their pilgrimage prematurely (Numbers 14:1) but present pilgrims must not throw away their confidence.

The point is clear: there is no turning back from the new covenant regulated gift of the Spirit without the loss of the promise. The author confronts the Hebrew believers with that looming danger and he refers to the spiritual resources, available from God, present with them through his word and Spirit. They had been partakers of the Holy Spirit, indeed, these contemporary Jewish believers had genuinely experienced God's presence just as wilderness Israel had (cf. God's placing of the Spirit on the elders of Israel, Numbers 11:16–30). But retention of that presence for wilderness Israel was contingent on continuing obedience. In the same way, Jewish Christians needed to persevere with the journey if the Spirit was to remain in them (cf. Exodus 15:24–16:13 and 17:3 where Israel had an actual return to Egypt in mind). The present pilgrims—like wilderness Israel—are in danger of losing the promise of their heavenly citizenship if they fall away (6:6), that is, if they cease to be pilgrims and throw away their confidence. Moreover, the Hebrew believers knew enough to keep them faithful for they had the atoning sacrifice of Jesus and the continued support and strengthening of the Holy Spirit. They had been redeemed. But redemption needed to be maintained. There could be no such thing as eternal security without faithful conduct.

Like wilderness Israel, these Jewish Christians may fail to enter the land by terminating their pilgrimage prematurely (Numbers 14:2). If the Hebrew believers throw away their confidence (10:35-36) then, just like the wilderness generation, they are not genuine believers. But now they are still on their way and must continue for there is no turning back without the loss of the promise. In this way the author confronts them with the peril of apostasy. God is now present in them through his word and Spirit but the continued possession of these great blessings is conditional on obedience. They must persevere with their journey if the Spirit is to remain with them.

The inward energy of the Holy Spirit will be the dynamic evidence of their spiritual growth (6:4-6). The Holy Spirit was the heavenly gift that believers had tasted (aorist), indeed, they had become sharers in the fellowship of the Holy Spirit as believing new covenant Jews. The powers of the world to come (6:5) are, specifically, the gifts of the Holy Spirit manifested to them. Their present heavenly experience and their heavenly destination are at risk if they retreat from the gospel in an attempt to be acceptable in their culture.

The Holy Spirit reveals the benefits of the new covenant (9:8)

The Holy Spirit has now clarified for their time the purpose of these former cultic provisions. So long as the outer sanctuary of the old covenant 'is standing'—that is, the 'first tent' or the holy place—access to God in the inner sanctuary was precluded. The present tense of the Greek participle 'still standing' (9:8) is used to convey that the way into the holy of holies has not been disclosed. The writer is outlining the relationship of the holy place and the holy of holies prescribed by the old covenant priestly law. By the use of the present tense, he is indicating that old covenant temple worship is continuing in Jerusalem (perhaps with Christian involvement) and this continuation of old covenant worship is a problem that is raised continually. This problem is, therefore, a contemporary issue; that is, the author was not raising an issue about cultic performance prior to the cross.

When Jesus died, the division between the two compartments of the sanctuary was removed (Mark 15:38) indicating that the way into God's presence—into the holy of holies—was from that moment available to believers. But Judaism continued liturgical and theological separation between the two compartments in its temple worship. This showed that Israel was still under the now defunct old covenant, uninfluenced by Jesus' ministry and death.

It is from this post-cross perspective in Hebrews that Jewish temple worship is being proscribed and contrasts drawn. The readers of Hebrews must understand that, so long as the old covenant remained valid, direct access to God for Judaism was not possible. Importantly, 9:8–9 encapsulate the cultic argument of the book. The argument of Hebrews regarding the criticism of the cult of the old covenant has been regularly misunderstood in that it is generally argued that 9:8–9 is dismissive about the Old Testament cultus as it operated historically during the era validly regulated by the old covenant (that is, the old covenant era before the cross). But this cannot be the case. By the intertwining of cult and two covenants in Hebrews 8:1–10:18, the argument is referring to the change which has come with the inauguration of the new covenant which is validated and introduced by the cross.

9:8–9 convey the irrelevance of continuing the Jewish model of temple worship after the cross because Jewish temple worship was always supposed to be an expression of a future reality. But the promised future has become present reality since Jesus' entry into the divine throne room of heaven. Up to the death of Christ, the old covenant still operated with validity—indeed, the life of Jesus was lived in the shadow of the old covenant. But by his life, Jesus pointed Israel to the way forward into the new covenant intimate presence of God by the mercy of God through the agency of the Spirit.

The Holy Spirit cleanses the conscience (9:14)

The interpretation of 'through an eternal spirit' (9:14) is very difficult. There are two possibilities. It is either through his own eternal spirit,[333] or through the Holy Spirit. One alternative, the Holy Spirit, gains support from Jesus' anointing at baptism which prepared him for the ministry which led to his death as a mediating sacrifice. The other possibility is that the 'eternal spirit' was Jesus' own essential nature as both human and, yet, truly divine and thus eternal. The moral and spiritual disposition of the offeror made the sacrifice what it was, a death for all. But Christ was not merely a good man—better than any appraisal—rather, the preferable alternative is that Christ was a divine man who was a party in an atonement mystery

---

[333] Eternal (*aionios*, 9:14) means a reality that comes in time but is then everlastingly valid (cf. Sasse, 1933, 209).

involving the Spirit that cannot be fully explained.[334] But, regardless of explanation, the collaborating work of Christ and the Spirit was effective in offering a perfect sacrifice which is continuously powerful to cleanse the guilt of a believer's dead works conscience thereby enabling the believer to engage in service that is acceptable to God.

The Holy Spirit witnesses the new covenant to us (10:15-18)

The Scripture relating to the new covenant (10:15) sums up the expectation. Jeremiah's new covenant prophecy (10:15-18) is referred to as the living and continuing voice of the Holy Spirit (10:16-17). The quotation differs from both Hebrews 8 and Jeremiah 31:33ff as it has been adapted to the argument. The re-quote of Jeremiah 31:33-34 indicate that the Old Testament future expectation (8:7-12) with regard to dismissal of the sacrificial system has now become (cf. 8:1ff) an article of faith in the experience of the Christian community. In 10:16-17 (cf. 8:8-12), the accent is placed on the forgiveness of sins. 10:16-17 is introduced as a testimony from the Holy Spirit (10:15; cf. 'he says', 8:8). Beginning with Jeremiah 31:33, the author omits the earlier verses about the failure of the first covenant and reference to the house of Israel is omitted in favour of the more general third person plural pronoun. More importantly, after the reference to the inwardly inscribed Torah, the author skips to the conclusion of the prophecy: the assurance of divine forgiveness. The transition is normally made more smoothly in translations by the addition of something like 'then he adds'. A new category of transgression appears—*anomion* (lawlessness) in lieu of *adikiais* (unrighteousness, 8:12)—to mark the dismissal of the covenant of law in its Mosaic form. Jews looking for moral direction after the cross are now law-less. The author's concluding statement reinforces the promise of complete and definite forgiveness (10:18), that is: 'where there is forgiveness of these there is no longer any offering for sin'.

The inability of the sacrificial system under the old covenant to provide for the maintenance of that covenant had led, as Jeremiah had prophesied, to the conclusion of the new covenant by way of sacrifice. So law (implicitly) and prophecy (explicitly) pointed to the same need: a new covenant. God has written the law in the hearts (minds) of the new people, as he had done for his Old Testament saints, and he would remember their sins no more. Now the new covenant was not national but, rather, a personal

---

[334] cf. Davidson, 2002, 186.

spiritual reality just as the old covenant had always been a personal spiritual reality for old testament saints.

The necessary conclusion is that, if forgiveness has been completely provided for, then no further sin offering is required (10:18). So the sacrifice of Christ continues to benefit new covenant believers because we are still in daily need of forgiveness. New covenant believers now live on the basis of the one sacrifice of Jesus. So the new thing in this new covenant is not the law in the heart for, indeed, the law in the heart was always the gift for believers in the Old Testament as well as in the New. What is new in the new covenant is that God will not remember sins (10:17). This is more than forgiveness of sins for which the debt has been paid on the cross, rather, at the end of human history and with the return of Jesus there will be a complete elimination of the human disposition to sin as a product of the cross.

To sin wilfully is to insult the Spirit (10:28–29)

There follows a comparison of punishment under the old and new covenants (10:28–29). The author returns to the tenor of 2:2–4 in a how-much-more argument (10:28). Those who disregarded the Mosaic legislation died without pity on the evidence of two or three witnesses (Deuteronomy 17:2–7; 13:8). Clearly, new covenant transgressors are more blameworthy. They have spurned the blessings of the new covenant brought about by the better sacrifice of Christ himself, by which their future was secured. This involves contempt for all that Christ had done. This will incur a dreadful penalty, since apostates put their confession of Jesus as Son of God contemptuously under their feet. New covenant transgressors also profane the blood of the covenant, taking an apostate attitude of unbelief towards Christ.[335] To sin wilfully is to insult the Spirit (cf. 9:14) through whom Christ had offered himself. By Christ's sacrifice, the grace of God in Christ has been applied to us and our access into the new holy of holies has been obtained. But the fate of those who have turned back to the old covenant and thereby profane the blood of the new covenant is dire. God has planned something better than rich cultural/religious traditions which have no power to save (11:39ff), namely, membership in the new covenant and the blessing of spiritual union with Christ the life-giving Spirit.

---

335 Rhee, 2001, 170.

1 Peter

The Spirit applies the benefits of the gospel of God (1:2-4)

Through sanctification of the Spirit (1:2), the conversion experience had led to their present lively hope grounded in the resurrection of Jesus (1:3) and its heavenly significance for believers (1:4). The Father, the Spirit and Jesus Christ work together in conveying the grace and peace which are the heavenly blessings of belonging to the triune God (cf. Ephesians 1:3). The gospel is the Father's plan for effectual grace in salvation and as such is called the gospel of God (Romans 1:1); and certain aspects of this plan are only known by the Father (1:2; Romans 15:16).[336] The Father's plan is enacted by Jesus Christ as the Son provides his own blood as the effective element for righteousness in the new covenant (1:2);[337] so the gospel is also called the gospel of Christ as it is the Father's plan about Christ (cf. John 3:16),[338] that is, the gospel of God is the gospel of Jesus Christ. The application of the benefits of the Father's plan in the gospel of Jesus Christ is the work of the Spirit as he sanctifies believers so that they now belong to God (1:2).[339] Throughout history, the Spirit has also communicated the plan of the Father's gospel in Jesus Christ (1:11-12; Romans 15:19; 1 Thessalonians 1:5).

God is the Father of our Lord Jesus Christ (1:3).[340] The Spirit is ontologically related to God but the Spirit of God is also the Spirit of Christ (cf. 1:11; Romans 8:9). Christ and the Spirit do not share the same ontological association as God and the Spirit, so the Spirit of Christ in revelation makes explicit the mind of God.

---

336 cf. Luke 22:42; Matthew 24:36.

337 cf. Matthew 26:28; Luke 22:20; Revelation 5:9; Hebrews 9:12,14.

338 Mark 1:1; Romans 1:16; 15:19,29; 1 Corinthians 9:12,18; 2 Corinthians 9:13; 10:14; Galatians 1:7; Philippians 1:27; 1 Thessalonians 3:2; 2 Thessalonians 1:8.

339 cf. Romans 15:16; 1 Corinthians 6:11; 2 Corinthians 3:3.

340 cf. 2 Corinthians 1:3; Ephesians 1:3.

Preaching the gospel requires Spirit empowerment (1:11-12)

The Old Testament prophets had prophesied the salvation to come at the instigation of the Spirit of Christ in them, predicting two states: the sufferings of Christ; and the glory to follow (1:11). These Old Testament prophecies have been fulfilled in Christ's humiliation and glory. Just as the Spirit of Christ was required within the Old Testament prophets for them to reveal essential elements of the gospel so, too, the preaching of the gospel in the present era requires personal empowerment by the Holy Spirit (1:12).[341]

The Spirit of glory resting on persecuted believers (4:14)

There is a blessing that accrues when the believer is reviled because he carries the name of Christ (3:14; 4:12; cf. Matthew 5:11-12), in particular, the reproached believer is blessed because the Spirit of glory and of God is resting on him (4:14). The Spirit of Christ in the Old Testament prophets pointed to the sufferings of Christ and the glories that would follow (1:11). Paul gave up everything to know Christ, including personal knowledge from the fellowship of his sufferings with the hope of being included in the glory of the final resurrection (Philippians 3:10-11,21). In the new covenant, by the Spirit of the Lord (2 Corinthians 3:18), all believers are being transformed into the image of the glory of the Lord. Jesus' crowning glory occurs through the suffering of death (Hebrews 2:10).

---

341 cf. Romans 15:19; Hebrews 2:4; 1 John 4:2; 5:6.

2 Peter

The Spirit inspired men to write infallible Scripture (1:21)

When the inspired authors wrote they were 'carried along' by the Holy Spirit so the Scripture has dual authorship: the Holy Spirit and the inspired person. What the inspired authors of the Bible wrote as they were moved by the Spirit is the only infallible rule of faith and practice for the Christian. Various passages reveal that this divine superintendence extends to the very words (verbal symbols) used by the authors (cf. Matthew 5:18; Galatians 3:16). The question of how the Spirit guided the authors in their writing is far from clear and hence not required for saving faith or walking in the Spirit. The style and theological emphasis of the individual writers shine through their writings indicating that the Spirit worked with and through the personality of the human authors to convey the divine message.

1 John

The anointing of the Spirit abides in the believer (2:20-27)

The fully incarnate reality of Jesus' coming and his continuing existence is experienced (endorsed) in the believer by an anointing from the Holy One (that is, the Holy Spirit). Similarly, Paul states that we need the Holy Spirit to know and make the confession that the incarnate Jesus is the exalted Lord (1 Corinthians 12:3). John writes to encourage Christians—young or old in the faith—in their witness because they have received an anointing from the Holy One (2:20) and hence they all know the truth. What is the truth that they know? They know the Father and the Son and the Spirit by the anointing that gives them knowledge of all things (2:23).

This anointing of the Spirit abides in the believer (2:27). So they know Christ through the Spirit and they know the gospel of Christ by revelation of the Spirit. Hence, believers do not need further teaching on this subject—that Jesus is the Christ—and they do not need to fear the false claims of others who deny Christ.

The Spirit communicates the indwelling Christ to us (3:24)

John is writing from the apostolic community to the next generation of believers in the church. The indicative statement about the next generation is that those who keep the commandments are abiding in Christ and Christ is abiding in them. Their holy life is ipso facto evidence of their relationship with God. But the indicative statement is not the next generation believer's assurance, rather, the believer is assured of being in new covenant relationship by the intimate presence of the Holy Spirit given to us by Christ. The Spirit directly communicates the indwelling Christ to us. The Spirit that now abides in the believer also confirms the apostles' testimony as eye witnesses of Jesus' life, death, resurrection and ascension (4:13-14).

Evidences of the indwelling Spirit of God (4:1-21)

The next generation church is given two criteria to test the spirits so that they can recognise believers operating in the Holy Spirit as distinct from other spirits (4:1). The first criterion is that those who are inspired by the Holy Spirit will bear witness to the fact that Jesus came in the flesh (4:2), that is, they will acknowledge: the virgin birth; the miracles in Judea; the teaching with authority; the confrontation of religious hypocrisy; the trial before the leading Jews and the Roman governor; the crucifixion; the resurrection; and the ascension.

The second criterion is that those who know God place themselves under apostolic doctrine (4:6). The authorship of 1 John is, essentially, plural. The authorial community claims to have seen Jesus with their own eyes and touched Jesus with their own hands (1:1) so the community from which this letter stems must be the original apostolic community (the twelve plus Paul), probably with John as their spokesman. The audience for the letter appears to be the next generation church—that is, those who have not been eye witnesses but who, nevertheless, are given opportunity to enter into fellowship with the apostolic community and with the Father and with his Son Jesus Christ (1:3). A false prophet will not accept the witness of the apostolic community as it is recorded in the New Testament (cf. 4:13–14).

The witness of the Spirit on earth and in heaven (5:6–8)

In heaven there is Trinitarian witness to the truth about all things. The three that bear witness in heaven are the Father, the eternal Word and the Spirit (5:7) and these three are in agreement. We have access to this Trinitarian witness by the Spirit (5:6; cf. Hebrews 4:16). All that is revealed in Scripture of God's eternal purposes can be relied on and is overwhelmingly wonderful to contemplate and moves us to the kind of worship that we read of in Revelation as all bow down and sing their new songs of praise around the heavenly throne.

And on earth there is also a form of Trinitarian worship. The three that bear witness on earth are the Spirit, the water and the blood and these three are in agreement. Water may refer to the heavenly witness to Jesus at his baptism and, no doubt, blood refers to the public crucifixion. Alternatively, water may refer to Christian baptism and blood may refer to the celebration of Jesus' sacrifice in Christian communion. Irrespective, the witness is about what God has done on earth in Jesus Christ for us and for our salvation. The witness on earth is—by geographical and spiritual proximity—more available to believers and those who have not yet responded to the gospel. The common witness in heaven and on earth is the Spirit. The Spirit agrees with Trinitarian testimony in heaven and the Spirit agrees with Trinitarian testimony on earth, so testimony in heaven and testimony on earth speak a common theme about God's wonderful plan to form an eternal fellowship of love through Jesus Christ (1:3; 4:12). The Spirit is a witness on earth (and in heaven) so the Spirit is as close to us as the incarnate Jesus was to the apostles—also, the Spirit is as close as the material symbols of his covenant (bread and wine in communion) are to us today. And the Spirit bears witness to us (5:16) so that we can truly know that God's gospel in Jesus Christ invites us into fellowship with him and his church.

Jude

Those who cause divisions do not have the Spirit (19-20)

Those who cause divisions in the church are sensual, that is, of the flesh (19) and if they are of the flesh then the Spirit of God cannot be in them (cf. Genesis 6:3; John 3:6; 6:63; Romans 8:1-13). True believers, on the other hand, should build themselves up in their most holy faith by praying in the Holy Spirit (20). Praying in the Holy Spirit will keep them in the love of God (21) for the Spirit will communicate the love of God to them as they pray. As they pray in the Holy Spirit they will also look ahead to the wonderful mercy of eternal life (21) in a resurrection body like that of our Lord Jesus Christ for the Spirit will communicate future heavenly realities to them as they pray.

The word that Jude uses to describe those who cause divisions is *psuchikos* (natural or physical existence that is not infused with the Spirit, 19) which is also used by Paul in the context of the divided Corinthian church to describe those who do not receive the things of the Spirit (1 Corinthians 2:14) and consequently become the source of envy, strife and divisions in the church because they are still of the flesh (*sarkikoi*, 1 Corinthians 3:3; cf. the *psuchikos* wisdom of those in the church who evidence bitter envy and selfish ambition, James 3:14-15). The *psuchikos* or *sarkikoi* behave in accordance with not having a living connection with God. Paul elaborates on the *psuchikos* in an anthropology that acknowledges a *psuchikos* (mere flesh existence) body and a *pneumatikos* (in the image of God, infused with the breath of God) body (1 Corinthians 15:44-46). Those who are *pneumatikos* are not less natural—not less flesh, not less body—but the body is brought to a new dimension of life by Jesus' life-giving Spirit, indeed, this new dimension of life is in the image of Jesus Christ (1 Corinthians 15:49) which is equivalent to in the image of God which was the original intent and therefore the fulfilment of God's purpose in the creation of humanity. In a church that appears to have been divided by some of the more eye-catching gifts of the Spirit, Paul emphasises that those who are truly of the Spirit will exercise their gifts with humility in harmony because all the gifts are from the same Spirit (1 Corinthians 12:4,11,13).

Within the church there are those who do not have the Spirit who prefer to manage a natural religion based perhaps on ethics and standards—like the Jews in the early church who tried to impose the defunct old covenant laws on new covenant Gentile believers (Galatians 3:2). They will cause division in the church because they are not related to the one Spirit who is the source of unity in the church. But also in the church, like in Corinth, there are those who appear to be filled with the Spirit because they appear to be exercising gifts of the Spirit which evidence the presence of Jesus Christ among them (such as words of wisdom and knowledge, faith, healings and miracles, prophecy, discernment, tongues and interpretation; 1 Corinthians 12:8–10) but, in fact, they are no more spiritual than those who reject the necessity of the ongoing activity of the Spirit because the unity of love which is the hallmark of life in the Spirit is not evident in their contribution within the church (1 Corinthians 13; Philippians 2:1–2; Jude 12). They cause division as they seek to be puffed up by a spectacular flesh contribution which they control rather than exercise the power of what is received from the Spirit in the unity brought by the Spirit. Then Jude refers to those who appear to be spiritual (dreamers, 8) but who are actually using the church as a resource for satisfying their own base desires. They cause division by their corruption. It is probable that there is some ambiguity on all sides in the complexity of life prior to the Parousia during which life can only ever be partially led by the Spirit as in a mirror dimly (1 Corinthians 13:12; Jude 16). So we all have a responsibility always to encourage each other to walk in the Spirit (Jude 22–23), evidencing holiness by faith, displaying the fruits of the Spirit, and ministering with the gifts of the Spirit in the unity of being one body of Jesus Christ together in the process of being formed by the one Spirit.

Revelation

John is in the Spirit and the Spirit is speaking to the churches

The Book of Revelation (*Apokalupsis*)—as a revelation of Jesus Christ (1:1) from God to show his servants—is marked at the beginning and end (1:3; 22:7,10,18) as a massive Christian prophecy that is required spiritual reading for believers. The book reports the words of the ascended Christ (1:11,17ff) which, at the same time, is what the Spirit says to the churches (2:7,11,17,29; 3:6,13,22). John's visions point to the coming Parousia towards which contemporary church life must focus. The prominence of the Spirit is a feature of this Apocalypse compared with other contemporary apocalyptic works, hence, the Spirit contributes significantly to the eschatological perspective of Revelation.[342]

John advises his readers that this prophetic revelation must take place soon (1:1). The introductory phrase 'in the Spirit' indicates John's prophetic stance when he receives different aspects of the content which Christ is speaking to him (1:10; 4:2; 17:3; 21:10).[343] Elsewhere 'in the Spirit' means in the Spirit's control or the temporary experience of the Spirit's power in prophetic speech or revelation (Matthew 22:43; Luke 2:27; Acts 19:21). The expression *egenomen en pneumati* (to be in the Spirit; 1:10; 4:2) is best understood as a technical term for the visionary's experience of rapture by the Spirit. John was *en pneumati* in the sense that his normal sensory experience was replaced by visions and auditions given him by the Spirit. Translation to the heavenly court (cf. 4:1ff) was a common claim of apocalyptic visionaries. Ezekiel's experience in the Spirit (Ezekiel 3:12,14; 8:3) parallels John's transportation *en pneumati* (17:3; 21:10). In neither case is the human spirit involved, rather, the Revelation is communicated entirely by the Spirit of God. John's usage of *en pneumati epi oros mega* (in the Spirit to a great high mountain, 21:10) is modelled on Ezekiel's parallel vision of New Jerusalem city from the perspective of a very high mountain (Ezekiel 40:2).

John is not like other apocalyptists in that he does not describe the experience of receiving the vision psychologically. John's purpose was not to describe how he received the revelation but to communicate it to his readers.

---

342 1:10; 4:2; 14:13; 17:3; 21:10; 22:17
343 Bauckham, 153–154, 1993.

The parallel formulae of 17:3 and 21:10—reminiscent of Ezekiel's vision of the new temple—are intended to highlight the antithesis of Babylon and Jerusalem, that is, they are included for literary effect and theological significance rather than to show a special role for the Spirit at these points in the Revelation. Simply put, John's theological claim was that the whole revelation came to him *en pneumati*.

The Spirit of prophecy (19:10) speaks through John bearing the testimony of the exalted Christ to his people on earth—endorsing on earth the words of the heavenly revelations and directing the prayers of the churches to their heavenly Lord. These are the functions of Christian prophets who, according to Revelation, are a special group within the churches (11:18; 16:6; 18:20,24; 22:9). Accordingly, the Spirit of prophecy within churches is envisaged as having life-giving and life-changing effects for the Spirit brings to the church the powerful word of Christ rebuking, encouraging, promising, threatening, and directing the lives and prayers of Christian communities towards the coming of Christ. The living voice of the Spirit speaking through prophets is characteristic of Christian churches as eschatological communities in which the age to come is dawning. Joel 2 had promised that the prophetic Spirit in the last days was not to be the endowment of the select few only so the prominence of prophets in the Apocalypse reflects not only the important role of those specially called to be prophets within the churches but also a conviction that the vocation of the church as a whole is prophetic.

The seven Spirits represent the fullness of God at work in the world

Distinctively in Revelation, the Spirit is also described as the 'seven Spirits' of God in connection with the heavenly throne and God's mission on earth (1:4; 3:1; 4:5; 5:6). There is much discussion as to whether the seven Spirits are angels or the Holy Spirit but it seems most probable that they are symbolic of the Spirit of God (cf. Isaiah 11:1–5).[344] In the Old Testament, 'Spirit' generally denotes God's action as an extension of his personality. 'Seven spirits' indicates the fullness of God in his powerful working in the world. The sevenfold Spirit before the throne identifies the Spirit as the one always ready and able to manifest the presence of God in the world (4:5).

---

344 Bauckham (1993, 164–166) references the seven lamps of Zechariah 4:2. The eyes of the lampstand are the Lord's seven eyes (5:6) which range through all the world by Christian witness empowered by the Holy Spirit.

God's worldly rule is thus to be imposed not by might but by the Spirit (Zechariah 4:6). Since his Spirit will act in and with the human spirit, God will principally carry out his intention by interaction with human beings. The Spirit is now the presence and power of the Lord in the world, bringing about God's kingdom by implementing the Lamb's victory throughout the world.

The seven lamps of Zechariah's lampstand (Zechariah 4:2) become the seven spirits of God blazing before the throne (4:5) of the Lord of the earth. John also sees seven horns and seven eyes with the seven Spirits of God (5:6) which indicate the range and power of Christian witness as opposed to the horns of the dragon and the beasts (12:3; 13:1,11). In heaven, the seven Spirits burn before the throne of God (1:4; 4:5) like the seven-branched lampstand that burned before the Lord in the earthly temple (Exodus 40:25). The seven Spirits are the horns and eyes of the Lamb, active throughout the earth through the Lamb's followers as they bear witness to Christ's victory through his death. In the Lamb's followers who are on earth, the Spirit of prophecy maintains the witness of Jesus in the world. They are not only olive trees filled with the Spirit but also lampstands (1:20; 2:1,5; 11:4) burning with the light of the Spirit in the world. Therefore the 'seven Spirits' (5:6) does not refer to the Lamb's omnipotence independent of his church, rather, the 'seven Spirits' refers to the Lamb's presence with those whom his death has ransomed for God (5:9)—through their witness the Spirit of God goes out into all the earth, continually expressing the Lamb's conquest. The ministry of the Lamb by the Spirit in the churches (2:1) is through the effectiveness of believers as his witnesses in the world (11:3ff).

The Spirit mediates the victory of the exalted Christ, the Lamb, through the church of Christ. The Spirit declares Christ's word to his people in vision and prophetic oracle. The Spirit leads the prayers of Christ's people. The Spirit inspires the missionary witness of Christ's people to the world. The Spirit's role is eschatological, constituting the Christian churches as the community of the age to come. The eschatological outpouring of the Spirit into the world is derived from the victory of Christ in his death and resurrection (5:6). Likewise, the Spirit's activity in and through the churches is directed towards the fulfilment of this victory of Christ in the eschatological future.

The Spirit's message is for overcomers at the Parousia

Each of the proclamations from Christ that John is instructed to deliver to the churches concludes with a message, directly from the Spirit, that relates to ultimate gifts for 'overcomers' who have endured in their faithfulness to God's enabling invitation into gospel life. The messages are from Christ, conveyed by the Spirit. The promise of the Spirit to overcomers is eternal life. At the Parousia, the Spirit gives to overcomers fruit from the tree of life which is in the middle of God's Paradise (2:7); the tree with fruit that Adam and Eve were not given opportunity to eat (Genesis 3:22) because they had not been washed and regenerated and sanctified by the Spirit in preparation for eternal life. Indeed, the Parousia marks a permanent transition in which death no longer has any power to hurt overcomers (2:11; 20:6,14; 21:4). At the Parousia, the overcomer partakes of the hidden manna (2:17) which is the bread of life come down from heaven—the flesh of the Son of Man—and whoever eats this bread will live forever because they are living in Jesus (John 6:32,35,48,50–51,56,58). The overcomer's name is recorded forever in the Book of Life (3:5).

The messages directly from the Spirit indicate the eternal identity and state of being of overcomers in their forever life with Christ. At the Parousia the adoption of overcomers is forever secured as they are given a new name in the family of God (2:17) and are together named as the bride of Christ (3:12; 21:2), indeed, Jesus speaks up for overcomers by specifically mentioning their names to the heavenly Father in the presence of angels at the Parousia (3:5). There are temptations to immoral faithlessness from those who seem to be spiritual even within active churches that overflow with good works and love, so in these churches there is a challenge not to be deceived by the depths of Satan. Those who overcome in this context will, at the Parousia, rule with Christ who shall be forever in their hearts (2:26,28; 3:21; 2 Peter 1:19). Indeed, overcomers are given white garments indicating that—from the Parousia onwards—overcomers are no longer in a state of contending with their own sinfulness or temptations to sinfulness from others within the congregation (3:5; 14:13), indeed, their righteous acts are now unambiguous (19:8). Overcomers who have remained faithful—even though they had little personal strength in the face of strenuous opposition—will, at the Parousia, be pillars of strength in God's forever household (3:12).

The Spirit of prophecy (19:10)

In post biblical Judaism the Spirit of God is especially the Spirit of prophecy, the Spirit who speaks through the prophets.[345] In Revelation, the witness of Jesus—which is the content of Revelation (cf. 1:2; 22:16,20)—is the Spirit if prophecy (19:10). The angel says that the testimony borne by Jesus provides what the prophetic Spirit must proclaim. The name Jesus—which occurs fourteen times in Revelation—is used principally with regard to his humanity, referring to his faithful witness (1:5). Believers have the prophetic Spirit by which they must proclaim the testimony of Jesus (1:9). Witness is primary verbal (11:7; 12:11) and the consequence of speaking the testimony of Jesus is expected to be martyrdom (2:13; 6:9; 17:6; 20:4). Those who bear witness are not just the prophets (19:10) but also Christians in general (12:17). Prophecy and bearing witness are equated (11:3) for the witness of Jesus communicates the Spirit of prophecy (19:10). The characterisation of the Christian community as those who bear the witness of Jesus seems therefore to attribute a prophetic vocation to the whole community.

It may well be that a distinction is to be drawn between the special vocation of the Christian prophets to declare the word of God within the Christian community and the general vocation of the Christian community as a whole to declare the word of God in the world. David Hill has argued, not convincingly, that John's role is unique while the prophet's role would be to understand and mediate John's message to others.[346] But 1:3 implies that Revelation was read aloud without any need for mediation and the natural sense of *humin* (to you, 22:16) is not 'to the prophets' but to all in the church who have been directed to hear the prophecy—especially the members of the seven churches (1:4,11). Indeed, the Spirit of prophecy speaks through the prophets to the churches and then through the churches to the world (10:11; 11:3-13). The story of the two witnesses represents the vocation of the whole church in its missionary role in the world. The whole church in the Apocalypse is endowed with the Spirit of prophecy so that it may bear the witness of Jesus in the world.

So the Spirit mediates the activity of the exalted Christ through his church: declaring Christ's word to his people in vision and prophetic oracle;

---

345 Sjoeberg, TDNT vi 381ff. cf. 1:1 with 22:9 for the similar identification of Jesus.
346 Hill, 1967, 413f and 417f.

leading the prayers of his people; and inspiring his people's missionary witness to the world. In all of this the Spirit's role is eschatological, constituting the Christian churches as the community of the age to come. The victory of Christ in his death and resurrection produces the eschatological outpouring of the Spirit into the world (5:6) so the consummation of Christ's victory in the eschatological future is brought about by the Spirit's activity in and through the churches.

The eschatological role of the Spirit in Revelation is not simply that of predicting the events of the end. The purpose of John's prophecy is to enable Christians in the seven churches to bear witness of Jesus, and this could only be done by directing their sight and their lives towards the coming of the Lord. The point was not so much to enable them or us to foresee the future as to enable them to see their present new covenant position from the perspective of the future.

The Spirit and bride together pray for the Parousia (22:17)

The bride (22:17) is the church, the true people of God,[347] seen from the perspective of the Parousia. There is a stark contrast between the generally unprepared seven churches of Asia and the church at the Parousia, now prepared as a bride by the Spirit for her husband Christ (21:2). Indeed, the function of the Spirit is to direct the church towards her eschatological reality. The church is chosen for salvation by God to be set apart and made holy by the Spirit (2 Thessalonians 2:13). God's message is preached by prophets who have been sent from heaven and enabled to communicate good news from God by the Holy Spirit (1 Peter 1:12). The love of God is poured into the church by the Holy Spirit given to us so that the church obtains a hope that does not disappoint (Romans 5:5), indeed, the church abounds in hope in the present by the power of the Holy Spirit (Romans 15:13). By the Spirit, the church is washed, sanctified and justified (1 Corinthians 6:11). The washing of the Spirit is for rebirth into a new and renewed life (Titus 3:5). The church is able to hold on to the good that has been committed to her by the indwelling Holy Spirit (1 Timothy 1:14), even more, the church is now being transformed towards the image of the glory of Jesus Christ by the Spirit of the Lord (2 Corinthians 3:18). Lust threatens to break up the proposed union between believers and God in Christ so the Spirit who dwells in us yearns jealously to keep us loving God with all our hearts,

---

[347] Beale, 1999, 370.

monogamously (James 4:5; cf. Exodus 20:3–5). Holy men of God spoke prophecy as they were moved by the Holy Spirit, and all of the prophecy recorded in Scripture is essential for ongoing correction and encouragement if the church is to remain faithful (2 Peter 1:21).

The hearer of Revelation—that is, all believers as all are instructed to read this prophecy—is to join his own voice to that of the Spirit so that the eschatological church may become a present reality (22:17). The prayer for the Parousia is at the heart of contemporary Christian living according to the Apocalypse. The invitation to the thirsty is also a call towards the eschatological future foreshadowing the new creation gift of the water of life (21:6).[348] The focus of this end-time promise is the Lord's 'I am coming soon' repeated three times (22:7,12,20).

---

348 cf. John 4:10; 7:37–39; Isaiah 55:1.

Bibliography

Aune, D E. *Prophecy in Early Christianity and the Ancient Mediterranean World* (Exeter: Paternoster, 1983).

Barrett, C K. *The Gospel According to St. John* (London: SPCK, 1955).

Bassler, J M. '1Cor 12:3– Curse and Confession in Context' *Journal of Biblical Literature* 101 (1982) 415–418.

Bauckham, R J. *The Climax of Prophecy: Studies on the Book of Revelation* (Edinburgh: Clark, 1993).

Bauckham, R J. 'The Role of the Spirit in the Apocalypse' *The Evangelical Quarterly*, 52.2 (April/June 1980) 66–83.

Beaton, R. *Isaiah's Christ in Matthew's Gospel* (Cambridge: CUP, 2002).

Bennema, C. *The Power of Saving Wisdom: An Investigation of Spirit and Wisdom in Relation to the Soteriology of the Fourth Gospel* (Tübingen: Mohr Siebeck, 2002).

Brawley, R L. *Luke Acts and the Jews: Conflict, Apology and Conciliation* (Atlanta: Scholars, 1987).

Brown, P E. *The Holy Spirit and the Bible: The Spirit's Interpreting Role in Relation to Biblical Hermeneutics* (Ross-Shire: Christian Focus, 2002).

Brown, R E. *The Gospel according to John: Introduction, Translation and Notes, 2 Vols* (Garden City: Doubleday, 1966 & 1971).

Caird, G B. *The Gospel of St. Luke* (Middlesex: Penguin, 1963).

Chae, D J. *Paul as Apostle to the Gentiles* (Carlisle: Paternoster, 1997).

Chiu, J E A. *1 Cor 12–14: Literary Structure and Theology* (Rome: Pontifical Biblical Institute, 2007).

Cho, Y. *Spirit and Kingdom in the Writings of Luke and Paul* (Milton Keynes: Paternoster Press, 2005).

Clark, A C. *Parallel Lives: The Relation of Paul to the Apostles in Lucan Perspective* (Carlisle: Paternoster, 2001).

Cole, G A. *He Who Gives Life: The Doctrine of the Holy Spirit* (Wheaton: Crossway Books, 2007).

Carson, D A. *The Gospel According to John* (Grand Rapids: Eerdmans, 1991).

Ciampa, R E. *The Presence and Function of Scripture in Galatians 1 and 2* (WUNT 2/102, Tübingen: Mohr Siebeck, 1998).

Davis, J A. *Wisdom and Spirit* (London: University Press of America, 1984).

Davidson, R M. 'Inauguration or Day of Atonement? A Response to Norman Young's "Old Testament Background to Hebrews 6:19-20 Revisited"' *Andrews University Seminary Studies* (40/1, 2002), 69-88.

Davies, J G. 'Pentecost and Glossolalia' *Journal of Theological Studies* (III/2, 1952), 228-231.

Dumbrell, W J. *Covenant and Creation* (Exeter: Paternoster Press, 1984).

Dumbrell, W J. 'The Spirit in John's Gospel' in Webb, B G. *Spirit of the Living God* (Homebush West: Lancer, 1991), 77-94.

Dumbrell, W J. *Search for Order: Biblical Eschatology in Focus* (Grand Rapids: Baker, 1994).

Dumbrell, W J. *The Faith of Israel* (Grand Rapids: Eerdmans, 2002).

Dunn, J D G. *Baptism in the Holy Spirit* (London: SCM, 1970).

Dunn, J D G. '2 Corinthians 3.17- 'the Lord is the Spirit'.' *JTS* (21/2, 1970), 309-20.

Dunn, J D G. 'Spirit and Fire Baptism' *NovT* (14, 1972), 81-92.

Dunn, J D G. *Jesus and the Spirit* (London: SCM, 1975).

Dunn, J D G. *Christ and the Spirit Vol 2: Pneumatology* (Grand Rapids: Eerdmans, 1998).

Fatehi, M. *The Spirit's Relation to the Risen Lord in Paul* (WUNT 2/128, Tübingen: Mohr Siebeck, 2000).

Fee, G D. *The First Epistle to the Corinthians* (Grand Rapids: Eerdmans, 1987).

Fee, G D. *God's empowering presence: the Holy Spirit in the letters of Paul* (Peabody: Hendrickson, 1994).

Ferguson, S B. *The Holy Spirit* (Downers Grove: InterVarsity Press, 1996).

Forestell, J T. *The Word of the Cross: Salvation as Revelation in the Fourth Gospel* (AnBib 51, Rome: Biblical Institute Press, 1974).

France, R T. *The Gospel according to Matthew: an Introduction and Commentary* (Leicester: InterVarsity Press, 1985).

Gaffin, R B. Jr. *The Centrality of the Resurrection: A Study in Paul's Soteriology* (Grand Rapids: Baker, 1978).

Gaffin, R B. *Perspectives on Pentecost: Studies in New Testament Teaching on the Gifts of the Holy Spirit* (Phillipsburg: Presbyterian and Reformed, 1979).

Goldingay, J. 'Was the Holy Spirit Active in Old Testament Times? What Was New about the Christian Experience of God?' *Ex Auditu* (12, 1996), 14–28.

Grabbe, L L. *Judaic Religion in the Second Temple Period: Belief and Practice from the Exile to Yavneh* (London: Routledge, 2000).

Grindheim, S. 'Wisdom for the Perfect: Paul's Challenge for the Corinthian Church (2:6–16)' *Journal of Biblical Literature* (121, 2002), 689–709.

Grigsby, B H. '"If Any Man Thirsts …": Observations on the Rabbinic Background of John 7:37–39' *Biblica* (67, 1986), 101–8.

Grudem, W A. *The Gift of Prophecy in 1 Corinthians* (Washington: University Press of America, 1982).

Hafemann, S J. 'The Comfort and Power of the Gospel. The Argument of 2 Corinthians 1–3' *Review and Expositor* (86, 1989), 325–344.

Hafemann, S J. *2 Corinthians: The NIV Application Commentary* (Grand Rapids: Zondervan, 2000).

Hafemann, S J. *Paul, Moses and the History of Israel: The Letter/Spirit Contrast in the Argument from Scripture in 2 Corinthians 3* (WUNT 81, Tübingen: Mohr, 1995).

Hafemann, S J. *Suffering and Ministry in the Spirit: Paul's Defence of His Ministry in 2 Corinthians 2:14–3:3* (Carlisle: Paternoster, 2000).

Hafemann, S J. '"Self-Commendation" and Apostolic Legitimacy in Dialectic?' *NTS* (36, 1990), 66-88.

Hafemann. S J. *Suffering and the Spirit*. (T-bingen: Mohr, 1986).

Hamid-Khani, S. *Revelation and concealment of Christ: a theological inquiry into the allusive language of the Fourth Gospel* (WUNT 2/210, Tübingen: Mohr Siebeck, 2000).

Hamilton, J M. *God's Indwelling Presence: The Holy Spirit in the Old & New Testaments* (Nashville: B&H Publishing Group, 2006).

Harris, M J. *Raised Immortal: Resurrection and Immortality in the New Testament* (Grand Rapids: Eerdmans, 1985).

Harris, M J. *The Second Epistle to the Corinthians* (Grand Rapids: Eerdmans, 2005).

Harris, M J. '2 Corinthians 5:1-10: Watershed in Paul's Eschatology' *TynBul* (22, 1971), 32-57.

Hawthorne, G E. *The Presence and the Power: The Significance of the Holy Spirit in Ministry of Jesus* (Dallas: Word, 1991).

Hemer, C J. *The Book of Acts in the Setting of Hellenistic History* (WUNT 49, Tübingen: Mohr, 1989).

Hengel, M. *Acts and the History of Earliest Christianity* (London: SCM 1979).

Hill, D. *Greek Words and Hebrew Meanings: Studies in the Semantics of Soteriological Terms* (Cambridge: Cambridge University Press, 1967).

Holmberg, B. *Paul and Power: The Structure of Authority in the Primitive Church as Reflected in the Pauline Epistles* (Philadelphia: Fortress Press, 1980).

Holwerda, D E. *The Holy Spirit and Eschatology in the Gospel of John* (Kampen: Kok, 1959).

Isaacs, M E. 'The Prophetic Spirit in the Fourth Gospel' *Hey J* (24, 1983), 391-407.

Jeremias, J. *Jesus' Promise to the Nations* (London: SCM, 1958).

Jervell, J. *Luke and the People of God: A New Look at Luke-Acts* (Minneapolis: Augsburg, 1972).

Jervell, J. *The Unknown Paul: Essays on Luke-Acts and Early Christian History* (Minneapolis: Augsburg, 1984).

Johnson, L T. *The Acts of the Apostles* (Collegeville: Liturgical Press/Michael Glazier, 1992).

Litwak, K D. *Echoes of Scripture in Luke-Acts: Telling the History of God's People Intertextually* (London: T&TClark, 2005).

Marcus, J. *The Way of the Lord. Christological Exegesis of the Old Testament in the Gospel of Mark* (Edinburgh: T&T Clark, 1992).

Martin, R P. *2 Corinthians* (Waco: Word Books, 1986).

Marshall, I H. 'The Significance of Pentecost' *Scottish Journal of Theology* (30, 1977), 347–369.

Marshall, I H. *Acts: Tyndale NT Commentaries* (Leicester: InterVarsity Press, 1980).

Meier, J P. *The Vision of Matthew* (New York: Crossroad, 1991).

Meyer, B F. *The Aims of Jesus* (London: SCM, 1979).

Meyer, B F. *Christus Faber: the Master Builder and the House of God* (Allison Park: Pickwick Publications, 1992).

Meyer, B F. 'Did Paul's View of the Resurrection of the Dead Undergo Development?' *TS* (47, 1986), 363–387.

Moo, D J. *The Epistle to the Romans* (Grand Rapids: Eerdmans, 1996).

Neyrey, J H. 'John III—A Debate over Johannine Epistemology and Christology' *Novum Testamentum* (23, 1981), 115–127.

Nygren, A. *Commentary on Romans* (Philadelphia: Fortress, 1949).

O'Day, G R. 'The Gospel of John' in *The New Interpreter's Bible Vol 9* (Nashville : Abingdon, 1995), 491–865.

Packer, J I. *Keep in Step with the Spirit* (Leicester: IVP, 1984).

Pao, D W. *Acts and the Isaianic New Exodus* (Tübingen: Mohr Siebeck, 2000).

Porter, S E. 'Can Traditional Exegesis Enlighten Literary Analysis of the Fourth Gospel? An Examination of the Old Testament Fulfilment Motif and the Passion Theme' in *The Gospels and the Scriptures of Israel JSNTSup 104* ed. Evans, C A. and Segner, W R. (Sheffield: Academic Press, 1994), 398-428.

Rhee, V (Sung-Yul). *Faith in Hebrews: Analysis within the Context of Christology, Eschatology and Ethics* (Studies in Biblical Literature Vol. 19; New York: Peter Lang, 2001).

Resseguie, J L. *The Strange Gospel: Narrative Design and Point of View in John* (Leiden: Brill, 2001).

Rosner, B S. *Paul, Scripture and Ethics: A Study of 1 Corinthians 5-7* (Leiden: Brill, 1994).

Sanders, E P. *Paul and Palestinian Judaism: A Comparison of Patterns of Religion* (Philadelphia: Fortress Press, 1977).

Sandnes, K O. *Paul – One of the Prophets?* (Tübingen: Mohr, 1991).

Sandnes, K O. *Belly and the Body in the Pauline Epistles* (Cambridge: Cambridge University Press, 2002).

Schatzmann, S S. *A Pauline Theology of Charismata* (Peabody: Hendrickson Press, 1989).

Scheffler, E. *Suffering in Luke's Gospel* (Zurich: Theologischer Verlag, 1993).

Scott, J M. *Adoption as Sons of God: An Exegetical Investigation into the Background of Huiothesia in the Pauline Corpus* (WUNT 48, Tübingen: Mohr Siebeck, 1992).

Seccombe, D P, *Possessions and the Poor in Luke-Acts* (Linz: A Fuchs, 1983).

Smit, J. 'The genre of 1 Corinthians 13 in the light of classical rhetoric' *Novum Testamentum* (33/3 July, 1991), 193-216.

Spicq, C. *Theological Lexicon of the New Testament* (Peabody: Hendrickson, 1994).

Strack and Billerbeck. *Kommentar zum Neuen Testament aus Talmud und Midrash, Vol 1 (das Evangelium nach Matthaus)* (Munchen: C. H. Beck, 1922).

Strauss, M L. *The Davidic Messiah in Luke-Acts: The Promise and its Fulfillment in Lukan Christology* (Sheffield: Sheffield Academic Press, 1995).

Stuhlmacher, P, 'The Hermeneutical Significance of 1 Cor 2:6-16' in Hawthorne G F. *Tradition and in Interpretation in the New Testament* (Grand Rapids: Eerdmans, 1987), 328-347.

Tannehill, R C. *The Narrative Unity of Luke-Acts: A Literary Interpretation* (2 Vols., Minneapolis: Fortress, 1986/90).

Thielman, F. *From Plight to Solution: A Jewish Framework for Understanding Paul's View of the Law in Galatians and Romans* (NovT-Sup 61; Leiden: Brill, 1989).

Thiselton, A. *The First Epistle to the Corinthians* (Grand Rapids: Eerdmans, 2000).

Theissen, G. *Psychological Aspects of Pauline Theology* (Edinburgh: T & T Clark, 1987).

Thrall, M E. *The Second Epistle, to the Corinthians Vol 1: Introduction and Commentary on II Corinthians 1-VII* (Edinburgh: T & T Clark, 1994).

Tiede, D L.'The Exaltation of Jesus and the Restoration of Israel in Acts 1,' *Harvard Theological Review* (79, 1986), 278-286.

Turner, M M B. 'The Concept of Receiving the Spirit in John's Gospel' *Vox Evangelica* (10, 1977), 24-42.

Turner, M M B. 'Jesus and the Spirit in Lucan Perspective' *Tyndale Bulletin* (32, 1981), 3-42.

Turner, M M B. 'Spirit Endowment in Luke/Acts: Some Linguistic Considerations' *Vox Evangelica* (12, 1981), 45-63.

Turner, M M B. 'The Spirit of Christ and Christology' in Rowdon, H H. *Christ the Lord: Studies in Christology presented to Donald Guthrie* (Leicester: IVP, 1982), 168-190.

Turner, M M B. 'The Spirit of Christ and "Divine" Christology' in Green, J B and Turner M M B. *Jesus of Nazareth: Lord and Christ* (Grand Rapids: Eerdmans, 1994), 413-436.

Turner, M M B. '"Empowerment for Mission"? The Pneumatology of Luke-Acts: An Appreciation and Critique of James R. Shelton's Mighty in Word and Deed' *Vox Evangelica* (24, 1994), 103–122.

Turner, M M B. *The Holy Spirit and Spiritual Gifts: Then and Now* (Carlisle: Paternoster. 1996).

Turner, M M B. *Power from on High: The Spirit in Israel's Restoration in Israel's Witness in Luke-Acts* (Sheffield: Sheffield Academic Press, 1996).

Turner, M M B. 'The Spirit in Luke-Acts: A Support or a Challenge to Classical Pentecostal Paradigms' *Vox Evangelica* (27, 1997), 75–101.

Vos, G. *The Teaching of Jesus Concerning the Kingdom of God and the Church* (Grand Rapids: Eerdmans, 1951).

Wenham, G J. *Genesis 1–15* (Milton Keynes: Word, 1991).

Wescott, B F. *The Gospel According to St. John. The Greek Text with Introduction and Notes*, 2 Vols (London: John Murray, 1908).

Wilson, S G. *The Gentiles and the Gentile Mission in Luke-Acts* (Cambridge: Cambridge University Press, 1973).

Wright, N T. *The Climax of the Covenant: Christ and the Law in Pauline Theology* (Edinburgh: T & T Clark, 1991).

Yates, J E. *The Spirit and the Kingdom* (London: SPCK, 1963).

Young, F and Ford, D F. *Meaning and Truth in 2 Corinthians* (London: SPCK, 1987).